24

# THE
# HEART OF THE CONTINENT :

## A RECORD OF TRAVEL ACROSS
## THE PLAINS AND IN OREGON,
## WITH AN EXAMINATION
## OF THE MORMON PRINCIPLE

*Engraved by V. Balch. from a painting by A. Bierstadt N. York.*

COLLECTED WORKS OF
FITZ HUGH LUDLOW

VOLUME 2

THE

# HEART OF THE CONTINENT :

A RECORD OF TRAVEL ACROSS THE
PLAINS AND IN OREGON,

WITH AN

EXAMINATION OF THE MORMON PRINCIPLE

WITH ILLUSTRATIONS BY ALBERT BIERSTADT

EDITED BY
DONALD P. DULCHINOS AND STEPHEN CRIMI

COLLECTED WORKS OF FITZ HUGH LUDLOW

VOLUME 2

THE HEART OF THE CONTINENT:
A RECORD OF TRAVEL ACROSS THE PLAINS AND IN OREGON,
WITH AN EXAMINATION OF THE MORMON PRINCIPLE

BY FITZ HUGH LUDLOW

EDITED BY DONALD P. DULCHINOS AND STEPHEN CRIMI

LOGOSOPHIA, LLC
90 Oteen Church Road
Asheville, NC 28805
www.logosophiabooks.com
logosophiabooks@gmail.com

Library of Congress-in-Publication Data
Ludlow, Fitz Hugh, 1836-1870
*Collected Works of Fitz Hugh Ludlow, Volume 2: The Heart of the Continent*
Crimi, Stephen, and Dulchinos, Donald P. , Editors

ISBN 978-0-9966394-4-6
Distributed by Small Press Distribution
Non-Fiction

Cover design by Jack E. Taylor
Interior layout and design by Susan Yost

Cover art: *Looking up the Yosemite Valley* by Albert Bierstadt, courtesy of The Haggin Museum.

# INTRODUCTION

1.

FITZ HUGH LUDLOW burst on the literary scene in 1857 with the unlikely best seller *The Hasheesh Eater*. Written when he was just 20 years old, the book swept Ludlow into a career as a prolific novelist, short story author, arts critic, travel writer, journalist and editor. His friends and colleagues ranged from Walt Whitman to Brigham Young to Mark Twain. The material published in Ludlow's Collected Works displays a depth of observation, a breadth of erudition and an appetite for extreme experience applied to the emerging modern American nation. *The Heart of the Continent*, published in 1870, book-ended his brief but prolific 13-year career.

*The Heart of the Continent* is a sweeping treatment of the American West on the cusp of its full settlement and exploitation. Ludlow's view was up close, gritty and personal. He spent several weeks on The Overland Stagecoach, from Atchison in the Kansas territory to a San Francisco catching its breath just 15 years after Sutter's Mill. He brought back the first shocking tales of "free love" in the new Mormon Zion of Utah, and equally shocking but more violent views of lynchings, Indian massacres and the Wild West. And the trip upon which the book was based became, in retrospect, the defining event of his life, impacting his writing career, his health and even his marriage.

Ludlow's *The Hasheesh Eater* had a major impact on the public in 1857, and shaped his personal life in many ways. It launched Ludlow's career, in the short span from 1857 to 1870, as a prolific short story writer, serial novelist, and journalist for the newly born popular magazines as well as many of New York City's newspapers. Fitz Hugh had appeared often in *Harper's Monthly Magazine* with short stories in a romantic vein. This was the bread and butter of his professional life. He published sporadically in several of the New York daily newspapers, a number of shorter-lived magazines, and his best humorous novel was serialized in the new *Vanity Fair* satirical magazine. He lived an urban, Bohemian lifestyle that scandalized some, including the father of his new bride.

To supplement this fiction income, he worked as an editor and journalist for the *New York Commercial Advertiser*, and later *New York Evening Post*. While at the Advertiser, he obtained a commission to write a travelogue of his trip to Florida, which he had undertaken partly for health reasons. Ludlow had a frail constitution since childhood, which had always fed his bookish nature. The travelogue was christened *Due South*, lasted for 25 installments, and was to become a template for *The Heart of the Continent*, mixing commentary of travel modes and accommodations, detailed descriptions of scenery, and much dialogue with local characters met along the way. In traveling through the deep south, Ludlow the son of an Abolitionist minister related encounters with slaves who took him into their confidence, and even attended a lively early gospel meeting. These experiences informed some later commentary of his on political subjects, although that was never a focus.

After the outbreak of the Civil War, Ludlow landed a position as arts critic for the *Home Journal*, a weekly magazine of the leisure class (ultimately to become *Town and Country* magazine.) He spent five months at the end of 1862 and early 1863 covering music and theatre performances, which had so far kept drawing audiences early in the war period. But then the *Home Journal* was forced to raise prices as their audience dwindled, and by February they discontinued the relationship with Fitz Hugh. Now money was running short, and Fitz Hugh landed a clerk job in the New York Customs House.

On a less personal but equally deadly note, Congress passed a national draft law that spring. The law exempted from service those who paid into the federal treasury the sum of $300 (the better part of a year's wages for laborers, the same laborers for whose jobs the freed slaves would likely compete). Fitz Hugh may have made such a payment, although he was also likely to have been excused for general poor health.

The draft began on July 11th, and promptly on the 13th a mob wrecked the Provost-marshal office, raided a "colored" orphan asylum, and then attacked another enrolling office. The riots began in a district filled with Irish laborers (Democrats), workers who were looked down on by other northerners. Fitz Hugh himself had satirized them in stories. The mob also attempted to sack and burn the offices of the *New York Tribune* (Horace Greeley was among the staunchest of abolitionists), and then began chasing and lynching Blacks in the streets. The state militia was called in and the riot quelled, but not before as many as 100 people had died. Ludlow saw blood in the water, an eerie echo of his father's experience as an Abolitionist preacher whose church was ransacked by anti-abolitionists just two years before Ludlow was born.

2.

"Go west young man, and grow up with the country," wrote Horace Greeley in the *New York Tribune* in 1851. The west-ward movement had begun in earnest in the 1830's as the early generations of colonists began to feel crowded. The Gold Rush erupted in the 1850's, setting the stage for a sea change in American culture that was only briefly slowed by the lack of information flow back to the East.

The Civil War had slowed the westward movement, but it was still in this frame of mind that Ludlow looked to the West. It was a new physical frontier, with an attraction similar to the spiritual frontiers opened by hashish. And it was a new cultural frontier, with inspiring perspectives on the eternal verities that were sure to fertilize Ludlow's pro-gressive thoughts as the breathtaking Rocky Mountains had begun to inspire artists.

The most notable of those artists was painter Albert Bierstadt, one of the Hudson School of landscape paint-ers. Bierstadt's trip to the West in 1859 had given him a whole new land in which to apply his techniques. Bierstadt's paintings, such as "Rocky Mountains—Lander's Peak," had captured the fancy of the patrons who visited the studios at the Tenth St. Studio Building where Bierstadt and the others entertained. It was there, and among the Genteel Circle, that a friendship developed between the painter and the hasheesh eater. Soon Ludlow was writing reviews of Bierstadt's work. In May of 1863, Fitz Hugh described "Mountain Brook" in glowing terms in the *Evening Post*, possessing "nearly the same degree of excellence as his marvelous 'Light and Shadow' in last year's [National] Academy [of Design]."

Bierstadt's growing reputation convinced a number of patrons to finance another western trip for the artist. Bierstadt offered Fitz Hugh the role of literary accompanist to chronicle the trip and whet the appetite of prospective art buyers with tales of the works in progress. Fitz Hugh convinced Godwin of the *Evening Post* to publish his commentary on the trip, and signed on to the expedition.

However, Ludlow's wife of five years, Rosalie, was not a part of the plan, even though the couple was still without children. The stagecoach was no place for a lady certainly, but Ludlow was so caught up in the excitement that he did not really consider that Rosalie would do anything but faithfully wait for his return. But there may have been more to it. In one short story, Fitz Hugh appeared to address his wife: "It is very hard for a man to become accustomed to the truth that a woman may regard him with veneration for other qualities than physical prowess." One of Fitz Hugh's motives for his journey to the West, at least in part, may have been to prove to Rosalie that she had not married some chronically ill bookworm, but a more robust adventurer. Rosalie's admiration for men of action in their circle, like Edmund Clarence Stedman and Bierstadt himself, added some jealous energy to Fitz Hugh's proposed trip.

The trip seemed to instantly attract more respectability in Ludlow's direction. Wells Fargo had made special arrangements for Bierstadt and Fitz Hugh to travel via the Overland Mail Stagecoach. The growing interests of the company lay in the expanding exploitation of the Western territories. Bierstadt's paintings, like Greeley's editorials, represented terrific free advertising for the lands made accessible by the conveyances of Wells Fargo and others. On a more scholarly note, the recently formed Smithsonian Institution had contacted Ludlow and Bierstadt to request their assistance in mapping the western territory. The party took with them materials to help with this topographical contribution.

The group began their eight-month journey in May. Ludlow sent off regular dispatches to the *Evening Post*: "In the dressing-gown and slippers of civilized life, I look through my window across the Missouri to a land which is the front-yard of barbarism." Ludlow was indeed embarked on a new life, unlike any he'd known before. The day of their arrival in Atchison, "we were invited to a hanging." Soon after, the men embarked on a buffalo hunt to provide Bierstadt his first subjects of local color. And they stayed with settlers in Kansas for a taste of frontier home life.

Their stage continued across Kansas to Denver, a total of 650 miles from their starting point in Atchison. Within days, *Rocky Mountain News* editor William Byers took the travelers and Bierstadt seventy miles west of Denver into the mountains, where Bierstadt made several color studies of a mountain of "over 15,000 feet, or considerably taller than Mont Blanc," and Ludlow wrote:

> That glorious roseate mountain stood nameless among the peaks in its virgin vail of snow; so Bierstadt, by right of first portrayal, baptized it after one far away from our sides, but very near and dear to our hearts — a gentle nature who had followed us clear to the verge of our Overland wanderings at Atchison, and parted from us bravely lest she should make our purpose fainter by seeming moved. Henceforth, that shining peak is MONTE ROSA.

The party took seven more days to make the trip to Salt Lake City, crossing the great divide through Bridger Pass.

Ludlow immediately became aware that "nothing happens along the great avenues to Salt Lake, of which Brigham Young does not get the earliest advices…The secret police system of France was never more efficient than Brigham Young's. And not long after that came a first encounter with a polygamous family. Fitz Hugh's "poor monogamic brain…felt like the three-thousandth homeopathic dilution of monogamy."

His writing was very complimentary of how the Mormons had carved a thriving settlement out of the desert, but he was highly critical of the society's autocratic nature. Ultimately, he was convinced that "Mormonism *is* Brigham Young." Brigham's power was absolute in Fitz Hugh's view not only because Brigham chose to wield it, but because Mormondom would perish without it. "The instant he crumbles, Mormondom and Mormonism will fall to pieces at once, irrevocably."

The remainder of the journey was colored by the discovery of an Indian massacre.

> Under a heavy cloud of black, clinging smoke, lay the charred beams and smouldering rafters of the house—while a little further off, the ruins of great trusses of hay were still steaming above the conflagration of the stables. On that further pile lay the mangled remains of all the stage stud—ten or a dozen fine animals who had perished with their halters unloosed; and nearer by, among the burning planks of the house, were stretched the bones of six horribly mutilated men, the flesh still partly adhering to them, and the whole mass rapidly becoming undistinguishable, roasting into our nostrils with the smell of mingled man and beast-hood, a loathsome holocaust to the Demon of Primeval Innocence.

The encounter colored his view of Native Americans forever after, though of course he had not seen nor heard of any of the similar massacres that had been historically inflicted *on* the local tribes. After a high-tension journey through the rest of Indian territory, they arrived in San Francisco in late July.

On August 2nd, a San Francisco weekly paper called *The Golden Era* took notice of the arrival of Bierstadt and Ludlow. *The Golden Era* was published by Joseph Lawrence, who had gathered about him a stable of young writers. One of these writers was an ex-steamboat captain who called himself Mark Twain. The travelers were immediately adopted. The writers nicknamed Fitz Hugh the Hasheesh Infant. After having read *The Hasheesh Eater*, all the western writers expected an aging, dissolute, world weary man, and instead found a bespectacled and erudite young man eager for new sensations. Not long after arrival, a local prize fight had the town talking, and Inigo wrote in his column a challenge to Mark Twain, the "Washoe Giant" and Fitz Hugh, the Hasheesh Infant, for a journalistic battle.

Before departing for Yosemite, Ludlow contributed his first piece to the *Era*, "On Good Living." The truly spiritual man is he who lives well…"[but I] comprise all depths of gastronomic degradation in this one formula: Fries its steaks!…The missionary is sadly needed…to smash those false Gods, the frying pans." Had the martyr St. Lawrence fallen into the hands of the heathen, "they would have fried him in a pan with some of the cold grease of yesterday's Christian." It was this kind of irreverence cheek-by-jowl with classical East Coast learning that won over Twain and the others, and from then on there was nothing but appreciation for a peer in one sense, and respect for a model of prestigious literary success in another.

The Overlanders spent time in Yosemite park, gold mining towns like Yreka, and then left California for Oregon. It was here that Ludlow's frail constitution again let him down. The overland journey, he wrote, had "frightfully undermined" his constitution. They had struggled on horseback for about a week along the foothills of the Cascade Range when Ludlow collapsed, coughing and feverish, about thirty miles south of Salem. He fell from the saddle with "a violent attack of pneumonia, which came near terminating my earthly with my Oregon pilgrimage." Bierstadt eventually got him back to San Francisco, somewhat recovered.

On November 8th, Ludlow began to take his literary leave of the city with the first of several essays giving his opinion of San Francisco. The essay was entitled "Plain Talks—No. 1, How It Strikes One." "The candid visitor must regret that the grading of San Francisco seems to have been done by a Giant armed with a fish slice and a coal-scoop under the influence of Delirium Tremens."

Ludlow wrote a "Goodbye Article" which appeared in the *Era* on November 22nd. He continued his Plain Talk there, and his strongest words were for "that Irresistable Washoe Giant, Mark Twain," who "takes quite a unique position. He makes me laugh more than any Californian since poor [George] Derby died. He imitates nobody. He is a school by himself." Twain took the encouragement to heart, and subsequently wrote to his mother in January, 1864:

> And if Fitz Hugh Ludlow (author of The Hasheesh Eater) comes your way, treat him well. He published a high encomium upon Mark Twain (the same being eminently just and truthful, I beseech you to believe) in a San Francisco paper. Artemus Ward said that when my gorgeous talents

were publicly acknowledged by such high authority I ought to appreciate them myself, leave sage-brush obscurity and journey to New York with him, as he wanted me to do. But I preferred not to burst upon the New York public too suddenly and brilliantly, so I concluded to remain here.

Critic Franklin Walker summed up Ludlow's impact thusly:

During his four months' visit he influenced the isolated community of San Francisco writers in a subtle, pervasive way, entangling himself in the web and woof of Western literary tradition. He was a voice of encouragement from the outside world.

Ludlow and Bierstadt took a steamer home to New York from San Francisco in December of 1864.

### 3.

In his dispatches in the Evening Post, Ludlow had begun to grow his reputation in new directions. After his encounter with Twain et al, he began writing for *The Golden Era* and continued to do so after his return to the East, with a series called "Reminiscences of an Overlander." But as his reputation grew, he finally came to the notice of *The Atlantic Monthly*, long the epitome of everything the Bohemian Fitz Hugh hated about Boston, but the premier journal in America nevertheless.

The April, 1864 issue of *The Atlantic Monthly* saw Fitz Hugh's debut in the premier showcase of literary America with a piece entitled "Among the Mormons." The style was a little less blunt, a little more respectable, and also indulged Ludlow the pedagogue, dilating in academic detail on subjects ranging from rock formations to Mormon social mores. Ludlow continued to publish four more essays on his western trip for the rest of 1864, including one where he successfully predicted the final route of the transcontinental railroad as built some ten years later.

The affiliation with the *Atlantic* led Ludlow to ignore his long affiliation with the Harpers book publishing arm, and contracted with Hurd and Houghton (now Houghton Mifflin) to collect his travel writings into one epic work in two planned volumes. Some of Bierstadt's sketches were being converted into woodcuts for Ludlow's book. Bierstadt meanwhile was finishing some paintings, such as Mount Hood from the Oregon trip, at reported prices of ten thousand dollars each, dwarfing Ludlow's writing income.

Around the same time, Ludlow added another marketable skill to his repertoire by initiating a lecture tour. *The Golden Era* of February 19th reported that "Fitz Hugh Ludlow recently delivered a lecture called 'Across the Continent' at Dodsworth's Hall, New York. It describes his overland journey from the Atlantic to the Pacific Coast." Lectures in the U.S. at this time often featured such luminaries as Henry Ward Beecher, but "Artemus Ward" and others of Fitz Hugh's acquaintance had broadened the field.

One part of Ludlow's life that had not improved upon his return from the West was his marriage. Ludlow and Rosalie had not resolved domestic troubles that had arisen well before the western trip, and neither had discouraged the attentions of others.

On one of his lecture trips, Fitz Hugh met the mysterious Mrs. Ives. Cousin Ellen Ludlow filed the following report in a letter in March, 1864.

Several weeks ago he decamped from New York with his new lady, privately, & after a while, a relative of Rose saw, in a hotel register at St Joseph's, Missouri, this entry, viz. "Fitz-hugh [*sic*] Ludlow, wife & servants." After this, he was seen by one who knew him at Leavenworth, in Kansas. The next we hear of him is again in New York & we learn that he left his affinity in Kansas…The uncle of the new lady says that she will remain with Fitz as long as he can furnish her an abundant supply of money. When that fails, she will desert him for someone else. He occasionally writes to his father, maintaining his great dignity & the propriety of his proceedings & pouring curses upon the head of poor Rose.

While Fitz Hugh and Rosalie's six-year history of flirtation and transgression, and no children, contributed to the separation, the Western trip may very well have raised the stakes. The "Free Love" aspect of the Mormon culture was not lost on the two Bohemians. Reading between the lines, one can imagine Bierstadt and Ludlow resolving to propose more open relations among the two men and Rosalie herself, who had been on the minds of both men throughout the trip, whether as Camp Rosalie or Monte Rosa. Perhaps Ludlow's dalliance with Mrs. Ives was contemplated as part of a more open relationship all around.

Rosalie walked out on Ludlow sometime in the winter as the Civil War came to an end. He remained in the apartment on Stuyvesant Square, from which to base his lecturing forays to the west as well as continuing to write. As Fitz Hugh wandered through upstate New York, he continued to rework his various travel writings into book form. However, publication was further delayed by bad luck. Another book was reported in preparation based on a similar 1865 Western trip of Speaker of the House of Representatives Schuyler

Colfax with newspaper editor Samuel Bowles. Ludlow felt compelled to write to Colfax.

> I have a favor to ask of you. My illness has retarded the completion of my book of travels. My publishers are getting very much alarmed because they say that your book will entirely supersede mine.

Indeed, *Across the Continent* by Bowles was published in 1865, and Ludlow had to find more writing work, and so returned meekly to Harper's. Several of his more conventional short stories appeared there, now flavored with topical color furnished by the Western trip.

But alas, in May came the following:

> DIVORCED—At the last term of N.Y. Supreme Court, a divorce was granted against Fitz Hugh Ludlow, the well known writer, on the petition of his wife, Rosalie H. Ludlow, daughter of Mr. A.O. Osborn of this village. The defendant was charged by the plaintiff with adultery with a Mrs. Ives both in New York City and in the West.

This was hard enough to take, but just six months later came this news:

> MARRIED—In Waterville, on the 21st inst., by Rev. Dr. Meachum, rector of Grace Church, Albert Bierstadt of Rosalie Harper, eldest daughter of Amos O. Osborn, Esq.

Free love indeed. Ludlow never really recovered. The Atlantic severed its ties with Ludlow. And the initial Oregon health collapse re-appeared in what now is understood to be a recurrence of tuberculosis. The remaining writing output of Ludlow's writing career came in spurts of several months of writing, alternating with several months in a sickbed.

During the illnesses, Ludlow began taking opium for the pain and seems to have developed a drug dependence as well. Toward the end of his life, he became known as an expert on the topic and was consulted and published about possible opium "cures." In 1867, he married an older widow, Maria Owen Milliken, who together with Ludlow's sister nursed him until his death.

Finally in 1870, at long last, Fitz Hugh's book on the Western journey of 1863 was published as *The Heart of the Continent*. The book collected and revised articles on the cross-country trip with Bierstadt from the *Atlantic Monthly* as well as the notes and the letters in the *New York Evening Post* and *The Golden Era*.

The book contained a frontispiece engraving of a mountain lake by V. Balch "from a painting by A. Bierstadt." Another engraving of Cho-Looke, the Yosemite waterfall, was rendered from a Bierstadt painting as well, although it must have been a remarkably diplomatic publisher who convinced Fitz Hugh to have any trace of Bierstadt in his book. Indeed, mentions of Bierstadt in earlier articles were completely excised from the book, occasionally replaced by reference to "the artist." But the worst was reserved for Rosalie. In an *Atlantic* article published in June 1864, there is a passage:

> Here we pitched our first Yo-Semite Camp,—calling it "Camp Rosalie," after a dear absent friend of mine and Bierstadt's.

In the book, the passage was savagely rewritten as:

> Here we pitched our first Yo-Semite camp,—calling it "-
> *Camp Rattlesnake," after a pestilent little beast of that tribe which*
> *insinuated itself into my blankets, but was disposed of by my artist*
> *comrade before it had inflicted its fatal wound upon me.*

Bierstadt and Rosalie remained together until his death. They also had no children together.

*The New York Times* reviewed the book favorably:

> We rejoice to see a book of American travel of which we can speak in terms of almost unqualified praise. Mr. Ludlow, while careful and deliberate as to the facts which in such a work are of chief consequence, has not been regardless of the graces of style or of the advantages to be gained through them in the way of influence and circulation. This book is, therefore, not only useful but is thoroughly interesting.
>
> The occasional picturesqueness of his manner gives great zest to Mr. Ludlow's book, and for this, among many other excellent qualities, he will be indebted for what we are confident will prove an abundant measure of success.

Other reviewers said, "He is one of the few thoroughly good descriptive writers we have," and "the chief merit and the peculiar charm of the 'Heart of the Continent' arises from the fact that the author is a many-sided, versatile man; a close and original thinker, a man of no mean scientific attainments, and, what is better than all, a profound and earnest observer of nature in her every feature."

Only a review in the July 1870 *Atlantic Monthly* was not so enthusiastic, and in fact was downright hostile. The break that ended Fitz Hugh's publishing career there was still remembered, and the use of material originally published in the *Atlantic* was not to be forgiven:

Since Mr. Ludlow made his explorations, some ten years ago, the Heart of the Continent has been visited by such numbers of travellers that it is well nigh as stale and battered as the heart of a coquette entering upon her fifth or sixth season of flirtations. And shall a man whose passion is ten years old make us listen to his superannuated raptures about buffaloes, and sage-bush, and alkali, and antelopes and parks, and the giant pines and domes of the Yosemite, and Brigham Young's capacity for self-government, and all the rest?

It is rather late for Mr. Ludlow, we must confess, and we think that five hundred and six pages are a good many.

Oddly, no mention was made that half the book first appeared in the *Atlantic*, but Fitz Hugh was still listed in the ads for the *Atlantic* as late as 1869 as a contributing author of "Papers on Science and Art." In any case, this is the only largely negative review Fitz Hugh ever received.

To the modern eye, the book remains a remarkably encyclopedic view of the old West. The geological details drag on a bit too long, but the freshness of the scenery to the traveler comes across, and Fitz Hugh's light and leisurely style still entertains. Nevertheless, unlike the perennial interest in *The Hasheesh Eater* (more than 10 editions in the 20th century), only one new edition of *The Heart of the Continent* has seen print, from AMS Press in New York in 1971, part of a series of reprints of 19th century Americana.

It is a little surprising there have been no other reprints, if only just for the Bierstadt illustrations that have drawn new interest as Bierstadt's artistic reputation was rehabilitated in the late 20th century. He is the subject of a permanent exhibit at the Brooklyn Museum of Art, where the love triangle with Rosalie is the topic of some of the commentary.

Perhaps also, the contemporary close up view of polygamy might be of interest in these tabloid days of *Sister Wives* and *Big Love*.

Ludlow was a Pioneer, not only in the exploration of drug effects, but more literally as one of the first journalists and commentators on the scene of the emerging Western United States.

– Donald P. Dulchinos

# CONTENTS

# TO THE READER

IT was my original intention to have published these notes of my journey in the two-volume form, comprehending much additional material which would have made the work a complete and minute survey not only of the entire region traversed by the Pacific Railroad, but of much of the incalculably valuable and interesting region tributary to it on either side. Of the latter part of my journey,—after leaving Salt Lake City,—I have here, however, had room to give only the more salient features; and by the same circumstances which rendered it advisable to reduce the book to a single volume, I have been compelled to throw much of the matter relating to the Mormons, their home, their problem, and their destiny, into what to most readers is the least attractive and most superficially noticed form—an Appendix.

It is principally on behalf of this Appendix that I utter a word of prefatory remark. The engrossing question, "What shall we do with the Mormons?" is, so far as I know from personal reading and information obtained at the best hands, treated in this Appendix from an entirely new point of view. I may say frankly that I believe my solution of the question the promptest, the most feasible, the least productive of violent dislocation and suffering, which has yet been offered. Because I so believe and am desirous to have the fact tested by other minds, and because there is much in the small type at the other end of my book which is full as worthy of the larger typographical honors as anything which precedes it,—because, in fine, I think the reader will agree with me in calling the Mormon Matter at least as interesting as the rest of the volume, I here venture to ask that it may be read at least no more superficially than that.

– F. H. L.

# CHAPTER I.

## The Setting Out.

I MIGHT pass over without a word the whole line of railway communication between New York and Atchison, on the Missouri River, were it not that the uniform kindness of its officers to the party of which I was a member, and their interest in the artistic and scientific purposes of our expedition, deserve to be as well known by our acknowledgement, as their roads are without our mention.

The moment that we stated our project to Mr. Scott and the other officers of the Pennsylvania Central, they not only presented the entire party transportation over their own road to Pittsburg, but gave us letters of introduction which insured our being treated with similar courtesy on all the remaining roads to St. Louis.

To them, to the officers of the Crestline route between Pittsburgh and Cincinnati, and to Messrs. Larned and M'Alpine of the Cincinnati and St. Louis road, we owe recognition, no less for the fine spirit of appreciation and helpfulness in which they received our enterprise, than for the diminution effected by their kindness in the burdens of a necessarily very expensive journey. There can scarcely be a better indication for the future of Science, Art, and Literature in our own country, than the cordiality which such a course as that of these gentlemen shows existing between those professions and Commerce. I might add that Commerce herself has reason to note this indication as gladly; for Science, Art, and

Literature are daughters of the same mature civilization as she, and together they flourish or decay.

At St. Louis we found a letter awaiting us from Colonel William Osborne, formerly of the Hannibal and St. Joseph's road and then President of the Platte County Railroad, extending between St. Joseph and the Missouri border opposite Atchison. This letter introduced us to Mr. Sturgeon, President of the Northern Railroad of Missouri, and, by the combined courtesy of these gentlemen, we were forwarded freely all the way to the Kansas terminus of railway communication. I shall have other courtesies to acknowledge as our journey proceeds.

At St. Joseph we completed our outfit by the purchase of additional blankets and ammunition; and after a few pleasant days spent in a family of personal friends, went down by rail to the starting-point of our Overland Journey.

Atchison is a small town, but a lively one. We had scarcely touched the ferry-wharf on the Kansas side before we were invited to a hanging. Lynch, C. J., was to sit that afternoon upon a couple of bushwhackers. His is a most impartial tribunal, which, to avoid giving offense, acquits nobody. The accused were, first, a man of fifty-five or thereabouts, a gray person who, in a more advanced state of society, might have bulled the gold market and cheated his acquaintance under the ægis of eminent respectability without the wagging of a reprobative tongue; second, a young fellow of imperturbable address, whom Wall Street would have esteemed highly in the position of confidential clerk to the foregoing. Neither of them had any look of the popularly conceived criminal,—probably neither of them were any worse than fifty men in the crowd who clamored for their death. I heard one man, enthusiastic upon the even-handed justice of the occasion, who, if he had the theme of his eulogy meted to himself, would swing higher than Haman, or leave locks of his gray hair dabbled in blood upon every threshold in Atchison,—a man with the effrontery to live under the very noses of citizens whose crape for brothers slaughtered by him in the border-ruffian times was scarce yet rusty on their wide-awakes. I speak thus, not because I deprecate stern frontier justice, but because the hands that administer it are nerved, almost invariably, by brute fury or caprice. In a new country, the indomitable pioneers who build the basement of civilization, have too much to do with subduing nature to bother their heads especially regarding government. But government, while mankind stays selfish, never can regulate itself. While the workers are felling trees, breaking roads, and building cabins, the knaves and do-nothings get into political power. Before long the judge sits only to intimidate the just and excuse the villain. The sheriff's baton becomes a finger-post to loop-holes for the escape of thieves and murderers. The jury and the malefactor wink at each other wink at each other across a rail. The governor stands waiting with a pardon to poke a hole through the coarse legal sieve which has casually caught an exceptional rascal across a wire. The legislature pass laws with cunning quirks in them, provident against a day when these shall be convenient for themselves. When this occurs, and the honest men find it out, Lynch-law is the only practical transition to a good form of government. A most horrible thing in the abstract, it become the sole thing in the concrete. Perhaps it is essential to it that it should in most cases be administered by a furious mob; but that is the most horrible part of its horror to a stranger.

Nearly two thousand people were assembled in a deep ravine indented in the rolling plain back of the town, around a lone cotton-wood tree, under which stood the fatal wagon. Such a dreadful multitude may God keep from the death-scene of every man whose guilt is not double-dyed! There was no attempt to classify it. Shaggy-bearded horsemen trampled under hoof swarming footmen, boys, and, shame to say it, women. Here and there stood the unhitched wagons of whole families who had come from distant ranches to make gala-day of the execution. These were the objects of general envy, for the view from their pedestals was not only more commanding, but more comfortable. It was a selfish sort of enjoyment to sit one's saddle at such a place. Stern Justice and Domestic Felicity were both satisfied in the little family party which sat—grown people on boards, children on knees, babes in arms—cracking grim jokes with each other till the dreadful melodrama should begin.

The trial was a short one. It was testified that the two accused had proceeded to the ranch of an old farmer living twenty miles out in the wilds back of Atchison; had beaten him insensible with a pistol-butt; knocked his wife down with a chair; and then hung his boy, a child of twelve years, till, to save himself from suffocation, he consented to reveal the hiding-place of the farmer's funds. Taking these, which amounted to forty dollars, and all the horses in the corral, they had returned to the Missouri, converted the animals into cash, and, without the least attempt at absconding, began to enjoy their gains in speculation. Three days from the date of their crime they were in the hands of Lynch.

These facts having been announced to the crowd, an opportunity, as they say in other assemblies, was given for the brethren to make a few remarks. One man on horse-back, better dressed and more refined in his appearance than the rest, held the attention of the crowd with a speech of equal force and freedom from temper, in which he drew a sketch of the defenselessness which would result to the set-tler if, in his lonely cabin, he could not be sure that prompt and certain vengeance hung over his would-be assassins. The people heard him with a running fire of murmurs,—saying, "Good!" "That's it!" and "I'm there too!" when he concluded his little speech with a vote for the instant death of both the bushwhackers. He was followed by others who spoke less ably, but all to the same point; and the crowd finally decided that the younger man should be executed at once,—the elder have respite till the next day but one succeeding. I may be uncharitable to communities of incipient civili-zation, but the respite seemed to me granted rather with a view to thrifty economy of pleasures than for the sake of pity and completed shrift. Indeed, one person told me, "If we hung 'em both on Thursday, we shouldn't have anybody to hang on Saturday."

The sentence being determined, its subject was asked by the immediate committee in charge, what he had to say for himself.

"Nothing," he replied, in a tone of nonchalance; only that you're going to murder a better man than any of yourselves."

He was lifted to the wagon; surveyed the stony faces of the crowd with a quick glance that took in no single look of pity; the rope was adjusted, the wagon driven away, and there, a horrid fruit of man's hateful passions, he hung, uncovered to all vengeful eyes, and the pure, sweet, but unhelping heaven of May, quivering from the limb of the cotton-wood.

This is the wickedness of Lynch executions. Like old Tyburn, they rear more gallows-birds than they intimidate. The horribly hardening effects of public deaths was visible, audible in all the crowd. As the poor wretch swung there, now past injuring them, and to all noble natures an object of pity, if only for the first time, the men cracked their brutal jokes, and women laughed at them. Mothers pointed their boys to the tree, not as to a warning, but a spectacle.

"This is not, nor it cannot come to good!"

With glutted eyes and unmoved hearts the crowd slowly withdrew from their place of fascination; but, as their murmur lessened, the air was broken with wails of agony which might have melted a Marat. Lying at full length in a wagon outside of the crowd's former hem, a young woman, without friend or comforter, was crying aloud for a husband whom she called God to witness had been cruelly murdered.

These things are too horrible to dwell upon. We, at the East, are apt to think that the punishment of our old national transgressions is all condensed in the war which has smitten us so sorely. But I felt within myself that day at Atchison, that the bitter seed sown by ruffians under the aegis of our Federal Government never bore fruit more poison to the constitution of society than such executions as had just taken place. It is but little wonder that the contempt for law, as the sum of all atrocities under a sanctified disguise, which was studiously cultivated among the people of Kansas by a past Administration, should breed to-day all manner of cruelties, though the powers that be have changed. Barbaric habitudes of society cannot be nurtured for years, and then uprooted in a week. The arrow has been withdrawn from her heart; but "bleeding Kansas" bleeds still.

I know all the palliations which a young society may plead for its excesses; but I must say that the recklessness which met me in the street, at the business places, in my hotel, after the execution, made me wonder whether I was on earth or in hell. Women in the dress of ladies leaned across the tea-table and asked, "Have you been to the hanging?" with as much *sang-froid* as a New Yorker might say, "Have you seen Faust?" Then, between sips of tea and bites of biscuit, such as had been, regaled those who had not, with particulars that made a stranger sicken at his food.

I was expressing my surprise to an indigenous acquaintance made that morning, when he replied, "Haven't been long in Kansas, have you?" "Six hours," I informed him. "Thought so. Lord bless you, nobody thinks anything of being hanged in this country! Why, in one Kansas settlement there lived an old man who was too lazy to do anything for his living, and whose neighbors had to support him, until finally they got tired of sendin' on him things, and concluded to put him out of his misery. When he stood on the wagon, with the rope around his neck, one new settler in the crowd took pity on him, and called out, 'Hold hard! ye needn't hang him. I'll give him ten bushel o' corn.' 'Is it shelled?' drawled the old man in his old, lazy voice. 'No, 'ta'nt,' says the settler. 'Drive on with your wagon,' says the old man."

After which veritable history, my new acquaintance looked up at the sky, remarked that it was a pity they didn't hang both the bushwhackers, "it was such a nice day for hangin'," and bid me good-by with regrets that I could not stay over to-morrow.

To turn an Eastern man's notions still more completely topsy-turvy on the subject of tribunals and government, as we went down to the coach-office to arrange for our places overland, we met an agent, whom we had expected to transact with, going over to Leavenworth between two dragoons, to answer before the Brigadier-General of the Department for having violated some freight contract on the stage-route. I began to wonder whether, if we stayed a little longer in Atchison, we should not see a soldier tried for desertion in a justice court, or a church-member turned out of the fold for heresy by a surrogate.

The Massasoit House, though far enough from resembling its ever-memorable namesake in Springfield, was still a very creditable hotel for a place on the extreme borders of civilization; and we should have slept well but for the fact that a party of ranchmen and wagon-drivers, who had come into town for holiday, saw fit to end their pleasantly stimulating afternoon by a night of carouse in a neighboring rum-shop. Fiddles, that were a fortuitous concourse of wood and cat-gut, without any attempt to systematize them or their noise; the sound of heels in the breakdown, loud swearing and yells for drink, kept us awake till a late hour of our last night on the Missouri River. It was not astonishing that, after a series of such unimagined horrors as we had passed through, an Eastern lady just arrived should have asked us next morning, "whether those were bushwhackers next door."

The hour of eight saw us embarked upon our vehicle, with all the baggage which it was absolutely necessary to carry: our commissary stores in boxes under our feet, where they might be easy of access in any of those frequent cases of semi-starvation which occur at the stations between the Missouri and the Pacific. Our guns hung in their cases by the straps of the wagon-top; our blankets were folded under us to supplement the cushions. To guard against any emergency, we were dressed exactly as we should want to be, if need occurred to camp out all night. We wore broad slouch hats of the softest felt, which made capital nightcaps for an out-door bed; blue flannel shirts with breast-pockets, the only garment, as far as material goes, which in all weathers or climates is equally serviceable, healthful, and comfortable; stout pantaloons of gray Cheviot, tucked into knee-boots; revolvers and cartouche-boxes on belts of broad leather about our waists; and light, loose linen sacks over all. I may here anticipate, in order to dismiss the subject, by saying that a few hundred miles made some changes expedient in our attire. We doffed our sacks, and rode in our hunting-shirts; we took off our belts, and slung them with holsters and ammunition beside our guns; and exchanged our boots for loose slippers which are much less galling during a protracted wagon-journey, keeping the former close at hand for use when we had, as sometimes happened, to ease the horses over a hard piece of road by walking ourselves.

The Overland Mail vehicle is of that description known as the Concord wagon,—a stout oblong box on springs, painted red, with heavy wheels and axles, having a flat arched roof of water-proof cloth erected on strong posts, like those of a rockaway, and to this are attached curtains of the same fabric, which in bad weather may be let down and buttoned so tight as to make the sides practically as proof against storms as the top. In fine weather, when the curtains are up, no airier arrangement or more unobstructed view could be desired. The seats of the wagon are three, the passengers at the end sitting *vis-a-vis*; those in the middle looking forward, with their backs against a strap hooked to the side-posts, as in the old-fashioned stage-coach. Six persons can ride comfortably inside, if they are only used to sleeping in an upright position; but the great pressure of travel to Denver often at that day compelled passengers to ride three on a seat,—an arrangement calculated to give one the liveliest ideas of the horrors of a negro hold on the middle passage. By the politeness of Messrs. Ben Holladay and Center, we were furnished with such letters to the Atchison agent of their line as insured us a stage to ourselves as far as Denver; and Mr. Munger, the superintendent between Atchison and Fort Kearney, did everything in his power to make our ride as comfortable as it could be. Just before we set out, we became acquainted with a Denver gentleman, Mr. Kershaw, and a lady in his charge, who were both anxious to reach Colorado by the earliest conveyance. We accordingly offered them our remaining seats, and had no occasion to regret the hospitality, finding them most pleasant companions as far as they went with us, and becoming afterward indebted to them for many courtesies in Colorado.

Just before we left, Mr. Munger got word from further west that the buffaloes had started northward for their summer resorts, and were now reported upon the south bank of the Republican Fork of the Kaw. We immediately made up our minds not to lose their visit, as we might have no second chance of seeing them in their glory, perhaps none of seeing them at all, if we went on to Denver without stopping, and returned from the Pacific coast—as was then possible, and eventually proved actual—by the way of Panama or Nicaragua. We accordingly made arrangements with Mr. Munger to lie by and wait for him about one hundred and eighty-five miles west of Atchison, at Comstock's Ranch in Nebraska. He, meanwhile, would make some final preparations for the proposed foray on the Kaw, and meet us at the ranch, or overtake us on the road in his light double buggy. The good sense of this course was afterward proved to our great satisfaction, as we never again saw buffaloes in a state of nature after leaving the Republican Fork, passing Fort Kearney, where the main herd makes its most frequent transit to the plains north of the Platte, some weeks before they crossed the road there.

The Concord wagon rambled out of Atchison, and we were fairly on "The Plains." For a while we were accompanied by picket fences; but these, in despair at the idea of limiting immensity, soon gave way to rails, and by the time we reached Lancaster,—a station merely, not a town,—ten miles out of Atchison, the rails themselves had succumbed, and we were running through an unbroken waste.

"The Plains" are very different in their character from the Prairies. Nowhere, after leaving the Missouri River westward, does the traveller behold such stretches of grass running to the horizon, everywhere level like the sea, as he finds in Illinois. The great sedimentary deposits which form the prairies proper, were laid in a period of long quiet, and denuded of their superadjacent water by a slow uniform upheaval, or equally slow evaporation, which embraced much larger tracts of country than the formative influences further west. As might be expected, the land gives evidence of more spasmodic and irregular disturbances the nearer we approach the great spinal mountain-chain of the Continent.

The grass around us was long and rich. Prairie-hens abounded in it, seeming almost as tame as barnyard fowl.

They were continually coming to the road and running ahead of the horses, so close to us, indeed, that, had we chosen, we might have bagged the whole party's supper from the wagon as we rode. The common plover were only less plenty, dodging about in the grass with their peculiar culprit manner as we approached. The mourning dove, a little creature of lovely shape and typical color, whose haunts embrace the entire Plains region, fluttered or hopped constantly about us in pairs. Several varieties of hawks, one of which we afterward discovered to be a true falcon; some large ravens, and a species of meadow-lark, were the other principal birds which attracted our attention on this day.

The air was delightfully soft, the sky clear, and the road in excellent condition, even without considering that Nature and the wheels of travel are here the only menders of highway. In some places it was as compact and smooth as the finest gravel roads of the East. Indeed, with the exception of the portion traversing the terrible desert of Utah, and a few shorter pieces elsewhere, the entire route astonished me by its excellence.

Just after sundown we arrived at Seneca, a settlement as well as a station, sixty miles from Atchison. Here we took tea in quite an ambitious frame tavern, and our eyes lay lingeringly on the shingle of Civilization's last justice of the peace. There was a tin-shop in Seneca; I think a lawyer's office; and there were several dwlling-houses.

After the darkness came on, and we rolled away from Seneca into its darkness, I began to realize that we were not going to stop anywhere for the night. It was a strange sensation, this; like being in an arm-chair, and sentenced not to get out of it from the Missouri to California.

I do not know whether it is necessary to inform anybody that the Overland Mail travelled night and day. I had known it always, but I never felt it till about twelve o'clock the first night out, when my legs began growing unpleasantly long, and my feet swelled to such a size that they touched all the boxes and musket-butts upon the floor. When these symptoms were further accompanied by a dull heat between the shoulders, and a longing for something soft applied to the nape of the neck, I wondered whether this was not what people on shore called wanting to go to bed. The facilities for such a gratification were so amusingly scanty that I concluded I must be mistaken. The back cushions of the wagon were stuffed as hard as cricket-balls, and the seat might have been the flat slide of a bat. I tried fastening my head in a corner by a pocket-handkerchief sling; but just as unconsciousness arrived, the head was sure to slip out, and, in despair, I finally gave over trying to do anything with it. At Guittards', a station famous among such passengers as have reached there in proper season for delicious suppers, we to-night stopped only long enough to change horses, and I took advantage of the halt to climb to the box. Here I rode the rest of the night, convinced that I could not surrender to Sleep until he had made a more protracted siege around the outworks. I felt convinced that my friends inside would not miss me, they having, some time before, reached that stage of sensation in which a stage-floor seems piled with human feet. When the fresh team started out with a plunge, and the fresh night-breath of the Plains began fanning my forehead, the fever of unsuccessful sleepiness left me, and I enjoyed myself as much as if I were not sure it would return to-morrow.

During the night, near a small settlement called Marysville, we forded the Big Blue, one of the largest streams in this portion of Kansas—timbered with cotton-woods, sycamores, oaks, and occasional elms—and, a little after sunrise, stopped at "Seventeen Mile Point," one hundred and eleven miles from Atchison, and the last station this side of Nebraska.

The stations on the Overland Road, between the Missouri and Denver, generally consist of a single wooden house, with stables attached, and a large corral, or inclosed yard, just adjacent. Some of the more ambitious station-keepers cultivate several acres of land adjoining, in which case the traveller is delighted by the entrance of fresh vegetables into a bill of fare, which is elsewhere unqualified pork and greasy potatoes. Occasionally, too, the station-keeper has both time and penchant for hunting; the happy result being buffalo-hump, antelope-steaks, and fricassee of prairie-chickens. But the majority of these important personages seem to have retired from the world under the influence of an ascetic spirit, and take grim delight in visiting the wrongs inflicted upon them by the society which they have left, on the innocent wayfarer compelled to pay for their hospitality. Many of them have married copartners in their social grudge; stern females, who boil bad coffee in an affronted manner, and hand you hot saleratus biscuit with an air of personal insult. All their principal supplies are drawn from Atchison by the Mail Company's conveyances; and it is no unusual occurrence to lack sugar as well as milk in your tea, because "that stage" hasn't brought up the last order. The station-keepers charge variously from fifty cents in Kansas to a dollar in Nebraska, and westward, for every meal, without regard to quality. Their charges upon the passengers they collect personally (though it is possible to buy meal-tickets at Atchison for the whole route); the board of the drivers is paid by the Company, who keep an account with the keepers for them and the stable-tenders.

While breakfast was cooking, I loaded a shot-gun, and started out for a short excursion in search of prairie-hens. Though we had seen numbers of them all along the road, I was unable to start a single one in the grass. This I found to be the ordinary case at this hour of the morning and season of the year. They wait till the sun is high and warm before they come out to strut and coquet with each other,—being the dandies and people of elegant leisure in the social system of the Plains. I got back to the station-house with the charge in my gun, yet with pleasant sensations of willingness to be charged myself, due to more than a mile's tramp through the rich grass of the breezy divide.

Just beyond the breakfast-place we entered Nebraska. The country now became wilder and some-what more sterile. The signs of human occupation disappeared entirely, and with them the prairie-chickens became less and less abundant. These fowl, as may be known, flourish best in the neighborhood of settlements,—sometimes, like quail, relying principally, over tracts of many miles square, for most of their subsistence, upon gleanings from the rick and stubble field. When found to any extent in perfectly wild regions, they occupy some secret spot far in the bosom of the Plains, where their natural food is steady and abundant; but they always prefer grain when they can get it, and will accompany wagons or stages for miles to pick up the droppings. Though the prairie-fowl diminished, the plovers and doves were still abundant.

At Virginia City, one hundred and thirty miles from Atchison, the stage stopped for dinner about noon; but our

COMSTOCK'S RANCH.

recollections of a station breakfast were not sufficiently fascinating to tempt us into sitting down at table. We now had occasion to congratulate ourselves on our provision in the matter of commissary stores, for, opening one of the boxes under our feet, we lunched, *alfresco*, under lee of the station-barn, on pilot-bread, sardines, and canned peaches. Our travelling larder contained, beside many duplicates of such a lunch as this, apple-butter, put up by the Shakers; preserved green corn and tomatoes; jars of assorted pickles, tamarinds, and cans of beef, prepared by a process which left nothing but salt and heating necessary for the creation of a capital ragout. Before these stores were exhausted we had repeated occasion to thank them for three meals a day, several days in succession. Indeed, wherever we stopped long enough to do, or get any cooking done, on our behalf, we always varied our else carnivorous meal by something succulent from the Shakers' tins.

By this time the whole party were greatly distressed from loss of sleep. A more sad-eyed, out-all-nightish set I never saw anywhere. But all of them except myself were just far enough gone in fatigue to take cat-naps against their strap or in their corners. My head was swollen with fever, but I could not succumb. After half an hour's vain attempt at sleeping in a heap, I left my room to the others who were in a condition to prefer it to the company of the best of friends, and once more sought the stage-box, where it was blowing a gale of wind that made fever and hats alike difficult to hold on to.

Our driver was a terrible fellow, with all the fingers missing from one hand,—the most profane man and the greatest braggart I ever saw. He alternately drank from a black bottle and praised his own driving, until the reins dropped out of his remaining fingers, and he himself would have gone headlong from the box, had I not grasped his collar. We had just crossed a high bridge without parapets over one of the numerous streams in this region, called Big or Little "Sandy"; the leaders stopped, and began facing the pole, and we were in imminent danger of being tipped over or backed down the steep bank. I jumped down upon the pole, and caught the reins just in time to save us; our Denver friend leaped out with his pistol drawn, and induced the driver to descend a little quicker than liquor and gravity combined would have brought him; after which, with a word of explanation directed around the side to our friends within, we left the fellow who had nearly murdered us, cursing his tortuous way along the road, and drove to the next station ourselves. In mentioning this occurrence, I should say, as an act of justice to the company and its drivers, that it was a very exceptional case to see a drunken man on an Overland box. The only repetition of it in our whole journey occurred in the Rocky Mountains, just beyond Fort Bridger, and then without any accident. It is due to the drivers as a class to say that they usually astonished me by an abstemiousness, under circumstances of great solitude, monotony, and temptation, which would have done credit to any man of business in an Eastern city. Many of them, on principle, or from a sense of their responsibility, would not drink at all.

Between Big Sandy and Comstock's we got our first experience of a thunder-storm on the Plains. At sunset the clouds were piled into an ebon staircase, draped with gold, mounting from the western horizon to the zenith; and as the daylight declined, the massive steps became tessellated every now and then with lightning working across them silently in strange patterns. The weather had been very warm all day, and we thought likely that this exhibition would prove nothing more than the heat-lightning of our Eastern summer evenings. But about nine o'clock we were undeceived. The sky "meant business." The agency that wrought those delicate traceries of golden sprig and anastomosing vein-work began to have a voice. At the foot of the great stair came a rumbling and a groan, as if the giants were beginning to climb. It grew louder, and here and there step parted from step, then the structure lifted at the base and descended at the top, making a series of black blocks and boulders, hanging downward from the same level of sky with lurid interstices between them, through which the upward depths looked awful. Never in my life did I see cloud distances graded with such delicacy. One could almost measure them by miles from the inky surface, hanging with torn fringes of leaden vapor just above our head, up through the tremendous chasms flecked along their wall, with dying gold and purple color, with wonderful light and shadows, and marked by innumerable changes of contour, to the clear but angry sky that paved the farthest depth of the abysses. I rode on the box for an hour looking into these glorious rifts with fascinated eyes. Then between their walls began a hurrying interplay of lightning, and the great artillery combat of the heavens commenced in earnest. At first the adjoining masses had their duels to themselves,— battery fighting battery, pair and pair. Half an hour more, and the forces had perceptibly massed,—their fire coming in broader sheet, their thunder bellowing louder. An hour, and the fight of the giants became a general engagement. The whole hemisphere was a blinding mass of yellow flame at once, and the reports were each one instantaneous shock, which burst the air like the explosion of a mine. Then the wind rose to a hurricane; and before the dust could be set whirling by it, there followed such a flood of rain as I never saw anywhere, on sea or land. Sitting on the box still, for I had much rather be soaked than desert such a spectacle, I found my breath taken away for the first minute, as if I had been under a waterfall. It was not drops, nor jets, nor a sheet; it was a mass of coherent water falling down bodily. Five minutes from the time it began to wet us, the horses were running fetlock-deep, with the road still hard under their hoofs, for the soil had not yet had time to dissolve into mud. Torrents were flowing down every incline; where the plain basined, the water stood in broad sheets revealed by the flashes, like new ponds suddenly added to the scenery. Still the storm did not spend itself in wind and water. The lightning got broader, and its flashes quicker in succession; the thunder surpassed everything I have heard, or read, or dreamed of. Between explosions we were so stunned that we could scarcely speak to or hear each other, and the shocks themselves made us fear for the permanent loss of our hearing. One moment we were in utter darkness, our horses kept in the road only by the sense of feeling; the next, and the vast expanse of rain-trampled grass lay in one embrace of topaz fire, with the colossal piles of defied cloud out of which the deluge was coming,—earth and heaven illumined with a brightness surpassing the most cloudless noon.

Suddenly there appeared before us a portent, of which I had read accounts in scientific annals, but which I had never seen before and never expect to see again. There was a temporary lull in the conflict above us. Into the blackness there rose out of the ground, apparently from a high divide, not a mile beyond our leaders, a column of lightning sized and shaped like the trunk of a tall pine. Straight and swift, but with a more measurely motion than that of the higher discharges, it shot up, shedding its glare for many rods around, and making a sharply cut band of fire against the black background of the clouds, until it struck the nearest mass of vapor. Then, with the most tremendous flash and peal of the whole storm, its blazing capital broke into splinters, and went shivering across the area, right over our heads. If it were only possible to paint such things! But on canvas they would seem even more theatrical than they do in these inadequate words. In all the wrath of nature,—mad hurricanes and thunder-storms, on sea or land,—there never visited me anything to compare in awful splendor, and the impression of ungoverned power, with this upward lightning-stroke on the Nebraska Plains.

Out of the deluge, the flame, and the roar, we suddenly saw a corral and log-house, at our right-hand; a small stream, swollen to a torrent, under tall cotton-woods, upon our left. The former were "Comstock's"; the latter was the Little Blue. Drenched to the skin, but happy with the memory of the greatest night in my life, I jumped down, and passed one of the box-lanterns inside to be lighted, for the first time, by my comparatively dry companions. This effected, we opened the curtains sufficiently to let them escape; with the assistance of the driver, got out of the boat all such dunnage as we intended to stop with us; and by the time everything was disgorged but our guns, succeeded in awakening the occupants of the ranch to a sense of our needs. Comstock came to the door with a lantern of his own, and as soon as we pronounced the words "Munger" and "buffalo hunt," welcomed us with a cordiality as cheering as dry stockings. A moment more, and all our belongings were whisked out of the torrent into a long apartment, floored with hewn plank and nicely weather-tight; the whip cracked on the off leader's withers; and saying good-night to our late comrades, with an accompaniment of thunder, we saw them whirl away into the glare, and shut the ranch door between us and the storm.

A tall ladder led up from the kitchen, reception-room, and bed-chamber we had just entered, into the "men folks'" loft, above. Ascending it, under Comstock's guidance, we found a number of sturdy ranch-men snoring defiance to the outer storm, and without ceremony dropped down in our blankets on the intervals of floor between them. As we have seen, it can thunder in Nebraska,—but not loud enough to break such slumber as then and there fell incontinently upon our prostrate forms!

## CHAPTER II.

## Comstock's.—A Buffalo Hunt.

Comstock had the early habits, without the aggressive and proselyting spirit, of most pioneers. He pitied our Eastern weakness, and let us sleep late, which, in Nebraska, means the sybaritic hour of eight A. M. It was still raining when we arose; but it was only a trickle compared with the night before. A Euphuist, indefatigable in hunting metaphors to earth, might have said that the sky looked like a battle-field the day after an engagement, where the exhausted clouds lay still, mangled with lightning, and bleeding lymph from all their wounds down upon the world below. Or he might have compared it to a great ball-room, where the dancers had waltzed themselves to death to the music of the thunder-band, and were now strewn prostrate on the floor of their late revel, amid the drippings of ruptured goblet, flask, and wassail bowl. To the matter-of-fact person, it was simply raining, and after a style which promised steady continuance all day; but whether the "tireless heavens" looked fagged to him or not, he must have acknowledged that he felt so, had he been of our party. We had not yet reacquired the old muscular tone of former forest-camps, which makes sleep, on a log-floor and a blanket, as refreshing as on the springiest mattress. We were a little lame, and, though we said nothing about it, were unable to regard eight A. M. an hour so luxuriously late as it appeared to our sturdy host, our last late breakfast having been eaten, like others of the series, at half-past eleven in New York. Yet we were undeniably refreshed from the sore, wide-awake sleepiness of the day before; and a capital meal of stewed buffalo-hump and antelope-steak, washed down by coffee, surprisingly realistic for this latitude of pease and chickory ideals, creamed, moreover, from the sumptuous and unmistakable udders of nature, proved palatable to us in the highest degree.

I like so much to think of the Comstocks—one of the best, truest, kindest families of pioneer people we met in our whole journey, and having no equals for typical character or native goodness in our experience, short of Sisson's delightful ranch at the foot of Shasta Peak, in California,—I enjoy their memory so heartily, that I am fain to spend a portion of this rainy Nebraska day in making their portraits for my readers.

Comstock himself is a man about sixty-three, with a head and face like the pictures of De Quincey. In contour only, not in expression; for in the wrinkles around his eyes lurks a Yankee waggery, which no English face, even the shrewdest, ever simulates. His hair is grizzled and wiry, such as belongs to the iron temperament. He is of the medium height, compactly made, and in every limb and lineament shows the training of over half a century's pioneer life, hardship having braced instead of shaken him. He began his history in the western part of New York State, when bear-hunts were still an accessible pastime to people in the vicinity of Rochester, and all the now smiling lawns and meadow-lands of the region were howling wildernesses, here and there intersected by a bridle-path. From his earliest manhood he has been pressing the front of barbarism. He has lived successively in Michigan, Wisconsin, Minnesota, Texas, and Nebraska. As fast as civilization has come up to his stake set in the wilderness, he has pulled it up, and travelled to some newer domain, beyond the atmosphere of artificial society. There is that in him which cannot tolerate fine gentlemen, town-meetings, political claptrap, and the gossip of mixed communities. As his eldest son said of himself, so he might say, "I cannot breathe free in sight of fences: I must be able to ride my horse where I like." Yet, for all this, there is nothing about him of the barbarism he has been fighting; nothing of asceticism or misanthropy toward the society he has left behind. He is a devouring reader. The crannies of his log-house are full of old magazines—newspapers of ancient date—well-read and re-read books. He takes the liveliest interest in everything that concerns the East; he is thoroughly acquainted with the names that have figured most largely in our public records, and has a general knowledge of recent literature which surprised me. He was never tired of hearing about New York, Boston, Philadelphia, their prominent people and institutions. I think he felt the same kind of interest in them that a boy feels in the Island of San Juan de Fernandez. An ideal blessedness surrounds Robinson Crusoe, to our youthful fancy, although on stern logical considerations, we should not care to be cast upon an uninhabited island ourselves. Nothing would tempt Comstock to live in a great city; yet its diminished roar, heard far off on the rear of the buffaloes, fascinates him like weird music. He was driven out of Texas by the corrupt manners of the slavocracy around him, and he loves Freedom as he loves air. He never tires of talking about people who have helped her at the East. "I would go further," said he one day, "to take a look at Henry Ward Beecher, than to see the biggest old buffalo-bull that ever ran."

Comstock is a widower, with a large family of children, most of them living with him, and two of them having children of their own under his roof. On the Plains there is none of our Eastern necessity of leaving home to push one's fortune. There is plenty of pushing to be done in home's immediate neighborhood,—plenty of room to push, where a family is surrounded everywhere by league on league of the most fertile soil, which has never been appropriated, recorded, or even surveyed for the market. The Little Blue is fringed with cotton-wood of lofty growth: men and axes are the only remaining conditions for a house and a corral. To be sure, cotton-wood timber has one unpleasant idiosyncrasy: even while it is growing, all the crevices of its bark swarm with that wretched insect which has received its name from the slovenly beds of corrupt civilization, and conferred on them their main horror; but a good seasoning removes the pest, and I must say for Comstock's that I never found an individual of the species while I stayed there. As for grain-land and pasture-lot, the only problem with the family is the point of the compass towards which they shall run the plough or drive the cattle; the consideration of how far never once intrudes upon their minds. The absence of fences makes it necessary to keep a tolerable stud of horses for the chase of stray steers. Occasionally a herd of emigrant cattle goes past, along the Overland trail, and not altogether unbeknown to its drivers, who are never celebrated for clear notions on portable property, absorbs a nice yoke of Comstock's animals, who chance to be feeding by the wayside. These have to be followed up and reclaimed,—a matter which may cost a day's rough riding, but nothing in the shape of litigation, where there are no courts or lawyers, and little in the nature of altercation, where everybody has so many cattle that two, more or less, are not worth a squabble. This is the main anxiety affecting the Comstock mind. It is quite unbothered with cumbersome and costly preparations for the wintering of stock. It needs and builds no barns or stables. The climate is at no season so severe that animals require more than the shelter of a corral or an open shed. All over this region the luxuriant grass cures on the ground, and makes inexhaustible winter feed, without the trouble of mowing and stacking. The snows never last long enough to starve out the herds left running at large. They sleep, as well as graze, on the open plain, all the year round, never being driven in, save to yoke, brand, or milk them. These facts make the pastoral life almost Arcadian, as far as labor is concerned. When a pioneer, like Comstock, has secured a few fine breeding animals, he is in possession of the easiest managed and most rapidly increasing capital in the world.

Beside his herds, Comstock attends to farming, in a moderate way,—raising sufficient corn for his horses' use, when work takes them out of pasture, and grain enough to keep his family supplied with flour. He has a vegetable patch, just across the Little Blue from his corral, whose deep, rich loam and thrifty crops would delight the heart of any suburban market gardener.

The necessities of life press a man so little in this bounteous region, that a comparatively small proportion of any day is devoted by the Comstocks to actual labor. Comstock himself is as sturdy at sixty-three as he was at forty, and goes out to the patch, across his log bridge, with a hoe over his shoulder, stepping as elastically as if he had pastime before him. His boys go with him; and after a forenoon of steady work, all come in to dinner, and seldom return again to any heavier labor than breaking colts, hunting, or chasing estrays. Within an hour's ride, across the Blue, antelope are nearly as plenty as anywhere on the Plains; and one afternoon's good sport will replenish the Comstock larders with the best fresh meat known to wild or civilized bills of fare.

George Comstock, the eldest son of the old pioneer, lives with him in a partition of the ranch-house,— whose front is devoted to miscellaneous emigrant supplies, while its rear is the sitting-room of a thrifty Mrs. George and the nursery of a rising family. In all the delightful old genre pieces of the Dutch artists, and the eccentric old places in Wapping and Holborn which the character-novelists of London love to paint, there is nothing more original than the sight of that shop and dwelling-room combined: where slouching teamsters take their pull at the beer-mug or Jamaica bottle, on their way to California, across a counter where the family bread-batch rests *in transitu* to the oven; where a pile of hickory shirts lies for sale on a shelf beside the family tea-kettle; where the cradle and the cooking-stove are inextricably mixed with vinegar barrels and meal-sacks; where the babies play Hide-and-seek behind piles of wagon canvas, and the house-wife's work-basket is flanked by rows of Osgood's Cholagogue. In this *omnium gatherum* of commerce and the family I found most unsuspectable things: copies of the "New York Herald," fresh with all the bloom of last month; a luxury of advanced civilization known as ready-prepared egg-nog; a sewing-machine; all kinds of canned fruit from the Shaker settlements; Sunday suits of great gloss, with a certain tenuity in the legs and arms, the very thing for a rotund, muscular lover, fearless of exhibiting his outlines; bandanna handkerchief shaming the flamingo; plug-tobacco in great swarthy cubes; trace-chains, ox-yokes, frying-pans, Little Songsters, beaver-skins taken in barter, looking-glasses, felt hats, ticking clocks,—but let me not attempt the inventory of a collection which surprised me as much out on the rim of the buffalo herds as it would have surprised Crusoe to have been washed ashore from the wreck into the front door of a branch of A.T. Stewart's. The shop is a house of call to all the emigrants and drivers on their way westward, and adds not a little to the revenue of the Comstocks, who deserve everything they can make, since people fairer and less huckstering in their nature exist nowhere.

To return to the other side of the house. The ménage of Comstock, Senior, is in charge of his two daughters, Frank and Mary, who for skillful housewifery, sterling common sense, and native refinement, are surpassed by few women whom I ever met at the East. It was a perpetual surprise to me to hear girls whose whole life had been spent on the Plains or in the backwoods, talk Longfellow and Bryant, Dickens and Thackeray, Scott and Cooper, when they came in from milking, and sat down in their plain calicoes to knit the masculine stockings or mend the infantile pinafores. Nobody could talk more understandingly, criticise more justly, or appreciate more fully everything in their authors that related to natural feeling; and if this book ever gets out to them (as I mean it shall), I shall be more interested in knowing their opinion of it than that of most critics who shall overhaul me in the cities. It is the pride of our American system that such womanly culture can coexist in the Nebraska wilds with those sturdy administrative qualities

ANTELOPES.

PRAIRIE DOGS.

which subdue savagery into a home, and fight the battle for a civilization which shall presently come and build cities on their conquered field. Place on the frontiers of any other country in the world a family of women isolated from all the luxuries and softening influences proper to their sex, and after a few years have gone over their heads you will find a set of female boors living in a slovenly hut. But "the peasantry" have no status in America. The nearest approach to them which we found in all our journeying was here and there a houseful of unfortunate "Pikes" or "Butternuts," whom slavery had degraded below the black level before they escaped from its miasma, and the first generation of whom still lay entangled in the accursed traditions of an accursed system, while the second and third were gradually struggling out into the light of new ideas. But even here there was a dim sense of something better to be had for the trying which does not exist among the disheartened lower strata of social Europe. As for the Comstocks, they were truly typical American people. They understood the science of pioneering as a chemist understands analysis and reactions; but just as one of our chemists would bestir himself, and make his way up in the world, if ill-fortune drove him to the gold-diggings, so would they within three years' time adapt themselves to any social conditions into which fate might force them, and lay the foundations of a family whose position would be prominent in any town where it might live. I was hourly surprised to see the self-reliance of these sisters. They were sometimes left alone in the ranch for a day at a time, all the "men-folks" being off on a hunt or elsewhere out of call. On several such occasions a detachment from one of the numerous Indian bands who make this region by turns a neutral and a fighting ground, poured in to make the "lone women" a compulsory visit. Now, an Indian visit is no joke. Even where a tribe pretends to be friendly, its only distinction between that and the hostile bearing is, that instead of scalping you first and robbing you afterward, it takes all the property it can lay hands on, and leaves your hair for a more convenient season. A band of "friendly" Sioux comes to a small settlement, stops at the first house, emaciates itself by drawing in the cheeks and abdomen, denotes by sepulchral grunts and distressed gestures that it has had nothing to eat for "three shneep" (whereby three *sleeps*, or entire days and nights, are intended), seizes on everything edible and, if the white feather is shown it, everything portable which it can appreciate beside; confiscates guns, ammunition, and whiskey, and, having cleared out house number one, goes in succession to every other dwelling with the same emaciation, gesture, and appropriation, until it departs at the other end of the settlement stuffed beyond the elasticity of all conceivable animals save Indians and anacondas, and loaded with the materials for a month's barter and a fortnight's "drunk." I asked Mary Comstock if she was not afraid of such visitors. "O no!" she replied; "we always get the guns out of sight when we are left alone by the men-folks, so that if the Indians come we needn't be robbed of what must defend us on a pinch; and if we see them coming, we bolt the doors, and talk with them through the shut window. Sometimes they steal a march on us, and the first thing we know they're swarming in like bees,—asking for everything they see, hunting for something to eat, and begging to be "treated." We generally give 'em everything they want to eat, but when it comes to liquor,—not we! One young Indian last summer got mighty sassy when his band came here, and insisted on having something to drink. At last I got a bottle of Perry Davis's Pain-killer, and handed him that. He just threw his head back, and took it down at one swallow. The next thing he gave *such* a yell, bolted through the door, and after that he never troubled *me* much."

Comstock has two sons with him beside George, both excellent specimens of the young pioneer,—one about twenty, the other about sixteen years old. They are fine shots, fearless horsemen, industrious farmers and herdsmen,—with the same rich veins of original humor and strong common sense which run through all the other members of the family. Their manners are frank, self-respectful, and, in the highest sense of the word, gentlemanly. There is a cordial kindness and a native refinement in all they do or say, as far from the artificial politeness or elegant puppyism which we too often find in our city boys at the East, as from the rustic greenness and awkwardness with which the traditions of romance and the stage invest the young backwoodsman.

Beside these children of Comstock's and others of the third generation, the log-cabin shelters a number of ranch-men and hunters, who assist in caring for the crops and herds, and purveying for the family with their rifles. A young Philadelphian, William Butler, who built the ranch as an emigrant trading-post, selling it to Comstock on the death of his brother and partner, lives here when he is not in the saddle or in camp. Willard Head, a dashing horseman, rejoicing in gorgeous leather breeches of Mexican manufacture, adorned with shiny bell-buttons all the way up the leg, makes this his rendezvous while awaiting promotion to the box of an Overland stage. Last, but as characteristic a pioneer as any of the family, comes John Gilbert,—a weath-er-bronzed youth of twenty-five, with the most resplendent set of teeth, blue eyes full of uncontrollable waggery, and a pair of hands skilled in every department of frontier craft, from throwing a lariat to building a house. His sight is as keen as an Indian's. This by itself makes him a capital shot, and, combined with quick intuitions and great experience, a guide unsurpassed by any I ever saw. Crowning his excellent physical qualities are a dry wit and inexhaustible backwoods' humor which would keep a camp cheerful if reduced to mule-meat and wild onions.

The second day after our arrival at Comstock's proved as fair and sunny as we could desire. Everything had been pre-pared for our expedition to the buffalo country. A sack of flour, a small keg of salt pork, a box of hard-tack, a grid-iron, two frying-pans, some camp-kettles, a pile of tin plates, and a lot of knives and forks; a judicious selection from our own party's private stores, consisting of pickles, canned fruits, condensed milk and coffee,—all these, and numerous small boxes containing the condiments for a reinforcement of nature's hunger-sauce, stood in a pile that looked like moving-day, at the door of the ranch by seven o'clock in the morning. Munger of the Overland Road had reached us with his double buggy and two fast horses on the eve-ning before. After breakfast we immediately set out in the following order. The artist of the expedition, Munger, and myself, with a pair of rifles, a shot-gun, and the large col-or-box which accompanied our entire journey, occupied the buggy. Butler, George and Ansell Comstock, John Gilbert, and the two remaining gentlemen of our party went in a couple of large farm-wagons drawn by teams belonging to the ranch. Willard Head, and Thompson of the Overland station to the eastward of us, which bore his name, escorted us as skirmishers, each on his own horse.

We forded the Little Blue just across the road from the ranch, passed the thrifty vegetable patch which supplied the Comstock table, and at once struck south over the trackless plain. The grass was tall and luxuriant, but not so close as to impede our animals. In spite of the recent rain-storm, the ground, matted with grass-roots, bore our hoofs and wheels as firmly as a trotting-course. Everybody was in high spirits. To men just out of the hot-house of New York life, the air and sunshine were fairly intoxicating. Life swarmed around us more luxuriously at every step. The wild flowers of the Plains were a perpetual source of happiness to the eye. They made royal splashes of high color on the sunny sides of all the divides; they checkered the rich green of the ravines with delicious contrasts; and every now and then, as the grass waved, glowed upon us out of their secret nurseries among the tall blades, like tangled sunshine getting woven through the herbage by the shuttle of the wind. Before we left home I had deeply regretted our failure to include a practical botanist in our party; I regretted it still more when we were among the lavish Flora of the Plains; and most of all, having to describe so inadequately what might have been treated so well, do I regret it now. But this makes no pretense to be a purely scientific book, and I must not omit to rehearse the beauties which rejoice the tourist, because I cannot say how they would strike the botanist.

Over all the higher lands of the rolling plain which we were traversing abounded a pink, purple, crimson, or sometimes nearly white blossom, known here as the Indian pea.

It grows on a long, villous flower-stalk, around which both blossoms and leaves are symmetrically arranged; its pistil is carried in a sheath, with the stamens about its base, and its fruit is a pod in shape like a large flattened gooseberry, containing seeds of the size of a pin-head. This pod is edible when boiled in salt water; at least, it is eaten, though to an Eastern epicure its taste is undisguisably rank. The Indian pea at this season, when in full blossom, both from its profusion and the variety of its tints, is one of the most important contributions to the beauty of the Plains.

Prairie roses are abundant everywhere on this portion of the Plains. I found the yellow, white, and pink varieties, all of which are luxuriant in blossom and deliciously fragrant. The tiny blue star-grass lurks everywhere among the taller herbage; and in many places I saw a variety of sorrel (*Oxalis acetocella*) bearing yellow blossoms as large as a good-sized buttercup, though in every other respect it appears quite identical with our Eastern plant. Along the borders of the small streams, especially where the ground was shaded, grew a small variety of our evening primrose, of several tints, from pale straw-color to nearly orange; and in low, moist spots I noticed several specimens of a flower only differing from this in the possession of black spots and a carinated structure dividing the corolla into segments, upon the middle of each of the petals. Another plant, which seemed to me a species of the abutilon, had handsome cupellate blossoms of a deep-orange color, striated longitudinally along the petals with delicate pale yellow. Here and there grew a white species closely allied to our garden "rocket"; and a wild sunflower, with a root which I found quite as edible and as flavorous as our Jerusalem artichoke, was very common on all the slopes of the divides.

But the two most charming flowers of the region, the one for its perfume, the other for its color, were a tiny species having the habits and appearance of the water-lily, to whose family I supposed it to belong, and a crimson cup as large as a small althea, whose only name among the ranch people was "the ground poppy," though whether it be really allied to that plant I regret my inability to state. Its plant-leaves are multilobed, and somewhat like those of our own poppy; but it grows upon running stalks close to the ground, and to unscientific eyes seems quite as closely connected with the mallows. It appears in patches varying from a few feet to several rods in circuit, and wherever these occur, the ground is one gorgeous mass of magenta fire. It is the glory of the fertile plains in May and early June, and we afterward found it extending for miles among the barren sand-dunes beyond Fort Kearney, encroaching upon the territory of the cacti and the gramma-grass. Wherever it appears, it is the chief visual delight of the Plains, Flora. The tiny water-lily above mentioned, I only found once in all our progress to the buffalo country. We had halted at the bottom of a wet-draw to water our horses. I went above the place where they were drinking, to quench my thirst at a brown pool which appeared a trifle less stagnant than their watering-place, and, lying down with my face over the water, noticed an exquisitely subtle fragrance like that of tuberose and orange-flower combined. On pushing away the weeds which grew out over the pool, I found a nest of lovely white blossoms, smaller than the smallest strawberry-flower, shaped like an Eastern water-lily in miniature, with delicate yellow stamens and pistil, and moored on the water by slender green filaments rooted in the ooze of the pool. No American blossom that I am acquainted with, not even the trailing arbutus, possesses such an indescribable ethereal fragrance as this tiny water-lily. I sought in vain to preserve specimens of it. The pages of the note-book in which I pressed them, absorbed the petals as if they had been dew, and only stains were left, having none of the flower's characteristic odor.

We had been travelling less than an hour, and had crossed a wet ravine, called "White Ash Draw," between our original divide and the next further south, when we saw our first antelope. He was a mere glancing spot on the sunny side of a slope two miles off, and disappeared too soon to be resolved by the field-glass. From that time forward we were continually uncovering pairs or groups of these lovely creatures, and before noon got near enough to some of them for a shot. Butler's rifle brought down a fine young buck. We laid him in one of the wagons, and continued our march.

It is perhaps no exaggeration to call the antelope the most beautiful as well as the swiftest animal of our American wilds. His size is that of a young red-deer doe; his color a compromise between buff and fawn, shading here and there into reddish-brown, with a patch of pure white on the buttocks which gives rise to the Western term expressive of his stampede, "showing his clean linen." His ears grow far back on his head, are long, and curve so much that at a distance they appear like horns. The horns themselves grow so immediately over the supra-orbital projection as to seem coming out of the animal's eyes; they are long, slender, have a comparatively slight retro-curve, and show no sign of branching, save a little bud which is developed, as in the engraving, near the root, when the antelope is about two years old. The older bucks are occasionally found with other rudiments of this kind.

The chief peculiarity of the antelope is his lack of a "dew-claw." His feet have no rudimentary hoof like the deer's. He is almost or quite an anomaly in this respect among the tribes with which he is allied. Whatever that deficiency may amount to, it certainly does not interfere with his speed, which is almost incredible, even to an eye-witness. We could scarcely believe that our sight had not deceived us, when, at one moment, we saw one of these little creatures plainly with the naked eye, browsing on a slope fifty yards off, the next beheld him dwindling to a mere speck, and the next lost sight of him altogether. His flight was more like that of a bird than a quadruped, sometimes rather like a rocket than either. Occasionally we surprised a pair of antelopes on a wide area of even ground, where we could watch their stampede for a longer period without obstruction; and the study of their motion became a perfect delight to the eye. They seldom or never leapt like deer, but ran with level backs, and in smooth rhythm, like sheep,—their legs glancing faster than sight could follow. We got no expression for this peculiar gait till George Comstock, looking at a flock of them in full flight, ejaculated, idiomatically, "Lord! *don't* they open and shet lively!"

It was quite amusing to see them baffle the attempts of one of our mounted men, whose enthusiasm overcame his experience. Clapping spurs to his horse, he rode with all his might at a flock of them, feeding within long rifle-shot, and came about eighty yards from them before they snuffed him and turned tail. For nearly ten minutes they treated him as a butterfly treats a school-boy. Putting half a mile between them and his panting horse in as little time as it takes to write it, they paused, stood with their noses in air, and seemed to be having a quiet laugh among themselves; let him approach nearly as close as before, and then floated away, on a line at right angles to their former retreat, tempting him with the delusion that he might head them off. As often as he turned, they repeated these tactics, until at last he stopped, quite provoked at himself, and with his horse thoroughly winded, to see their "clean linen" flash for an instant in the sun, as they went out of sight among some thick cotton-woods, on the edge of a distant run. It was about as hopeful a piece of business as trying to run down a telegraph message.

Later in the day, we learned the only way to hunt antelope with unvarying success. It is an old Indian method, and the white men on the Plains have learned as much adroitness in it as their exemplars. The antelope is not afraid of horses; and by walking in the cover of his saddle-animal, the hunter can get quite near a flock without being discovered, provided he approaches against the wind. If the wind blows from him, it is astonishing how quickly their scent warns them of him, without the least aid from their eyes. Having got as near them as he dares in this way, he throws the coil of his lariat down from the saddle-horn, crouches and pickets his horse with a sharp stake, always carried with him for the purpose. Lying in the grass, he ties his bright colored bandanna (a strip of white cloth will answer, *faute de mieux*) to a tall sunflower stalk, his ramrod, or a stick of any kind. If still too far off to attract his game, he crawls low on his hands and knees, dragging his rifle by his side, until he reaches a spot of such prominence that they would be sure to see him in an instant if he stood up. There he quietly lies down again on his stomach, and lifts his extemporized flag as high as he can reach. The antelopes see it, stop browsing, raise their heads, and peer forward with bulging eyes, but show no signs of fright. The flag is for a moment dropped out of sight into the grass. The beautiful creatures lower their noses, and attempt to resume their dinner. But there is something on their minds. After one or two distrait pulls at the sweet grass-roots, their heads are again lifted, and again they peer earnestly forward. Up goes the flag once more, and this time perhaps with a slow waving motion. The antelopes' curiosity is now thoroughly excited. For an instant they pause irresolutely, then make two or three hesitating steps in advance, snuffing as they go. Again the flag is lowered. They turn to each other, and seem to be holding a parley. Their inevitable conclusion is that they will pursue their reconnoissance, and see what strange bird that is fluttering above the grass. When the flag is once more lifted, they advance again, and finally, unless the wind shifts, or the recumbent hunter finds his patience ebbing, come up almost within pistol-shot of his ambush. Crack goes his rifle; and he must be a poor shot indeed if one of the beautiful quarries before him does not turn a summerset and tumble headlong. I have known a single rifle-ball do the business for two antelopes, where they stood in range. If now the hunter does not discover himself, one at least of the remaining antelopes is often easily bagged. The survivors dart away for a moment from the side of their fallen comrade, but do not go far, often return, and nearly always stand still, to satisfy their own curiosity, within easy rifle-shot of the hunter. But unless he actually needs the meat at once, or can avail himself of it before it spoils, the thorough-going hunter of the Plains is too chivalrous and merciful (to say nothing of economy, in a country where game is as plenty as at creation) to slaughter a beautiful animal for which, despite his own rough exterior, he has a true, even poetical, admiration. I never found a hunter on the Plains (I am not including boy-tourists and foreign emigrants) who would not blush to emulate Gordon Cummings.

About six miles south of the spot where we encountered our first antelope, we saw our first buffaloes. John Gilbert, the wariest hunter of the whole party, rode alongside of our buggy, and quietly pointed to eight or ten scattered black dots on a divide, nearly three miles away, to our right. Our glasses revealed their character; and I should be almost ashamed to let an old hunter know what a fever of enthusiasm that far-off glance communicated to my blood. It was such a strange jumble of feeling to remember operas, National Academy pictures, and the crowd on Broadway, so close on the heels of these grand old giants, who own the monarchy of the Continent's freest wilderness. I felt as happy as a green boy, and trembled all over. Buffaloes—indubitable buffaloes—feeding on that vast sunny, fenceless mead, in as matter-of-fact and bovine a manner as any New England farmer's cows on one of Coleman's or Shattuck's elm-dotted pasture-lots. They were too far away to take any notice of us, and proved to be only the outposts of the herd,—the extreme advance of venerable bulls, pushed across the Republican to reconnoitre.

Just after we saw the buffaloes, I had a remarkable instance of John Gilbert's delicate Indian training as a guide. We had been steering all the morning, since we left the Blue, by the points of compass, but following the main divides for the sake of a good track as closely as we could without inconvenient aberration from the ford on the Republican, for which we had been making. The ground now began rising before us, and we came to a place where the divide forked. We had not yet seen the Republican, nor the timber which marked its first bottom. It became a question to us which way we should turn, east or west, as nothing more entirely without landmarks than the Plains out of sight of timber can well be imagined.

John Gilbert was called upon to decide, while the party halted. He rode about in the tall grass for a few moments without any particular appearance of scrutiny, and finally remarked,—"We'll keep to the eastward, I reckon. Some fellow's gone wrong hereabouts lately. I wonder who it could be. Munger, when you were coming along the road, did you pass a big covered wagon and a small ambulance,—a four-mule team hitched to one, and a span o' horses on t'other?"

Munger hadn't, but Thompson had seen such an "outfit" camped near his station the day before.

"Well, that's it: it's come on down and turned off in the wrong d'rection, just hereabouts."

"*What's* IT?" asked the uninitiated, "and *where* is it? There's nothing to be seen of that kind."

"O yes, there is," replied John, positively. "I've just found the tracks. Here's one set o' narrow wheels, with eight big hoof-marks between 'em; and a sorter mixed up with that is a set of broad wheels, with sixteen small hoofs in between *them*, a comin' after one another. One's the ambulance and horses. T'other's the wagon and the mules. Then, just a little divided from them, and turnin' easterly, is the old track our wagon made when we come down a shootin' from the ranch, ten days ago. So easterly's our way; and the other fellows'll get lost, I reckon."

To satisfy my curiosity, I jumped down from the buggy, pushed the high grass away, and among its matted roots discovered something like the marks he described. From the height where he sat on horse-back, they were as invisible to any ordinary eye as if they had been at the bottom of the sea; and when I did discover them, they would have been as illegible to my understanding for any pathfinding purposes as if they were cuneiform inscriptions on a slab from Nineveh. Still, every word John Gilbert said was afterward substantiated; and how good reason I personally had to thank my stars that those "fellows" *did* go astray, as well as who they were, and other matters concerning them, will all plainly appear before the close of this chapter. For the present, I refer to our quandary only as a remarkable illustration of the intuitional sixth sense acquired by a man like Gilbert, in protracted frontier experience. It must be remembered that since the ranch-wagon had passed down to the Republican, "ten days ago," the tremendous rain-storm, through which we came to Comstock's, had beaten the prairie hard enough to obliterate any vestige of travel on an ordinary road.

We kept to the easterly, following John Gilbert's lead, passed the rise in the divide of which I have spoken, and came to the brink of a lofty bluff, from the base of which a broad plain extended two miles to the now clearly visible cotton-wood fringe along the Republican. We were compelled to ride along the edge for nearly three miles further, before we found a draw running back into the divide with sides sufficiently gradual to permit our descent to the river's first bottom. But none of the time demanded by this detour was thrown away. The view from the brink was one of the loveliest in nature. Broad level sunshine flooded the green plain below us, and drifting cloud-shadows brought out the contour of the lofty bluffs, which alternately projected into and receded from the plain on the river's further side. Here and there the fringing cotton-woods broke away, and let up to us pure blue glimpses of the river, itself reflecting the deeper sapphire of the summer sky. The air was wonderfully clear,—distance deemed partially annihilated. The White Rock Buttes, which we knew to be many miles away to the southward, came out clear and strong, so that we could see the undulations of their surface almost as plainly as if they were in the near foreground. The whole extent of territory within our vision was as fertile in appearance as the finest meadow-lands of the East, and so closely simulated cultivation in its smooth rolling downs and level fields that the eye continually looked for signs of human residence, and found ever fresh astonishment in the utter loneliness of the landscape. It was as if some great agricultural nation had suddenly been driven out of its ancient possessions, or stricken quickly asleep by magic in the deep green groves along the river-bank. But without apparent hyperbole it is impossible to convey the strange impression of this lovely region of lawns without mansions, and farms without grange or barn.

I am wrong in saying "without mansions"; for on our descent to the broad alluvial level below the bluffs, the faces and voices of merry little colonists greeted us on every hand. The river-bottom was so riddled by the burrows of the prairie-dogs that we had to drive cautiously lest our horses should sink mid-leg deep at every step. I have travelled for miles in Nebraska and Colorado through the villages of these marmots; but I never saw their life so teeming, and their habits so active, as here on the utterly undisturbed and unfrequented border of the Republican. The little creatures made the air lively with their chattering, which is a peculiar short shrill squeak rather than a bark, and the honeycombed soil as far as the eye could see was in motion with their antics. They were to be seen in every variety of position. Here sat one on the top of his burrow, completely out of his hole, resting on his haunches, nearly upright like a squirrel, and peering curiously at us with a pair of shiny black eyes till our neighborhood grew too close for his nerves. Another showed both head and tail out of his door, keeping his more vulnerable middle below the edge of the earth-pile; and the still more cautious dog exhibited a mere nose-tip above his entrenchment, chirping at us occasionally in a querulous manner, as if he were asking what in the world could be our business in his municipality. We made several attempts to get specimens, but failed here, as we indeed did everywhere else where we attempted the thing. In the first place, it was almost impossible to calculate one's aim for an object projecting so short a distance from the ground; and in the second, when one's shots did not go over or fall short, there was always enough life left in the little animal to tumble him down his hole beyond the risk of capture. So we soon abandoned the job. The people on the Plains have an effective but rather tedious way of catching prairie-dogs alive. They draw a barrel of water to some isolated hole that does not communicate with the rest of a village, and drown the occupants out by deluging their cul-de-sac. A couple of days' confinement tames them so thoroughly that they can be handled with impunity, and when they are let loose again they cannot be driven from the neighborhood of the house, but burrow somewhere about the foundation or under the doorstep, coming at a whistle to be fed with corn as fearlessly as a house-bred puppy. Though called dogs, they have of course no right to the name, belonging to the rodents, and resembling in all respects the Eastern woodchuck more closely than any other of the tribe with which we are familiar. We shall find them repeatedly hereafter in our progress to the Rocky Mountains, and have occasion to speak of their habits in various localities. I was offered a very pretty and well tamed pair of them at a station two hundred miles east of Denver, and much regretted my inability to close the bargain in consequence of unwillingness to hamper myself with pets all the way to California.

We found the Republican a clear stream, about fifteen rods in width at the place where we struck it,—full of sandbars and quicksands, with treacherous banks of black and yellow loam, which came near casting our horses when we tried to ford. We managed, however, to get across without "sloughing" where the water was only a little above our hubs. The southern edge of the stream was well timbered with fine old growths, mainly of elm and cotton-wood, under whose shadow we made our camp, and picketed our animals. We were on the Sioux hunting-ground; and although our numbers and armament were sufficiently formidable to warrant us presumably against any attack, in accordance with frontier habits we disposed ourselves between the river and our large wagon, and stacked our guns within easy reach.

Here the Eastern members of our party made their first acquaintance with an animal we had known by reputation since the earliest days devoted to the perusal of Mrs. Trimmer. The gifted beaver had left his "sign" on every tree adjoining the bank. If a workman may be known by his chips, the admiration which we felt for an animal hitherto familiar only in the form of old-school hats, was thoroughly well grounded. We saw many trunks a foot in diameter, and some as thick as eighteen inches, gnawed through with an even bevel all round the girth, as neatly as an experienced wood-chopper could have cut them with an axe. Beside the trees, which the next strong wind or another night's felling-bee of the beavers would tumble to the ground, we found immense numbers of logs, varying from the full length of the trunk to three feet, lying near the severed stumps, awaiting deportation to some projected dam, or further truncation by the tools which had felled them. A neater workshop or nicer work than this on the bank of the Republican never existed among the professors of any handicraft. Where the logs had suffered their final reduction, they were of as uniform length as if they had been cut by the gauge, and their conical extremities of such polished smoothness that one had to examine closely before perceiving the channels made by the ivory gauges of the little workmen. With true human dishonesty, we helped ourselves freely from their wood-pile, and in a few moments had a blazing camp-fire and a kettle singing pleasant prophecies of coffee.

Before the water boiled, and while the antelope was dressing for dinner (the last he should ever be invited to, poor little fellow!) a few of us strolled out beyond the timber with our field-glasses. We did not need them to discover that the crown of the whole adjoining bluff was alive with buffalo. There were certainly quite a thousand in plain sight; yet these were only the second line of outposts,—the first, as we had seen, having already been pushed across the river as skirmishers. Some of them stood on the brink of a clay precipice, fifty or sixty feet high, surveying the horizon, but without any apparent emotion in view of our presence, while the farther ones cropped their way slowly through the grass without raising their heads. Two miles of plain and the height of the bluff intervened between us and them, accounting for a nonchalance far greater than that of any other absolutely wild animal I am acquainted with. A herd of elk, deer, or antelope would have tossed up their heads and been away down the wind before we could have snapped our fingers at them. This bovine stolidity, as we shall see hereafter, is no result of misplaced confidence in human goodness, but a well based faith in the most admirable strategic arrangement known to the gregarious tribes of the brute world.

My first experience of antelope-steak, was a gastronomic sensation, surpassing all the luxuries offered the palate by civilized bills of fare. The finest venison, the most delicate mountain mutton, afford no just comparison for it, though it possesses all the game flavor of the one, and the tenderness, without the inevitable *tallowy* suggestion, of the other. Spring-chicken, quail-breast, or frog's hind legs, are not more delicate; and there is a flavor in the juice quite indescribable, belonging in fact to the idiosyncrasies and monopolies of nature. We had our antelope cooked in several modes: steak broiled on a gridiron; a rib-roast, made by spitting the meat on a sharp stick thrust into the ground before the fire; liver, as exquisite as sweet-bread, *sauté* with a few scraps of salt pork; and large collops fried with the same relish to suit the hearty appetite of our frontiersmen. The only condiments we had with our meat were pepper, salt, and a can of the Shaker peaches, brought from our own party's commissariat; nor would sauce of any piquant kind have been anything but an unwarrantable intrusion on the inmost Eleusinian mysteries of gourmanderie. But I can imagine Soyer looking down on us from some fifth sphere of the world, where he is inventing a five hundredth method of treating ambrosia, and saying with tears of still human regret, "Ah! I died too soon!"

After dinner, the artist opened his color-box, and began making a study of the antelope's head, which had been left entire for his purpose, while the two other gentlemen of our Overland party, accompanied by John Gilbert, Ansell Comstock, Butler, and myself, shouldered our guns and started for the bluff, to try stalking buffalo on foot. The afternoon was very warm, and the tramp through the grass of the river-bottom by no means easy; but the enthusiasm of a first hunt would have carried our neophytes cheerfully twice as far.

We made our way to a precipitous draw, entering the bluff at a distance of three miles from our camp, and halted at its mouth to consider our course. On all the commanding prominences of the divide was stationed a giant bull, motionless, as if carven in bronze, noting our every gesture with red, inevitable eyes. We determined to hide in the cover of some low scrubby bushes, and wait until one of these sentinels came down from his post to drink (the only calculable relaxation of his vigilance) at a neighboring puddle, which lay stagnant in a hollow of the draw. Having distributed ourselves, we waited with held breath for nearly an hour. The sentinel had forgotten us, we thought, for he began moving toward our ambush on a slow stately walk, and descended the side of the draw. We crept along behind the bushes on our hands and knees, intending to flank him, and get to the top of the bluff among the herd without his knowledge. Just as we came abreast of the puddle where he stood irresolutely snuffing, with an evident suspicion weighing on his crafty mind, we looked upward at the post he had just left, and there was another bull, as large and wary as the sentry off duty. We were out-maneuvered, after all; and in revenge for our calloused knee-pans, I regret to say that we poured one simultaneous volley into the buffalo at the puddle. But even an old bull-steak, or the juicy hump and tongue, which were the only valuable part of him, were denied us by an excitement which confused our aim. Revenge must be cool to fire straight. As it was, we had the mortification of seeing him lash with his tail such inconsequential portions of his surface as we had hit at the shamefully small range of one hundred and fifty yards, and without apparent inconvenience shamble away on a leisurely cow-trot, up the draw toward his comrade.

"Cuss his tough hide!" ejaculated John Gilbert. "Why didn't we shoot for him in the first place, instead o' trying to creep round? Then we'd a' had a good tongue for supper at least. Now we hain't got nothin'."

Some one suggested that we had intended to find better game in the herd,—if we had got there.

"*Ef*—that's very good—*ef*," said John Gilbert. "Well,—we *didn't*. Now I don't believe in throwin' away a chance that's clost to you, for a maybe ten mile off. It's too much like Thompson's colt, that swam a ráyvin [ravine] to get a drink, 'cause he'd allays been watered on t'other side."

Both the bulls had now moved out of sight, leaving their late sentry-station unoccupied. We concluded to move up the draw as fast as possible, and get to the top of the bluff before the panic had become general among the herd,—there to lie down out of sight, while confidence was getting restored, and finally to creep through the grass, near enough for another shot. We ran up the draw at double quick, bending as low as possible, and had nearly reached the upper debouchment, when a turn to the right uncovered us to another prominence, and there lowered another pair of vengeful red eyes, burning out of a shaggy fell of hair! We dropped down in an instant, but too late. With a leisurely step, the grim old vedette retreated in good order on the main body.

To gratify new men, whose desire to see and capture buffalo was greater than any possible belief in human experience, our frontiersmen, telling us all the while that it was useless, assisted us for three hours in twice as many repetitions of this maneuver. We might as well have attempted to surprise Grant or Napoleon. Our failures were good for us; for they taught us more of the habits of the buffalo than we could have learned at home from a course of lectures, or a monograph of many pages devoted to that animal.

Had we not learned it with our own eyes, we never could have regarded a true statement of the case as anything but a traveller's tale, and would have filed it alongside of stories about the Gyascutus, or the pelican feeding her young with blood from her own breast.

In very truth, the disposition of the buffalo troops is not surpassed by the most skillful general's arrangement of his forces. On the moment of reaching a new feeding-ground, they fall into an order which seems rather the result of masterly strategy and deep-laid plan than any unconscious result of mere brute instinct. If, as is the case at the season when we visited them, the cows are running with newly dropped calves, the sucklings and their mothers are placed in the very centre of the herd. Just outside of these is a series of lines occupied by the weaned calves and yearlings. The next concentric layer consists of the young bulls, able to fight and shift pretty well for themselves, but not yet to be trusted with state secrets, or the keys of a defensive position. Outside of these come the veterans of the corps,—venerable bulls, who have crossed the Arkansas and the Platte many successive summers,—who know all the good feeding-grounds, and can exercise a general direction and supervision over the cows and the youngsters on the march for their first or second time. These form the advance of the army proper. From their ranks, by a principle of natural selection as unerring as Darwin's, come the skirmishers, who reconnoitre for the advance, and the pickets, who protect the main body. For both these functions, the very oldest and most wary bulls are chosen; but even here a distinction is made which it is interesting to notice. I repeatedly found maimed and invalid bulls among the veterans on picket-duty, but never once among those thrown forward as skirmishers. A tacit conviction seems to exist among the buffaloes that, while age and experience are necessary for responsible posts of observation, perfect soundness of physique must accompany these to constitute the proper pioneers of a campaign. A bull, carrying in his hip the ten-years' souvenir of an ounce ball, or an arrow-head, can limp back from a sentry-post, a mile or two outside the grazing herd, in time to stampede them by intelligence of an enemy; but nothing short of perfect wind and limb consists with the duty of going five or ten miles ahead of a corps, to scent and discover pasture. I have noticed their arrangement so widely that it is no mere theory with me, arising from an admiration which insists on pushing to the extreme a parallel between human and bovine sagacity.

The bulls selected for sentry duty take up their position on all the prominences of the divide, leaving unoccupied, as we discovered on the day referred to, and always after-ward, not a single point from which an approaching enemy may be commanded. The buffalo, widely different from the antelope, depends scarcely at all on his scent; but those great round eyes of his, glowing in their earnestness or anger, like balls of fiery asphaltum, possess a length of range, and an inevitability of keenness, scarcely surpassed by those of any quadruped running wild on our continent. Crouch and crawl where you may, you cannot enter the main herd without half a dozen pair of them successively, or at a time, focusing full upon you. Instant retreat of their owners follows; at first no faster than a majestic walk, but, if your pursuit be hot, with increasing gradations of speed up to the heavy cow-gallop; and then comes the stampede of the late quietly feeding herd, in a cloud of dust, and with a noise of thunder, like a general engagement.

I have said it is impossible to get by the sentries; but there is an exception for the case of a hunter, who, disguised in a wolf or antelope skin, is willing to crawl slowly, dragging a rifle, for two or three miles; or the still rarer case of one who, lying down completely out of sight in the grass, wriggles himself painfully along, like a snake, till he gets within range.

Being somewhat of an enthusiast in hunting as well as everything else, and having no animal disguises at hand to aid me in the former method, I resolved, after our repeated failures recorded above, to try the latter manner of approach. Nobody cared to join me. The rest of the party went around the foot of the bluff to watch the success of Munger, who had just come from the camp on horseback, and was charg-ing with carbine slung and revolver drawn, up another draw about a mile to the north of our first advance. I stayed on top of the divide, and, lying down close to the grassroots, began to work myself toward the herd.

I kept my secret so well that a coyote passed only a little over pistol-shot from me before he suspected danger. I crawled and rested at intervals for more than an hour, the herd getting all the time in plainer sight, until finally my patience became exhausted, and several buffalo wandered as near me as four hundred yards. My rifle was the Ballard (a weapon of whose excellence I shall hereafter have occasion to speak more at large), and put up for five hundred yards, though I have killed an antelope with it at six hundred. I was sure I might rely on it at my present distance, if the buffalo-fever could only be held in check. I took deliberate aim, and succeeded in hitting a fine bull, though the ball went too low for his final settlement, and he walked away laboriously to lie down where I could not follow him. Just at that moment a pair of rifles spoke in quick succession lower down the bluff. Two old bulls on the edge of the herd gave as many jumps, and began lashing their sides and shaking their heads after a most expressive manner. They had evidently been made to tingle somewhere, but were only provoked. For a moment they stood confronting each other, and considering themselves for the probable cause of the disturbance. Then the idea seemed to strike each simultaneously that the other had in some mysterious manner committed the insult and forthwith they rushed headlong against each other's adamant skulls with a shock which might have caved in an ordinary brick house. Then they locked horns, and pushed with such strength as nearly to lift each other on their hind legs; then they tossed each other's heads sideways, broke hold, trampled the ground savagely, and joined their heads with another crash in desperate tourney. Another pair of shots broke up the comical misunderstanding, and set the whole detachment stampeding out of sight, after which I picked myself up a much more fatigued but decidedly a wiser man on the subject of penetrating herds, and joined my comrades just at the foot of the bluff, to find Munger and a gentleman of our Overland party responsible for the practical joke on the old bulls, at whose memory we were still laughing.

It was long after sunset when we got back to camp. Our artist had made two or three studies of game and horses while we were "wasting our time" (as people always say to hunters who return light, though I notice that a nice pair of grouse or saddle of venison greatly dignifies the pastime); George Comstock had the remainder of the antelope cooking at a glorious fire, supplied as usual from the beavers' wood-pile; and the aroma of our condensed coffee, just prepared by turning a gallon of water into a pint of paste, gave the wild pure air of the Plains a strangely incongruous but delicious flavor of civilization.

After finishing our meal, we spread our blankets for the night, and lay down upon them to smoke and talk away that nice mezzotint hour which in camp shades away from supper to bed-time. From the "Noctes Ambrosianæ" down to the last book on the Adirondacks, Literature delights to dwell on such occasions. The romance and poetry, the wit and wisdom, of the camp-fire belong to a specialty as individual and charming as Boswell's Johnson and the gossip of Leigh Hunt I wish I could believe myself adequate to the analyzing of our camp palaver; for it was so racy that no tyro can hope to do it the least justice, and even an old hand might shrink from attempting to redraw the most original of frontier originalities.

The magical beauty and the strange suggestions of our place and time seemed to open every heart, infuse some genius into every mind. He must have had a vulgar nature indeed who could not be caught up into one short inspiration by the mere reflection upon where we were. Half a score of white men all alone in the heart of the virgin continent; some far Sioux camp and the vast cohorts of the buffalo our nearest neighbors in place or sympathy. Above us was the great, pure dome of a heaven so free from all taint of earthly smoke that the stars seemed to have been let down like cressets leagues closer to our heads than in the city, and burned in diamond points without veil or trembling. The air was of that strange sweetness which, having no scent and being absolutely limpid, is still called spicy and balmy by hyperbole straining vainly for an adequate name. Our fire leaped up gladly, as if it tasted the young original oxygen with our own human relish; and across its faint, vanishing edges came spectral glimpses of shivering trees along a distant bend of the Republican; while boldly beyond the flame, the purple-black bluffs rose against the clear dark sky, their promontories merged by night into one long wall of shadow. Nothing broke the silence save now and then the yelp of a coyote, a night-bird's scream, our own subdued voices, and the lulling gurgle of the river at our feet, on its way over dusky sand-bars to carry the message of the Rocky Mountain snows to the soft current of the Gulf and the mad waves of the Atlantic. We lay half-way between great mysteries, —in the lap of a loneliness as profound as the caves of the Nereids.

But this loneliness mellowed instead of oppressing the quaint Western minds which were around us in the firelight. Some trifling remark about the hunt led to a queer idiomatic answer; we began to laugh, and the fire of humor was straightway kindled to such a height that yarn after yarn, joke on joke, surprised the solemn dignity of nature. The simplest saying of any man who has lived like these pioneers much away from his kind takes the form of an aphorism. He has not been where he could give away the sap of his reflections before it crystallized; he has not emptied his brains in loose small-talk; he has much bethought himself,—boiled himself down; and when he speaks, be sure that it is "sugaring-off"' time. I fancy the amount of thought is much the same in all men of quick intellects; they differ mostly in quality of thought and in the measure of its condensation. There is less difference between the Yankee mountaineer and the Western plainsman than their local varieties of scene and habit would lead one to expect. The terseness and epigrammatic smack of both comes from isolation, and their talk has many resemblances.

Ansell Comstock was lamenting the loss of his lariat. Butler saw it lying on the ground beside him, and called his attention to the fact by the figurative utterance, "If it were a snake, it would bite you." Before I left, I had heard Ansell reproving one of his children for a greasy face, by asking him if he wasn't ashamed to sprain all the flies' legs that lit on him. Metaphors like these were common speech at the Comstocks'.

Some of the best stories and *bonmots* told by our frontiersmen had reference to "Old Trotter," an eccentric genius who drives on the first stage out of Fort Kearney westward, and whose deeds and sayings will in future time become as historical as those of Tom Quick in Sullivan County, New York State, Jim Beckworth in Colorado, or any other original elevated by pioneer tradition among its demigods. Trotter improved on the old yarn to the effect "The weather would have been colder if the thermometer had been longer," by saying that he had been where it was "so cold that the thermometer got down off the nail." He once stopped his stage, and steadily gazed into the sky until all the passengers alighted and began gazing with him. Somebody said, "What's the matter, driver? what are you looking at?"—"Can you see the comet?" rejoined Trotter, earnestly. Again for a space everybody made thorough search through the heavens. Finally the most impatient passenger answered, "No! I can't! Where is it?" The rest assented to him, upon which Trotter very quietly said, "Wall, if none of us can find it, I don't believe there's any there,—so s'pose we g'lang." On one occasion, Trotter took a vacation and came down to Atchison for the purpose of recreating in that gilded capital, and beholding the gay world of fashion as displayed upon its costly Boulevards. It was immediately after pay-day, and Trotter was flush. After casting about for some method accordant with his original turn of mind by which his earnings might be dissipated with the highest degree of voluptuary satisfaction, he discovered that a band of minstrels was about to delight Atchison with a concert. He immediately went to the treasurer of the company, prevailed upon him to limit his number of tickets, and, forestalling the market, bought up every one of them himself. Having thus effected what the brokers would call "a corner" in the world of amusement, he repaired to the hall at the hour of performance, occupied a seat in the centre, and had the entire concert to himself. Having thus experienced the sensation of solitary grandeur usually confined to kings and high dignitaries, he expressed himself fully satisfied with his money's worth, and the next morning departed for Fort Kearney, to drive until next pay day without a penny in his pocket.

By far the most entertaining practical joke told of him (for the above has rather the complexion of a luxurious solemnity) is his stopping a man on the road who drove a miserable team of sick and aged little mules, with the ejaculation, "Look a'here, pilgrim! I know a man that would give eight hundred dollars if he could only see them mules!" "Why!" exclaimed the man, startled by such an unexpected prospect of luck, "Yeou da-on't say so! Who is he?" "*He's a blind man*," said Trotter; "g'lang!"

With such stories as these, and many others belonging to that category of which a well known *bel esprit* once said to me, "O, if one could only print the good things which mustn't be printed, what a book that would be!" our frontiersmen kept us lively until the fire burned down to coals, and we felt ready to wrap ourselves in our blankets.

The next five minutes, and we were as sound asleep in that divine bed-chamber of all-out-doors as any baby that ever lay in its cradle, ignorant of human woe. O the change from the lately abandoned vigils and labors of long city nights,— from the three-o'clock retirings, the nervous tossings, the unsolved problems that write themselves on the bed-curtain of him who lies down without any extinction of his business impetus, or cooling of life's competitive fever! It was a return to childhood; and the mother nature stroked our foreheads into slumber with a hand of soft sweet air, the moment that we touched our rugged pillows. Years had blotted out the memory of true sleep from us: now it returned as a new sensation.

With the earliest rays of spring sunshine we were on our feet again, and but a little later saw us as deep as we could get in the clear, bracing water of the Republican. Thoroughly refreshed, we made our breakfast off our own stores,—supper having dismissed the antelope,—and prepared for he grand foray against the buffalo herd, of which yesterday had been only the burlesque; to which, indeed, yesterday was related in much the same sort of way as Mrs. Trimmer and natural history apprenticeships in general are related to actual experience of lions.

The two horses which had been attached to Munger's buggy were both of them well trained hunters of our present game. They were accordingly put under saddle,—Munger retaining the chestnut, a fine animal named Ben Holladay, after the Overland Stage proprietor, and giving me "Nig," an excellent black horse, whose pluck and endurance I afterwards thoroughly tested. I owed this kindness partly to the fact that in my own private capacity I was very anxious for one good hunt on a horse that knew buffalo, but mainly to Munger's willingness to do a "courtesy to the Press," whereof, before leaving New York, I was a member. It both amused and gratified me to see the influence and interest of journalism extending so far beyond the reach of latest editions. No higher compliment could have been paid the profession. The last time I had used my press privilege was in going to my parquet stall in the Academy of Music, past a smiling doorkeeper, who took tickets of other people. Here I vaulted to the saddle of one of the best hunters in the American wilderness, from the same professional spring-board; and the two courtesies were but three weeks apart.

Our artist, though a good shot, and capable of going to market for himself wherever there was any game, as well as most people, had seen enough buffalo-hunting in other expeditions to care little for it now, compared with the artistic opportunities which our battue afforded him for portraits of fine old bulls. He accordingly put his color-box, camp-stool, and sketching-umbrella into the buggy, hitched a team of the wagon-horses to it, and, taking one of our own party in with him, declared his intention of visiting the battle-field solely as "our special artist." Thompson and John Gilbert accompanied us on their own horses. The rest stayed behind to watch camp.

Fully recovered from the stampede of yesterday, the outer bulls of the herd, guarded by their sentinels, were grazing in plain sight along the top of the bluff It was arranged that our four mounted men should lead in open order toward the foot of the bluff upon a quiet walk, and the moment the sentry bulls walked away to give the alarm, charge up the nearest practicable gulch that entered the bluff, getting to the top as quickly as possible. There each of us was to select his own bull out of the herd, and ride him down till he got within easy range. The buggy was to keep as close on our rear as it was able.

Following this arrangement, we marched out from the shadow of the cotton-woods, and began pushing slowly through the grass toward our game. The sentries focused all their eyes on us before we had gone a quarter of a mile from cover, but did not think us worth solicitude until we were a hundred and fifty rods closer. Then they began to paw uneasily, lash their sides, and stretch their necks with unequivocal earnestness. The buggy still kept right behind us, and we walked our horses about fifty feet apart. We were a quarter of a mile from the foot of the bluff, when the first bull in front of us walked majestically away. A few rods further on, and all the sentries began a dignified leave-taking. "Now!" cried Munger, and the four horsemen spurred at once. We all took the same ravine, and scrambled up its sides (steeper than any hill where I had ever seen a horse pushed before) in hardly more time than I have taken to write the fact. We gained the top of the bluff just before the sentries had reached their lines. The herd itself was not stampeded until we came m sight of its front. In an instant some uncountable hundreds of black, shaggy monsters threw their heads into the air with a force which lifted them on their hind hoofs, and, making these last pivotal, whirled about, as John said, "Like as if they had springs in 'em." Then, with a ponderous trot, the whole line was away. We were about two hundred and fifty yards from them when the stampede became general.

This was altogether too far for effective shooting from the saddle, except for an Indian, or some exceptional white man who had spent his life with the herds; and even such ride as close as possible before using bow or rifle. So we again clapped spurs to our horses, and hammered on toward our game, just as the buggy succeeded in climbing the bluff.

The buffalo heard us, and quickened their flight to that clumsy cow-gallop of which I have before spoken. In a few minutes we were putting them to their trumps. They continued to lead our horses for a mile, running quite at the rate of ten miles an hour. But our animals had not yet "got their wind"; and so long as the bulls kept on tolerably even ground where we could follow them, every minute brought us fresh advantage. If they reached the jaws of some unexpected draw, they would plunge thirty feet down its almost perpendicular sides with as little hesitation as we would leap a ditch; but no such ill luck befell us. They showed signs of distress in about five minutes from the first burst, and blew hard, though there was no diminution in their speed, while our animals were warming into their work splendidly.

I selected the bull nearest me, each of the other horsemen picked his quarry, and for ten minutes more I knew nothing, in the heat of my first buffalo fever, but streaming wind, a great oscillating patch of hair and hide beyond me, and a sound of trampling like steady thunder. My horse was crazy with enthusiasm. He snorted as he ran, and his eyes bulged full of fire. I had got within a distance of my game where I should have been ashamed to miss a hat-crown at standing fire. I whirled my carbine round from my back, and dropping the reins let drive for the back of the foreshoulder. Good intention! The slug went harmlessly far over my old monster's neck, as the plunge of my horse threw the muzzle into the air. I was disgusted with the world, but sought to retrieve myself by one more effort. My breech-loading Ballard, the best arm for sport of all kinds that is made on the continent, had another cartridge in it within ten seconds. I was still within fifty yards of my buffalo, and again I fired. This time, in spite of my greenness at shooting on the gallop, I put a ball home, but not in the right place. It struck too low in the flank, and just bled the buffalo without stopping him. A third time I fired, and without any more valuable effect. The one or two places in which an ounce ball *will* stop a buffalo-bull, bear a charmed life to the tyro in saddle-shooting. My horse began to be fearfully winded,—this was his first time out during the season; he was a generous loan; and though the buffalo was rapidly tiring, I desisted from the chase in a state of dissatisfaction with myself only commensurate with my previous enthusiasm.

As I sat, the Knight of the Rueful Countenance translated to Kansas (I omitted to say that our ride from Comstock's had once more taken us out of Nebraska), Thompson rode up, and invited me to go and look at *his* success. Well, I never wished to be mean; it was pleasant to see somebody's success; and I accordingly rode with him a mile away, to find a magnificent bull stretched dead as a smelt on a high grassy knoll where he had fallen with one unerring shot, right through the heart. Through the right portion of the heart, it is necessary to add; for I felt a little less ashamed of myself on learning that a buffalo will travel, and get clear of capture, with a slug through the apex of that organ, nothing short of disturbing its valvular arrangement having the immediate effect to bring him down. For the first time I came close enough to a wild native buffalo to examine him minutely, and was obliged to confess that he was one of the noblest specimens of the brute creation. Upright, the hump of this bull must have stood over five feet high. It was the hair-shedding season, and all abaft the hump his body was as bare, save in two or three isolated patches of frowzy, faded wool, as a Chinese dog. This fact was advantageous to the examination of his anatomy; and though he carried a head and chest only less ponderous than a young elephant's, I found a beautiful shapeliness of curve about his haunches, a cleanness of line, and even slenderness in his hind legs, that looked rather like a member of the deer or elk family than any of the bovine tribes.

I stood admiring him and felicitating Thompson, when Munger appeared upon a distant divide, beckoning me to him. I left the dead bull, and rode to ask what was wanted. When I got within earshot, Munger hollowed his hand before his mouth and roared, "Bring along your painter." Glad to be of more use to somebody than I had been to myself, I set out in search of the buggy. About a mile away, I found it rolling placidly along through the grass, after the well-meaning but veteran wagon-team. I told our artist that Munger had something for him. At the news the buggy axles creaked joyfully; the little old horses sprang forward on a gallop, with all the recalled freshness of their youth; and in something less than a quarter of an hour, we stood, or sat, beside Munger and the champing Ben Holladay.

That makes two: there were three of his company. He had ridden upon as big a bull as ever ran the Plains, stopped him with a series of shots from a Colt's army revolver, and was holding him at bay in a grassy basin, for our artist's especial behoof. He, on his part, did not need three words to show him his opportunity. He leapt from the buggy; out came the materials of success following him, and in a trifle over three minutes from his first halt, the big blue umbrella was pointed and pitched, and he sat under it on his camp-stool, with his color-box on his knees, his brush and palette in hand, and a clean board pinned in the cover of his color-box.

Munger's old giant glowered and flashed fire from two great wells of angry brown and red, burning up like a pair of lighted naphtha-springs, through a foot-deep environment of shaggy hair. The old fellow had been shot in half a

BUFFALO CALVES.

WOLVES ATTACKING A WOUNDED BUFFALO.

dozen places. He was wounded in the haunch, through the lower ribs, through the lungs, and elsewhere. Still he stood his ground like a Spartacus. He was too much distressed to run with the herd; at every plunge he was easily headed off by a turn of Munger's bridle; he had trampled a circle of twenty feet diameter, in his sallies to get away, yet he would not lie down. From both his nostrils the blood was flowing, mixed with glare and foam. His breath was like a black-smith's bellows. His great sides heaved laboriously, as if he were breathing with his whole body. I never could be enough of a hunter not to regard this as a distressing sight. Yet I could understand how Parrhasius might have been driven by the devil of his genius to do the deed of horror and power which has come down to us through the centuries. I seemed to see Prometheus on his rock, defying the gods. Kill a deer, and he pleads with you out of his wet, dying eye; a bear falls headlong with a grunt, and gives up his stolid ghost with-out more ado, if the bullet is mortal; but here was a monster whose body contained at least four deathly bullet, yet who stood as unflinching as adamant, with his face to the foe. It was the first time I had seen moral grandeur in a brute.

Munger, Thompson, and I rode slowly round the bull, attracting his attention by feigned assaults, that our artist might see him in action. As each of us came to a point where the artist saw him sideways, the rider advanced his horse, and menaced the bull with his weapon. The old giant low-ered his head till his great beard swept the dust; out of his immense fell of hair his eyes glared fiercer and redder; he drew in his breath with a hollow roar and a painful hiss, and charged madly at the aggressor. A mere twist of the rein threw the splendidly trained horse out of harm's way, and the bull almost went headlong with his unspent impetus. For nearly fifteen minutes, this process was continued, while the artist's hand and eye followed each other at the double-quick over the board. The signs of exhaustion increased with every charge of the bull; the blood streamed faster from wounds and nostrils; yet he showed no signs of surrender, and an almost human devil of impotent revenge looked out of his fiery, unblinking eyeballs.

But our Parrhasius was merciful. As soon as he had transferred the splendid action of the buffalo to his study, he called on us to put an end to the distress, which, for aught else than art's sake, was terrible to see. All of us who had weapons drew up in line, while the artist attracted the bull's attention by a final feigned assault. We aimed right for the heart, and fired. A hat might have covered the chasm which poured blood from his side when our smoke blew away. All the balls had sped home; but the unconquerable would not fall with his side to the foe. He turned himself painfully around on his quivering legs; he stiffened his tail in one last fury; he shook his mighty head, and then, lowering it to the ground, concentrated all the life that lasted in him for a mad onset. He rushed forward at his persecutors with all the *elan* of his first charges; but strength failed him half way. Ten feet from where we stood, he tumbled to his knees, made heroic efforts to rise again, and came up on one leg; but the death-tremor possessed the other, and with a great panting groan, in which all of brute power and beauty went forth at once, he fell prone on the trampled turf, and a glaze hid the anger of his eyes. Even in death those eyes were wide open on the foe, as he lay grand, like Cæsar before Pompey's statue, at the feet of his assassins.

We then returned to Thompson's bull, where our artist sat down to make another study, leaving the buggy to return to camp and send out a wagon for our meat, and ourselves to set forth in search of new adventures.

One of Thompson's intensest yearnings was to get some cow-meat. This laudable desire had been frustrated in all the hunts he had joined since the buffalo left the Arkansas this season. He liked hump and tongue very well, but naturally preferred game which he could use more economically than simply to cut out these, and leave the carcass. So he proposed a flank movement, by which we might get nearer to the herd.

Munger had an equal anxiety to lasso some young calves. He had been very successful in this sport several summers before, and secured some capital specimens to send East, for curiosity, or to domesticate among the ranches for breeding. I was surprised to learn how frequent was the latter practice in this region. Numbers of the settlers between Atchison and Fort Kearney had reared buffalo calves, and crossed them with domestic cattle, the hybrids proving very serviceable working-cattle, somewhat surly and unmanageable at times, but possessing greater speed and endurance than the common ox. I was further told, on excellent authority, what seemed hard of belief, and under the circumstances was impossible of tangible demonstration, that this hybrid had been found perpetuable. This is a curious fact, when we recollect how much more the cow and the buffalo differ from each other than the horse and the ass, whose mules are still sterile. I was equally anxious with Munger to get a nice pair of calves, as we were sufficiently near railroad communication to have sent them East to await our return.

Accordingly John Gilbert and ourselves set out in a nearly southwesterly direction, leading diagonally between the main course of the Republican and a line of tall, conical mounds, called the White Rock Buttes, parallel with the river six miles further south. We had gone about three miles across a rolling country much like the plain traversed from Comstock's, without seeing anything but the rear of the herd lately stampeded by us, when John Gilbert caught sight of a much larger herd, feeding a little nearer the Republican than our line of march. He proposed that we should separate, and, by alarming this herd at different points, stampede them in such confusion as to break up their order, make them spread out and open their centre to attack. Munger looked through his field-glass, and was sure he saw calves; Thompson took a look, and beheld the cows necessarily accompanying ; I saw buffalo of some description or other, which was all that was needed to make me join the rest in assent to John Gilbert's proposition.

Munger, Thompson, and myself went to the southerly; John Gilbert alone took toward the river side, with the intention of stampeding the herd back into our hands. We had gone a little over a mile when the thundering of hoofs announced that John had succeeded, and the next minute the herd came tearing over a high divide right toward us. As they saw us, they checked their impetus; but so near us did they get that each of us might have shot his bull without difficulty, had our design been so childish and murderous. As it was, we left our rifles alone, not intending to use them again till we could use the lasso with them. Still, no calves nor cows were visible. I began to despair of ever seeing them.

As the herd reached us, it swung its front round at right angles, and made about westerly. Munger, Thompson, and

I immediately rushed at it with all speed, and it separated into roughly divided detachments, one of winch each of us selected to chase down. The herd was larger than any we had yet seen. It was impossible that our glasses should have deceived us. There were cows and calves somewhere in the herd, and this was the way to find them.

In five minutes after I had selected my squad for attack, I was entirely separated from my companions. The ground was in splendid order for running; the lay of the land as favorable; my horse had acquired his "second wind," and his enthusiasm fully equaled my own. I never knew the ecstasy of the mad gallop until now. Like young Lochinvar, "We stayed not for brake, we stopped not for stone." Some draws which we crossed, made me shudder afterward as I thought of them. Now we were plunging with headlong bounds down bluffs of caving sand, fifty feet high, and steep as a fortress glacis, while the buffalo, crazy with terror, were scrambling halfway up to the top of the opposite side. Now we were following them in the ascent, my noble Nig using his fore-hoofs more like hands than any horse I ever saw before, fairly clawing his way up, with every muscle tense through passionate emulation. Now we were on the very haunches of our game, with a fair field before us, and no end to pluck and bottom for the rest of the chase, the buffalo laboring heavily, and their immense fore-parts coming down on their hoofs with a harder shock at every jump. Now we saw a broad, slippery buffalo-wallow just in time to leap it clear; now we plunged into the very middle of one, but Nig dug himself out of the mud with one frantic tug, and kept on. Still we came closer to our buffaloes, and suddenly I heard a loud thunder of trampling behind me.

I looked over my shoulder: there in plain sight was another herd, tearing down on our rear. As I afterward discovered, this was the herd stampeded in separate columns by Munger and Thompson, joined again after making their detour. For nearly a mile in width stretched a line of angry faces, a rolling surf of wind-blown hair, a row of quivering lanterns, burning reddish-brown. The column was as deep as the line. I quickly bethought myself: It is death to get involved in a herd if my horse stumbles. If I have both pluck and luck to ride steadily in the line of the stampede until I can insinuate myself laterally, and make a break out through the side of the herd, all may go well with me, as it has with several hunters of my acquaintance, caught in this predicament. It was death to turn back. I should be trampled and gored to death. I should be wiped out like a grease-spot, and Nig with me, for the terror of the herd was too extreme for me to hope to re-stampede them, with Munger and Thompson probably somewhere close on their rear.

All this flashed through my mind in an instant. Nig was steadily shortening the distance between me and the herd ahead. I had just made up my mind to ride as long as he would stand in the line of the stampede, when the herd before me divided into two columns to pass around a low butte I had seen before. Quick as lightning this providential move of theirs suggested the means of my salvation. I made for the mound, reached its summit, and to Nig's great disgust, though he was fearfully short-breathed, and trickling with rivulets of sweat, halted him instantly to await the rear column. I had not many minutes of anxiety. The herd saw me fifty rods off, but, as I expected, paid no more attention to me than if I had been a grass-blade. Nor could they if they would. All stampedes are alike, whether of men or animals. For the front line to swerve is to be knocked down and slain instanter. This *vis a tergo* gives the van a courage of despair, while it takes away all option of movement So the angry front line of faces saw me without fear. I had only a minute of certain life. The next would see me safe or beaten to a mummy. I dismounted, held my horse's head away from the coming herd, and faced it myself, with the rein over my arm and my rifle poised. As the herd got within a hundred yards of the mound, I delivered one steadily aimed ball at the fore-shoulder of the nearest bull. He gave a single wild jump, and began limping on three legs. I had done for him. For a few seconds, fear of his pressing comrades gave him enough extra speed to keep up with the rest; but before the line reached the foot of the mound, he had tumbled, and the whole host was rushing over him. This obstacle, and the terror of his fate, sent the first lateral panic into the hearts of the herd. Once more, as the front line came so close that I could almost have jumped my horse on to their backs, I fired my rifle again. The ball did no damage to any but itself, flattening like putty on the thick-matted Gibraltar of one old bull's frontispiece, but it served my turn, and split the herd. They divided just in time to avoid being crowded over the mound by their rear, and in a moment I was standing on a desert island, in a sea of billowing backs, flowed around on either side by a half-mile current of crazy buffaloes.

Here was abundant opportunity to shoot, but not the slightest anxiety for doing so. I was safe; I had such a view of buffaloes as I never could have expected, never would enjoy again. This was all-sufficient to me. I stood and studied the host with devouring eyes, while my horse snorted and pulled at the bridle in a passion of enthusiasm.

The herd were about five minutes in passing me. During that time I saw the calves which Munger was looking for, and Thompson's much desiderated cows, beside numerous yearlings and two-year-olds, both bulls and heifers. There also appeared here and there a veteran bull, carrying about him the marks of battle in the form of a stiff or broken leg, or a bad scar in the flank. One old fellow made as good time on three legs as any of his comrades on four, though his useless member was in front, where most of the strain falls in running. His progress was absolutely comical. He reminded me of an aged ape hopping, with one hand on the ground to steady him, and his countenance wore the most whimsical expression, his mat of hair being torn off in places, so as to disclose more of his features than I ever saw in any other buffalo. As he scrambled past in steady-by-jerks, Dundreary style, he seemed saying, "To be bothered in this way at my time of life!"

When the herd had passed, and joined the body I had lately been chasing, the combined force stopped about half a mile ahead. I turned, as the last laggards panted by the mound, and, for the first time since I reached my elevation, paid attention to the westward. Then I understood why the stampeders had halted so soon. They had come up with the main herd!

Yes, there, beyond peradventure, in my plain sight, grazed the entire buffalo army of Middle Kansas. As far as the western horizon the whole earth was black with them. From a point a mile in front of me their rear line extended on the north to the bluffs bounding the Republican, on the south to the very summits of the White Rock Buttes, an entire breadth of more than six miles. I had no way of measuring the unbounded plain, looking westerly; but a man on horseback, in the clear air of the region, and with a field-glass of Voigtlander's as good as mine, can recognize an object of the size of a buffalo at ten miles' distance. I will not add my name to the list of travellers who have stated undeniable truths that nobody would believe. When I say that a hundred square feet of room was an exaggerated average allowance to the individual buffalo in the close-packed herd before me, I have contributed all the elements necessary to each of my readers for his personal calculation of the number in sight. I never saw any Eastern acquaintance who would credit me when I stated my own estimate diminished by one half. Let it be enough to acknowledge that it reaches millions. As for comparisons, flies on a molasses barrel, ants on an ant-hill, tadpoles in a puddle, all these strong but vulgar similitudes fail to express the ideas of multitude awakened by looking at that mighty throng. Arithmetic is as petty to the task as the lightning calculator to the expression of a hurricane. I have seen the innumerable herd of laughing waves in a broad sunny sea; I have seen the same multitude lashed to madness by a tropical cyclone; I remember my first and my succeeding impressions of Niagara; but never did I see an incarnation of vast multitude, or resistless force, which impressed me like the main herd of the buffalo. The desire to shoot, kill, and capture utterly passed away. I only wished to look, and look till I could realize or find some speech for the greatness of Nature that silenced me.

I had gazed for nearly an hour, when it suddenly occurred to me that more than twice that time had elapsed since I saw any of my comrades. I referred to the sun, for I had no watch in my hunting-shirt, and saw that it was at least three o'clock in the afternoon. I took one last look at the buffaloes, and came down from my mount of vision. The way back I was quite certain of. It seemed the easiest thing in the world to retrace my step. I remounted Nig, and began pushing for home.

I remembered that our camp was nearly due north from a certain characteristic butte of the White Rock range. I resolved to bring this butte abreast of me, travelling down the middle of the plain, between it and the Republican, then to strike due north for the river, over the ground which had become familiar to us through two days' hunt.

This matter was easier to promise than accomplish. I little knew the deception of which a traveller was susceptible on these endlessly uniform divides. I might almost as well have hoped to travel by foam-marks on the waves of the sea as by any idiosyncrasies in this rolling sward. But as yet I was ignorant and happy.

My chief troubles were the now plainly apparent fatigue of my horse, reacting from his late enthusiasm; a pair of badly sun-burnt hands, the bridle one of which, being more more exposed, was swollen into a very respectable red velvet pincushion, and felt as if it had been dipped in a jar of aqua-fortis. I was also exceedingly hungry, and had been unwise enough to leave camp without so much as a piece of hard-tack in my pocket. I might at least have brought out a canteen of pure water; but not having anticipated a protracted absence from the river, I had neglected even that, and began to have a tongue like a tile. My horse gradually became so used up, that I lay down with his long halter in my hand, and let him crop his dinner by piecemeal while

I rested, for fifteen minutes at a time. I found a large sun-flower, whose root I pulled up and ate; but the food was rather scanty, and whetted my appetite as a relish, instead of satisfying it like a meal. But my greatest suffering presently came on in the form of intense thirst.

Before I reached the point abreast of the White Rock Buttes, whence I was to commence my northerly course, I was in veritable torment. I felt like a German Zwieback, dry-rusked through and through by a sun which pelted mer-cilessly on that shadeless waste, hot as our Eastern July. I was reduced to such a deplorable demoralization that I cheer-fully, nay joyfully, consented to relieve myself over and over again, in a way at whose very mention I had shuddered when the old hunters told me of it in camp. I lay down by the side of those stagnant rain-puddles which stand in basins of hard-pan on the top of the divides, and, plunging my face in to the very eye-brows, drank ravenously, right over the hoof-marks of the buffaloes. Sometimes the water was thicker than cream with mud; sometimes red with the dejec-tions of the herd; always as hot as blood,—yet I thought no more of these things than if I were a buffalo myself. For the first time I fully understood the sufferings of travellers in the desert. When I afterward came to experience those suffer-ings myself, I found them but little worse than that trial on the Kansas Plains.

Reaching the line of range I had selected, I struck due north for the river, sure of finding our camp and overjoyed at the prospect. I looked from the edge of the bluff, after a toilsome trudge of three miles on a tired horse, and saw everything to convince me that my course had been cor-rect. Between the bluff and the river stretched a swale of dry grass, bounded by two expanses of green herbage; the first bottom of the river descended by two well-marked curving terraces; there was a fine old cotton-wood grove, with a pair of gaps in it where the beavers had been felling; above this grove I saw a broad yellow sand-bar running diagonally half-way across the Republican; and to the eastward the river made a short curve toward me, narrowing the view of its bank to a mere strip, which was studded thickly with new timber-growth. Every feature which I have related was the facsimile of a corresponding environment about our camp.

I descended, as I thought, through the very draw by which we had yesterday approached the buffalo on foot. The likeness became more and more perfect as I went down. The same grotesque forms presented by the profile of a precipice of indurated sand, the same arrangement of bushes, the same puddle to which the relieved sentinel came down when we fired our first shots, the same well-worn buffalo-path leading through the draw to the river.

I chirruped cheerfully to Nig, as in assurance that we should soon reach home, and struck into the broad river-bottom with renewed patience. I reached the river without seeing any novel feature in the landscape, entered the cotton-wood grove, came to the very water's edge,—and found nowhere a trace of human kind.

I thought it must be a joke. The party had played some trick on me. They were punishing me for my long absence by hiding in the timber near by. But then where were the wagons? Where the horses, the wheel-tracks,—above all, where was the burnt spot left by our camp-fire?

I had to confess that this was not our camp. It needs no explanation to understand how with that confession came a full assurance of the fact that I was about as badly lost as it is possible for a man to be. If there were one place exactly like our camp, there might be fifty. And so there were. Should I go up or down the river?

I concluded on the latter course. I calculated as nearly as possible my distance from home when I reached the main herd, and found it unlikely that I could have made enough return with my tired horse to have brought me abreast of the camp again. I set off along the edge of the river timber, at the best rate my horse could travel. A mile down I was stopped by an impassable swamp, running entirely across from the foot of the bluff to the river bottom. The water vegetation in it was almost tropically rank, and its pools swarmed with ducks. I had no time or thought for shooting. I dismounted from my horse, and, finding the bluff loose and sandy ten feet up, I led him along its slope around the marsh, in momentary danger of his falling on me, and both of us going into the bog.

We now entered a thick wood, containing some of the grandest old trees I ever saw in my life. They were mostly elms and cotton-woods, with an occasional oak, primeval in their size and luxuriance, making the ground under them black with the shadow of their dense foliage, and exhibiting tree-forms which might fill an artist with rapture. They grew entirely without underbrush, on a damp, velvety lawn of short grass, expanding their immense arms at the top of shafts a hundred feet in height, locking them together into their impenetrable roof, with graceful curves and grotesque angles, that surpassed anything in human architecture. It was one of those places continually met with in this region, which so strongly simulate human cultivation that the traveller finds it almost impossible to believe he is not in the park of some lordly demesne. To this feeling all wild animals contribute, but far beyond the rest, the gregarious buffalo, by making paths so like those of a well regulated country-seat that everybody exclaims at the first sight of them, "Inhabited after all!" These are thoroughly well beaten, straight as a gardener could lay them out, or following the conformation of the land in curves that could not be bettered. To add to the human suggestions of the delicious grove I had entered, two such paths crossed each other in its centre, I found one of them a pleasant relief to my tired horse.

Pursuing it for half a mile, we emerged from the grove, or more properly became immersed in a thicket. Thorn-bushes hanging covered with wisps of buffalo hair recently scraped off, alternated with springy saplings, which in turn tore and flogged us, till I should have been driven back had there been any way out of the fix except forward. Patience, and an occasional use of my bowie-knife, at last hacked us out to daylight; but the view that broke on me was as little satisfactory as the thicket. A narrow rift, eight feet deep and three wide, its nearer side a moist, springy clay, opened at my feet, discharging a small stream into the river. I tied my horse for a moment, plunged down into the fissure, and drank till it seemed as if I should burst. Climbing up again, I surveyed the opposite bank. It was the side of the main bluff itself, thirty feet high, and slanting at an angle of little less than seventy degrees. The river had curved around to meet it past the marsh and wood which I had just traversed, cutting away the first bottom entirely. But this I did not know till afterward. I explained the nearness of the river to the precipice, by supposing that the bed of the former had fallen within the last two miles sufficiently to bring the first bottom as high above it as the bluff here appeared. Upon this, I reasoned that I must, after all, have struck the stream too far below our camp. Still, rather than turn back through the thicket, I would try crossing the rift and ascending to the top of the bluff, where I would have smooth ground for my return. The difficulty was how to get my horse over. There was no standing-room for a single pair of hoofs at the base of the bluff across the ditch. I accordingly built myself a bridge. In the first place, I flung lumps of clay from the springy side into the fissure, until I had a surface nearly enough even with the edge to receive a superstructure of sticks hacked from the thicket. On this treacherous fascine, which it took me a perspiring hour to complete, I managed to support the hind hoofs of my horse till he could dig his front ones into the bluff. I then ran before him, caught his bridle, and scaled the height, with the noble fellow scrambling up after me as deftly and almost as perpendicularly as a climbing monkey. I never saw a horse east of the Mississippi that could have comprehended and met the situation like Nig. Whoever came after us to our bridge of fascines, must have thought that a very badly educated company of beavers had been there.

I wandered for a quarter of a mile down the river. The banks grew higher and higher with every rod. I found no sign of human life anywhere, save the remains of a Sioux camp. The occupants had not been long gone; some of their lodge-poles lay in a bundle near the fire-place, and around it were still standing the crotched sticks on which they hung their pots. I had no anxiety to meet the Sioux; and as the hope of encountering my companions seemed increasingly slight in this direction, I turned and began retracing my steps, leading my horse by the bridle. Poor Nig was so battered by his day's strain and hunger that I could make better time in this way than on his back.

A new misfortune now appeared to me. What scriptural writer says that trouble does not come out of the ground? He had never contemplated a series of draws, with precipitous sides, running a mile into the heart of a bluff upon whose edge he was travelling with a tired horse, and used-up personality. Here was a trouble resulting from the ground, which might well excuse imprecation.

Did none of my readers ever get into a situation where Nature's obstacles seemed to have been created on purpose for him? I had descended one of these reëntrant draws at imminent peril to my neck, and climbed the other side with a difficulty only conquered by desperation; I had made a detour of at least a mile, to get around another one, which looked absolutely untraversable; I now came to a third, with sides literally precipitous. Its walls were fifty feet high, and ran sinuously, eating about into the plain further than I could see, with numerous lateral ramifications. After several vain attempts to flank these trenches of Nature, I came back to the edge of the bluff, and considered myself. I was lost, faint, sick; my horse quite worn out, and the sun not an hour high. I was uncomfortably near the Sioux, who a few days before had taken a Colorado soldier, on a hunt from Fort Kearney and lost like myself; had robbed him of horse, ammunition, arms, all he had in the world; pulled out his beard, and left him naked as he was born, forty miles from the nearest white trapper. I made up my mind that I would descend the first practicable draw, cross the river, picket my horse, make a supper of sunflower-roots and wild onions, and camp down under my saddle-blankets, and with the returning light renew

JEAN BAPTISTE MONCRÉVIÉ.

PORTRAIT OF COMSTOCK.

my search for our camp, along the northern and more level bank of the Republican. I was pretty sure that I could find the ford we had crossed, by hunting for our wheel-tracks. I accordingly led my horse down the nearest ramification of the great draw, and with great difficulty, for the bottom was a perfect slough, escaped from my embarrassments upon the low level of the river bank.

Before I leave this entanglement of horrors, I must not omit to say that just before descending, I shot my first antelope. He was grazing on the side of a divide, quite six hundred yards off, to the naked eye appearing only a small brown spot in the sunshine. I wanted meat so badly that I never asked myself the question how I was going to get round to him, and pack him home. He had not seen or scented me when I lay down in the grass and poised my Ballard, which nominally put up for five hundred yards, but at that distance invariably threw the ball above, unless allowance was made for its habits. I spent as much time in calculating my aim as a boy of ten over a sum in division, and fired resting on my elbows. My brown spot went up into the air with one convulsive spring, turned a cart-wheel, and fell on his side in his tracks. The next moment I saw how impossible it was to get him, but went down the draw excusing the murder by a promise to go after him to-morrow. When that morrow came, he was a clean skeleton, picked by the wolves. Though I had not the meat, I had gained a pride and a confidence in my weapon which were everything to a man in my position,—and hugged it close to my breast ere I swung it round to my back, not knowing how often it might have to save my life before I saw camp again. I had many occasions to love that rifle afterwards; and I should be ungrateful indeed, if I did not say that the Ballard breech-loader is, without a single exception, the best arm for Western work that was ever invented. In good hands, it fires seven balls a minute with perfect accuracy, having all the advantages ever practically used in a repeater; it is the simplest in its mechanism of all breech-loading weapons, and never once got out of order during a daily use of eight months. Its breech is absolutely powder-tight, through the very construction of its cartridge; this cartridge is an entire load, including percussion material, and cleans the bore in leaving it; nothing can be more portable, simpler, safer. The man who is competent to us a rifle at all need never miss with it, and one who has made its acquaintance will never be without it in the wilderness. If this be high praise, I can only say that every expert who has seen its performance agrees with me. Over and over again in the far West, old hunters became so enamored of it as to offer me its original cost, several times told.

I was half way across the first bottom when the sun went out of sight. Simultaneously with his disappearance, the wolves seemed to be assembling for jubilee. In every quarter I could see one of either the big gray or the coyote variety. They did not seem alarmed at me, and sat up on their haunches like so many shepherd dogs, in a circle around me and poor tired Nig, making the air dismal with their discordant howls. I was not afraid of them, for they never attack a man unless mad with hunger; but their presence, worn out as I was, filled me with gloom and foreboding. They seemed like harpy old women at a country funeral, crowding around to get a last look at the corpse. Moreover, they might attack my picketed horse in force during the night; and personal affection for him after my trial of his intelligent faithfulness, to say nothing of my own loneliness if he were killed, made me very anxious not to lose him.

Despite the depression begotten of he wolves, my spirits had still to touch their zero point. Crossing the river bottom about a hundred rods from me, I presently saw a man, coatless, hatless, and, to my field-glass, of a rich-brown complexion, black-haired, and carrying a gun. So this was the meaning of the deserted Sioux camp on the bluff! How far off were the rest of the band?

I knew it would not do to show the white feather. I leaped on my horse, whom I had still been leading, and rode toward the savage, hallooing with all my might. He stopped for a minute, eyed me curiously, took down his gun, thought better of it, and left for the neighboring timber. Upon this I put spurs to poor Nig, who met the exigency with all his reserve capital of speed. In five minutes more I was on the brink of the river.

Directly opposite, on the northern bank, stood a snow-white tent, and above it floated St. George's Cross!

If Robinson Crusoe, in one of his goat hunts, had suddenly come to the office of the British consulate, he could not have been taken more aback by that sight than I by this!

I rubbed my eyes to make sure that it was not a dream of exhausted nerves and an empty stomach. But my horse gave a joyful neigh, which was quickly answered by several of the same sort, in the tent's immediate neighborhood. I knew horses were not given to nervous hallucination, and, without any attempt to explain a verdict which could not be impugned, plunged Nig into the Republican, and forded to the opposite shore. A bluff, jolly Englishman, of undeniable Pall Mall flavor, hailed me as I touched the bank, and pointed out the access to his camp. This was pitched on high ground, surrounded by a slough except at one narrow pointy which was covered with the densest forest and undergrowth. If an Englishman's house is his castle, his camp in this instance was still more so. Twenty resolute white men could have defended it against a thousand Sioux. Nothing in the defenses of Washington was stronger by natural position. If the Rev. Clarence FitzPotts, with his love of the Medæval had been there, he would have erected a ruined donjon keep upon it immediately.

With all the aid of friendly showing, I spent a full half-hour in getting round to shake the hands I had seen extended to me on my landing. I never knew that the sight of a British flag, and the sound of the British accent, could make me as glad as I was when I reached the camp. I was received with a genuine cordial welcome, which made me forgive Liverpool and the "Morning Post." My new acquaintance and his comrades were members of Lord Lyons's embassy, out on a buffalo hunt like myself. They had come all the way from Washington to see a herd, but as yet had not sighted a single bull. I was able to give them cheering news, and encourage them with the prospect of approaching reward for a difficult journey. They had turned off in the wrong direction from the high northern divide, and found a series of bad draws and rough hammocks, which much hampered their progress. It was as John Gilbert had said. His unerring eye had not failed him. I now saw what a good thing for me it had proved that they went astray. Such a happy providence is not vouchsafed to one man in a thousand as this discovery of white friends and civilized shelter, when lost in the wild heart of the Continent.

It is hardly necessary to say that the Indian I had seen proved to be an attaché of the party. He had gone out hunting, and, when he returned, had a story as interesting as my own, about a savage figure starting from the grass.

My horse was picketed. I had made amends for the day's inanition by a hearty supper of Yarmouth bloaters, Scotch marmalade, toasted pilot-bread, canned beef, and English breakfast tea. There was a dreamy quiet over the whole twilight landscape, and I sat in it smoking my pipe, with a sense of perfect rest, only broken by my appreciation of the anxiety which would be felt for me by my party.

I had finished my pipe, and sat chatting with one of the party, when another member came from the tent with a troubled face, and asked me if I knew anything about medicine.

"Too much," I replied: "who is sick of it now?"

"Mr.——has just been attacked with terrible distress in the epigastrium. He is suffering from wretched cramps, and I don't know but he may be in serious danger."

I saw that his trouble was only one of our ordinary Western summer affairs, and, knowing that it would presently cure itself, set to work to relieve the immediate pain. I had one of the servants build a roaring fire, and set on it a camp-kettle full of water. In about five minutes this was scalding hot, and I kept a steady express-train of towels, freshly wrung out of it, running between it and the epigastric station referred to.

This treatment was an instantaneous success in more senses than one. It not only quieted the patient's pain, but brought relief to the anxiety of his friends. When the bright fire I had made leapt up into the dark, it became a beacon to two despondent horsemen, who were searching vainly for me on the southern bluff. They immediately pushed for it; and nearly an hour after the first towel had started from the kettle, Munger and John Gilbert appeared at the further bank of the river, and shouted, "Halloo!" I left my patient sinking into a pleasant sleep, and disclosed to them myself and my safety, after which I had the pleasure of piloting them round the slough by the same path which had led me to camp.

They were as glad to see me as I to see them. I found that they had been in search of me for three hours, having returned from their hunt to dinner, and started out again to look me up soon after that. I introduced them to my new friends, got them supper, and then we all camped down under our blankets (my friends had thoughtfully brought mine out to me), to await the daylight that should enable us to return.

The impression in our own camp had been that I was killed or horribly mangled by some old bull, whom I had brought to bay. Such things happen every season; and the fact that Nig was famous for his pluck in riding up to the very head of the buffalo whom his master had wounded, did not diminish the fear of my friends in my behalf.

I further found that I had been within a mile of our camp, when I struck the high bluff where I found the deserted Indian camp. I learned a new fact about the bluffs of the Republican. They do not run parallel with the river, but alternately recede and approach, making the river bottom a succession of amphitheatres, the ends of whose semicircles rise precipitously from the water, like the bluff in question. Had I known this fact, I should not have been misled by the conformation of the land. The very next amphitheatrical bottom below the Indian bluff was the one on which our party lay encamped.

This had been a day of curious good fortune to me, though I regretted to think that it all arose from some corresponding misfortune on the part of my British friends. If they had not diverged from their course on the northern divide, I should have crossed the river to-night, only to change my place of desolation; there would have been no British flag here to gladden an American eye. If my friend had not been attacked in the epigastrium, I should have built no fire. Had I built none, my comrades would have turned back to camp in despair. They had just concluded to do so, when my beacon flamed up through the dark. I thought of these things with a tendency to philosophize, but Zeno himself would have gone to sleep after such a day as I had spent. In five minutes, thoughtless and philosophers, we were all "sawing gourds" together in the land of Nod.

The sun was not half an hour high when our blankets were strapped behind our saddles, and we ourselves had shaken hands with our kind hosts. We had gone as far as Turkey Draw, a wet ravine about four miles from the English camp (and very well named, as the rapid departure from their nests of several turkey-hens at our approach convinced us), when we caught sight of two fine buffalo on the broad meadow, bordering the opposite side of the draw. I felt glad of an opportunity for retrieving myself, and bringing a little meat home to camp, after my long absence. So I stole quietly across the stream into its fringing timber, and, dismounting from Nig, took steady aim at the nearest buffalo. He was grazing with his haunches toward me. The ball broke his right hip, and he plunged away on three legs, the other swinging useless. I leapt on my horse, put spurs to him, and was in three minutes close on the bull's rear. To my astonishment, and the still greater surprise of the two old hunters who came after me, the unhurt bull stuck to his comrade's side without flinching. I fired another shot, which took effect in the lungs of the first buffalo; the second sheered off for a moment, but instantly returned to his friend. The wounded buffalo became distressed, and slackened his pace; the unwounded one not only retarded his, but actually stopped, came to the rear of his friend, and stood with his head down, offering battle! This was the first instance of such fidelity known to Munger, John Gilbert, or any old hunter to whom I have related it.

The buffalo bull, in pairing season, will forsake his wounded cow; the cow will not stand a moment to protect her hurt calf; yet here was a devotion which had no instinct to inspire it, an ideal camaraderie rare even among men. The sight was to all three of us a sublime one. We could no more have accepted the challenge of this brave creature than we could have smitten Damon at the side of Pythias. Epic bull! Bull worthier of heroic bronzes than half the manmade heroes who prance in brass on public squares! I had once in college a bosom friend like thee. How strangely the grotesque intertwines with our life's dearest things, and becomes transfigured above laughter, when those things are consecrated of death! My friend was called, in the rude style of man's endearment, "Our little Buffalo Bull,"—for he was strong, vital, impetuous, and came from the Lake City of New York State, which gave him the former half of his sobriquet. If that man were by my side in peril, brave bull, he would stick by his friend to the death, as thou by thine. But he fell at Seven Pines, in the front of his regiment, with a ball through the bravest forehead that ever faced friend or foe. Go, noble bull! I cannot shoot! I wish I had not slain thy brother!

The wounded buffalo ran on to the border of the next wet draw, troubling us little to keep up with him, and in attempting to cross fell headlong down the steep, oozy bank, and never rose again. Not till that moment, when courage was useless forever, did faithful Achates drop from the side of his Æneas, and consider his own safety in flight. We took off our hats to him as he walked sullenly away, and gave three cordial cheers to his departing form as it vanished beyond the fringing timber.

Having cut off the hump and the tongue of our game, we continued our way to camp, reaching it after about four miles' further travel. Persons desiring to know how I was received, will please consult "The Lost Heir," T. Hood author. Next to having thought your friend dead, and found out you were correct, there is nothing more disagreeable than to think so and find it a mistake. "So much good tears lost," as Talfourd said of a lady who cried all the way through Mrs. Siddons' "Rosalind," supposing it to be her Lady Constance. However, my recent mis adventure resulted well, in having convinced us all of the propriety of a compact never hereafter to stray away from our own party on the Plains.

When I had received the full measure due me of felicitation and scolding, the horses which, just as I arrived, had been put under saddle with the intention of going out to look up Munger and John Gilbert, as well as myself, were brought back to their original positions, and, breaking up camp, we all set out for a meadow five miles further down the Republican, on the same side. Our prevailing motive was to gratify Thompson's inextinguishable enthusiasm for cows. If he had been Juno's œstrum poor Io would have fared even more pitiably than the poets tell us. Thompson was a capital

THE OVERLAND MAIL COACH.

fellow and shot; but if I were called on in a court of justice to testify what I regarded the salient point of his character, candor would force me to confess "cows." Despite the failures of yesterday, he was as certain that a promised land of cows was flowing with milk and calves just beyond the far timber as if he had been permitted to stand where Moses stood, and view the landscape o'er. It was impossible not to catch the infection of such certainty. To be sure, I had seen the main herd in a diametrically opposite direction, and all the stampeded detachments fled that way; but how so much conviction could be based on an entire absence of cow was a psychological problem we felt inadequate to solve. So we blithely set forth with Thompson, a boö-scopic fervor gleaming from every eye.

Our way led along the first bottom through a broad dry slash of last year's grass, yellow as a wheat-field. We occasionally sent a turkey-hen rattling from her nest, as we approached a timbered draw, and saw an antelope or two, but no fresh buffalo-sign appeared, or anything else of striking interest. An hour's ride brought us to one of the forward-curving extremities of the high bluff, and we were compelled to ford the river to the low bottom on the other side. We had great difficulty in getting our wagons across. The middle of the most practicable ford we could find, proved to have as treacherous a quicksand bottom as one ever sees. Our horses fell, and were only kept from drowning by the most vigorous efforts to keep their noses perpendicular. Our wagons sank so rapidly, that, to save their tires from following their hubs out of sight, we were all compelled to strip ourselves, plunge in, unload them, and carry their contents to the shore. The water rose over the bottom-boards, and there stopped as we got the last box of hard-tack safe to land. We then hitched our saddle horses, which with the buggy had crossed safely, by extempore breast-straps and their picket-ropes, to the tugs of our struggling wagon-teams, and managed to unslough them just in time.

The sun was as bright, the sky as clear, as yesterday, and all the party, more especially myself with a red-hot pincushion for a hand, were greatly fatigued and perspired. Halting our horses to rest under the shade of some fine old cotton-woods between the river and the open, we plunged hack into the Republican, and sucked refreshment through every pore, during a bath which lasted nearly an hour. Over and above this delightful relief, our swim had some interesting scientific results, which I transfer almost verbatim from the hurried pages of my field-book, apologizing for any deficiency which may be found in definiteness of nomenclature, by the fact that in such circumstances as ours an amateur scientist has neither books nor tests, except his own memory and intuitions.

1. Along the river banks, and in holes of its bed, we found several strong chalybeate springs, with bog-iron about their spiracles. Everywhere we discovered iron ore of some kind in immediate proximity to the water. Much of it was peroxide mixed into a yellow mass with clay; but we found some specimens of black-scale that were almost virgin-pure,— certainly, I should say, reaching ninety per cent. of metal. It appeared in large enough quantities to make its working indubitably valuable, when the Pacific Railroad shall have given an outlet to the products of the Plains.

2. We found, both above and under water, slate in every stage of its formation, from the soft layer of clay, newly

compacted into a slab, to the hardest kind of uncrystalline shale. When we dug down and brought up masses of the river bottom, they were laminated in parallel bands of varying color, which showed us plainly, as if written in characters of light, the successive periods of changing detritus brought down by the stream. Some of the masses cracked across with a true slaty fracture, square and straight, breaking under slight pressure. Some bent like fresh clay. All laminated easily. A large number of specimens contained shells; some of the older masses had them fossilized; and in none did they belong to any species whose living representatives we could find along the stream. Most of them were acephalous,—allied to the clam; some of them had corrugated valves; one or two, the cardinal expansion of the scallop. Several were *ostracidæ*. One particularly hard lump of clay-rock, which laminated with comparative difficulty, was a perfect congeries of gasteropod univalves, both fossil shell and cast remaining perfect. What surprised me most was to find slate containing these obsolete shells, so soft and so inchoate in its own petrifaction; also to find such abundance of perfect fossils in clay-shale at all. All geologists know that throughout our Eastern region this friable rock is the poorest possible receptacle for the preservation of remains. I ascribe the durability of the matrix in the present instance to a small per cent. of lime acting as a cement.

3. Numerous flat plates of a yellow argillaceous limestone came up from the bed of the river, and were found *in situ* on its bank. These did not laminate, but broke across with as square a fracture as the slate. The lime was in combination,—probably an impure gypsum; but as to that, in the absence of chemical tests, I could only judge by a sulphurous taste and smell at the fracture.

4. Everywhere in the river appeared a very remarkable conglomerate, and like the slate in exhibiting all the stages of formation. The matrix was the blue clay of the bank, the rubble was the gravel of the bottom. It was most interesting to read the history of its formation in the progressive specimens. A lump of heavy clay breaks off the shore, and is rolled over the pebbles of the bed by a rapid shallow current, which presently gives it a spherical, oval, or cylindrical contour, and studs it with a mass of small imbedded stones. As these sink deeper, the clay laps over them, and begins catching a new layer of pebbles on its fresh surface. Some less recent balls which we brought up from the bed were two feet in circumference, and little else than a mass of pebbles, cemented by hardened clay. Several were so compacted and indurated that the surface seemed nearly as homogeneous as porphyry, the matrix having become little less hard than the flintiest pebbles.

This sight staggered me in my own preconceived view, and that of many geologists, regarding the igneous origin of the harder conglomerates. From what I saw I could well conceive how the very hardest might have been the result of mere water-operations. I had regarded the pebbles of igneous origin, found in conglomerates, as presumptive proof of the same origin for the whole mass. But the pebbles in any conglomerate might easily have been the detritus rolled from hypogene rocks down the bed of a stream with tenacious clay banks like the Republican. This view opened to me a new field of speculation upon the aqueous and igneous theories of many formations.

5. The pebbles and breccia-like detritus which inhere in the above conglomerates, are exceedingly diversified. I found

among other water-worn detritus, appearing in patches between the clay and quicksand of the bottom, every possible kind of silicious material, such as agate, pure quartz crystal, smoky, rosy, and cloudy quartz, cornelian (impure), cellular quartz, and quartz united with feldspar and hornblende, or both, in all proportions and manners. One specimen of the cellular kind, associated with fibrous hornblende, was peculiarly beautiful, and resembled some of the rich auriferous specimens which I afterward found in the Colorado mines (Gregory and Bob-tail lodes). All these minerals I regard as brought down by the ice and current from the head of the Republican, which, despite the United States Survey maps, is in all probability to be found as far west as Denver, and thirty miles south. They are all of Rocky Mountain formations, and resemble no outcrop in the region where I found them.

6. To a similar source may be ascribed the small particles of mica discovered in the ferruginous sand of the bed. In my field-book I wrote "must" instead of "may," but after discoveries made it necessary for me to suspend a decision. When I reached Fort Kearney, Lieutenant Davis, then garrison commandant, showed me a specimen of mica which he had found, with many others like it, in clay beds on the Republican, about twenty miles above our second ford. I could not gather from his description as to whether it lay apparently *in situ* or washed in with other debris. If the former be the true case, it opens the same interesting question regarding the aqueous or igneous origin of mica, which a little above was started about the conglomerate. If the formation of mica can be gradual and aqueous, like that of clay shale, Lieutenant Davis' specimen would be an excellent illustration of the mineral in its earlier stages.

It was so soft that, although in a tabular prism and nearly quite transparent, I could scratch it almost as easily as putty, and scrape its edges into powder with my nail, and without scaling off the laminæ. At first sight it appeared like calc-spar, and not till it refused to effervesce with acids did it occur to me to try its cleavage, when it laminated with ease to an indefinite thinness, each sheet showing a perfect micaceous iridescence on the surface.

7. I also found an immense boulder of almost pure feld-spar, the largest mass not distinctly crystalline that I have ever seen. It was as hard as iron, of a nearly similar weight, and about three feet in circumference.

8. Near our first ford I found a small outcrop of impure shaly-brown coal, of no apparent commercial value. Butler told me that he had seen an outcropping seam of coal on the Little Blue Bluffs back of the ranch. I had no time to go and examine it,—cannot therefore be certain that it is true coal,—but am inclined to believe both this and the Republi-can outcrop of the same period as contemporary with much which I afterward found near Denver, and which was indu-bitably tertiary. Of that we shall speak further.

From our ford we moved down along the north bank to the intersection of the Fort Riley and Fort Kearney trail with the Republican first bottom. In some places the track was so over-grown with grass that it needed John Gilbert's eyes to find it, and considerable imagination to conceive how it could have been but a few years ago a comparatively important route from the Kaw to the Rocky Mountains. At this point a decayed old bridge of logs overhung a small stream emptying into the Republican, and just above it the beaver dams were plentier and more interesting than we anywhere saw them during our journey. We here halted for dinner; and Thompson's cows not having yet turned up with any fresh steak, we were compelled to feed on canned provisions. These disposed of, Munger, the artist, and myself continued in the buggy along a beautifully smooth, grassy bottom, with gigantic cotton-woods fringing the river all the way, to a point about a mile above the junction of White Rock Creek with the Republican. Here we picketed our horses, and prepared to camp down, building a magnificent fire of old logs, with a hollow cotton-wood for a chimney. Thompson finally appeared to tell us that the others had got tired, and were camping four miles above, also to ask if we had seen any cows. We all the more regretted to say that we had not, inasmuch as the wagons contained our whole commissariat, and we were hungry enough to have done anything for a supper except reharness and ride back four miles after we had camped down for the night. Thompson returned to the base of supplies, and we went to bed supperless. Substance being denied us, we were fain to content ourselves with shadows. Our feet lay toward the river bank, and our magnificent, though purely ornamental fire made the gigantic white trunks and grotesque gnarled branches of the cotton-woods overhanging the stream dance and flicker like ghosts in a dream. I think this was one of the noblest chiaro-oscuro effects of firelight that I ever saw in my life. Below us murmured the river, repeating the sky's purple twilight on its smooth depths, and glinting with diamond sparks from our flame on its fretful shallows. The air was the perfection of breathableness,— softer, purer, clearer than anything east of the plains around Mount Shasta.

The next morning we rejoined our companions just in time to cook our breakfast on the remains of their kitchen. I began to feel terribly sick of meat, and, in my rage for vegetables, broke my bowie-knife digging wild onions. After this exploit, costing me a splendid weapon irreplaceable short of Denver, we made a ragout of onions and salt pork, which I cannot recommend to anybody living near Delmonico's, washed our dishes in the Republican, and turned north again toward the ranch.

We reached Comstock's about two in the afternoon, with less buffalo-meat than we should have liked, but an experience of one of the loveliest and most interesting regions on the Continent; a region which the Pacific Railroad will make the most valuable farming-land between St. Louis and California.

## CHAPTER III.

# FROM THE BUFFALO COUNTRY
# TO THE GOLD MINES.

ON the 29th of May, our party were obliged to divide. We had waited several nights without finding a westward stage which would contain us all. Accordingly two of us stayed behind, while our two friends squeezed themselves into an overcrowded coach, where one at least of the passengers took it as a personal insult, using language unparliamentary and profane. Munger had promised to send us on an empty coach from Atchison, during the next few days; for this our friends were to telegraph when they reached Kearney.

I was not sorry to stay with the Comstocks a little longer. We were both of us charmed with their original and kindly characters, and they never tired of hearing us talk about the great East. Apropos of that, John Gilbert told me that next year he was going east on a visit. I gave him a cordial invitation to come and see me, when he replied naïvely, "I don't think I shall get beyond Chicago." What a revelation! How far west must we be, when going to Chicago was going east! And yet we were only two hundred miles on a road numbering more than as many thousands.

From the Comstocks we learned more of the social condition of Kansas and Nebraska than all editorials and speeches had ever taught us at the East. To a remarkable extent this family had kept the good of frontier life, and shed aside the evil. I regarded them as in all respects trustworthy and unbiased historians of the events of the last few years; yet they revealed to me a condition of affairs which was appalling. Nobody could suspect them of a bias toward the accursed system which had originally caused all the border troubles; so I was obliged to believe them when they said that bushwhacking, robbery, murder, jayhawking in general, had been committed under the sacred name of Liberty and the detested name of Slavery alike. Border Ruffianism had spread far beyond its original clique. In every small settlement or settled region, the party in power for the time had called to its aid all the means of violence which coerced the first Free State men. If a settler did not lend himself to the tyranny in vogue, he was marked for plunder or destruction. Armed parties surrounded his house in the night, brought him out and shot or hanged him, confiscated his goods, drove off his cattle, and sent his family into the bush. This was done in the name of the cause most popular at the time, and for much of it no cause was responsible. It was mere organized pillage under a convenient party name, and got so lucrative that jayhawking absorbed into its profession all the bold, unscrupulous spirits who spurned the slow rewards of industry; and it became as dangerous for a hard-working *bonâ fide* settler to become a "suspect," as honest people found it in the French Reign of Terror. The Comstocks had seen men in whose loyalty to the Union and freedom they had as much confidence as in their own, utterly broken up and ruined by jayhawkers, pretending to represent those holy interests; they had sheltered from the halter and the pistol hunted acquaintances, whose only crime was the possession of property which the jayhawkers found valuable.

For the last three days of our stay at Comstock's, a very interesting man was visiting there. Jean Baptiste Moncrévié, the Indian interpreter, is sixty-eight years of age, yet looks scarcely over fifty; full of French grace, fire, and vivacity, grafted with American humor. He was educated in Paris, married, came over to this country to make his way in one of the professions, lost his wife in her first child-bed, and became insane. He recovered his sanity after a protracted period, but the energy of his life was gone. He had no further ambition; the thought of succeeding in the world was a mockery to a man who had lost the world's highest success. To get away from old associations, he went West with Audubon, and became so well acquainted with frontier life that at the close of the ornithological tour he determined to stay among the Indians. He is now perfectly conversant with six different Indian languages,—the Sioux, Pawnee, Arapahoe, Blackfeet, Crow, and Flathead. He furnished me with some vocabularies, valuable not only in the practical, but the philological point of view. All the material which we procured in this specialty, during our entire tour, we forwarded to Mr. George Gibbs, of the Smithsonian, whose book on the Indian languages must only be worthy of the opportunities he has enjoyed, and the erudition he possesses, to be the most complete dictionary, grammar, and comparative philology of savage speech ever issued in any country. Moncrévié's stories amused us much. I never heard a man describe an Indian "soldier-feast" as comically as he did. For the benefit of the uninitiated, let me say that this happy banquet consists of a series of the most frightful messes which ever entered a witch cauldron. For instance, there will be a ragout of dog, flavored with mud and sole-leather; a soup of lizard, pig-gristle, and wild onions; an enormous *salmis* of old mule and sunflower leaves. Your host is most generous with his provender. He heaps your plate with the nauseous delicacies until you sit aghast. If you cannot eat your portion, you are technically said to be "killed," and have to buy some other convive to eat it for you with a valuable present. One elastic Indian of long practice will sometimes eat two other men's portions beside his own, and feel no more inconvenience from them than an anaconda from a goat *au naturel.* Moncrévié had once to pay the most valuable horse he had, to get his mess eaten by a Sioux brave. As these are debts of honor, the most capacious glutton goes to a soldier-feast with all the avidity felt by a gray Wall Street bull for a "corner" in Harlem.

Nowhere on our travels did we find better opportunities for studying Western tree-formations than along the banks of the Little Blue. The varied structure of the cotton-woods was a perpetual surprise to us. They seem by their heart-shaped leaf to be near relations of the poplar family; but they have none of that tribe's stiff, unyielding individuality. The poplar, especially the Lombardy, is the Mr. Dombey of our sylva, but there is nothing of the starched-shirt-collar school in the attitudes or expressions of the cotton-woods. They are protean in simulations. One whose butt we used for our rifle-target, about forty rods from Comstock's door, passed for a magnificent white-oak until we got near enough to examine its foliage; and everywhere in the neighborhood these mimetic trees wore the mien of the elm, the ash, or the hickory. Nature on the Plains, like the poet Saadi, has but a limited vocabulary, yet makes a wonderfully polytoned music with her scant material.

It was about eleven o'clock on the night of May 30th, that we broke away from the cordial grasp of our friends and entertainers, to resume our places in the Overland Coach. To give some idea of the cheapness of board and the generosity of soul existing in the Comstock ranch, I will chronicle that our bill amounted to twenty-five cents a meal for the days spent in-doors, nothing at all for our lodging, as little for the share of transportation and edibles which we had enjoyed during our hunt; and that for the days elapsing between our return from the Republican and our resumption of the road, we could only obtain the privilege of squaring our account by depositing the debt as a concealed keepsake in Frank's and Mary's hands, and running away before they discovered what it was.

We were fortunate enough to find our favorite box-seats unoccupied, and mounted to them with great satisfaction, thus avoiding the dreadful grudge which is created in the minds of a stageful of insides, by new-comers entering at an inhuman hour, with a proposition to re-sort their heads and legs.

For the first forty miles our road lay along the Little Blue. The light-and-shade effects on its dense fringe of foliage, and occasional glimpses of its gliding water, were well worthy of an artist's enthusiasm. Every turn of the road brought us into some new loveliness: some deep embowered dell, scented with the ethereal spice of the wild grape-vine; some lofty bluff leaving us just space to pass by a dug-way between it and the river (one such place, called the Narrows, awakens some anxiety in the breasts of travellers who have not been case-hardened to danger farther west); some broad stretch of rolling plain, where the distances were vague and mystical,—and ours was the only living spot in the great solitude.

Our first driver told us that Munger, on his way back to Atchison from the ranch, had run down, with his buggy, drawn by Nig and Ben, a pair of young antelope kids a fortnight old, captured them, and carried them home with him in triumph! That was indeed a buggy superior to its birth. What tales it will have to relate, when it finally gets invalided among the veteran stage-coaches in that Chelsea of vehicles, a wagon-shed! how their venerable doors will open with astonishment at a buggy that has hunted buffalo and captured antelope!

During the night we accomplished three stations, Little Blue, Liberty Farm, and Lone Tree. We rode at the average Overland Stage rate of a little over one hundred miles in twenty-four hours. Our second driver was a fine-looking young fellow who interested us much. A year before, he had been at the very bottom of the pit of drunkenness,—as apparently hopeless a case as existed on the road. From that horror his good angel had brought him up once more to his perfect manhood; and now he refused the proffer of liquor from one of the passengers, with an earnest "O no! no, I thank you," which only seemed brusque to those who did not know his history, and contained in it the significance of a whole youth of misery. Many times afterward, on stage-boxes between Nebraska and California, I thought of that handsome young face, hoping to Heaven that its frank brown eyes might be beclouded by death before liquor should redim them. He impressed me as a soul whose inhabiting devil would be no common fiend. His face was so written with the possibilities of extreme feeling that it haunted one like Guido's "Beatrice."

It grew light enough, before we reached the breakfast station at Thirty-two Mile Creek, for us to see at wide distances apart several ranch houses and corrals, one at least of which was steadily inhabited. This appeared at our crossing of Pawnee Creek, a shallow affluent of the Blue. Here, too, we found real pathos in the sight of a rudely inclosed little grave-yard, containing one large and one small headstone. Even in this loneliness a man might be left still more alone!

The country in general was as uninhabited as we saw it about Comstock's. Antelope abounded on all sides, scouring out of sight from within easy rifle-shot at every turn of our road. The day before, a hunter had shot an elk on the river bottom, but a few miles from Thirty-two Mile Creek, so large that he had to return to his camp, and send back a wagon for him.

The journey from Thirty-two Mile Creek to Fort Kearney (a distance of thirty-five miles) disclosed to us increasing barrenness in the soil, accompanied by a corresponding change in the zone of the flora. Cactuses became a prominent feature on all the hot sand dunes; a peculiar desert species of the Asclepias here and there began showing itself; and wherever the arid ground yielded any herbage, the succulent grass of the Little Blue region was replaced by the short, wiry gramma. This little plant is the main support of the herds along the Platte. Both the emigrant cattle and the buffaloes are very fond of it, though their attachment seems rather eccentric to anybody who has ever examined it. If you can imagine an inventive genius who had discovered a method of making an article for army rations, called "Desiccated Corkscrews," his products would be an approximate imitation of the gramma. If I ever felt like decrying that intolerable old fallacy to the effect that figures don't lie, it was when I heard a ranchman mention the avoirdupois of an ox who had fed on gramma entirely. How it can be nutritive, needs chemistry to show; that it is so, all the plainsmen aver, and their cattle seem to prove it.

The ground rose perceptibly between breakfast and Fort Kearney. We climbed several of the loftiest and longest hills we had seen since leaving St. Louis. About twenty miles east of the fort, we seemed to reach the top of a new terrace, and thenceforward rode nearly all the way on a level sand-plain, extremely barren, very hot and dusty, and quite distressing to the horses. This plain was interspersed with bare sand-hillocks from five to twenty feet high, making it look as if it were the now abandoned dumping-ground of some pre-Adamic race of genii, who followed the dustman's trade for the rest of the solar system, and came to this world to unload. Beyond the hillocks, perhaps a distance of eight miles southerly, rose a much higher range of equally barren bluffs, giving us, for the first time in our journey, a sensation of mountain scenery, and, so to speak, striking the resolving chords between the low plains of Kansas and the high plateaus of the Rocky Mountain region, whither we were tending. On our northern hand, about fifteen miles from the fort, we saw for the first time bounding our horizon the fringe of trees along the Platte. At first sight this river appeared as wide as the Hudson at Tappan Zee, or the St. John's below Pilatka. Its further banks were enveloped in a misty veil, and looked languidly soft, like far islands seen through tropical fog. Atmospheric distance never deceived so completely. The charming grandeur and tenderness of scale on which this view seemed constructed, were delusions of the mirage. Hot sun and mirroring sand had wrought up the scanty materials of the stream into a dream of beauty which had no geometric reasons. Our best dreams of beauty are generally of that sort, belonging to the soul, and not to the intellect. We hated to have this vision disturbed by Gradgrind measurements of space. "If this were a delusion, let us dream on!" I must confess that this region of mirage is almost the only place, till one reaches the Platte's ice-cold cañon, in the mountains of Colorado, where the river exerts any fascination on the tourist. It will presently lose the assistance of mirage and imagination, and turn out the most miserably uninteresting and feeble-minded stream to be found on the continent. If it were compressed into a single bed, instead of being vaguely dispersed about great and small islands, in all sorts of intricate channels, it would approach the size of the Oswego River at the city of that name.

About two o'clock, we passed a very picturesque party of Germans going to Oregon. They had a large herd of cattle and fifty wagons, mostly drawn by oxen, though some of the more prosperous "outfits" were attached to horses or mules. The people themselves represented the better class of Prussian or North German peasantry. A number of strapping teamsters, in gay costumes, appeared like Westphalians. Some of them wore canary shirts and blue pantaloons; with these were intermingled blouses of claret, rich warm brown, and the most vivid red. All the women and children had some positive color about them, if it only amounted to a knot of ribbons, or the glimpse of a petticoat. I never saw so many bright and comely faces in an emigrant train. One real little beauty, who showed the typical German blonde through all her tan, peered out of one great canvas wagon cover, like a baby under the bonnet of the Shaker giantess, and coqueted for a moment with us from a pair of wicked-innocent blue eyes, drawing back, when the driver stared at her, in nicely simulated confusion. Several old women, of less than the usual anile hideousness of the German

Bauerinn, were trudging along the road with the teamsters, in short blue petticoats and everlasting shoes; partly to
unbend their joints, as was evident from the pastime alacrity
of their gait, and partly to oversee a crowd of children who
were hunting green grass with sickles, and conveying their
scanty harvest to the cattle by handfuls at a time. In the
wagons all manner of domestic bliss was going on. A young
teamster, whose turn it was to ride, sat smoking a pipe and
wooing his bashful dear, thus uniting business and pleasure
in an eminent degree, under the shadow of a great wagon top,
and on a barrel of mess pork. Many mothers were on front
seats, nursing their babies in the innocent unconsciousness
of Eve. Old men lay asleep on bales of bedding, with their
horn spectacles still astride the nose; old women, with similar aids, read great books of theoretical religion, or knitted
stockings of the practical kind. Every wagon was a gem of
an interior such as no Fleming ever put on canvas, and every
group a *genre* piece for Boughton. The whole picture of the
train was such a delight in form, color, and spirit that I could
have lingered near it all the way to Kearney.

About three o'clock we arrived at Fort Kearney, and again
halted. The comparatively light-loaded stage which Munger
had kindly promised to send on to us, would arrive the next
day. After dinner at the Overland station, we walked over
to the fort, which is a mere inclosure of boards, containing several barrack buildings, and stores belonging to the
trading-post. It is not intended to resist assault, but would
probably furnish sufficient protection to settlers who might
flee to it for asylum, from the Indian mode of warfare.

Lieutenant Davis, then in command of a garrison of about a
hundred Colorado troops, received us very politely, and asked

us to make the fort our head-quarters. In the yard of his house we found a pair of nice little buffalo calves, which his men had captured in their last expedition against the Sioux. With the engravings before us, it is needless to remark how strong is their resemblance to the calf of our domestic cow, at the same age. These are supposed to be about a month old. Our artist held two *séances* with the little creatures on the afternoon of our arrival and the next morning, transferring them to canvas in every variety of attitude, and getting their *animus* and typical distinctions as well by heart as he had succeeded in doing with their belligerent sires. They are stupid little creatures, with the usual vituline concentration of sense in their mouths and nose, and no very clear idea of the system on which their legs were planned; but they have a slight suggestion of their future hump, and a certain spunkiness of demeanor, which, to the close observer, bound them off from the common calf. Their coats, too, are rougher than his, and show symptoms of coming curl; but they are of a reddish-brown color, which is not uncommon in our barn-yards.

Punctually at the expected time, our stage came along, and, to our great satisfaction, contained only a couple of passengers. Our dreams of luxurious space were rudely disturbed by the appearance, while we were dining, of the coach from Omaha, which here intersects the main Overland road, with a cargo of passengers mostly intending to keep on further west, and clamorous for their shares in our vehicle. After protracted negotiation, we compromised by receiving two of the new lot, who, with our party of four and the original occupants, crowded us into wretchedly tight quarters.

For the thirty-six miles to Plum Creek station, the road continued to run through a country of only less aridity than preceded our entrance to Fort Kearney. The only spots of brightness on the dreary waste of sand and gramma were the crimson flowers of the ground-poppy, which afford such diversified beauty to the Plains about the Little Blue, and which here fought for a bare existence with the thickening myriads of cacti, bursting up between the spikes and saffron-colored blossoms of the latter, like flames twinkling among pale cinders.

Again we went pattering out into the twilight, behind fresh relays. About nine o'clock, the moon rose among a swarm of small straggling clouds. About eight miles from Plum Creek, her light fell on a broad encampment of Sioux, silvering the dingy skins and occasional canvas of the smoky *tè-pis* into something like the Fenimore Cooper romance of Indian life. I could not help thinking that part of this illusion was owing to the early habits of the savage, which prevented any Indians from being in sight. It would take a good deal of moonlight to make an Indian look romantic. About the tents were a herd of picturesque, ewe-necked horses, feeding at their ease on the short, dry herbage, and showing their sides, mottled with the spots which character-ize what we at the East call a "circus-horse,"—still odder in the brood moonlight.

Just as we passed the last tent, a strange figure burst through the narrow slit in it used as a doorway, and hailed our driver, who stopped for him, and took him on the box. He wore a handsome buckskin hunting-blouse, profusely embroidered and dangling with leather tags, a low slouch hat, and a beaded belt, from which peeped the butt of a six-shooter. His complexion was so bronzed, and his hair so long and black, that until I had looked him full in the face, and heard him speak, I took him for a Sioux. He was a white man,—or white as a man can be who has lived much with the Indians of the Plains,—and had in his countenance one of the most singular mixtures of good-fellowship and desperadoism that I ever saw. I should have liked to see him on my side in a Plains fight, and been sorry to think he was on the other; but there was an Iago quality in his restless black eyes and the iciness of his laugh, which must have made any student of human nature uncomfortable in a protracted acquaintance with him among lonely surroundings.

About eleven o'clock, while we were about half a mile from the station called Willow Island, the moon became as suddenly obscured as if she had been put out with an extinguisher. The clouds grew inky black, and simultaneously the wind rose to a tempest. I never saw in my life such dispatch in getting up a storm. Another minute, and the clouds were pelting down on us hailstones as large as musket-balls. The mules became frightened, and plunged furiously. It was too black to see the heads of the leaders, but there was nothing to be done except advance; so by coaxing, cursing, and whipping, the driver finally persuaded the team to take us as far as the station. We jumped down from the box, and in the dark, after imminent danger from the hoofs of the madly kicking wheel-mules, managed to unhook the traces instead of cutting them, as we had contemplated the necessity of doing. It will seem almost incredible to anybody who has not seen a hailstorm on the Platte; but after we had got the team loose, and were standing by their heads, while the inside passengers used up half a box of matches in getting the lanterns lighted, the stage heavy with mails, seven inside passengers, and all their baggage, was forcibly blown back by the wind a distance of several yards. I could compare its effect on myself only to having a stable door pressed steadily against my person; and if I had not held on by one of the most obstinate of nature's animals, I should have been sent scurrying out of sight in the direction of Fort Kearney.

Just as our patience began to give out under the buffets of the wind and the sound whipping of the hail, our friend in the buckskin made his voice heard through the roar, and a stable-keeper appeared with a light, which was instantly put out. By this time our lanterns were lighted, and we managed to get our mules into their stalls without any accident more serious than a graze on one of the shins belonging to our driver.

It was quite out of reason to attempt going on in such a tempest. Accordingly we let our relays stay in the stable, and went back to tell the insides, penned into darkness and uncertainty by tightly buttoned carriage leathers, that we had concluded, after the manner of the Connecticut River mate, "to anchor our end of the schooner." This seemed to meet as much approbation as they had to expend upon anything under the circumstances. They resigned themselves to an upright sleep against the straps and cushions, while we, who had still enough wakefulness in our legs to hunt up something better, betook ourselves to the stable, and lay down on clean straw in some empty stalls. I blessed the hailstorm which was pelting outside, for it had given me a chance to stretch myself. Dearest opportunity to the over-lander! I have known hours when I speculated curiously on the torture of the rack, and wondered how the old martyrs could have found it so disagreeable. Certainly it seemed to me that any amount of relaxation could not be so painful as that sense of being shortened up, driven in, and clinched on the other side, which results from twenty-four hours' constancy to a bent position. I accordingly welcomed the chance of extending myself on the Willow Island straw, with a delight which would have scarcely been lessened, had the bare boards been substituted as a lying-place.

About three o'clock in the morning I was awakened by a tumbling and groaning in the next stall to mine. I rose, and felt my way to the sufferer, thinking that he had a fit. In the dark I put out my hand; and touched a leathern fringe. It belonged to our new passenger. He continued to toss and twist; he got into deadly combat with the wisps of straw under him; I heard him send home three or four well-meant blows with his fist against the side of the stall, and then he muttered in a voice of horror, "Murder! murder! O God, murder!"

I caught him by the shoulder, and shook him soundly. As he woke, he felt for his pistol. I held his hand, and explained the facts of the case. "O thank you!" said he; "I sometimes have the nightmare very badly, and then I remember,—O *such* disagreeable things—everything in fact that I ever saw in my life."

It was broad daylight when I woke the second time. My friend of the next stall had disappeared, and did not join us when we again put ourselves *en route*. The hail had ceased, but had left a gray, greasy, despondent heaven, and a sullen, sobbing wind. We rode through a sterile country, with distant bluffs of dun sand bounding our plain on either side, till at Midway Station we stopped for breakfast.

One of the greatest puzzles of the Plains is their nomenclature. You stop at stations called something "Spring," and look in vain for anything to drink but stagnant water. When you come to anything "Lake," you are nearly sure to find no expanse a pig could wallow in. If you discovered a station named Brown's, you might be very sure that no one had ever lived there but a family of Johnsons; And there is no better Western reason for calling a station Pratt's Hill than because it is a hollow occupied by Joneses.

We reached Cottonwood at dinner-time, but our previous experience gave us no encouragement to alight. We satisfied appetite with canned peaches, hard tack, and that charmingly portable little fish which so invariably accompanies Western immigration that its empty tin coffins are seen scattered around every station door; and the name for a spindling little fellow, whom the plainsman does not wish to compliment, is "*You Sardine.*"

The country around Cottonwood is more undulating than any we had seen since leaving Comstock's. For miles both east and west of it, we continually climbed and descended hills, and passed through a series of sand cañons, beginning to assume the typical look of the mountain galleries further west. We observed projecting from the side of one of these, the first limestone outcrop we had noticed west of the Missouri River.

Just west of Cottonwood, the Platte River is formed by the junction of its north and south forks. In the neighborhood of the confluence, the land begins rising westward perceptibly. About ten miles from Cottonwood, I got my first sensation of ascent toward the Rocky Mountains. There was a solid, under-braced look in the hills, a firm, resonant quality to the road, which did not belong to alluvial bluffs. I felt as if I were standing on the first fold of the old fire-serpent, who ages ago wriggled himself up under the crust, and protruded his flaming crest in the form of the Rocky Mountain summit. We continued passing over extensive undulations all that afternoon, though the harder formations made no visible outcrop.

It was just after sunset when we ascended a considerable elevation to the station of Fremont Springs, 29 miles west of Cottonwood and 379 from Atchison. We were now close beside the South Fork of Platte, and thenceforward to Denver, a distance of 274 miles, were hardly ever out of its sight. We stopped here to change horses, and take delicious draughts from the finest spring between the Missouri River and the Rocky Mountain snow-peaks. We found it carefully enshrined, as if it were a Greek god; for a clear, cold, living fountain may well demand apotheosis at the lips which have cooled their fever in it in the midst of the journey beside those stagnant pools and that dull, creeping, muddy river, which are the lot of every passenger across the Plains. The station-keeper was faithful to his precious trust; and the crystal water was so well protected under a little house of boards, that neither sun could heat nor impurities sully a single ripple of its ceaseless gayety. It was like a baby's soul cradled in from the world's evil; a joy without reaction, an abandon without danger. It sang temperance lectures without knowing it, inspired in its sleep. It was a homily on good living, a parable of pure-heartedness; without didacticism going straight to the point. People with flat flasks in their breast-pockets felt disgusted at them, and, for miles after we left the spring, could not bear to take its taste out of their mouths.

We bade adieu to the beautiful fountain and the little lakes into which it ran on its way to the Platte, all alive with wild ducks, and mirroring the exquisite pink and salmon hues of a beautiful sunset. We rode on twenty-five miles further, to Alkali Lake, where sleep so thoroughly overpowered me that instead of going into the station to take an Overland supper, I threw myself down on the stable straw, and slept a sleep like death, until the driver awakened me by protracted shaking. The sensation of having to get up and go on again, was one of the most miserable I ever knew. After all our experience, I could not learn the trick of sleeping upright in the stage. I kept on the box, and my whole nature fought slumber as if it were a disease. Nor did I ever learn; and but for the necessity of the case summoning up all the Yankee ingenuity which was in me, I believe my comparatively uninitiated constitution would have given out before I got to Denver.

I may say, in passing, that Alkali Lake was one of those places, now growing more frequent, where salts of soda and potash exist in nearly saturated solution with stagnant water, or occasional springs, in shallow basins along the banks of the Platte. The Platte itself is not alkaline; yet where the trail runs at any distance from it, emigrant cattle often suffer so much from thirst, that unless great watchfullness is used, they temporarily satiate themselves at the pools before they can be driven to the river, producing a disease of the stomach and intestines, which carries off multitudes of them every summer. The entire road along the South Fork is strewn with bleaching heads, whole skeletons, and putrefying carcasses, which mark the effects of this malady, heat, and overdriving. As for the human passenger, though in most cases his caution prevents him from an injurious gratification of his thirst, he still suffers intensely from the very inhalation of the air carrying alkaline particles. Few manias, it seems to me, were ever more intense than my longing for pickles, lemons, tamarinds, vinegar, anything which could correct the alkaline excess in my blood. The rest of us suffered nearly as much; and we found that the acid stores which we had used the precaution to bring from the Missouri River were, as long as they lasted, the most invaluable portion of our commissariat. At times I have ridden for twenty miles in a state of absolute wretchedness, with the taste of soda crusting my entire mouth and throat as perceptibly as if I had just taken a teaspoonful of the commercial article. To the traveller on this part of the Platte, canned fruit, the sourer the better, is an absolutely indispensable portion of his outfit.

The use of that word "outfit," is curiously broad upon the Plains. It means as many things as the Italian "roba," or the French "chose." It may seem a very natural amplification of significance that this term, originally taken from an emigrant's preparation for the road, should come to be applied to a suit of clothes, or even the ranch which a man had put under cultivation. But it is rather amusing to hear a Durham bull referred to as having rather a short outfit of horns; a mother threatening a refractory child with the worst outfit he ever got in his life; or a stage-driver saying that he has a big outfit of passengers. I was still more interested to have a man in Colorado tell me of a friend of his who had been living among the Indians, and had come home "with just the prettiest outfit of small-pox that he ever see."

The moon rose late, and was very light. At any other time I might cheerfully have sat up with her. In my present state of feeling, I wondered how poets could ever have lingered out of bed long enough to write about her. A pumpkin cart full of moons, reinforced by a Barnum's museum of nightingales would not have been the least inducement to a man in my situation. We emerged from the hilly country we had been travelling since the middle of the afternoon, and came out upon a sterile-looking plain of sand and buffalo-grass, which resembled the country about Fort Kearney. It was after midnight when we reached Diamond Springs, a station four hundred and twenty-seven miles from Atchison, and another of the topographical misnomers before referred to, possessing, so far as I could discover, as little that was valuable in the way of springs as of diamonds.

It had, however, its uses to me. It meant bed. My mind was made up, that is to say, what mind I had left. It all rallied to the final support of my life's now one remaining idea. I jumped down from the box, stuck my head inside the leathers, and woke my friends from the miserable cat-nap they were indulging, to bid them goodnight till we met in Denver. They were too sleepy to be much surprised, and plead with great moderation for my continuance on the vehicle of torture. As for myself, I did not wait to see the horses change, but tumbled as well as I was able into the station-house, and was stretched on a bunk under my camp-blankets beside a sleeping stable-keeper before the wheels rolled away.

It was eight o'clock in the morning before I awoke. I think I never slept so much or of so excellent a quality in the same time. I was a new man when I stood on my feet, and the idea of breakfast began to dawn in on me like a dissolving view, replacing that of bed.

After breakfast, which was made a little more luxurious than the usual Overland meal by the addition of some very nice Indian meal flapjacks, I posted up my journal, and then went forth to survey the land. Trenck amused himself with spiders, and in "Le dernier Jour d'un Condamné" much food for meditation existed within four stone walls. The human eye is a wonderfully adjustable instrument, becoming a telescope for broad generalizations, and a microscope for details. I brought mine to the latter focus, and went hunting for objects of interest over a tract which more perfectly represented Platitude and Inanity, reduced to their geographical terms, than anything east of the Goshoot Desert.

I dwell on this Thohu Va-vohu a little longer because, if I can at all approach its painting in words, I shall have succeeded in conveying to my readers an idea of the sand and gramma plains skirting the South Platte, better than any which could be rendered by an engraving.

I emerge from a one-story house of logs, fifty feet long, fifteen broad, twenty feet to the roof-peak. It has no pretense of a fence, but a corral about a hundred feet west incloses a barn and two company stables.

In front of me stretches a waste of sand, midway in color between an ash-heap and the Rockaway Beach, illimitably flat to the east and west, bounded on the southern horizon by a range of equally gloomy bluffs, which may be six miles off, and a hundred feet high. In all the view is no tree, no vegetation of any kind which a grown man would not have to stoop to touch, no living thing or sign of any; for the very antelope, which usually put a locomotive spot of interest somewhere on such voids, had retired out of sight into the ravines of the bluff. Behind me, a hundred steps to the north, crept the Platte River, here apparently confined to a single channel about three hundred yards wide. It sneaks along between low banks, like an assassin river going to drown somebody. It does not woo or cajole; it is a murderer who has lived past the arts of fascination; a cruel courtesan, old, wrinkled, hateful, too life-weary to think of pleasing, yet loving to kill. And it has killed. It has proffered fords, and given quicksands; it has engulfed in its treacherous bottom horse, rider, wagon, herd, all that was trusted to it. Fascinated by its ugliness and the story of its crimes, I come close to its edge. The oozy paste of loam which banks it curves glibly away from under my feet, and I am in the water before I know it. It is well I have not slipped off in a dark night, or how the greasy mud and the dribbling sand would toy with my fingers, and let me slip easily away! I scramble up the bank by main force with a shudder. I was longing for a bath—had meant to try the Platte, though the ranchmen had informed me that it was only knee-deep, save in holes; but I gave up the idea on looking at that water-fiend, *a Lorelei* with all her treachery remaining, and all her graces gone.

There is another reason why I should not go in. Across the desert waste from the southerly bluffs a torrid wind is blowing ten knots an hour. It is like a hot blast of the Cyclops' furnace escaping above ground. It comes so freighted with microscopic sand-grains that it is not as much the old school definition of wind—"air," as it is earth "in motion." I have been out five minutes, and there is not a pore of my body which it has not stopped. I feel dry and caustic, a sort of mineral deposit rather than a fleshly man. If I went into the Platte, I should be stuccoed like a cheap country seat before I could use a towel. The river, too, is as bad as the air. It is a saturated solution of sand; a gray sirup of silex, which drops dust on your hand wherever you stop a ripple. The Platte is never entirely dry in the usual sense; but what river can be rationally drier than this, which is composed, one particle in ten, of the driest thing on the globe?

Let me take stock of this pathless waste before me. When they are right under my feet, I can see the cork-screw curls of the gray gramma. I walk a little further, and begin to make distinctions. Everything is gray, but not all of it is gramma. A little furzy plant, the undersides of its leaves covered with a dry down that rubs to powder between the fingers, of name unknown, but resembling the artemisias; a true artemisia, from six to eighteen inches high, also woolly; a single spot of orange color as large as a half-dime, seeming to be a poor relation of the marigolds; a stinted sunflower; a few sickly cactuses; this is the vegetable inventory. The beautiful ground-poppy, and all other flowers which might enliven a landscape, had entirely disappeared.

Despite the nakedness of the land, it swarmed with ants, whose industry was manifest in cones a foot high, though it was impossible to see any practical application for it in the shape of food asking storage. The same famine supported myriads of cheery grasshoppers, with red wings and legs, which made them, when they flew, the only bright objects in the landscape. A reddish-brown species of cricket also abounded, its size averaging a little larger than our black insect of the States. Here is the animal inventory. I looked for lizards, and found none, though they may only have retired to private apartments in a temporary fit of disgust at their situation, since it seems almost inconceivable that some member of the family should not exist in so congenial a habitat. I was disappointed more especially not to find the horned toad, so called. A friend of mine in a Western expedition had discovered it on the Plains of the North Platte, considerably east of Fort Laramie; but we saw none in our present journey until within a day's ride of the Rocky

Mountain Watershed, though repeatedly passing over tracts where they might reasonably be looked for.

That night the wind blew more violently, if possible, than it had at Willow Island. The ranch-house rocked under it, and such tempests of sand came flying with it, that every crevice of the walls streamed with little jets, and every object that lay untouched for an hour was powdered half an inch deep. The air was intensely dry and irritating. At sundown it began to thunder and lighten. The flash and roar soon became almost continuous, and remained so till after midnight. With all this commotion came not a single drop of rain. In the States the water would have fallen half a foot deep. Here, though the sky was black as iron, it was equally hard and pitiless. The people told me that for years at a time the storms were equally severe and rainless with this one. I could think of nothing, when I looked at the heavens, but the agony of a baffled yet unrepentant soul.

Through the tempest of wind and sand, an east-going stage struggled about tea-time, bearing half a dozen miserable passengers, every one of whom looked like a cast of himself in silex, unflattered in expression. They had come all the way from California; and I shuddered to think whether I should have grown as reckless as they by the time I was equally near my end of the journey. Some of them seemed merely hanging on to life by the neck of a pocket-flask. Solitary confinement, with a Chinese gong beaten at fifteen-minute intervals, day and night, for six months, near one's bunk-head, could not have reduced victims to a more deplorable state of despair and defacultization. One passenger, who, being now only four hundred miles or so from home, felt as if he were beginning to catch sight of familiar chimney-pots, sold his blankets to the station-keeper, under an impression that he would have no further use for them. They were of the best California variety, a handsome blue, little worn, and could not have been purchased originally for less than ten dollars in gold. As I soon after bought them of the station-keeper for two dollars and a half in greenbacks,—and nobody ever does anything out there except at a tremendous profit,—I am led to conclude that the passenger must have lost much of his hold on life. I felt sorry for him whenever I wrapped myself up in his handsome spoils, though they proved an invaluable addition to my own during the bitter nights we afterwards spent next the snow-peaks.

Beyond Spring Hill, the South Platte makes the nearest approach to beauty which you find in it till you see it issuing from its lofty cañon back of Denver. All the way that we skirted it during the remainder of the afternoon, it was studded with picturesque islands, green as emerald. When the sun declined so that its level rays overlooked, instead of pointing out the arid plains, and the carrion carcasses of dead cattle which pollute them, the view became quite fascinating. It was like fairy-land when the sun disappeared entirely, and the whole west became glorious with gold and purple, green and salmon, reflected in the slow-creeping water between the islands. Whatever else may be lacking on the Plains, the sunsets are magnificent. To be sure, the natives cannot be held responsible for that; if they could get at them, they would fry them. As it is, Nature triumphs over all; and the two hours I used to sit on the stage-box worshipping her sunset divinity, were compensation enough for a whole day of discomfort.

For twenty-five miles beyond Spring Hill, we rode through a solitude broken only by one station-house, a few antelope, and innumerable jackass-rabbits. The latter came tamely out to bathe their immense ears in twilight, squatting among patches of gramma and artemisia, or leaping across the road so close to us that if we had had time to stop and cook them, we might easily have shot a dozen as we toiled by them through the deep sand.

About day-break we drew up at Beaver Creek Station, five hundred and thirty-three miles from Atchison, and a hundred and twenty from Denver. The station consisted, as usual, of a single house with the company's stables and corral attached, and is situated about three miles east of the Beaver Creek laid down on the maps. The light was vague when we first stopped, but sufficient to reveal a picturesqueness in the immediate landscape which set my heart bounding, after the experience of the past two days. Nature, for a little respite, had repented her of neutral tints, and forsaken the Society of Friends. The Platte had made a concession to our rebellious æsthetic sense, by sending out from the main channel, where it crept eastward, some forty rods north of the house, a sinuous lagoon terminating in a marsh near the road. All along the borders of this still but living water, the grass was green and thick even to rankness, and its high banks bore in profusion succulent weeds, congeneric with those that haunt our Eastern morasses. As the sun grew nearer the horizon, this pleasant feature showed to better advantage. The eye rested on the broad borders and patches of living greenness, with a feeling of comfort that no Eastern imagination can appreciate. The rosy hues of as lovely a sunrise as I ever saw, bloomed slowly out on the spotless mirror of the water, with the effect of a developing daguerreotype or a dissolving view. The lagoon became iridescent upon one side, remaining black as night under the shadow of the opposite bank; and when a light mist began rising under the touch of growing light, the colors shone through breaks in its dancing masses beautiful as a dream. Still a little later, then the rosy changed to golden; and when the sun first showed his edge, the water was turned to a sheet of topaz fire.

With advancing dawn, large game broke into view. I thought I had seen ducks before, but the lagoon and the river swarmed with them to a degree which quite corrected my views on that subject. Two or three varieties of teal, the ruddy duck, a mallard, and a small diver were represented in the great argosy that rippled the smooth, glowing water; and beyond my immediate ken, there may have been detachments from numerous others, Colorado possessing fourteen distinct species of the bird. Every step of my way along the margin of the main stream sent the quacking mistress of some future family scurrying off her loose-built nest, until the water was alive with gliding motion of exquisite grace, and colors of the most varied beauty. The cinnamon teal and the ruddy duck were rich warm patches that slipped past like tinted vapor; while the green and blue-winged teal shone cool and steely in the dawn which had come to waken them with me. It seems to me that I have never seen bird-life more plentiful or lovely.

We were all seated on or in the wagon, when our scarred driver pointed westward across the Plains, now all aflood with the gold of the risen sun, and said,—

"There are the Rocky Mountains."

I strained my eyes in the direction of his finger, but for a minute could see nothing. Presently sight seemed adjusted to a new focus, and out against the bright sky dawned slowly the undefined shimmering trace of something a little bluer. Still, it seemed nothing tangible. It might have passed for a vapor effect on the horizon, had not the driver called it otherwise. Another minute, and it took slightly more certain shape. It cannot be described by any Eastern analogy; no other far mountain view that I ever saw is at all like it. If you have ever seen those sea-side albums which ladies fill with algæ during their summer holiday, and in those albums have been startled, on turning over a page suddenly, to see an exquisite marine ghost appear, almost evanescent in its faint azure, but still a literal existence which had been called up from the deeps and laid to rest with infinite delicacy and difficulty, then you will form some conception of the first view of the Rocky Mountains. It is impossible to imagine them built of earth, rock, anything terrestrial; to fancy them cloven by horrible chasms, or shaggy with giant woods. They are made out of the air and the sunshine which show them. Nature has dipped her pencil in the faintest solution of ultramarine, and drawn it once across the western sky, with a hand tender as Love's. Then, when sight becomes still better adjusted, you find the most delicate division taking place in this pale blot of beauty, near its upper edge. It is rimmed with a mere thread of opaline and crystalline light. For a moment it sways before you, and is confused. But your eagerness grows steadier, you see plainer, and know that you are looking on the everlasting snow, the ice that never melts. As the entire fact in all its meaning possesses you completely, you feel a sensation which is as new to your life as it is impossible of repetition. I confess (I should be ashamed not to confess) that my first view of the Rocky Mountains had no way of expressing itself save in tears. To see what they looked, and know what they were, was like a sudden revelation of the truth, that the spiritual is the only real and substantial; that the eternal things of the universe are they which afar off seem dim and faint.

Soon after leaving the breakfast station, we struck a low range of tiresome sand-hills resembling those about Julesburg. Through them runs to the Platte, Beaver Creek, the first of a series of short streams, laid down on the maps as draining a broad plateau south of Denver, and communicating with the river in nearly parallel lines. Bijou, Kiowa, and Cherry Creeks are the three others noticed; and there is a fourth, which does not appear on any United States map, emptying into the river near Denver, and called Coal Creek. I have said that Beaver Creek runs, but this is hyperbole. It just trickles. A thirsty mule might have stopped at one of the holes in its bed, and in five minutes drunk it dry, to stay so for an hour. Its pulse was feeble as syncope. As to Bijou, I do not feel that I am anticipating by its mention, for when we got to it there was nothing to anticipate; while Cherry Creek, running through part of Denver, is a mere bed, dry as Sahara, save when some express train of a snow-melting freshet comes thundering down from the range, to surprise human life and property in its murderous rush, as it did in 1864.

At Junction, the next station west of Beaver Creek, we left the Platte, and took a cut-off to Fremont's Orchard, twenty miles across a succession of high sand-hills, on which the sun pelted and the dry hot wind blew more mercilessly than anywhere on our previous journey. I had left my canteen behind me at Diamond Spring; one might as well look for water in an ash barrel as anywhere along the cut-off; and before we were half-way over it, I suffered from a thirst, only paralleled hitherto by the experience of my buffalo hunt. But for the misery of a parched tongue, a throat like a glass-house chimney, lips cracked by the alkali atmosphere, and the lassitude of a perfectly shadeless ride on the hottest day of the season, I should have enjoyed the new nature opening to study throughout this tract, with much zest and enthusiasm. From the time we left Junction till we struck the Platte again, we seemed to be in a new zone, both botanically and zoölogically. If we had altered our latitude by a hundred miles, we could hardly have entered a fauna and flora more widely differing from those of the Plains proper than we attained by the present slight change in our topographical conditions. We found on the long sand-hills which we now had to climb, a greater variety of plants than we had discovered over all the comparative level between O'Fallon's Bluff and Beaver Creek. Among others were by far the handsomest asclepias I ever saw, with profuse pink blossoms; a beautiful rose-colored cactus of the branching kind, several of the globular varieties, and the common yellow variety in great profusion; a blue daisy, seen here for the first time, in all but its color nearly resembling the white millefoil daisy of the East; several sunflowers, and varieties of flowering bean and pea; a blue flower, apparently of the larkspur family; another poor relation of the marigolds, like that noticed at Diamond Springs; star-grass here and there; and a very singular blossom, quite unknown to me, which consisted of a fusiform central sack of fibrous tissue containing pulp, and attached to this three membranous wings, like those of a maple-seed, but much larger and softer, as well as differently colored, a pale flesh tint characterizing the fresh specimens.

These plants all grow out of a soil which might have rivaled the mountains of Gilboa for ignorance of either rain or dew, and with a desolate, hot exposure, where utter sterility might have been pardoned. Though they flourished, and I was informed that cattle could subsist themselves across this waste, I saw nothing in the shape of herbage which even a charity broadened by appreciation of the gramma, could have called edible food.

For the first time lizards appeared plentifully. A little brown-and-yellow variety, occasionally tending toward red, and in shape, as well as agility of motion, resembling the so-called chameleon of the Southern States, was the chief enlivener of all our toilsome climbs, darting across the road at our approach with great velocity, and whisking under the shadow of some fat cactus which hid everything but its beady eyes and betraying tail. The naturally expectable horned toad still failed to make its appearance. The air was merry with red-winged grasshoppers; great liver-colored crickets basked on all the little sand-hummocks; one old familiar friend of Eastern roadsides, the "tumble-bug," was here and there seen rolling its balls into a happy rotundity, under much more trying circumstances of ground than its relation in the States; a very handsome lady-bird beetle, in size considerably surpassing our own, and a small painted beetle of the pumpkin-bug appearance, finished the more obvious catalogue of insect life on this tract. Less apparent to the eye, but abundantly sensible to feeling, were the minute buffalo-gnats, which at intervals during the past three days had much annoyed us along the Platte, but now became a nuisance justifying imprecation. As if we had not enough to suffer from parching heat and thirst, mules tired to death, deep sand, and a surly driver, these pestilent little creatures swarmed around our heads and into our hair, stinging us on neck and scalp like so many winged cambric needles dipped in aqua-fortis, and utterly scouting the obstacle of a green barege veil which I had brought from Atchison for defense against them. Wherever there was the minutest crevice in the barrier, they swarmed through without the mosquito's warning hum; and the first sign that these microscopic Philistines were upon us, was an itching which no slaps or scratches could appease.

Ravens, crows, here and there a variety of black-bird, and a small ground-sparrow were the region's only contributions to ornithology, so far as I observed. The only mammalia anywhere to be seen were a herd of antelope, faultlessly constant to desolation, which crossed the road at lightning speed about a hundred yards ahead of us, on their way to drink at the Platte, an hour before we reached Fremont's Orchard. Prairie-dogs and jack-rabbits either did not exist in the neighborhood, or had the wisdom and good taste to keep their settlements away from the cut-off, and themselves out of the torrid sunlight.

The last three or four miles of our way led us through a series of arroyos, or deep channels, to which I have before referred in describing the Plains formation, running towards the Platte, and evidently at some remote geological day the drains of rapid water-masses, though they have not been moist within the memory of man. Everything in their direction, their shape, and the successive terraces of their banks, suggests a series of water-courses only recently dried up; and not until one has traversed them entirely to the fine old cotton-woods at Fremont's Orchard does he give up the notion that he must be near some temporarily exhausted affluent of the Platte. They are, all of them, larger than the channels laid down on the maps as creeks, and, to all appearance, might as well discharge some water from the plateau at longer or shorter intervals; yet their thirstiness is a matter of ages, not of years.

At Eagle's Nest, a station eleven miles from the Orchard, I observed, for the first time since leaving Cottonwood, a stony outcrop from the universal sand. It was a friable sandstone, abounding in iron, and possessing a curious conchoidal cleavage, which, with a little delicacy of manipulation, enabled me to separate a large piece of it in concentric basins or belts. Its solidification was very recent, probably belonging to a post-tertiary period.

From Eagle's Nest to Latham, a distance of twelve miles, we rode almost immediately along the banks of the Platte, which here began to compress itself within narrower boundaries, and rejoice in higher, much better timbered, and more picturesque banks. Just west of Latham, the main trail to California crosses and leaves the South Platte, the river itself making an abrupt bend of nearly 45° from the southerly direction. The road to Denver, a distance of sixty miles, follows up the Platte, Denver being at the junction of that stream with the spasmodic and semi-mythical Cherry Creek. Reaching Latham about dark, I abandoned the stage which had brought me thus far westward, and awaited another, which was to start for Denver on the arrival of the eastward passengers. It was ten o'clock before this happy prerequisite was fulfilled. The interval of waiting I was only too glad to consume, after a tolerable supper at the station-house, in a straight-out slumber among the grain-bags of the company's stables, having first feed the driver of the Denver stage to wake me when he got ready for the start.

I was surprised to find the Platte becoming quite a nice stream soon after we left Latham. Its banks hid their sandy monotony under a fine cotton-wood fringe, which, without any extensive gap, continued all the way to Denver. The river was very narrow, in some places not half its width at Diamond Springs, and began to assume the clear, forcible look of a true mountain stream. Regarding this bright young brook, which should shortly become a melancholy sewer, I felt like some prophetic soul who sees the future outcast in the innocent child. It was sad to reflect what the Platte would come to.

The night was a deliciously temperate one, the moon at its full, and I the only passenger who shared the driver's seat; so I enjoyed unbounded facilities for feasting on the new landscape. There were many signs in it of cultivation. Ranches had dropped into the lap of nature; and though their surrounding meadows were far from what we should call green in the States, attempts at irrigation had been made here and there, and the grateful ground responded to the extent at least of a small vegetable garden. The land was a smooth rolling prairie, without high hills, and in some places generous enough to support a noble clump of trees at the distance of half a mile from the river.

Nothing of any importance occurred during the night. The mountains, which had been growing plainer all day, were almost dimmed back into their morning romance of spirituality. Long's Peak, one of the loftiest in the range, rose ghastly on our immediate right; and from the point of high light on its snowy head, the Sierra retreated into increasing mistiness toward the south, becoming a mere film of moon-lit cobweb behind the invisible town of Denver. I talked with the driver as far as Fort Lupton,—a stockaded rendezvous and trading-post, now abandoned, situated on the east bank of the Platte, about thirty miles from Denver,—and then curled myself up in the front boot, found fortunately empty, to finish the nap interrupted at Latham. Waking after a couple of hours, I found the dawn up before me, and resumed my seat on the box for the last fourteen miles.

A few miles out of Denver the signs of civilization began to thicken fast. The inclosed ranches became more frequent. One island in the Platte had been brought under cultivation, and adorned with a house and garden which would not have shamed a neighborhood of Eastern country seats.

Finally, as we ascended a hill, Denver broke upon us. It was a larger place, in its first impression on me, than I had expected to find. It lay scattered at the bottom and about the slopes of a basin formed by the lowest foot-hills of the Rocky Mountains; and its white dots, relieved against the rich brown of the hills, made a very cheerful contrast. At six o'clock in the morning, we bowled over the rim of the basin, and rattled down to the stage office. At the door of the adjoining Planters' Hotel I met some of our party. They had reached Denver, as we expected, just a day before me, without any unusual accident or adventure.

CHAPTER IV.

## PIKE'S PEAK AND THE GARDEN OF THE GODS.

In a few days we were so thoroughly rested that we became tired of having nothing to tire us. We proposed to ourselves at least two subordinate trips out of Denver before we should finally leave the place for Salt Lake: the first to Pike's Peak, with the remarkable scenery and geological formations lying between it and Denver; the second to the chief Colorado gold mines and their business nucleus at Central City.

Our kind friends at Denver took such a warm, practical interest in the former of these expeditions, that we had hardly broached its subject when the means of accomplishing it were put at our disposal. Governor Evans very kindly offered us his ambulance, a comfortable vehicle, strongly built, capable of accommodating four persons, and the very thing for our purpose, and a pair of stout serviceable horses, accustomed to territorial travelling. Mr. Pierce was obliging enough not only to pilot our expedition, but to contribute his own horse and buck-board to the service, taking our artist and his color-box beside him on the elastic machine. These two being provided for, Judge Hall occupied the fourth seat in the ambulance with myself and the two other Overlanders; and having abundantly supplied ourselves with food and ammunition, we set out for our seventy miles' journey to the base of Pike's Peak, on the 10th of June, after an early breakfast.

Our road led us out of the southern portion of the town, past the barracks of a detachment of Colorado volunteers, called Camp Weld, in honor of the late secretary, who had resigned in their cause. The camp was a pleasant and orderly one; the fine appearance of the men impressed us all.

There is a lofty divide and wooded table-land, which sheds off Cherry Creek upon the east, and Plum Creek on the west side. This divide terminates in a much larger and loftier one, running nearly east and west from the Rocky Mountain foot-hills, an unmeasured distance into the Plains. It is the opinion of many experienced frontiersmen that the Republican Fork of the Kansas River takes its rise out of the eastern extremity of this divide. When we remember the various masses of Rocky Mountain detritus discovered in our expedition to the buffalo country on the lower portion of the Republican Fork, it certainly seems improbable that the stream rises any further east than this. There are not lacking hunters and trappers who assert that they have drunk from the springs of the Republican on this divide; but there is a long tract to be explored before the connection can be absolutely established. All the attempts which had been made to track up the course of the stream prior to our visit at Denver, had failed on account of the extreme sterility of certain portions of its banks. One train, to which a large reward had been offered for the discovery of a route from the Missouri to Denver along the main Kansas and the Republican, was obliged to turn north and seek the old trail, after having wallowed for days through sand-hills, where the teams could hardly pull their load, and nearly starved for lack of herbage. If the Republican can be proved to take its rise where I have supposed, its course is perhaps the best natural line for that portion of the Pacific Railroad to be run between the main Kansas and Denver. Fewer engineering difficulties would exist on this line than on any other; the finest grazing-land in America would be opened to set-tlement on the lower portion of the Republican; and the barren land intervening between that and the high divide would offer no such obstacles to a railroad train as to make the route impracticable for cattle.

Our present road led us from Denver to the crown of the smaller divide, and thence along its surface, to its junction with the larger. I must not omit to say that this latter is the watershed between the Platte and Arkansas rivers. It is about half-way between Denver and Colorado City. We proposed to reach it by our first day's journey, getting to Colorado City at the close of the second.

Six miles of pretty level travelling brought us to the ascent of the Plum and Cherry Creek divide. By quite a steep rise we reached the top of the divide, and rested our horses while we enjoyed the scenery. From the foot of our lofty eleva-tion the Plains stretched for a hundred miles to the east and north, to our sight as level as the sea, and still more soli-tary. Standing where all minor details were lost, we could not see the sail of a single wagon-cover whitening the des-olate, billowless main; nor did there peer from it any little islets of green vegetation. It might have been the sea of the Ancient Mariner, and we "the first who ever burst" into its silence. The deception, if you choose to call it so, was quite perfect. But I do not like that word. Nature in her high-est moods runs the same idea into several creations. Great things resemble each other. The gods are of one blood, and the sea is like the desert.

A yet grander sight than the dead sea of the Plains invited us on our right. We had risen so far above the Denver basin that the foot-hills shrank out of sight, and the mountains behind the town uncovered themselves boldly to our view. From our position they appeared nearly on a level with us, a fact of perspective which enabled us to separate them into five or six distinct or anastomosing ranges between the level plains and the highest snow-peak. The arcs described by each range so intersected those of the neighboring ranges, that Judge Hall quite aptly compared our view to a herd of travelling dromedaries. Equally happy was another favorite illustration of the judge's, frequently used in his explanations of Colorado geology, in which he compared the unfolding of the several uplifts at our present point of vision to the opening leaves of the peony.

A book on the Rocky Mountains should say something about those mountains, yet I confess that I have deliberated well ere deciding to do so. The description I have given of their first assure blossoming on the sky west of Beaver Creek, is no dreamier than must be a reader's idea of the mountains seen close at hand, after the most vivid description that can be written. In the East there is nothing to illustrate the Rocky Mountains by. With the Rocky Mountains, the Alleghanies and the Taconic have no common terms. Here are none of those delicious, turfy glades, those enameled banks, which beautify the mountains of our Atlantic slope. The landscape is without a single patch of bright green. The mountains rise up in ragged, brawny masses, without the apology of color for a nakedness that is grand in itself. They oppress you with such sublime size, they are the evident stone-mask of such a tremendous force spent in the old centuries, that you do not miss color in them,—do not think of it. Every cross-twist in them is the cast of a muscle strained by the gladiator, Fire.

The gentler curves, the valleys that lead out of sight into mountain recesses,—these are suggestions of a gentler world-time, which came after the struggle. They are the kisses of the Water Nymph, and the dalliance of bland but treacherous Oxygen. The Rocky Mountains are full of infinite suggestion. Their presence makes a thoughtful man wish to sit down and learn from them; there is such genius in it, it so overawes one. You are surprised when you examine this feeling, and see how few of the qualities which made you admire other mountains, exist in these. What you see is a colossal mass of brown, and, in its highest lights, of amber, relieved against nothing, mediated by nothing, its wall bounding your entire western horizon. It is so consistently great, it is a congress of such equal giants, that you cannot compare it with any of the ranges you have seen before. When you rise to a higher plane of vision, this single leaf of grandeur becomes a book. You confess you have not seen the Rocky Mountains until now. Mountain billows westward after mountain, their crests climbing as they go; and far on, where you might suppose the Plains began again, break on a spotless strand of everlasting snow.

This snow indicates the top of the range. But of what range? Not the top of the Rocky Mountains, but only of a small minor range in that range. That glittering ridge yonder is but one of a hundred lying parallel with it to the westward. We have not even yet seen the Rocky Mountains.

I remember how the idea of crossing the Rocky Mountains used to look to me. It was an affair something like the steep grades between Altoona and Pittsburg, where it takes part of a day to go up, see the view, and come down satisfied on the other side. In spite of the atlas (or by favor of some of the earlier ones), I never could conceive of the Rocky Mountains except as a single range occupying a small line along the axis of the Continent. Comparatively little has been done for the geology of this region, so that scientific distinctions in that science have no more familiarized us with the multitudinous ranges than have those of geography. I suppose that to most Eastern men the discovery of what is meant by crossing the Rocky Mountains would be as great a surprise as it was to myself. Day after day, as we were travelling between Denver and Salt Lake, I kept wondering when we should get over the mountains. Four, five, six days, still we were perpetually climbing, descending, or flanking them; and at nightfall of the last day, we rolled down into the Mormon city, through a gorge in one of the grandest ranges in the system. Then, for the first time after a journey of six hundred miles, could we be said to have crossed the Rocky Mountains.

The only name for the system is "nation." "Range" does not express it at all. It is a whole country, populous with mountains. It is as if an ocean of molten granite had been caught by instant petrifaction when its billows were rolling heaven-high.

In some places the parallel ranges thin out, leaving a large tract of level country quite embosomed between snow-ridges, and, so to speak, *alcoved* into the very heart of the system. These are the "Parks"; and they form one of the most interesting as well as characteristic features of the Rocky Mountain scenery. Formations of this kind abound everywhere in these mountains; but the four principal ones form a series, running from a point considerably northwest of Denver quite into New Mexico. They are called, in their order, North, Middle, South, and San Luis Parks. They more nearly resemble the green dells of our Atlantic range than any other parts of this; but their imitation is an expansion on the scale of miles to the inch. You might set down one of our smaller States in Middle Park without crowding it.

The Parks are watered directly from the snow-peaks, being indeed only the inner court of those peaks, and catching the droppings from their eaves. The portions of the Parks most thoroughly irrigated, remain beautifully green throughout the year; and over the whole region herbage is abundant. The sheltered situation of the Parks insure them an equable climate; and old hunters who have camped out in them for months together, talk of life there as an earthly paradise. It will prove equally so to the farmer and grazier when Colorado finds time to develop her agriculture. For the present they are difficult of access, and the most beautiful as well as the richest hunting-grounds in the far West. Elk, deer, and antelope abound there; wild animals of the cat kind, headed by the Rocky Mountain lion, are common in the wooded ridges that skirt them; they are not stinted in respect to bears, wolves, or foxes.

Perhaps, too, the Parks may be said to bound the extreme western range of the buffalo. I saw a buffalo skull, to be sure, on a dry, gravelly plain near the Green River; and tradition still speaks of their having formerly extended all the way into Utah. But the climate is such an antiseptic that the remains seen by me may have been a hundred years old, being white as snow and hardly more than a perfect cast of head and horns in the salts of lime. It is certainly many years since a herd has crossed the mountains, many even since it penetrated them further than the Parks. It is not at all an every-day matter, at this time, to shoot a "mountain buffalo"; so little, indeed, that I could not get absolute certainty as to whether he is identical with the ordinary buffalo of the Plains or a distinct variety. Some of my informants described him as the same in everything but habitat, while others pronounced him much larger and fiercer. The probability is that this animal is only a descendant from strays left behind a herd that crossed the mountains, which gradually were adapted to the new conditions until they present an entirely distinct variety. The mountain buffalo is said not to be migratory. If this be true, the loss of such a strong race instinct is of itself sufficient to form the base of a variety distinction.

I have been betrayed into the artistic error (or excellence, according to your school) of painting more into my picture than I could see from my camp-stool; of adding after experience to the present facts of vision. But to see the Rocky Mountains means so much more than the view of any one mighty ridge or peak, that I might just as well give its idea by glancing across the whole billowy main as by stopping short where the undulations break on that ice-bound coast yonder, in clouds against the blue of heaven.

The divide we were travelling was unlike those of the Plains not only in being of much greater height and surface, but in its possession at intervals of deep ravines, finely timbered with pine, and bearing an underbrush of scrub-oak. The divide was outside of the lowest Rocky Mountain foothills, yet at the East it would have been called a mountainous country in itself. The pine was getting rapidly cleared away from the divide by teams and choppers for the fuel-market of Denver. We were every now and then, during the forenoon, passing great ox-loads of it on their way there. The oak was not that black-jack usually recognized as the scrub variety in our Atlantic sand barrens, but a tree with a comparatively delicate round-lobed leaf. An innumerable array of unknown peas and beans showed pretty scentless flowers along the road, in every shade of purple, blue, and pink. In some situations the ground was all aflame with the intense scarlet flowers of "the paint-brush."

About one o'clock, we descended into a valley of the divide, about twenty miles from Denver, in which, for the first time on our journey, we encountered those sculpturesque freaks of geology which form so large a field of interesting study throughout the Rocky Mountains, and were continually presenting themselves along our subsequent route to Salt Lake.

The steep sand-bluffs, down which our course ran from the high plateau of the divide to the valley, were curiously channeled into isolated groups and masses, whose form gave every possible scope to one's fancy. The simplest of these formations were mere sinuous galleries. Where the work of excavation had gone further, the sand rose in smooth cones or solitary pillars; and in yet more complicated cases, the piles took a statuesque shape, which, with a trifling effort of imagination, became idols, gypsies about their camp-fire, witches, or mummies in their coffins. At first sight these formations were a good deal of a puzzle to me; but as we advanced, and saw them not only in the various stages, but undergoing the processes of production, their explanation became possible on at least one hypothesis, to which I will refer further on.

A little beyond these statues, and in such plain sight of them that their moonlight view must have been like having a guard of honor composed of ghosts, we found "The Pretty Woman's Ranch" and its occupants, the Richardsons. The nomenclature of new settlers is unconventionally direct. They do not hesitate to say when they think a woman is pretty; and I am afraid they would assert the opposite, if true, with equal frankness. There is no doubt what their names mean; and when they call a name, it sticks. All the Richardsons may die; but future travellers will have no difficulty in knowing that a pretty woman was once the ornament of this solitude, or in finding the exact place on which to drop a tear for the evanescence of all things lovely. It is perhaps no betrayal of Coloradian confidence to acknowledge that Mrs. Richardson is the Pretty Woman referred to in the title. We stopped at the ranch which she has characterized, to give our horses their noon feed, take our own lunch, and, let it be confessed, to see the Pretty Woman, though of course solely as a geographical personage. The name is not inappropriate.

Richardson, the owner of a comfortable log-house, and the husband of the ranch's fair namesake, is so good a type of the indomitable class which turns our country's wastes into garden and pasture, that I cannot refrain from condensing into a few lines the simple account which, while we were resting, he gave us of his toilsome and eventful history.

He began his manhood (he is now a bronzed, wiry man of three or four and thirty) by entering the vineyard business with his father and brothers, near Catskill, on the Hudson River. After a year or two, the fever of adventure got into his blood, and he set out to seek a wider field. His way was westward, as that fever always drives an American, and his first halting-place a settlement in Wisconsin. Here he established a nursery, but was presently ruined (or what an Eastern man

would call so) through a protracted season of bad weather
and the failure of his trees. Taking all that he could scrape
together of the remnant of his property, he moved directly
to Denver, and opened, among the earliest there, a store for
the sale of groceries and provisions. Here bad weather came
to him in the human form. He failed again by trusting out
large bills to a set of scamps who were ostensibly buying an
outfit to commence business in the mines, but in reality only
wanted it to enable them to flee the territory, and get beyond
their creditors. They absconded, leaving him quite cleaned
out, without a particle either of pay or security. Indomitable
as ever, Richardson wasted no time in bemoaning himself,
but pushed still further beyond civilization to his present
place, determined to wring out of nature the justice he
could not get from man. The divide in whose valley he lies,
is the natural thoroughfare of all travel from Denver to the
Arkansas; and he occupies an excellent position on it for
the keeping of a "Pilgrims" hostelry. Oats or corn for horses
sell here at fifty cents the single noon feed (six pounds, or
nearly corresponding to our usual four quarts); so that it will
not surprise one to hear that by the end of his first year
in the divide, Richardson had laid by two thousand dollars.
But ill-luck had not done with him. With his savings he
bought a handsome lot of blood-cattle, and had just finished his preparations for adding the business of a grazier to
that of a landlord, when the vendor of the stock was discovered to be a thief, and Richardson's title to them smashed by
the appearance of an owner with the proper documents. I
know numbers of reputable business men who at this juncture would have refused to play any more at cogged dice
with Fortune, and wound up their affairs with the summary

process of a pistol. The idea never seems to have suggested itself to Richardson. When we stopped at the ranch, he had saved two thousand dollars more, and invested it in a stock of blood-sheep, which were then on the way to him from the Missouri River. If I had returned overland from California, I should certainly have made another visit to the Pretty Woman's Ranch, to satisfy my mind about those sheep. I felt as if it would be a pleasure to pitch in and do a day's sheep-tending for a man who had kept such a brave face toward his fate. I sincerely hope that his sheep arrived safely, and that they now thrive and multiply to the extent which his sanguine nature expected. I believe the hope fully justified by the character of the country. There is every reason why a flock of healthy sheep should do admirably on the dry grass of the divide and more succulent nibblings along the water-courses, or, if protected against wild beasts, even in the scantier pasturage along the lower mountain foot-hills. The character of the soil and climate is such that foot-rot would be most unlikely to originate here; and a few years would so thoroughly acclimate the stock as to make both its fleece and mutton valuable additions to the revenue of any virtually unlimited land-proprietor like Richardson. It is unnecessary to praise mountain mutton to any man who has ever eaten Welsh saddle, or chops from the Sierra Nevada. Stimulated by a cruel curiosity, I ventured to ask Richardson if he would be discouraged supposing his sheep failed. He answered no; that in that case he'd only return to the East, where he knew he *was* wanted, and go into the vineyard business again. He certainly had the greatest reasons which a man, according as he is gritty or not, can have for courage or discouragement, a wife and one little boy three years old,—a child of astonishing precocity, who insisted that his first name was Denver City, and would not be pacified until we had let him sit down with us after dinner, and smoke a pipe in proof of our confidence in that assertion.

We paid the worthy ranchman for our noon feed, and took his cheerful philosophy gratis. The debt we incur by seeing such men is one that cannot be paid. Their memory is a vigor. You are better for having talked with them; you make other people better, and the benefit goes on rolling up compound interest. The atmosphere of the Pretty Woman's Ranch is an anti-periodic to blue-devils. They certainly will not recur the day one baits there.

About a mile and a half southwest of Richardson's is a broad field, situated on the table-land, which in comparatively small compass contains some of the most interesting subjects for the geologist which are to be found in this country or the world. The entire tract is a fossil forest. Its trees, to be sure, are leveled with the ground; but their stumps and many of their prostrate trunks remain in a condition of stony metamorphosis which may challenge the Enchanted Groves of fairy lore and the Arabic legend of Aladdin's ruby fruit. Nothing can exceed the perfection with which the original vegetable characteristics have been retained in the petrified remains. Some of the trunks, full ten feet in length, have become so thoroughly infiltrated with silicates (chiefly of aluminum, having iron for their tinge), that at first sight they look more like exquisite imitations of trees in jasper, agate, or chalcedony, than the metamorphosed bodies of trees themselves. The translation from ligneous to stony substance has been so gradual, yet so perfect, that you are reminded of the famous jack-knife which retained its identity with a new blade and a new handle. Probably nothing does in reality exist of those trees' original tissue; but each portion of that tissue survived just long enough to act as a mould, and determine every faintest marking on the flinty jelly whose consolidated mass substituted it. The result is that we have in silicates of aluminum and iron as perfect a representation as could be given by original vegetable matter, of cotton-woods, firs, and pines, throughout all the sizes attained by those growths. Nothing among mineral treasures can exceed the beauty of some specimens we found here. Looking at the cross section of one of the stone saplings, the merest tyro saw at a glance the history of its growth, and the position which it had occupied in the arboreal scale,—whether it was an ordinary exogenous tree or a conifer,—and often, too, the age at which it became stone-enchanted. Its pores, its medullary rays, its pith, its rings of growth, and, in some cases, its outer bark, were preserved as distinctly as they were the last day it budded; and though it possessed the lustrous flinty fracture common to the semi-precious stones, across the sharp edges, faithful to its original direction, ran the old grain of the wood as plain as ever. I think it was here that I felt, for the first time in my life, the sensation of avarice, and at the same time realized the sternness of that double test of values, portability, convertibility. It hurt me to go away, and leave that fieldful of gems,—ten-fold more interesting to me than if they had been diamonds,—simply because I had no means of transporting so much as one poor cart-load of the finest to a place where they would give all the delight, win all the admiration, of which they are capable. Of course their beauty is greatest to a mineralogist; but they possess a beauty of marking and color quite apart from this, being intrinsically among the handsomest specimens of the agate and allied stones which I ever saw in cabinet or show-case.

It is somewhat difficult to account for this curious meta-morphosis upon any of the commonly received theories of petrifaction. The stumps are evidently *in situ;* so they cannot have been thrown up by any natural convulsion from a lower stratum, where they had been embedded and fossilized. To imagine them petrified by long submersion in a flood highly charged with silicates, is only to make another difficulty; for in that case what has become of the detritus which should surround them, and why did these exceptional phenomena occur here when the lower ground, which must have been simultaneously under water, exhibits no trace of similar operations? The most probable hypothesis may be that the whole tract was once covered with strongly silicated springs, and that as fast as death deprived a tree of its elaborating and selective apparatus, it became a mere mechanically acting bundle of capillaries, and sucked up the liquor of immortality, which made it a gem. I succeeded in bringing away but a few specimens. They are small, but among the most exquisite for color, lustre, and reproduction of the original tissue. They vary through every shade of purple, brown, yellow, red, and white; and almost any chance specimen that might be collected, would cut into an elegant ornament for the toilet or writing-table, for seal-ring or sleeve-buttons, of the kind for which blood-stone or onyx is usually employed.

Thirty miles from Denver, on a table-land of the divide, we came to a peculiar hill of the butte kind, a single cone, rising abrupt and solitary out of the level plain to the height of about four hundred feet, and crowned with a rude cube of red argillaceous sandstone, nearly five hundred feet in circumference and a hundred feet in altitude. Vasquez, a Spanish guide in Pike's Expedition, gave it the name of "Castle Rock," or rather the no-name, since new settlers are not sufficiently in communication with each other to be bothered about originality, and have illustrated the proverbial coincidence of great minds by fastening this appellation on every one of the multitudinous castellated formations between the tertiary clay of the Platte region and the granite mountains of the Pacific. Still, at a distance, this Castle Rock belies the title as little as any of its namesakes.

Accompanied by one of the gentlemen of my own party, I climbed to the very summit, while the ambulance halted for us below. We found the immense stone which formed the capital of the cone bare of soil and vegetation, save in crevices. On all sides it overhung the earth mound on which it rested to the distance of several feet, thus getting a look of being poised upon its centre, just insecure enough to increase its picturesque effect. By insinuating ourselves into fissures and making bold use of projecting knobs, we contrived to work our way around its sides to the upper surface. Here we found a fine breezy platform, perfectly level, and commanding a view in every direction, which amply repaid our trouble. Here and there through the gray Plains we could see a flock of antelope feeding quietly; one side of our pedestal was alive with screaming hawks, who built their colony of nests there, nowise counting on intrusion from such visitors as we; we could see the little hares playing below us in the ashen furze which thatched the cone; and we could have tossed a stone on the roof of the ambulance, dwindled to a speck, where it stood awaiting us at the foot of the butte.

The declining sun was bathing the great brown mountains in an amber glow; and still, far off to the west and southerly, Old Pike was baring his giant forehead of white and crystal, through a gap in our nearer ranges, to the common splendor. It was the quietest, sunniest, most satisfying mount of vision we had yet climbed.

We came down to find that the enterprising buck-board had come up with our ambulance, stopped to put Castle Rock in our artist's sketch-book, and preceded us in the direction of Pike's Peak and supper. We hurried on after it, and about nightfall came to a comfortable log-house, situated near the head of Plum Creek, here a mountain brook of considerable size, and not far from the junction of the divide on which we had been travelling with that which separates between the affluents of the Platte and of the Arkansas. The house is a neat structure of sawed timber, all of it got out in a steam saw-mill, imported by the proprietor, a man named Sprague, who, like Richardson, increases the income of a ranchman by the entertainment of pilgrims such as we. Here we had an excellent supper; and when we discovered that there were not enough beds to go round, those who were left out camped cheerily down on their blankets, and all slept equally well till sunrise.

We had now reached the grand divide between the Platte and the Arkansas. It seemed rather a spur from the mountains than one of their attendant foot-hills. Immediately about Sprague's the scenery was wildly rocky. The house stood at the foot of a magnificent gray crag, seven hundred feet high, densely wooded with evergreen along a series of gulches which channeled its face at angles that nearly made climbing impossible. Plum Creek was quite embowered in the willows and willow-leaved cotton-woods, which belong to the never-failing water-courses of the Rocky range. The valley through which it flowed was as green as a June meadow in the East; and the sweet, pure air was of itself enough to tell us that we had risen far above the level of Denver.

We left Sprague's early in the morning, well satisfied with his accommodations, and glad to have found, so deep in these solitudes a man who had evidently preserved many of the ideals of civilized life, who took a number of papers and magazines, had a good library, and was successfully toiling to make himself a picturesque and comfortable home.

A couple of miles beyond Sprague's, the rocks, which had been menacing us on the right, withdrew further west, and left a long sloping embankment next us, crowned by another of those remarkable geological freaks which I have before mentioned. On the plateau of the embankment, and not far from its edge, stood Windsor Castle.

The resemblance was astonishing. Towers, battlements, imposing façade, proportions, all were remarkably imitated. If the bareness about it had been broken up by fine old trees, and the royal colors had floated over the flag-staff turret, one might have been compelled to think twice before asserting that this was not the palace of the Old World transported bodily by magic to America. The structure stood so abruptly perpendicular out of the table-land, was so entirely unsupported and unexplained, that it was almost impossible to imagine it a mere mass of Rocky Mountain conglomerate or sandstone. Our road ran within half a mile of it, and at that distance little fancy was necessary to discern regular rows of windows, stately door-ways, and all other details requisite for completing the realization. It is very difficult to get any idea from an engraving of the impression produced by these castellated formations of the West. If the picture makes its mimicry as strong as the formation has it, it is apt to look less like a good picture of the formation than a bad picture of the architecture or sculpture imitated.

The divide continued tolerably level for about ten miles further, flanked on our right by a series of lofty undulations, crested with pine and fir, leading into the Rocky Mountain foot-hills. An occasional spot of more brilliant yellow on their amber slopes below the tree-line betrayed an antelope grazing in the sunshine; but otherwise the loneliness of the view was intense. An everlasting Sabbath bathed the silent brown mountains, climbing range on range to the far glittering snow. They were like the stairs of heaven after the last soul had ascended out of earth. Not the faintest cry of bird or hum of insect broke the stillness of the shining hills next us. It was so strange to look southward over placid fields, yellow with noon, and be sure that, in all that great receding stretch, man was a wanderer, a guest, and not a master; to think, as some deep gorge caught our eye, far up the range, what an unknown region lay there, virgin to man's tread; that it might be ages ere its quiet were disturbed; and that this was but one small spot among myriads as mysterious and inaccessible. The mountains seemed hopelessly apart from us, like the glories we try to grasp in a dream; yet this very hopelessness gave them all a dream's grandeur, and made them seem rather great thoughts than great things. To see the Rocky Mountains in bright sunlight, to drink from the vast, voiceless happiness which they seem set there to embody, is one of the strangest mixtures of pleasure and pain in all scenery.

On one of the rolling hills of the divide we stopped to get what we considered the finest view of Pike's Peak, obtained during our trip. We stopped our horses for an hour at the foot of the hill, and ascended on foot to enjoy the sight, while our artist took his box from the buck-board and made a color study.

In the midst of this virgin solitude, Nature kept repeating fantastic freaks of sculpture and of architecture, as if she were diverting herself with trifles from the strain of that mighty mood in which she brought forth the mountains. The strangeness of effect produced by coming suddenly on ruined temples or Moorish summer-houses in that untamed solitude, and against that tremendous background, is quite indescribable. You thought you were in the most untrodden wild of a late discovered continent; but here is Luxor, here Palmyra, here the Parthenon, Nineveh, and Baalbec. In one place the tawny columns of the ruin were arranged at regular intervals around an oblong; a well defined, though broken pediment, rested on the front row; and about the bases of the entire columns lay splintered shafts and shattered capitals. There was such unity in the design, and such a wonderfully natural posture in the ruins of this structure, that at the moment of first sight, its character absolutely posed one. Further on, a charming little country-house was nestled in just the nook an artist would have chosen,—an indentation of the hill-side, under the shadow of some fine evergreens. But the main architecture was all templar or monumental, as if Nature, even in her play, had not quite got down to the secular level from her mountain inspiration. But, though religions, she was still catholic in her taste, and moulded in Athenian or Egyptian, Gothic or Syrian, styles with equal largeness of appreciation. In these conglomerate structures I saw models belonging to the art of almost every country and time.

About noon we came to a small trickling rill, which was the first water flowing to the Arkansas from the grand divide. It was an affluent of the Monument Creek, which we were to intersect later in the afternoon. It was a miserable little rivulet. Any Eastern gutter would have leaked a healthier one, on an ordinary drizzly day. But water is precious in this almost rainless region; and even this poor rill has a family dependent upon it,—a family which takes in travellers too. There is a small log-house here, with a board over the door, on which, in rude black letters, appears the inscription, "P. Garlick." One of our company was anxious to know if P stood for Pill; as in such case it was an appropriate place for that noted party to live. The actual Mr. Garlick was not aware of any member of his family with that Christian name. He himself was a kindly dispositioned man of forty, who had edged over into Colorado from his native Virginia, taking Missouri on the way, and adding a sort of Pike flavor to his original chivalry. It was surprising to see either Pike or Virginia in such good flesh as he. He weighed about two hundred, though in height not much over five feet six. He was apparently contented with his lot, and complained of nothing except a pair of frozen feet, which had left him badly maimed the past winter. It required an easy soul to put up with that cabin, in the absence of any energetic soul to mend it. It seemed miserably dilapidated, had broken floors or none at all, was chinked by numerous yawning crevices, and in the winter must have been about as much shelter as a good picket-fence. Still, in this house a family of two grown people and their children were satisfied to spend their lives. I found it easy to tell, in all our journey through the wilds, which of the cabins were settled from the Free, and which from the Slave States.

Perhaps, in justice to the present occupants of the cabin, I ought to mention that they have struggled under one great disadvantage. We have noticed in the case of Richardson's place how plain-spoken Coloradian nomenclature is when intended to be complimentary; but it no more hesitates to tell the uncomplimentary facts of a case. During the occupancy of Mr. P. Garlick's predecessors, this cabin got the name of "the Dirty Woman's Ranch." I fear that the multitudinous seas, aided by what little water Mr. P. Garlick can bring to the task, will not wash clean the reputation of that ranch.

If it were possible for a Virginian Pike to be as neat as a Connecticut housewife, Mr. P. Garlick could not redeem the reputation of the Dirty Woman's Ranch. What's in a name? Dreadful things! I heard one Coloradian say to another, "Did you see the Dirty Woman?" and the other answered, "No; she isn't at the Dirty Woman's Ranch any more." What an acknowledgment of the hopelessness of Mr. Garlick's job! The ranch is still the Dirty Woman's, though the Dirty Woman has left forever. I was interested to see the Dirty Woman as a geographical landmark; but my nearest approach to such a view was when a Colorado City friend showed me a very respectable looking young woman on horseback, with the words, "That's the Dirty Woman's daughter." I think she must have been an improvement on the first generation, which was said to have licked the milk-pans, stirred people's tea with an unwashed finger, and deserved the inseparable *soubriquet* mentioned, in multitudinous other ways too

INDIANS ON THE MOVE.

unpleasant to chronicle. Mr. P. Garlick seemed to be aware of the name of his ranch, referring to the circumstances with a subdued air, as if he had once entertained hard feelings toward the Dirty Woman for living there before him, but had now partly succeeded in living the thing down.

We lunched on our own stores in the wagon, and I then stretched myself prone on a settee in the Dirty Woman's front cabin, with my head upon my hands, that in the intervals between napping I might detect the movements of certain occupants which I suspected in the cushion. In the midst of my siesta I was awakened at once by lively bites and a loud roar, and jumped up to discover that Mr. P. Garlick was in convulsions at a broad charcoal sketch of my sprawling figure made on the Dirty Woman's door. The likeness, considering point of view, was very excellent, and showed such a lively feeling for boots that in justice to our artist, I would insist on having it engraved here, only I could not bear to rob Mr. P. Garlick of the cartoon. On the other hand, so magnaminous was I that I explained to him its value as the work of one of our rising painters, and counseled him to keep it always. It would be a legacy for his children when the P. Garlicks had become Coloradian noblemen, with a gallery in their palace. He seemed to appreciate what I asked him, and promised me that he would never wash the sketch off. I don't think he would if I hadn't asked him.

For a couple of hours after leaving the Dirty Woman's, we travelled over a series of low spurs and broad sand-plains. Many of the former, along the course of Monument Creek, were so covered with imitations of sepulchral sculpture, which showed to fine advantage through sombre groves of pine, that illusion again became almost deception, and we might have been excused for fancying ourselves in the burying-ground of some extinct race. My remarks regarding Nature's catholicity of architecture in these simulations apply equally to her sculpture. This marvelous cemetery contained obelisks, little baby grave-stones a foot high, truncated columns, shafts, and urns, pedestaled statues, plain horizontal tablets, and royal sarcophagi. There was a variety about the style, and a naturalness about the grouping of the monuments, which seemed well-nigh inexplicable on the ground of mere geologic chance.

The broad plains which alternated with these spurs were alike distressing to our horses and ourselves. They were expanses of very deep and almost entirely barren sand, fenced a couple of miles to the west by high sandy bluffs just under the foot-hills. On this tract the day for the first time seemed oppressively warm, a state of things not bettered by a dry wind blowing sand into our eyes. Our wheels sank half-way to the hubs; and large horse-flies began to swarm about our poor animals, settling faster than the whip could knock them off, and making the blood trickle at every bite.

The barrenest tract which we crossed, bore abundance both of the cacti and soap-weed. Most of the former which I noticed, belonged either to the flat or globular species; but there occasionally appeared one of the branching varieties, which are found at their highest development considerably further south, in the gigantic "candelabra." In Mexico I afterward saw them attain the dimensions of a good-sized tree; standing thirty feet high, and twenty feet in circuit round the branches. The soap-weed (*Yucca filamentosa*) is the plant known in Florida as the "Spanish bayonet" bearing a profusion of tough, lance-shaped leaves, armed at the extremity with a thorn almost steely in its hardness and sharpness. A hedge of these plants is the most complete shelter against wild beasts or the assault of enemies. They are little used for purposes of defense, their main utility existing in the mucilaginous juice of their roots, which the Mexicans employ instead of soap for laundry purposes. A somewhat protracted acquaintance with Mexicans leads me to question whether the supply of yucca for that purpose does not considerably exceed the demand.

On this waste, for the first time since reaching Fremont's Orchard, we found a large colony of prairie-dogs. They were very saucy, and kept tempting us to shoot at them, with the usual result of wasting ammunition. Their mounds covered an area of several square miles, and all this surface was alive with their chattering frolic.

Apropos of these dogs and their habits, our party got at issue on a point which I have never considered entirely settled. Among all the old plainsmen I found a firm belief that the prairie-dogs are not only gregarious among themselves, but with owls and rattle-snakes. Mr. Pierce assured me that this notion was an entire fallacy. I had a great respect for his researches and opinion, but could not make up my mind to discard the popular view of the subject. I had heard repeated stories of both owls and snakes being driven out of holes where men were digging to examine a dog-town. I found at Kelly's Station a ranchman who, the year previous, had been badly bitten by a rattlesnake while incautiously feeling down a burrow into which he had just chased a prairie-dog. I am, however, perfectly willing to abandon the theory on proof, though its associations have become pleasantly comic and poetical, through the little domestic scenes which I observed at twilight in dog-towns along the Platte. It may be merely a coincidence that owls and dogs are found so constantly about the same burrows; it may be that their burrows are contiguous, but not shared. I am only repeating what my eyes saw, or thought they saw, a great many times. When the sun was well down, and a purple gray began softening hill, and sky, and river, the prairie-dogs who had been chattering their cheery good-night for the past hour in the sand-field at our side, whisked their last tail within the burrows, and became silent all at once. Then, to all appearance out of the same burrows, came one by one a troop of little grayish owls, who, with the low stealthy flight peculiar to night-prowling species, began gliding about the sand-banks and grassy borders of the river. Every now and then, one of them returned to the dog-town, dropped down at the entrance to some burrow, and went out of sight. For mile after mile, as long as we travelled through dog-towns, and had light enough to see the holes, these movements kept occurring. So that I came to regard the dogs as the boarding-house keepers of animal society; wondered whether they ever got into rows with their lodgers, were taken in by swindling owls pretending to large means, or let their apartments to crusty owls who grumbled about the way their beds were made. The owls became to me little Quaker bachelors going out for an evening stroll, or returning cozily at a not too dissipated hour, with their night-keys in their pockets. I own I should be sorry to find myself mistaken.

Soon after leaving the largest dog-town, we turned considerably to the westward, getting in among the mountain foot-hills, and continuing to thread them until we reached Colorado City.

Before we finally left the neighborhood of Monument Creek, I stopped the ambulance, and ascended one of the most practicable hills among the number crowned by sculpturesque formations. The hill was a mere mass of sand and débris from decayed rocks, about a hundred feet high, conical, and bearing on its summit an irregular group of pillars. After a protracted examination, I found the formation to consist of a peculiar friable conglomerate, which has no precise parallel in any of our Eastern strata. Some of the pillars were nearly cylindrical; others were long cones; and a number were spindle-shaped, or like a buoy set on end. With hardly an exception, they were surmounted by capitals of remarkable projection beyond their base. These I found slightly different in composition from the shafts. The conglomerate of the latter was an irregular mixture of fragments from all the hypogene rocks of the range, including quartzose pebbles, pure crystals of silex, various crystalline sandstones, gneiss, solitary hornblende and feldspar, nodular iron-stones, rude agates, and gun-flint; the whole loosely cemented in a matrix composed of clay, lime (most likely from the decomposition of gypsum), and red oxide of iron. The disk which formed the largely projecting capital seemed to represent the original diameter of the pillar, and apparently retained its proportions in virtue of a much closer texture and larger per cent. of iron in its composition. These were often so apparent, that the pillars had a contour of the most rugged description, and a tinge of pale cream-yellow, while the capitals were of a brick-dust color, with excess of red oxide, and nearly as uniform in their granulation as fine millstone-grit.

The shape of these formations seemed, therefore, to turn on the comparative resistance to atmospheric influences possessed by their various parts. Many other indications, together with such reports as I could get from old settlers, and the experience of so acute a student as Mr. Pierce, led me to narrow down all the hypothetical agencies which might have produced them, to a single one,—*air*, in its chemical or mechanical operations, and usually in both. Water cannot be conceived of for an instant among the producing causes,— except in its vaporous dispersion through the atmosphere. Rain falls too seldom here (never in some localities of the mountains where these structures abound) to work much change in even the most friable rocks; besides, rain is a leveler, not a sculptor. No freshet from the mountains has topped these lofty hills since the creation of mankind; nor are they accessible to any water-course. But an all-sufficient denial to the hypothesis of water is the shape of the mimetic structures themselves. Water in motion is not easily deflected, and acts like a plane, not like a lathe. These skillfully turned cylinders, spindles, and cones point to a tool far more manageable, more readily carried around curved lines, and more minutely delicate.

This tool, in Colorado and other portions of the Rocky Mountain region, is none other than air or wind. This agent has never thus far received in our geological dynamics the importance it deserves. The atmosphere of this region is a chemical solvent, as energetic in some directions as it is inert in others. Its oxygen is in a comparatively passive state. It will not rust iron exposed to it for years at a time, and the progress of pulmonary tubercle is often arrested in it at once. But over wide tracts it is charged with alkaline vapor, and, in virtue of that characteristic, possesses a power of decomposing the combinations of silex, which sometimes on our journey showed itself in ways quite surprising. I have seen large tracts in the heart of the range covered with crags and boulders belonging to a granite originally one of the most uniform and cohesive in texture among all our rocks, out of whose weather-worn faces the feldspar crystals could be scraped with the nail as easily as one would pick the seeds from a New Year's cake. Several large boulders seemed to have been corroded through and through. I kicked them to pieces as easily as the softest conglomerate.

The detritus resulting from such chemical decomposition has, during earlier ages, been brought down from the older rocks of the range in immense quantities, by the action of ice or floods. The whole region of the high divides we had been travelling from Denver, was thickly strewn with such detritus; and in some cases, like the conical hills beneath the monuments, the ground was entirely composed of it. In its earliest stage, it was probably all one vast rubble bed, whose surface became gradually comminuted into sand, as on the yucca plains; or triturated and weather-beaten into a coherent layer, like that which forms the capitals of the columns.

The chemical energies of atmosphere having been exhausted in forming, with the aid of water, this superficially compacted drift-bed, mechanical causes began to operate, in the form of wind. Those who think such an agency inadequate to the large and largely varied excavations which have taken place in the Colorado drift-bed, need only witness a whirlwind like those which it was my fortune to encounter both along the Platte and in the mountains, to make their minds entirely easy on the subject. There is no achievement of force beyond the capability of a Rocky Mountain tornado. It would take too long to investigate all the meteorological conditions which underlie this fact; but one abundant

reason exists in the contour of the mountains, and their relative position with the Plains. The Plains, over their whole
sandy surface, compose a vast radiator; discharging immense
quantities of heat into the atmosphere during the entire
sunny period of every day.

From dawn till night-fall the superjacent stratum of air
undergoes constant rarefaction, and, as it ascends to meet
the westerly current, is progressively carried into the higher
mountain region adjacent. Here it parts with a portion of its
caloric, but is pressed back by continuous rarifications from
below, until with darkness the process stops, at a state of
things like the following: an immense body of air condensed
among the mountains, but every moment growing colder
and heavier, a comparative vacuum existing immediately
over the Plains below. The result is an immediate wind-cat-
aract, falling from the height of about twenty thousand feet.
But this fall does not make a straight plunge, like Niagara.
It descends not over a precipice, but through a chasm. One
characteristic of the Rocky Mountains is its system of vast
indentations, cutting through from the top to the bottom
of the range. Some of these take the form of funnels, others
are deep, tortuous galleries, known as passes or cañons; but
all have their openings toward the Plains. The descending
masses of air fall into these funnels, or sinuous canals, as
they slide down, concentrating themselves and acquiring a
vertical motion. By the time they issue from the mouth of
the gorge at the base of the range, they are gigantic augers,
with a revolution faster than man's cunningest machinery,
and a cutting edge of silex, obtained from the first sand-heap
caught up by their fury. Thus armed with their own resistless
motion, and an incisive thread of the hardest mineral next to

the diamond, they sweep on over the Plains, to excavate, pull down, or carve into new forms whatever friable formation lies in their way. I can give no better idea of the efficiency of this instrument than by citing a few examples from actual experience. First, as to carrying capacity. That portion of the track between Denver and Pike's Peak which lies across the open Plains is every year repeatedly buried out of sight under gravel large enough to make it seem macadamized, blown from the foot-hills, a distance of several miles, by the ordinary winds of the region. It is no uncommon occurrence to see large trees in the path of the whirl-wind torn up by the roots, and carried, revolving as they go, a distance of several miles into the Plains. Stones of many pounds' weight are sometimes served in the same way, seeming to be retained in the vertical whirl with as much ease as a cloud of dust or a splinter of wood.

Second, as to the force of the wind-auger. I myself have seen a hole bored into a Colorado sand-bluff, several feet deep, and of sufficient diameter to admit one's arm, by a small spiral current which rose on a comparatively calm day, and without any general atmospheric perturbation. The work was done in a few seconds; and no machinery could have accomplished it more neatly. Mr. Pierce informed me of much larger excavations which he had seen effected with equal dispatch. But the account of his from which I gained my best idea of the exact composition and operation of the wind-and-silex auger, was to the effect that on a certain occasion, when he was stopping at a settler's cabin during the prevalence of one of these mountain whirlwinds, a spiral current, laden with sand-grains, impinged against one of the window-panes, and, after a few moment's revolution, left it as perfect a piece of *ground glass* as could be made by a man-ufacturer of lamp-shades.

It is to the agency of this wind-and-silex auger that I ascribe all the mimetic formations of the Colorado foot-hills. Though a tool of tremendous force, it possesses a flexibility which enables it to accept any curved path; and this is an essential requisite of the instrument which can create such sculptures. It is a far more delicate tool than run-ning water; for it acts by mechanical force alone, while water chemically decomposes the rocks whose surface it is abrad-ing, and crumbles them to pieces while it is channeling their outsides. I consider the wind-and-silex auger the cleanest tool that Nature works with. It corresponds to man's highest advance in a similar direction,—the lathe for turning eccen-tric surfaces. The work that it does, no other agency could do; and we are thus indebted for one of the most character-istic features of our contemporary geology to a force scarcely noticed in its dynamics.

About four o'clock in the afternoon we came into a nar-row valley between perpendicular uplifts of red and white argillaceous sandstone, which towered, bare as a house-wall, to the height of three or four hundred feet. The effect of the sunlight on these brightly colored precipices was splendid in the extreme. They guarded the sides of our narrow avenue for a distance of three or four miles, and only left us at the edge of the little settlement of Colorado City.

We drove to the one place of entertainment which the town possessed,—a small wooden structure, whose title of the El Paso House was an indication of our approach toward Mexican boundaries and Mexican manners. The latter fact was abundantly attested by the slovenliness with which the house was managed, the discomfort of its rooms, and the melancholy recklessness of its table.

But we were in no mood to grumble, having such food for the eyes and head as dispensed with the necessity of other aliment. The dozen buildings of which Colorado City is composed, lie in a sand plain at the base of the foot-hills which wait upon Pike's Peak. The grand old mountain itself projects its head of glittering snow, through a gap in the nearer ranges which surround it, to a height and loneliness which almost tire imagination. Its altitude is very differently estimated, but cannot vary much from sixteen thousand feet. The best view of it is not from the base of its foot-hills at Colorado City, for its full proportions are veiled at that point by intermediate ranges, but far out on the Plains, east of the town, where for more than a hundred miles the emigrant sees it standing, a solitary beacon, with every detail melted into one heaven-piercing cone. How prominent an object it is, may be inferred from the fact that it gave its name to this entire region,—the man who came to the Colorado mines being a "Pike's-Peaker," though his nearest lodes were situated a hundred miles from that mountain by the shortest access.

A mountain which I admire more than Pike's Peak (or at least the Colorado City view of it), is the grand Cheyenne, which rises a little further south, and is plainly visible at the rear of the El Paso House, from base to dome. Its height is several thousand feet less than Pike's; but its contour is so noble and so massive that this disadvantage is overlooked. There is a unity of conception in it unsurpassed in any mountain I have seen. It is full of living power. In the declining daylight, its vast simple surface became the broadest mass of blue and purple shadow that ever lay on the easel of Nature.

Having refreshed ourselves with a good night's rest, in which fatigue met fleas and came off conqueror, we took an early start from the El Paso, to examine the natural features of this most interesting region.

Our first visit was paid to a shale-bed on the Fontaine qui Bouille, in which I had heard through Mr. Pierce of the discovery of interesting tertiary remains.

Mr. Garvin, a man of varied experience as sailor, hunter, miner, and merchant, who had finally settled down among the Rocky Mountains, and was conducting a Colorado City branch of George Tappan's house, accompanied us in our examination, and much assisted us by his knowledge of localities. We were joined by another gentleman of the same name, but no relationship with the former, (a singular coincidence in so small a directory!) a Dr. Garvin, whose practice is probably more extensive than any physician's in the world,—bounded like a State, by the Arkansas on the south, the Platte on the north, the Rocky Mountains on the west, and some indefinite line on the Plains to the eastward. This is a case in which a doctor must keep his horse. How many calls can be accomplished in a day by a medical man who has one case of high fever on the top of the snow-range, and a low typhoid patient on the Plains of the Arkansas, may be imagined by merely consulting the atlas. Still another gentleman joined our explorations about the Fontaine qui Bouille—Mr. Sheldon, a resident engineer in Mr. Pierce's department, who shared his chief's enthusiasm for science, and had collected a small cabinet embracing some very valuable geological specimens.

The Fontaine qui Bouille (here pronounced "Fon-ten kee Boo'yeh") is a clear and rapid stream, about ten yards wide, and two feet deep, issuing from a cañon near the true base of Pike's Peak, and skirting the edge of the Colorado City settlement, with a southeasterly course towards the Arkansas. Half a mile below the El Paso House, it has been pressed into the service of a grist-mill by a rude dam of stakes and slabs. The little pond resulting from this arrangement gave us a nice opportunity to bathe. We were not slow to avail ourselves of it, and found the nearly snow-cold water the most delightful tonic we had enjoyed since our parching journey across the Plains. Having finished our bath with a cold shower below the dam, we dressed ourselves, and proceeded to work.

The mill, possibly owing to the fact that Colorado as yet buys most of her flour in sacks from the East, was not in operation, and did not seem to have been for a considerable time previous. This fact facilitated our investigations, some of the most interesting excavations being in the bank near the water-wheel, and at the bottom of the stream beyond the sluice.

The bank was a perpendicular mass of shale interspersed with alluvial soil (the former predominating as we went deeper), about fifteen feet high, immediately below the mill, and running a number of rods without much change of elevation. Through this mass the long fibrous roots of young willow and cotton-wood trees growing on the edge of the bluff, had penetrated and reticulated in all directions. The shale itself was almost purely argillaceous, and broke into cubes or scaled into laminæ with equal ease. A more friable matrix, one apparently less favorable for the preservation of remains, could scarcely be imagined. Every geologist at the East knows in what low estimation the softer shales are regarded as a store-house for fossils, and how little reasonable hope there is of finding perfect specimens there, especially of the more delicate sorts. This shale was a more unlikely looking one than the brittlest of our Eastern strata. Yet, by the aid of a common jackknife, a hammer, and a shovel, we extracted from it a better preserved and more interesting collection of remains than I ever got from an equal area with thrice the labor. The great bulk of them belonged to a single species of tertiary oyster, resembling our modern mollusk in shape, but larger and heavier, with a beauty of color on its inner surface not surpassed by the mother-of-pearl shells which adorn East Indian cabinets. I was astonished to find the delicate arragonite lining as perfectly preserved and freshly iridescent as if the animal had died an hour before. Not until the shells had been exposed to the air for several hours did the nacreous layer begin to scale off, and leave the coarser structure bare. Noticing this occur in some of the specimens, I gave the others a thin coating of glue which quite successfully arrested their further deterioration.

Patient digging in the shales was also rewarded by some fragments of an equally well kept ammonite. Though we succeeded in getting out no single perfect specimen, the remains were sufficiently complete to be characterized as *Ammonites jason*. In Mr. Sheldon's collection we found several specimens of this mollusk much larger and handsomer, one nearly entire, obtained near the place where we were working. But the most interesting remains of this shale are the baculites. Several found here have measured eighteen inches in length, and exhibit a clearness in their curious markings, points, and iridescence so startling that one can hardly credit them to an obsolete period, and might almost be led into hunting the bed of the creek for contemporary specimens. On our return from the creek, we availed ourselves of the kindly proffered house where Mr. Garvin was keeping his bachelor menage entirely alone, and passed a couple of hours in sorting, varnishing, labeling, and packing the results of our investigation among both the conglomerates and agates of our past two days, and the shales of the Fontaine qui Bouille.

On the following day, the same party went two miles and a half up the Fontaine qui Bouille to visit the springs which gave it its name. The road along the bank of the stream from Colorado City is a pure impromptu affair to every fresh corner; but by skillful driving we managed to steer between boulders, and get the ambulance into the neighborhood of the springs, accompanied by several gentlemen on horse-back.

The springs no doubt originally bubbled up from the bed of the river, but immense depositions of Glauber's-salts, or sulphates of lime and soda, have raised the principal fountains ten feet above the creek level, and they now rise in basins at the top of immense masses of this incrustation, standing perpendicularly out of the stream.

The Glauber's-salt taste of the waters is agreeably modified by a stream of carbonic acid, which jets up through the middle of the basin, keeping them constantly in a state of violent ebullition to the height of two or three inches. There are two of the main springs on the south side, and one on the north of the stream. The last is the most pungent. There are also along the base of the south bank, higher up, a number of small and comparatively quiet springs, one of which is an inky chalybeate, and the other a white sulphur. The alkali of the larger springs is evidently undersaturated with acid. We made as good lemon-soda water as I ever tasted, by filling in the liveliest part of the main spring, and corking up instantly a bottle, which we had previously charged with half a pint of lemon syrup and half a table-spoonful of tartaric acid. The water which we bottled without any mixture, and took back to the El Paso with us by way of experiment, resembled Congress water when opened an hour or two after, though lacking the saline flavor. The northern and more pungent spring somewhat reminded me of Vichy, and the chalybeate was rather like Pyrmont.

These springs are very highly estimated among the settlers of this region for their virtues in the cure of rheumatism, all cutaneous diseases, and the special class for which the practitioner's sole dependence has hitherto been mercury. When Colorado becomes a populous State, the springs of the Fontaine qui Bouille will constitute its spa. In air and scenery no more glorious summer residence could be imagined. The Coloradian of the future, astonishing the echoes of the Rocky foot-hills by a railroad from Denver to the Springs, and running down on Saturday to stop over Sunday with his family, will have little cause to envy us Easterners our Saratoga as he paces up and down the piazza of the Spa Hotel, mingling his full-flavored Havana with that lovely air, quite unbreathed before, which is floating down upon him from the snow-peaks of the range.

Leaving the springs of the Fontaine qui Bouille, we rode to a spot about two miles northward of Colorado City, which is called "The Garden of the Gods." This fanciful name is due to the curious forms assumed by red and white sedimentary strata which have been upheaved to a perfect perpendicular on a narrow plain at the base of the foot-hills, with summits worn by the action of wind and weather into their present statuesque appearance. There is not much garden to justify the title; but it would not be difficult to imagine some of the curious rock-masses petrified gods of the old Scandinavian mythology. These masses, upon their east and west faces, are nearly tabular. Some of them reach a height of four hundred feet, with the proportions of a flat grave-stone. Two of the loftier ones make a fine portal to the gateway of the garden. Their red is intenser than that of any of the sandstones I am acquainted with, in a bright sun seeming almost like carnelian. A rock of similar look and type which I have omitted to mention on the way from Denver, was at least four miles away, yet made as clear and conspicuous a blot of red against the mountain-side as if it had been laid on with a heavily charged paint-brush. This, from some fancied resemblance, was called "Church" or "Brick Church" Rock.

These "gods" rise abruptly out of perfectly level ground. The right hand or northern warder of the gateway is more wedge-shaped than tabular, and contains within it a cavern, which we penetrated with some difficulty by a small aperture opening near the base of the western side. Twelve feet of prostrate squeezing brought us into a vault about fifty feet long, ten feet high, and a dozen wide. We lighted our candles, but there was not much to see. The walls of the hollow were damp; but there was no dripping water, and of course, in a gritty rock like this, there were no stalactites or secondary formations of any kind. One of the other red rocks resembles a statue of Liberty standing by her escutcheon, with the usual Phrygian cap on her head. Still another is surmounted by two figures which it requires very little poetry, at the proper distance from them, to imagine a dolphin and an eagle aspecting each other across a field gules. The spine-cracking curve of the dolphin, and his nice, impossibly fluted mouth would have delighted any of the old bronze-workers. Quentin Matsys would have used him for a model in some civic fountain. The eagle, too, was quite striking. Together, we regarded these animals as the emblems of our national supremacy over field and flood, and named them The American Arms. Another rock resembles a pilgrim (poetical, not Plains' variety) pressing forward with a staff in his hand; another is supposed to look exactly like a griffin. Indeed, from the right point of view one feels that a griffin must very probably look thus, though the difficulty of comparing it with an original specimen prevents absolute certainty.

It was a great disappointment to some of our kind friends that our artist did not choose the Garden of the Gods for a "big picture." It was such an interesting place in nature that they could not understand its unavailability for art. Everywhere we went during our journey, we found the same ideas prevailing, and had to be on our guard against enthusiasms, lest we should waste time in getting at the "most magnificent scenery in the world" to find some solitary castle-rock or weird simulation of another kind, which, however impressive it might be out-doors, was absolutely incommunicable by paint and canvas, when the attempt to convey it, being simply the imitation of an imitation, must have looked either like a very poor castle, or a mountain put up by an association of stone-masons. But the artist's selective faculty is not to be looked for among practical men.

The morning after our visit to the god-patch, we bade good-by to our friends at Colorado City, and bnce more turned our ambulance, now considerably heavier by a rich collection of specimens, in the direction of Denver. Instead of keeping near the outer edge of that field of giant grave-stones between which we had picked our avenue on the way down, we followed the Fontaine qui Bouille up to its effer-vescent springs, took a last deep draught of the champagne which Nature keeps there endlessly on tap, and, steering inward, passed the gods in final, quick review.

Just as we got to the gateway of the Garden of the Gods, one of our ambulance horses broke his whiffletree by a sud-den start. His excuse was an alarm from a gun fired by a gentleman of our party at one of the numerous hares which we encountered in the furze about the Garden. He and the gentleman magnanimously divided the inconvenience of the accident; the one riding and the other letting himself be rid-den down to Colorado City for a new spar.

We were not sorry for an excuse to linger beyond our intention in one of the most interesting spots of the Con-tinent. In politeness to us, that portion of the expedition represented by the buck-board also halted. Pierce geologized, and the artist sketched. Judge Hall found sufficient employ-ment in the mere act of admiration; expressing himself with an enthusiasm in regard to the gods, which assured me that they were gods indeed, being no respecters of persons,—else had they risen and bowed to the Chief Justice of the Terri-tory. The other member of our party went hare-hunting with good success, using the gun which the gentleman in search of the whiffletree had left behind him,—a state of things which has its high moral illustration in the history of vir-tue from Hogarth down to the last Sunday-school book, or herein, where the bad little boy, who fires in an original style out of the coach, has to go away from the hares, and get a whiffletree, while the good little boy, who was careful not to fire till he could do it under the most proper circumstances, stays behind, and shoots a great many hares with the bad little boy's gun. We remarked to our bad little boy, on his return, that we regarded him as a lofty moral lesson. It was a very hot day to ride five miles in the open, on a hard trotting horse and bare-back; so that he did not wish to be a lofty moral lesson, and expressed that view strongly.

As for myself during his absence, I gave over all thought of business, and wandered around in a much more aesthetic atmosphere than yesterday. I visited the gypsum hill near by, and, instead of asking it questions, let it talk to me. The intense glow of to-day's sun made it more lustrous than I had seen it before; or else it may have been that my eyes were no longer occupied with minutiæ of structure, and gave themselves up to its entire impression. It was a beau- tiful object in the landscape; such an exquisite pure white, with such a fleecy look from the softening influence of the débris scattered over its crystals, that a poet would have called it one of the gods' sheep who had lain down in the garden when the doom came, and suffered petrifaction with his masters. I interested myself in the attempts which here and there were making by inhabitants of Colorado City to turn the level bottom below the Garden into a valuable tract for agricultural purposes. It requires little expense of time or labor to secure a foothold on Uncle Sam's soil in this Terri- tory. Four notched logs laid in a square on the ground, will keep a preëmpted quarter-section for a year, being to all legal intents, as has been decided, sufficient earnest of the fact that the owner purposes building "a house suitable for human habitation." During our present trip we saw several such squares of logs; and they were quite as well respected by new-comers as if they had been squares of infantry. At one time Mr. Garvin had set his stake in the Garden of the Gods, intending to enjoy the luxury of ownership in that great natural curiosity; but other business prevented his carrying out his plan of a large house there, and, not to interfere with actual settlers who might wish the spot, he finally withdrew his claim. George Tappan, some time before I came to Denver, preëmpted the section containing the springs of the Fontaine qui Bouille. But Nature is not quite as easy with the new settler as Uncle Sam. If she is to yield him anything, she demands pay beforehand. He can't put in his seeds, and give her a due-bill on Heaven to be presently paid in showers; but he must advance her moisture in the shape of irrigation, prior to all possibility of her growing a valuable crop. Through the low bottom immediately east of the Gods' Garden, I found a number of "sequis," or distributing ditches, already run, connecting with a small rivulet which came from Camp Creek Cañon, and fell lower down into the Fontaine qui Bouille. Along these grew a profusion of the willow-leaved cotton-wood, a tree so much resembling the common swamp willow of our Eastern States, that but for the character of the bark I should have taken it for an old friend. The cotton-wood with the cordiform leaf abounds around Denver, but is comparatively scarce here. Wandering through the thicket, I collected several of the largest and most gorgeous butterflies found out of California, and had my first open-air interview with a Colorado rattlesnake. He was so near me, as I stooped to put my hat over a giant papilio sucking from the mud of the stream, that if he had not been a noble enemy, he could have killed me more easily than I caught the insect. But he lifted his head out of his coil, rattled vigorously, and as I leaped back to break off a sapling for his benefit, slipped quietly out of sight into an overgrown "sequi." He was five feet in length; and though, as may well be supposed under the circumstances, I did not undertake to count his rattles, he had every look of a veteran. But for his noise, the ordinary observer, familiar with our Eastern and Southern snake, would not have taken him for a crotalus at all, the brown of his clouds being so much duller, and shading into ashen gray without the least yellow tinge in it. Besides, his length is never as great as that attained by our varieties, four and five feet being his average, and six feet a somewhat unusual measure. He is none the pleasanter pet for these differences. His poison is quite as deadly as his Eastern cousin's, though I must do him the justice to say that he is not such a bore, and keeps himself much further from the sight of civilization. In all our wanderings through the wildest parts of the Continent, I only saw one other living rattlesnake in the open air, and perhaps half a dozen that had been killed, and were lying in our track. The creatures showed every anxiety to get out of man's way, and, it is to be hoped, will never learn the habits of their Virginia congeners, who make a rendezvous of the rock foundation under a house, and a profession, on sunny days, of biting the children. One of our party, in an expedition to the mountains, had one of his ambulance mules bitten on the nose while feeding on a green bottom among the Wind River peaks. Everybody counseled him to shoot the beast, insisting that he could not save him. But he liked the mule, as possessing a somewhat sweeter temper and happier view of life than are usually enjoyed by his tribe, so he determined to cure him. In the first place, he tied a small package of gunpowder across the wound on the nose, bandaged the mule's eyes, and exploded the charge. Following this novel method of actual cautery, he bound upon the spot a paper of moistened fine-cut tobacco. Then, with the assistance of his men, he had the mule's mouth open, and poured an entire bottle of raw Bourbon whiskey down his throat. After that—he did nothing more. The mule lived to thank him, and pay his bill for medical services, by drawing him home to the white settlements; but I suspect that there were moments during the progress of the cure when Mr. Mule wondered seriously whether it was worth while. (In saying *Mr.* Mule, I do not intend to be eccentric; but really, over this entire region, that term of respect is so habitually applied to animals as to lose the slightest semblance of badinage. The old hunter says, "I up with my rifle, and down goes Mr. Antelope"; or, "Mr. Bear sat up, and took one of my dogs right across the scalp"; or, "Mr. Indian lay in the bushes waiting for the train." It is a title given to anything that has made the settler trouble, or in any way measured forces with him; given half in mockery of a conquered foe, but mostly, I suspect, with an instinctive veneration for the force of character which has made the victory costly. What did Mister originally mean but master? I am, however, getting too philological even for a parenthesis.)

We had been employed at the Garden of the Gods in our various fashions for a little over two hours, when our ambassador returned with a whiffletree. It was manufactured out of an old awning-post belonging to some discarded emigrant wagon, and had several holes in it, where the curtain-buttons had been screwed in. But it was neatly made, and the only thing we could get. The blacksmith of the settlement, who was also its wheelwright and general mechanic, had made a tour among all the ruins of his shop before he could find a piece of timber suitable for our purpose. It is a curious fact that no hard wood like our nut-trees, ash, and white-oak, is to be found among the native growths of Colorado. There is plenty of pine and cedar timber in the high mountain gorges, some spruce and fir; but all the work which has to endure strain, must be made from imported woods. It is not long since young hickory, not particularly well seasoned, sold as high as forty cents a pound in this region. An old pair of ash thills will often bring more money, for purposes of cutting up and making over, than an entirely new pair, of the best workmanship, would cost in New York. There seems to be a fine field open to any man who can resist the temptation of immediate and perhaps munificent returns offered by specu- lation and the mines, long enough to try the acclimatization of the hard woods in Colorado. There is but little doubt that a nursery of hickories, English walnuts, white-ashes, and oaks, would flourish almost anywhere between Denver and Latham, along the banks of the Platte. It certainly would take but little time and energy to commence the experiment, by planting the nuts, seeds, or acorns. No enterprise takes better care of itself from the first start; and if it succeeded, the proprietor would have the satisfaction of a fine source of revenue yearly, doubling its value before his eyes, with the certainty that in twenty years he might command the entire markets of Denver, Central, and Colorado cities, in virtue of the mere fact that he was first in the field. Vast quantities of hard wood are needed in Denver and the mines; yet the impossibility of getting it close at hand is so great that I have seen men come into George Tappan's store, buy half a dozen imported rakes, and break off the teeth and bows to make fish-poles of the handles. Nothing else sufficiently strong, light, and pliant was to be had for love or money. Every train of Tappan's, Byram's, or the other merchants running wagons from the Missouri, brings out a cargo of the hard woods; but these necessarily command prices which must long ago have stimulated Coloradian enterprise into attempting tree culture for itself, had not the one idea of mining hitherto absorbed every faculty of the people. This matter must and will right itself in time. At least, I hope so; for certainty is not quite possible to one who has seen the same destitution prevailing in parts of Oregon which have been much longer settled, have no excuse in the importunity of mining, and very little help to their condition from anything like a well perfected system of imports.

What I have said touching this matter may seem too large an excursion from the recital of our trip; but it is my object, so far as possible, to take the reader along with me, let him see what I saw as it occurred, and have him share the suggestions awakened within me as they arose on the spot. We shall thus be in less danger of overlooking many apparently trifling but still important traits of the country and people we travel through, which by their minuteness might slip the grasp of a more orderly and ambitious classification.

On the whiffletree having been adjusted, we resumed our line of march, turning, in about five miles from Colorado City, between shaggy precipices and thickets of low evergreen, to the cañon of Camp Creek. The character of the uplifts in the mouth of this cañon is even bolder than at the Garden of the Gods. The most remarkable columnar structure that I saw in our whole journey exists here, in an obelisk of the same brilliant natural brick which forms the material of the Gods, rising quite unsupported to the height of about four hundred feet, with a curious swell at its summit which much exceeds in circumference the lower portion of the shaft, and gives the whole structure a look of self-poise and strong insecurity in the face of natural laws, not excelled by the Leaning Tower of Pisa. I was compelled to sketch it for myself, there being so much more artistic work at hand for the artist's pencil; but I could not give with my black lines an idea of the color, however truthful the drawing in figure. How much is lost by the absence of color, may be conceived by imagining a shaft higher than the loftiest steeple of our metropolitan churches, red as blood from foot to capital, and relieved against dense green rock-pines, bare brown mountains, shining uplifts of the white variety, or the intense blue sky of a Colorado summer.

Behind the obelisk to the west, the cañon entered the mountains between heightening walls of an unrivaled savage beauty, its last glimpse being a lofty gap with serrated edges like a giant's staircase, formed by the great mass of schistose sandstone broken into square blocks. Neither in pictures nor landscape do I remember a more exquisite gradation between foreground and sky than that which led my eye from the tall red obelisk to the glimpse at the top of the cañon.

Nothing occurred on the return to Sprague's—our half-way house both going and coming—more important than the shooting of a fine sickle-bill curlew, which was floating over the long sandy dog-plain I have before noticed. The last place where I had held a curlew in my hands was far up the

St. John's River, among the tangled yellow jasmines and con-volvuli that border Floridian lagoons; and it was a singular sensation to see this bird so far away from all his (to me) famil-iar haunts. But the curlew is considerable of a cosmopolitan. In regard to this bird we were compelled to acknowledge a fact that often forced itself upon us afterwards. There is no use in attempting to collect such specimens, unless one goes specially provided for the purpose. You cannot satisfy your-self on the vast field between the Missouri and the Pacific by naturalizing merely *en amateur*. You must set out with something more than an empty box and a piece of arsenical soap. The climate, being anti-septic, is in your favor; but all else is against you. You have no adequate means of packing your skins, and keeping them from vermin; none for trans-porting them safely, on the wild routes which we travelled, and in the way we were compelled to travel them. Mineral specimens are all that the amateur can be sure of getting home to the States in good order. This vast field of the Cen-tral Continent must be beaten by specialists, each provided with his own definite plan, tools, and means of carriage. At the best, he will have to sacrifice much that it is a real pain not to carry away; for his collections accumulate faster than he will ever be able to forward them to the settlements till the Pacific Raiload has opened its great artery from Pike's Peak to the sea. So, despite our arsenical soap, this fine cur-lew eventually became so much deteriorated that we had regretfully to throw him away.

I will not stale these pages by a review of the route between Sprague's and Denver. We took dinner at the Pretty Wom-an's Ranch, and came down the slope of the Cherry and Plum Creek Divide just after sunset, getting in twilight a magnificent view of fires which were devastating the dense fir and pine growths of the mountain gorges behind Denver. The smoke and heated air from the vast chimney-draughts of the cañons were wafted full in our faces; and the leaping sheets of flame, or their flickering fringe along the forest top, almost crackled in our ears, and added to the evanescent orange of sundown a bloodier, baleful red.

It was about nine o'clock in the evening, when, after a ride through a perfect Shaker meeting of jumping hares, we got over the broad plain between the divide and Jim Beckwith's station, skirted the silent Platte lying steel-gray in twilight shadow, whirled past Camp Weld, and came into Denver.

## CHAPTER V.

# INTO THE ROCKY MOUNTAINS.

THE day before our party left Denver finally, was passed by myself in visiting, under Mr. Pierce's guidance, one of the principal coal outcrops thus far discovered in the Territory.

For a wonder, our dust was laid by a fine drizzling rain, which lasted the entire day. The ranchman at whose house we stopped to dine, was quite delighted by it. It was doubtless a godsend to his crops; but, æsthetically speaking, Colorado does not look well in a shower. The Plains seem surprised by it. There is none of that bright, thankful receptivity in them which rain meets from every grassy stretch in the East. There is no hope of their laughing back at bounty in a gayer green,—a green like our meadows, growing greener even while you look at it, and the rain still falls.

In spite of the drizzle, our blankets and water-proofs kept us perfectly comfortable on Mr. Pierce's buck-board. Sixteen miles of tolerably smooth driving, picked out by ourselves among the undulations of the Plain north of Denver, brought us to what was called "the Mine." Nobody was working it at present. It was situated on an entered quarter-section, and some uncertainty as to the title retarded its development.

Thus far the workings had been limited to a single lateral shaft, running into the face of a low bluff for the distance of thirty or forty yards, and laid with a wooden tramway, upon which were several small cars, still in good order. The coal was instantly recognizable as tertiary, and must have been among the latest lignite formations of that period. The nearest brown-coal layers are, I believe, generally referred to the miocene. This I think subsequent to the miocene. The vein was distributed through a bed of friable, bituminous shales and clay. Both the coal and the shales contained perfect impressions of still contemporary plants. We found numerous specimens of leaves from both the common varieties of cotton-wood and the swamp-willow; also of an entire plant belonging to the bulrushes. The coal deposit seemed surrounded by the shales mentioned, both above and below. It burns with a brisk flame and fragrant oily smoke, like the English soft coal, but has much less body, and consumes to ashes without coking. We saw enough of it, and heard sufficiently of other like discoveries near by, to be sure that this mineral is abundant about Denver, and may be profitably mined for domestic purposes.

I think it not at all improbable that petroleum will yet be discovered in the Plains of Colorado. Its origin is not yet among the certainties of science; but the only certain fact about it, that it is a result of vegetable decomposition under pressure, makes us look for it in the underdrainage of all such beds as that near Denver. It seems to play the part of molasses to the sugar of coal, comprising the carbon particles which could not be caught out of solution, and brought within the cohesion of the solid form. The underlying calcareous formations of the chalk and tertiary exist everywhere over the Plains, in basins which form the most natural reservoirs for a petroleum deposit, and are often sufficiently indurated to retain it.

On the way back to Denver, we found growing on one of the sand-hills a running verbena entirely new to both of us;

in form exactly resembling the scarlet variety of our gardens, but bearing profuse blossoms of a brilliant blue tint, which would have thrown into ecstasies any of those florists who have spent such effort to produce it artificially. We dug up several of the plants, and, the rain favoring, kept sufficient soil about the roots to transplant them successfully in Mr. Pierce's garden on our return.

The day before we left Denver, we had an opportunity to witness one of those periodic incursions of the Arrapahoe tribe of Indians, which led a new-come Irishman to ask on one occasion "whether that was the reason why Americans called the season Indian summer." In Denver nobody says "Arrapahoe." The wag who first misquoted "Lo the poor Indian" has perpetuated himself in Denver by the fact that Indians there are always called "The Lo Family." "How are you, Lo (or Mr. Lo)?" is the familiar address of a copper-colored warrior. Of a sudden, just about midday, the Messrs., Mistresses, Masters, and Misses Lo swarmed in the streets of Denver, with as little preface as seventeen-year locusts. They might have come out of holes in the ground. Some of the men had magnificent buffalo-robes, elegantly worked and stained on the inside; others had robes of wolf-skin; and I saw a number of fine blankets. But the majority of the tribe were half naked, and in a condition of squalid filth. One of the squaws entered a grocery store with a baby bound to her back, and a greasy blanket over all. In her hand she held some pieces of deerskin work for barter. Her eye wandered with a savage restlessness over the shelves, and fell to an open barrel of brown sugar. An Arrapahoe can no more resist sugar than a wasp. Mrs. Lo uttered a guttural of exultation, thrust the deerskin into the grocer's hands, whipped the baby out of his pouch in a jiffy cast her blanket on the floor, and after throwing into the middle of it all the sugar she could scoop before the grocer cried, "Hold!" tied it up composedly by the corners, hung it over one arm and her offspring over the other, marching out of the store with all the dignity of Penthesilea, and considerably fewer clothes than that royal Amazon wore on public occasions; in other words, nothing but a breech-cloth.

Towards nightfall might occasionally be seen a stalwart brave stalking out of the town towards the encampment, metaphorically speaking with his hands in his pockets, and a high-bred insolence in his carriage, followed by a trail of wives laden with babies and the day's shopping of the family. I was about to utter a sneer at the cruelty of savage life, when a question occurred to me whether women still carry the heaviest burdens in our own civilized society. Here is Mrs. Lo stumbling under twenty pounds of sugar and young Indian; but I have known white wives who had loads to carry for their lords something heavier and far less sweet.

On the 23d of June, two of us resumed our journey toward California, by the Overland wagon. The other two stayed behind to visit friends who had introduced Eastern farming to a well timbered tract of low bottom land on the Platte, near Denver. Our party was to reunite at Salt Lake or at some intermediate station.

Nothing noticeable occurred on the road to Latham to change the moonlight impression of it which I have heretofore given, with the exception of Arrapahoe Indians. They were on their way southward, and those we had seen in or around Denver were the mere skirmish line of the tribe. For the first forty miles out of Denver, we were perpetually meeting parties of them on horseback, or encamped under black skin tents resembling the Sibley, and having quite an improved style of egress at the apex of the cone for the smoke, which among some tribes has no means of exit but the front slit. They made no hostile signs, being for the present on their summer tour, and not their war-path; but I could not help thinking of them, as I have among lunatics in an asylum, or wild beasts in a menagerie, how little they knew their power, or how to exercise it. There were enough of them to have swept away every vestige of civilization between Latham and Pike's Peak. The puniest woman who could wield my Ballard's carbine was a match for ten of them.

We found tents pitched near several of the stations where we stopped to change horses, and took advantage of the halt to push our acquaintance with the Arrapahoes. I was particularly anxious to see the noble Indian. When a boy, I read everything that was ever written about him. At that time of life, I regarded him as a sort of every-day Alexander the Great, slightly tinctured with Damon and Pythias. He principally followed burning himself at stakes,—rather liked it than otherwise,—so much so that he was in the habit of requesting to be allowed to suggest whether hot pinchers would not be a neater method of ending the job. In his intervals of ennui, he did the lecture business on a free basis, visiting public lyceums known by the descriptive title of pow-wows, and affording much satisfaction to audiences, chiefly on the themes of "the Bounding Deer" and "the Blasted Pine." He was a poet, an orator, a prophet, a hero, a highly educated and accomplished gentleman, who, from native simplicity of character, went without his clothes on. The only screw loose in his whole construction was an unaccountable propensity to die off. This was called "fading before the advance of the cruel white man." When I thought of it, I felt ashamed of being white; I belonged to a cruel race that "advanced"; I wished that the cruel race would only listen to the good people who disliked "advancing," and consent to stop it. As for the female Indian, there was a period when I pined for her. I owe her many melancholy months between the ages of nine and twelve. I remained faithfuler to my ideal than my ideal proved to me. I remember what a solace Beadle's Dime Novels would have been to me then, just as I think how much better off I might have been, had chloroform only been invented when I had my first tooth out. "Wishky-Washky, or the Queen of the Pottowatomies," would have served me for one good dose. As it was, I read Cooper cumulatively to get the same effect. Every Indian woman was beautiful. All you had to do to equal the Venus de Medici was to turn the color of a new cent. The Indian woman lived principally on shady banks, with her feet in the water; but the same guilelessness of character which obviated a tailor's bill for her brother, guaranteed her against colds in the head. She was as pretty as anybody could be who was so pious; more pious than any white girl half so pretty. She contemplated alternately the Great Spirit in the clouds, and her own lovely face in the pool. If the half that was told of her was true, she could not be accused of wasting her time. How I longed to see her! I thought of her whenever I was in a grove. Would she steal out from behind that old chestnut, give me one quick antelope-look with the meltingest black eyes in Pagan-dom, and, laughing like the woodrobin's gurgle, be away again among the invisible Dryads and Fauns ? Ah, bright Alfaratta, you jilted me! You are a swindle, bright

Alfaratta! I don't like to say it to a lady, but you are, Alfaratta; you know you are.

I am obliged to disbelieve in the existence of a beautiful full-blooded Indian woman. I know that many excellent men, writing at a distance from Indians, have warmly imaged such a fact, and that a very few other excellent men, who have known Indians at home, speak enthusiastically of it. We must remember that almost any woman seems beautiful to a man who has seen none for three months, as often happened to the old voyageurs; also that the poet is quite independent of facts. *A priori* it would be possible to disprove a beautiful Indian. Neither in the physical, mental, or moral training of the Indian woman exist any of those conditions which underlie female beauty. She is man's drudge, and shows it in her face. Her husband can sell her or let her: she knows it, and shows that. She is ill fed, badly clothed, depressed by too rapid child-bearing; she shows from head to foot that she is all of these, or that her mother was before her. It is a manifest impossibility for physical beauty to exist under such circumstances by the operation of any known law. As to studying the question by observation, I can only say that I have looked in vain, through all that part of the Continent we traversed, for a single instance of anything which the utmost lenience could pronounce beauty in an Indian woman. Nothing can be a greater mistake than the popular notions regarding Indian maternity; the getting and rearing of a family break them down, and age them in their prime, to an extent more deplorable than among our frailest American women. Their health is poisoned by a congenital taint (which some philosophers have insisted in foisting upon the whites, but which is as independent of them as death itself); their habits are too slovenly to mention; their digestion quivers between gorge and fast; they become inured to the cold at the expense of stinted limbs, narrow chest, protruding abdomens, and a skin with the texture of rawhide. The assertions of the last sentence apply equally to the men. It would be hard for an imaginative artist to give an exaggerated idea of the extent to which the Arrapahoes carry the spindle-shanked and pot-bellied style of human architecture. The little children all seem consumed by *tabes mesenterica*. For one boy of six I could find no simile but a kettle-drum standing on two fifes, with the bulge forward. Most of the men were gaunt; many under-sized; nearly all were shrunken in the calf; and I saw none whose development in any way would have attracted notice in an Eastern gymnasium. They gave me the impression of a race on the decomposing grade, and a good way down the scale. Their faces were, without exception, gross, brutal, selfish, and sullen. Their occasional scanty laugh was a bad laugh. There was no suspicion even of prettiness in the face or form of either man, woman, or child.

The horses of the Arrapahoes and their appreciation of them formed their one strong point. Few of the wiry little animals were larger than a Kanuck pony; they were all of them ewe-necked, as is inevitable with pasture-feeders; here and there was a tympanitic little cob which seemed to have succumbed to the surrounding human contagion, and become pot-bellied out of complaisance; but their action was good, their color picturesquely patched and pied, their eyes intelligent, their training such that they were ridden without bridle (often without saddle either), guided only by a pat on the neck, and their bottom evidently immense. I felt some respect for a large warrior on thin legs who refused our offer of one hundred dollars for his stallion.

On one of these little fellows I saw a boy and a girl riding, with their little brother between them, the pony trotting away with as much comfort as if he were carrying an empty sack. I think he would not have objected if they had put him under a pyramid of the entire family. It is certainly in the Indian's favor that he belongs to one of the few races which make their horse their friend. An Arrapahoe baby takes much the same line of familiarities with his father's horse that a white child indulges towards his sister's poodle. An Indian horse hardly ever comes vicious to the stable of his first white owner. Not until the cruel bit has been substituted for the gentle hand-pat, and he has heard himself addressed in the new voice of enmity, does he learn to bite, kick, or practice the still worse vice of bucking. It is a pity that civilized nations should be compelled to learn the perfection of one of the manliest arts from the Nomads of Tartary, the Plains, and the Arabian Desert. The horse is as capable of friendship as the dog. The more that I see of him, the more I love his nature, and the more am I convinced that the true side for the trainer to approach him on, is his personal devotion to himself. The horse that cannot be approached thus, by wisdom and patience, I have yet to see.

The nearest approach to luxury among the Arrapahoes was a sort of horse-palanquin, made by suspending a hammock of skins between two of the lodge-poles, which are tied at one end to the horse's neck, when the tents are struck for a march. The other ends of the poles drag on the ground; and they possess sufficient elasticity to make the hammock no mean ambulance for a veteran or a sick person.

A little before sunset we pulled up at the one house and the stables representing Latham. Here we took tea from our own supply chest, and passed the time waiting for the westward stage in sketching and botanizing before dark, and writing letters after it. The stage arrived about ten o'clock, and to our great satisfaction we discovered only three inside passengers intending to go further. Night-riding in a stage is an occasion where misery decidedly does *not* love company.

Just after leaving Latham, we coiled ourselves into one corner for a nap, but had hardly began to nod before we plunged down a steep bank, and began fording the South Platte at a point where the water came just nicely over the floor of the wagon, soaking our boots, gun-cases, and blankets to perfection. The night was dark; but, to judge by feeling, the road during the first half of the night continued nearly as level as from Fremont's Orchard to Latham. We dozed up the steep grades, and got rattled wide awake down them, coming feverishly into the dawn during our first severely mountainous climb, along the bed of the Cache-la-Poudre. This stream is one of the most beautiful mountain torrents which we saw on our entire journey. It comes from the everlasting snow-line of the peaks about Cheyenne Pass; and its entire course to the Platte is a roaring sluice, broken by no great fall, but obstructed by gigantic boulders, with a tolerably even grade and considerable winding of direction. At Camp Halleck, where we arrived at sunrise, the stream was about thirty yards wide, and plunged through a densely tangled forest. The soldiers encamped at this station were a detachment of Colorado volunteers, sent out to watch the Utes and Snakes. I envied them their trout-fishing. The Cache-la-Poudre swarms with fine fish, and is the most mysteriously seductive of streams to an artist. We should have been glad to trace it up to the top of its cañon, but turned off its course shortly after leaving Camp Halleck, and ascended to a new level.

We now began to understand the significance of the title Rocky Mountains. We had reached a minor plateau between the snow-ridges, where the granite and sandstone outcrops projected from fifty to three hundred feet above the general sandy level, bare and perpendicular as the side of a house, varied by rolling buttes or ridges of similar height, thinly tufted with the gray gramma-grass, and dotted with clumps of sage brush. This was the first place where sage, so called (though I believe it is properly an artemisia), becomes the prominent feature of the Overland landscape, though it occurs previously at intervals all the way from Denver, and other wormwoods abound on the Plains much farther east. The sage rises from a tough gnarled root in a number of spiral shoots which finally twist together into a single trunk, varying in circumference from six inches to two feet, and tenacious as a hawser. The leaves of the plant are gray, woolly, and crisp, with a strong offensive smell, resembling true sage. From Camp Halleck to the Wasatch, almost the only vegetable life not distinctly arborescent greets the traveler's eye in the shape of limitless wastes abandoned to this scrubby sage, and the equally scrubby but somewhat greener "greasewood." For long stages between the high timbered snow-ridges, the only resource for fuel on which the emigrant can rely while following the Rocky Mountain trail, is this pair of dry, resinous shrubs; and they burn so freely as to be a great improvement on the method of boiling his kettle over dry buffalo droppings, which he was compelled to adopt on some level stretches of the Plains.

Where the sage was lacking, the plateau to which we had climbed from Camp Halleck was a mere clean skeleton of the world. Telescopes reveal to us a very similar tract in the moon, and geology takes us back to a time when the earth was all thus. I think that the man who stands where we rode on the 24th of June, need never be without a tolerably correct idea of the azoic period, nor use a glass to see the Lunar Desert. We might have been visiting this sphere by some magical anachronism before the first river flowed, or sea felt tidal fluctuation; when as yet there had been neither Ganoid, nor Euripterus, nor Trilobite. When we descended into a depression of the plateau, there was nothing but pure rock between us and the horizon. Vast stones lay heaped up into pyramids as if they had been rained from the sky. Cubical masses, each covering an acre of surface and rising to a perpendicular height of thirty or forty feet, appeared in strange series about a rude square, irresistibly suggesting the buttresses of some gigantic palace or prison whose super-structure had crumbled away with the race of its Titanic builders. The most remarkable instance of geologic record which I ever saw or heard of, occurred in a vast rectangular pile of altered red sandstone, which we encountered on this tract. It was a mass nearly the eighth of a mile in circuit, and stood nearly four-square to the height of a hundred feet or more above a basin of water-washed pebbles. It was a pile as entirely isolated as the dome of St Peter's, yet on its eastern face it bore the unmistakable signs of having once formed the wall of a mighty cataract. Its upper horizontal edge was channeled in polished grooves; its face was broken into ledges, and the angles of these worn again to curves; there were pot-holes on the top of the rock, and gravel strewn with boulders lining the conical basin at its foot; in fact, to one standing on the eastern side of the rock, there appeared every condition requisite for a Niagara, except the water. That was nowhere within sight or credibility. A poet might have fancied that he heard it; that it was an invisible fall, a ghost of some Old World torrent which roared gently as 'twere any sucking dove to the vulgar, but had rhythm and thunder for the ears which can hear the spheres sing. To scientific eyes it was such a wonder as the Niagara precipice might be if a cube of its present mass were cut away from the rest of the world on the American and Canada side and at the upper end of Goat Island, the surrounding country leveled to the plane of the lower river, and the water led by some far distant channel to the St. Lawrence. The man who, ten centuries afterward, looked on the scarred dry precipice resulting from such a process, beheld the deep furrows of the brink, counted the slippery shelves beneath it, yet heard no voice of water break the desert silence, would experience some such sensation as I did on beholding that Rocky Mountain stone-pile. Where did the water come from? Where were the successive terraces, where the cradling cañon by which the mighty freshets hurled themselves down from the snows to grind this silex into sand or crack it into ledges? To leap this wall with the force recorded, the water must have descended a succession of steep grades towering far above the precipice. Every vestige of such formations has been moved out of the way by some colossal agency, and one might as well look for a cataract from the roof of a house. Yet here stands the unanswerable record,—a witness which has survived cataclysm,—a monument, compared with which the Pyramids were things of yesterday, to a cataract whose very bed had departed, like its vapor, from the face of the modern world.

Another curious formation of this plateau was an uplift of trap-rock in the neighborhood of the sand-stone cataract, taking the form of a colossal steam-ship, much keeled to leeward, and rising the crest of a lofty billow of sandstone. At the distance of forty yards, the illusion was absolutely startling. We could see a handsome clean cut-water, a clipper bow, a main-mast broken off short at the cross-trees, a battered funnel, a hatch with its cover and combings, a pilot-house and a bowsprit, with a fragment of the jib-boom. Everything was made out with such mimetic distinctness that we seemed to be looking at some petrifaction where a ship, suddenly transformed to basalt, was foundering in a sea of sandstone.

I have mentioned only the two most important of many remarkable uplifts, simulating every variety of artificial object that is conceivable of execution in stone. The human face and figure seemed among Nature's most favorite subjects for burlesque. In all the wonderful suggestions of Doré's "Wandering Jew," there is nothing to compare with the frightful stone shapes and faces which occur on this plateau. On a bright sunny day like the one we spent in crossing it, the sensation of the traveller resembles a pleasant nightmare; he feels that if he stayed a night in this wilderness of naked blocks, he would depart mad. The tract is landscape gone demoniacal. Yet even this is weak art compared with the sculptures of trap and sandstone further on toward Salt Lake.

Ten miles of gradual climbing brought us out of this plateau to another region of rolling ridges, scantily timbered with cedar, and bearing a good crop of gramma grass. We found an occasional rivulet in the valleys, and strips of positive green along its course. Coming out of a quarry whose boundaries comprised a circuit of twenty miles, and whose blocks were hewn large enough to make a cathedral out of each cube, we breathed freer, and welcomed the sight of verdure like a balm. I had never understood before the epic sublimity of that expression, "They shall pray that the mountains may fall on them," nor had I appreciated the horror of that Arabian Nights' talisman which enabled evil magicians to keep their victims under the granite floor of the world. There was not even the piteous relief of moss or lichen, no sprig of wormwood or cedar, no green lamina of any kind, on all those tremendous buttresses, and slabs, and effigies. The slabs might have been hot tiles on the roof of some impenetrable Dantesque hell; the buttresses waited for another story to the prison which should build itself to heaven; the effigies were devil-sentries guarding the ramparts. No picture can be on a scale sufficiently large to give any idea of the effect produced by these formations on an eye-witness. Almost everybody of Oriental propensities has formed to himself some notion of the way Domdaniel, Vathek, and Aladdin caverns might be expected to look. But if any such person, of however vivid fancy, will pass from the head of the Cache la Poudre to Virginia Dale, without confessing that his most ambitious ideals have been utterly surpassed, and his mind fairly confounded, by the hard realities of trap and sandstone, I will be sure that I have not been modest in estimating other men's imagination by my own.

Between a series of perpendicular sandstone uplifts from two to five hundred feet high, and descending again to another green valley level, we reached Virginia Dale about noon. We had grown so fascinated with the scenery since daybreak that we resolved to leave the stage, and stop over till the next day. I do not know whether I have heretofore more than inferentially mentioned how great a convenience we found the Overland Company's license, always granted their travellers, to lie by whenever and as long as we pleased, without invalidating the contract for through passage. We had only to mark on our large baggage the address in Salt lake City where it should be left to await us, and take our minor traps, such as guns, artists' material, blankets, and small stores, into camp or ranch with us till we resumed our route. By stopping at Virginia Dale, we should give the remaining two of our party a chance to catch up with us, and have a better opportunity for sidewise explorations than might again be afforded us in the heart of the Rocky Mountain system.

The Virginia Dale Station is 752 miles from Atchison, and about 1300 from San Francisco. It is situated in a continuation of that lofty furrow of the range known as the Cheyenne Pass. A log-ranch and stables constitute the entire station. Beyond the buildings southerly, a mountain stream winds into a dense forest. Across the Overland trail, north of the house, rises a congeries of round gray mountains fifteen hundred feet in average height from the trail level, packed together in such close order that they resembled a school of porpoises coming up to breathe. Just below the house to the eastward, a little rivulet sang its way round coquettish curves to the large trout-stream in the far jungle, through a meadow golden green in patches where the water eddied back and the sun fell directly. We were told that trout swarmed within five miles of us; but there was not force enough at the station to spare us guides or escort, and we had moreover but little desire to catch fish when our finest crops of literary and artistic hay ought to be making. We were indebted for an unusually comfortable reception at Virginia Dale (not to speak here of other places) to the kind thoughtfulness of Mr. Otis, the Overland Road superintendent. We called on him at Denver with letters from his brother, the well known artist, author, and physician, our friend Doctor Fessenden N. Otis of New York; found him absent on the line, left the notes for him, and never afterwards were fortunate enough to meet him personally. Just as we resumed our route from Denver, a very pleasant letter of information and guidance was put into our hands; and we were not only instructed how to find the best things, but enabled to enjoy them comfortably by still another letter from Mr. Otis, addressed to all the employees of the road, enjoining them to grant us every facility for stopping to sketch or geologize which did not involve exorbitant delay of the mail, and to treat us, in every respect of fare and accommodations, as his personal friends. This courtesy on his part was so liberal and hearty, and showed such warm appreciation of our objects, that we were more surprised than we need to have been after knowing another member of his family.

At Virginia Dale we drew this kindly document for the first time, and presented it at the station-keeper, who instantly surrendered us the best bed he had in the house, with the exception of his own, and assured us we might have had that if his wife were not then sick on it with a violent intermittent fever. I could not imagine where a person could contract such a disease in this region, and found that it belonged to those rare cases which get settled in some one of the Western States too deeply to be cured at once by the Rocky Mountains. Poor little wife! What a terrible distance from everything to have chills and fever! I caught a single glimpse of the patient as her husband passed into the sick-room, and saw, through all the expression of suffering which her face wore, a delicate, refined prettiness most unexpected in this savage wilderness. Love, however, seemed to make that tract bloom in the teeth of ague. I never saw a man kinder to his wife than the station-keeper. He was obliged, in her default, to manage every detail of housekeeping; and conjugal fidelity raised him to the level of the occasion. I do not believe the skillfullest artist could scour a pan to begin with that unaccustomed male who learned it yesterday for his wife's sake. His success in the initial batch of tea-biscuit I regard explicable on the ground of inspiration. Confiding and clinging to the last, like all our sex, he took in the dough to be inspected by the invalid, who entertained an indulgent spirit toward it, and relieved him from apprehensions. He was not afraid of it any more, but put it in the oven, and stayed by it with no one else near him, till it came out a triumphant straw-color, and tasted less like equal quantities of lard and potash than any Rocky Mountain tea-cake which I ever approached with a consciousness of my imminent peril. But to see the station-keeper in his great dish-washing act was to witness the favorite spectacle of the gods,—a good man struggling under difficulties. A trifle redder in the face, but feeling morally developed, he came out of Destiny and the Dish-kettle without a nick in any of his crockery, left no grease-streaks when he wiped the plates, and lived fully up to his privileges in the fidelity with which he washed out the dish-cloth.

Beside this excellent man and his wife, there lived in the house a pair of stable-helpers and such drivers as stopped there transiently during off-hours. With these lodgers we were to share one of the three apartments into which the house was divided.

After dinner, (which in admiration of the station-man's great qualities, we cooked for ourselves), we set out to explore the porpoise-back mountains which rolled away to the northward of the road. We had under-estimated their height at starting, and found that the climb to their highest cone took us a full hour. Our way led along the upper course of the brook, which waters the meadow before the ranch, to a series of deep rifts or cañons channeled in the side of the mountains by freshets at the season of snow-melting, but now dry as ashes, and paved with enormous boulders. Up the steep incline of one of these cañon bottoms, and under the shade of occasional maples or aspens which still throve along the slopes on memories of last spring's moisture, we clambered to the bald gray top of the mountain. We were rewarded by a fine bird's-eye view of the country traversed since sunrise, and immediately below us stretched delicious green bottom lands watered by a third mountain brook. Everywhere our horizon is bounded by snow-peaks. We stand at the summit of mountain piled on mountain, but yonder are colossal ridges which look down measurelessly far to laugh at us. Still further on rise peaks as much higher than they as they than we, or we than Denver. As for matters right under foot, we find, in the first place, that these round mountains are a formation of flesh-colored granite, largely feldspathic, and existing, wherever it outcrops to the weather, in a state as friable and incoherent as the softest pudding-stone. This was the locality in which, as I have here-tofore mentioned, I kicked several large boulders entirely to pieces in a few minutes, leaving a mere gravel-bed of crystal. Wherever a granite mass outcropped above the thin sand and gramma, I observed that its form followed the same haystack or mushroom contour presented by the mountains themselves. Several of the outcrops were very narrow in pro-portion to their heights, standing in round-topped pillars five or six feet high, with nearly the proportions of a Bolo-gna sausage. The merest tap shook them down. From the similarity of their forms, I inferred that the mountains, as well as the minor outcrops, were masses of rotten granite which had been weathered into a spheroidal surface, though I had never before imagined the rock occurring in such quantity so completely decomposed. Several Rocky Moun-tain hares, a distant herd of antelope, a young elk, and a villainous looking gray wolf, who slunk on seeing us into the indistinctness of the similarly hued sage-brush, were the quadrupeds who came into our field; we saw several mourn-ing-doves and plovers; and, coming down into the valley again, made unavailing search along the brook for a wonder-ful "fish with hands," which the stable-boys had seen there, and which, from their poetical description, we hoped might be a new species of siren, or some other equally interesting amphibian.

The next day, our friends came along in the stage, and we rejoined them. Our road for the next fifteen miles traversed an undulating tract like that between the stony plateau and Virginia Dale, tolerably green and well watered from the snow-peaks. As we proceeded, the undulations became lower, and presently merged into the magnificent level of the

Laramie Plains. This is one of the world's largest and loftiest intra-montane plateaus. It occupies a surface of about fifty miles square; is as smooth as an Illinois prairie; and the sensation of finding such a lowland tract at the height of eight thousand feet in the air, is a bewilderment to all one's previous notions of physical geography. The plateau is an alluvial deposit, belonging, so far as I could learn from a perpendicular section on the west bank of Big Laramie River, to the late tertiary. This appeared to consist of alternating white and yellow striæ, representing two varieties of silt, the former almost purely cretaceous, the latter partly so, but mostly composed of alumina with a tinge of red oxide of iron or chromium. I nowhere noticed an outcrop of rocks belonging to the mountain system. The grass was nearly as luxuriant and green as a New England June meadow. Its level in the general view seemed uniform as the sea; and such special deviations as occurred here and there, were not of the ordinary rolling contour proper to the Plains, but rather seemed terrace formations. To understand the strangeness of such a landscape in such a position, it must be remembered that this vast plain not only stands at an elevation of eight thousand feet, but is walled on all sides by mountains nearly as much higher than itself. Just as we enter the Plain by its eastern boundary coming from Cheyenne Pass, we catch a glorious glimpse of the Laramie Butte, its snow shining like a white-hot mass in the dazzling sunlight; its form almost a perfect cone, its height rated among the loftiest snow-peaks of the range. It stands as a sort of northeastern bastion to the enormous square, and from it, westward, lead the giant ramparts of the Wind River range, with an occasional snow-crowned turret, towards Fremont's and Lander's Peaks. On the southern side of the plateau, in a direction nearly parallel to the Wind River chain, runs a long black range of rolling mountains, three or four thousand feet high above the Plains level, bare as the bumps on a phrenologist's cast, and possessing the rounded contour which I had found associated with rotten granite. Behind us the square is almost closed by the time we reach the lowest bottom, through the intervention of those crags and cones we have left around Virginia Dale. To the due westward rises a succession of rugged granite stairs climbing up to the mighty Medicine Bow Mountains, under whose snows we shall shiver to-morrow; and from the middle of the Plains, through a gap at the southwestern corner of our bounding walls, we get the most ravishing view of distant snow-ranges that was ever vouchsafed Nature's lover in this world. I have seen many isolated peaks which surpassed those of this particular view, but I never in my life imagined equal beauty in a range itself. These mountains belonged to the Uintah system, another transverse range like the Wind River, running from Green River, near the 109th parallel of longitude, to inosculate with the Wahsateh range near Utah Lake. This was our first view of Mormondom; and I could not wonder that when that strange company of enthusiasts, led by Brigham Young, caught such a glimpse as this of the land beyond them, they were filled with an ecstasy which spent itself in prayers, dreams, and prophesyings. I can think of no resemblance for it, save my childish impressions of an old steel engraving, called "The Mount of God." Mature taste may condemn such prints with the nightmares of Fuseli and the resurrections of Martin; but my propensity for the marvelous was too much gratified to let me be critical. So was it here. The view was not explicable by the ordinary ideal of terrestrial scenery; it was a fairy phantasm, a floating cloud, a beatific dream of paradisaical ranges let down out of heaven, not builded out of earth. The sunlight fell on it out of a spotless sky; every square inch of the range received its maximum of illumination, so that its shadows were only less relieved against greater lights, and seemed spots of vague turquoise, sapphire, or pale amethyst on a floating mist of diamond or opal vapor. These gross comparisons come as near the impression as words of mine can; but my reader must take a step in idealism for himself, and imagine all these gems glorified by distance into the spirits of themselves. The nearest peaks of the Uintah were at least a hundred miles from us, and rose from a lower level than ourselves; yet none of us needed to be told that they were among the grandest of the whole Cordillera. They vindicated themselves to the kingly title by the ermine of snow and the diamonds of ice, together making them one continuous splendor half way from foot to crest.

Our way lay across the southern third of the level. On each side of us the grass was luxuriant, and everywhere a nearer approach to Eastern meadows in its greenness than any of the herbage on the Plains proper. There were no settlements visible except at the stations; and these consisted merely of the buildings demanded by the road. We passed several large trains of cattle-wagons, all of them belonging to Gentile emigrants (the Mormon trains preferring the northern or Laramie route); and in one place, where they had halted for the day, the camp, with its snowy wagon-tilts, its leaping fires, its picturesque back-woodsmen, women, and children, and the oxen browsing or lying down in the sweet thick grass, made a very pretty spectacle.

The Indian still has free range over this delightful plain. The antelope abounds on it; every variety of grouse found in the range is plenty here; deer, bear, and elk are numerous in the fastnesses of the surrounding mountains; and so long as the sun shines warm, no tract can be a better antetype of the Indians' happy hunting-grounds. As if in recognition of this likeness, the tribes had here and there on the plain erected curious mausoleums for their departed braves, consisting of a high pole-staging, upon which the dead lay, wrapped in his blankets in the open air. In no case where we passed these strange monuments were we offended by odors of decomposition. This fact is one of the strongest illustrations of the character of the Rocky Mountain atmosphere, and especially of that part of it which floats dissolved with the purest sunlight over Laramie Plains. The air is different from that on the eastern slope of the Appalachians very much in the same kind that muriatic acid differs from muriate of ammonia. Muriate of ammonia contains acid which has been satisfied: the air contains oxygen in its passive state. There are some localities in the mountains where the ozone tests fail of a discovery for months at a time; throughout the mountains, and a distance of many miles eastward on the Plains, iron lies out-of-doors a year at a time without perceptible rusting; such consumptives as come to this region, and settle no higher up the range than they can preserve their ease of respiration, find their disease remarkably retarded. There are several theories looking toward an explanation of the passive oxygen accumulated toward the centre of the Continent. It has been found that the air interpolated between water globules contains a much higher per cent. of active oxygen. The vapor of the sea-board, on its way towards the Rocky

Mountains, undergoes progressive condensation upon every eminence, alternating with rarefaction over every heated plain. Both the water that ascends into the higher stratum of clouds to be wafted westward for final condensation on the loftiest snow-peaks of the Rocky range, and that which falls in showers between the Appalachians, or the Gulf margin and the rainless regions of the Platte, contain between their globules a large per cent. of all the ozonized air which they have met in their passage through the atmosphere. Thus in either case, whether the ozone goes entangled with the water into the soil or the supra-human regions of the atmosphere, all the middle space occupied by the range and its neighboring plains has suffered a defiltration of its ozone. If this view of mine be correct, we may naturally look for a powerfully ozonized atmosphere on the highest peaks of the Rocky Mountains. Another theory suggests that the ozone of the sea-board atmosphere is only an allotropic condition of all the oxygen present resulting from the decomposition of sea-water, electrical currents created by the friction of dry and wet air, or from both, and that with the removal of these conditions, as by transportation inland, the oxygen returns to its passive, and, on this hypothesis, its normal state. I prefer the former view, as consistent with the experiments of Schönbein and his theory of the duplex constitution of aërial oxygen by a plus and a minus element.

However we may philosophize about it, the fact is there. All the processes of Nature, which require abundance of active oxygen, are retarded, or even in some cases nearly arrested, in the Plains and the Rocky Mountain region below the snow limits. Tuberculous disease necessitates the oxidation of a larger amount of tissue than the digestion can replace. On reaching Colorado, the patient finds the equilibrium between waste and reparation partially restored, by what we may call the pacification of his inhaled oxygen; the tuberculous deposits are arrested at their present stage, the immature remaining nearly stationary, and the mature çicatrizing after a fashion which sometimes quite surprises the Eastern practitioner. This is not the place to inquire how far the unhealthy products of a strumous diathesis may accumulate elsewhere after they cease to be consumed in the lungs. As it is the oxidation rather than the accumulation which leads directly to a mortal result in such cases, when we have retarded oxidation we have lengthened life. To the consumptive patient, who has a particular interest in living as long as possible, the climate of Colorado offers one of the finest sanitaria in the world. This will be one of the leading advantages of the Territory as soon as our Pacific Railroad has made Denver accessible to invalids. I hope, before many years have elapsed, to see some of the pleasantest sites on the foot-hills between Denver and the Arkansas occupied by institutions for the accommodation and treatment of patients attacked by pulmonary diseases in the East. When the Parks become attainable by any ordinary means of transport, they may form territory for the regeneration of the race in this particular; scrofula dying out of the blood of successive generations reared here, until it shall be impossible to find a baby with the least congenital taint. To be sure, the Indians are decaying away over this identical tract; but their scourge is a worse one than simple scrofula, being none other than scrofula's worst and most invincible parent.

As a mere selfish matter, apart from the obvious humanitarian motives which I never yet found it necessary to urge upon any true member of the noble profession of medicine, I should strongly advise the physician whose studies had been specially directed toward pulmonary disease, if he wished to make himself a name and a fortune, to open a house for the reception of consumptives either at Denver or Colorado City. At the latter spot he might still further enlarge the sphere of his institution, by receiving the classes of patients in whose cases the various Fontaine qui Bouille waters can be employed with benefit.

To return to the Laramie Plains. This vast level has an interest beside its vernal beauty of herbage: its grand *entourage* of mountains; the exhilarating elixir of its air, which bears infallible evidence of coming fresh from the alembic, virgin from all lungs except one's own; the glorious glimpses of the snow-peaks toward Quien Hornet, and the far ghost of white-robed Laramie. The plain is one of those nodal points in the physical geography of the Continent which must always form the most engrossing objects of research to the catholic student or far-sighted originator of national enterprise. Where man can work with nature, he saves himself an immense deal of drudgery. When he discovers the natural system of communications on a continent, he possesses knowledge of the highest possible use to him in running his own artificial lines with facility. The study of the natural system leads him directly to the perception of certain nodal points on the earth's surface, to hold which is to hold all the empire between them. Thus, if it be conceivable that any new Alexander should arise to struggle for universal empire, he would practically succeed (in the present state of artificial communication) when he had possessed himself of the Straits of Gibraltar, the Isthmus of Suez, the entrance to the Red Sea, the isthmuses joining North and South America. Similarly the great passes and intra-montane plateaus of the Rocky range involve in their possession the power to dictate to New York and California upon many of their common matters, and the ability at will to unite them by the strongest ties of national cohesion, or eventually break up vital communication between them. The West side of the Continent is overwhelmingly loyal in its animus; proud of the American Union and its own position in it. But the Pacific States will in time grow to be self-sufficient. They will grow, manufacture, import for themselves; and when that maturity arrives, the homogeneity of the two coasts will and should depend upon the degree of facility afforded to intercommunication. So long as it remains a formidable undertaking to pass between New York and San Francisco, so long will there develop an independence of interest and feeling which, however gradual and imperceptible, cannot fail to result in two distinct nations.

The value to the future statesman and engineer of such nodal points as we have mentioned, is well illustrated by a description of the South Pass occurring in ex-Governor Gilpin's interesting book, "The Central Gold Region." Laramie Plains are a level of similar interest. This level is a justification of the Spanish name of the system,—Sierra Madre, or Mother-Range. It is one of a group of mothers occurring along the axis of the Range, out of whose loins come the grand rivers which irrigate the Continent. From the Plains of the South Pass, and the vast ranges on whose summit the plateau is upborne, flow the Missouri and the Yellowstone to the easterly; the Snake, or principal fork of the Columbia, to the westward; and in a direction south by westerly the Green, or main branch of the Colorado River. Either by themselves or their cañons and valleys, which radiate towards one common centre in the Plains of the Pass, these rivers facilitate communication between the Mississippi and the Great Salt Lake basins, offering a series of nearly connected galleries or grades rather to the revision than to the reconstruction of the civil engineer. The Laramie Plains form another level, important for the same reasons, if not in the same degree. The level and its inclosing mountains form a reservoir for far less voluminous and extensive streams than those rising out of the South Pass plateau, but offer better opportunities for the study of the phenomena of the system than if their own were more complicated. The mountain *mesa* which has the Laramie Plains for its upper surface, is almost cinctured by the North Platte River. The South Platte has its origin in South Park; its net-work of tributaries may almost be said to inosculate on the north side with those running into Middle Park for the formation of the Blue Fork of the Colorado; the Blue Fork receives another system of tributaries running southerly from North Park, and this system again interpenetrates that of the tributaries running northward to compose the North Platte in the area of the same Park. Behind that grim range of bare, black mountains which form the southern wall of the Laramie Plateau, the North Platte is winding in a general westerly direction out of the snow-peaks which nurture its infancy. Eighty miles west of the Laramie Plains summit level, it makes an abrupt bend to the north, and thence preserves this direction to the western butment of that noble range which forms the northern wall, taking in, near this corner, the Medicine Bow Creek, which has descended from a magnificent congeries of snow-peaks, to be climbed by us on the morrow, and has followed a higher terrace of the same slope as the North Platte across the entire west side of the *mesa*. A step further on, the North Platte receives the Sweetwater from the west, and, passing around a bastion of the Wind River system, turns nearly due east to enter the lower Plains near Fort Laramie, receiving *en route* innumerable further tributaries, all of which rise from the north slope of the Wind River system, excepting the Laramie River itself. This latter stream is formed by the junction of two forks, the Big and Little Laramie, both of which rise out of the Black Mountains, on the plateau's southern boundary, and traverse it completely from south to north, uniting nearly in its centre.

A careful examination of the best Government maps of this region will enable the reader to follow this description, and get an idea of the contour of the Laramie *mesa*, which may serve as the key to all other formations of the kind, including the Plains of South Pass and the three great parks south of Laramie. Upon such nodal points as these, all the internal river systems of the Continent are centred. Their contour and position are the important facts of the range to the theoretical, the all-important ones to the practical student of physical geography.

Big and Little Laramie, where we crossed the Plain, flow nearly parallel and about fourteen miles apart. Their width, at the bridges maintained by the Overland Route, is about thirty or forty yards. Their banks, but especially those of the latter branch, are enameled with flowers of a brilliancy unequaled, but of titles unknown in my experience. One variety was a scarlet vivid as flame, and at a distance resembled a salvia. The *leguminaceæ* were represented by several plants bearing the richest mauve and purple blossoms; besides which I noticed some flowers seemingly allied to the larkspur, of a deep-blue shade, and sparingly interspersed among the profusion of the others. The sun was just on the western verge of the plateau as we reached Little Laramie; and the effect of his level rays upon the exquisite cool verdure of the grass, with all these brilliant flowers dashed in for the high tones, was something out of which to manufacture peaceful memories for a lifetime.

During the next seventeen miles the ground gradually grew less even; but the general characteristics of the plateau were preserved until twilight gave way to starlight, and we arrived at the station of Cooper's Creek. Here the moon rose, and revealed to us one of the loveliest little dells in all the Rocky Mountain scenery. Along the bottom of a shallow depression ran, crystal-clear and icy cold, a small stream, rising from the same Black range as the Laramie, and belonging to one of three classes which abound in this immediate vicinity: the streams which lose themselves upon the Plain in "sinks," or lakes without outlet; those which penetrate the Black range to join the North Platte immediately; and those which flow thither indirectly, by emptying into Medicine Bow. For these three systems, the terrace including Cooper's Creek forms a nodal point on the small scale; to which of them the creek belongs, I am not positive. We ate our supper from the box of private stores, sitting dappled with the moon-shadow of the luxuriant cotton-woods which embowered the creek; and listening to its tuneful gurgling, or watching the silver flash of ripples break across an umber pool of shade, we could have forgotten that this was not the end of our wanderings.

The hoarse "All right!" of the driver startled us from our lotus margin. We had a great deal more before us; so we arose to shake the crumbs from our beards, and the romance from our souls. We turned back one lingering glance at the paradise of Laramie Plains. Far off we heard the shrill yelp of the coyote; and as far, a silver spark went shooting across the shadow of a grassy terrace, with that electric swiftness which denotes the antelope. The whole great level was powdered with silvery mist. The moonlight seemed to lie on the nearer grass in silvery globules. Moonlight was tangled into the texture of the grossest things. The ragged cotton-wood bark by the creek looked like strips of silver foil; the bleak station-house was soaked in a solution of romance and might have been let for a palace to Rasselas; there was antiquity and a sort of Gothic strength about the company's stables; while the very mules of the new relay seemed touched by the divinity of the hour, and became hallowed, or moon-mellowed mules, who might have walked into the traces out of some old Italian "Flight into Egypt," or "Adoration of the Magi."

With a sigh at turning our backs upon this lovely view, we drove across the creek, and immediately entered a rolling country. The transition between the general level of Laramie Plains and the intricately convoluted tract just west of Cooper's Creek, is almost as abrupt as the threshold of a door. The simple passage of a stream which does not wet our hubs, takes us at once into the view of an entirely new type of landscape. We are now, strictly speaking, out of the Laramie Plateau, and beginning to ascend toward Elk Mountain and the head of Medicine Bow, by the foot-hills of the range including them. We were entering the extremity of the Black range, which had imperceptibly swung round nearly a whole quadrant while we were crossing the Plains, to blend with the Elk Mountain range as we ascended. The evening had been bracing, but not unpleasantly sharp, upon the Plains. Ascending from an elevation of eight thousand feet, however, a man is not compelled to go very far for cold weather. We had not climbed an hour among the gray, cerebral convolutions of this tract, before the cold became intense enough, not only for overcoats, but for all the blankets we could wrap in. I was quite benumbed upon my favorite seat at the driver's side; and he himself suffered severely under a heavy-caped coachman's coat of pilot-cloth, his fingers aching and stiffening around the lines inside Indian mittens of thick buckskin. Yet we could scarcely have chosen a more favorable season to cross the range, and this was one of the pleasantest nights in the entire year. I expressed to the driver my sincere desire that I might never be here during the least pleasant ones, and climbed around through the stage door into the interior.

It was early daybreak when we stopped at the base of the great Elk Mountain. The air was perfectly clear, and so intensely cold that while our horses were changing, we collected the dead boughs of some stinted cedars, and made ourselves a jolly camp-fire, at which we simultaneously warmed our benumbed bodies, and extracted our breakfast coffee.

Just at our left and southernmost hand rose the rugged wedge of the Elk Mountain, save in occasional reddish-gray patches of protruding granite, snow-clad from base to edge. It overtopped our own lofty level by full three thousand feet, we ourselves being at between nine thousand and ten thousand feet of elevation.

The two most massive mountains which I saw during my entire journey, were this Elk Mountain and the Old Cheyenne, guarding the south approach to Pike's Peak. There are higher *peaks*, but no nobler mountains than these broad masses of bald or snow-clad rock, with a general trapezoidal surface, broken into splendid variations of light and shade, and having an almost horizontal sky-line, when the sunlight strikes its crest of eternal ice, defined as sharply as a razor's edge.

The base of the Elk Mountain is surrounded with forests, consisting of all the mountain species; and the water from its snow rivulets keeps the herbage fresh under the trees. As a result, game has always been very plenty here, the Elk Mountain hunting-grounds being famous alike to the Indian and the white man, who, by struggles not a few, have tested their relative rights of entry upon the domain. The animals which gave the mountain its name were abundant at this season, and the Colorado deer and antelope no less so. We had frequent opportunities to try the meat of all these animals, and found elk-meat a translation of venison into the vulgar dialect, while antelope was venison's apotheosis.

After leaving the Elk Mountain, we continued during the entire morning to traverse one of these desert plateaus, which are characteristic of the Rocky Mountain system, and to which I have already referred in the itinerary of the day before we reached Laramie Plains. It consisted of a series of terraces, casually mistakable for an effect of wind-blown sand, had not occasional ledges of trap shown that all belonged to one system of elevation, and that where the sand had heaped the rock out of sight, the dikes still kept their strike uniform. For ten miles the plateau was mainly covered with sand. Through this here and there projected a columnar mass, or a curious series of trapezoids, arranged stair-fashion; but its general effect was that of a level ash-bed, in which throve the pale saffron blossoms of the palmate cacti, and the delicate pink cactus flower, like a baby's finger-tips seen in sunlight, which grows on a globular body like an aristocratic artichoke. Add to the inventory of vegetable life an occasional whorl of gramma-grass, a scattering of dwarfed wormwoods, a patch of greasewood here and there, and a variety of those pale-leaved plants, covered with a soft sessile down, which, all over the barrenest tracts east of Salt Lake, cling to the ground so close that frequently they are not distinguished from it by the traveller.

For the first time on our journey, I found, crawling among the cactuses and sand-heaps of this plateau, that singular little animal, known vulgarly as the Texan Toad, or Horned Frog, though in reality he does not belong to the family of the Ranidæ at all, but is a nearer relation to the lizards and salamanders. The range of this animal is singularly eccentric. On the baked, droughty prairies of Texas, it is found under a semi-tropical sun; travellers have met with it as high north as the Sweetwater, and indeed, for aught I know, it may exist on many of the sand-plains between the South Pass and the Dalles of the Columbia; and frequent specimens of it are met with on the way between Julesberg and Fort Laramie, along the North Platte trail. This plateau, however, was the only tract on which we found them during our present expedition. At a height at least equal to that of Laramie Plains, surrounded visibly on almost all sides by snow-peaks, and itself snowed under for several months of the year, this waste still supports an animal whose type resembles those of the torrid rather than the temperate zone. The only condition on which he seems inclined to stickle is aridity; put him where there is apparently nothing for him to live on, and temperature is a secondary matter.

These "toads" have an earthy brown back, which is broader and flatter than that of the true garden reptile; a white belly; a small, twinkling black eye, not all ugly or malicious in its expression, and set in an almond-shaped slit, which in some of the older animals is inclosed by two dark lines of the same shape. This has an effect to enlarge the eye as if it had been penciled, and give it a soft look like that of a miniature sheep or antelope. The two retro-curved horns which arise out of the bony plate above the eyes, add still more to this odd resemblance. The skin of the back, and the long stiff tail, instead of being warty like the true toad's upper surface, are thickly set with thorny excrescences, sharp as those of a rose, and nearly as hard. That of the belly is not a soft mucous surface, like those of the frog and toad, but a dry, tough tissue, almost horny in its character, imbricated with exquisite delicacy in minute rectangular patterns, that give the little creature sufficient freedom of motion, and at the same time provide him with the most accurately linked and fitted of breast-plates. What all this panoply is for, I have never learned. The rattlesnake may be his enemy; but, if so, toady leaves the offensive to him. The little animal is so far from pugnacious, that he submits to being taken into the hand; in fact, if placed on it right after capture, will often stand there without an attempt to get away; and it is the easiest possible thing to catch him in the first place, his gait, over the loose sand of his haunts, not exceeding in speed that of a common box-tortoise. This, by the way, is an animal which I only twice saw between the Missouri and California: once on the road between Cottonwood (at the confluence of the North and South Platte) and Fremont's Spring in Nebraska; again far up toward the snow-range, among the mines back of Denver. Neither of these differed remarkably from our commonest Eastern variety.

Just as I had about finished my naturalizing, having a handkerchief full of lizards, insects, and plants, and a pail brimming with horned toads, the area about us became suddenly still more sterile, and within a few hundred yards the sand plateau gave way to one of almost absolutely bare rock, terraced or escaladed in right lines, but with such a gradual descent to the westward that our road in most places went down the steps easily without detour, débris having filled in the sharpest angles.

Nowhere do I recollect seeing a more colossal landscape of desolation. Both my artist-friend and I rode through it for a long way silent, because we were overawed.

It is difficult by an enumeration of details so to describe this tract as to give any adequate notion of it to a reader who has never visited the scenery characteristic of rainless plateaus in a lofty mountain region.

Our road followed the lowest indentations of the rocky uplifts, being in many places a mere wheel-scratch on their surface; and thus we might fancy ourselves upon a street, along which these trap structures had been erected. It was difficult not so to fancy when we noticed the remarkable symmetry with which the rocks were arranged. They mostly seemed of the same coarse trap variety as those of the Palisades, with an occasional streak of greenstone or of phonolite.

They had come up through the most curious net-work of dikes, in which the strikes crossed each other nearly at right angles, producing a four-square arrangement of masses which reminded one forcibly of architecture and city blocks. But neither a city nor an architecture that was human. Many single blocks of trachyte, standing isolated to mark the corner of a square, were fifty feet cube, and as regular as if they had been chiseled. In other situations I saw numerous series of tabular masses, arranged like a flight of stone steps each ten feet or more in height, and in all running to a height of at least a hundred feet. In still other places the uplifts have split perpendicularly, leaving fragments of a flat rectangular form, standing like the rugged tomb-stones of a giant's burial-ground, to the height of from twenty to a hundred feet.

As we penetrated further into this tract, the architectural appearances became so consistent, that one's fancy was compelled to construct a theory for itself, and did it very rationally to the effect that we were travelling through a deserted city of the conquered Titans. Those colossal square inclosures were the wine cellars and treasure-vaults of palaces thousands of feet high. In those acres of basement what vast wassail may have been held on the return of the masters from hunting megatheria, fishing for icthyosauri, or playing quoits with cross-slices off a volcano! That mighty cube of black fire-rock, which weighs a thousand tons, was but one of a single course of stones in the same rectangle, upon whose foundation the now down-tumbled house was built—high as the eaves of a tall city house itself, but only at the bottom of a structure whose roof menaced the gods.

The ruined staircases to which I have referred, often stood alone in such relative position to the basement rectangles that it required no stretch of the imagination to conceive of them as the former access to the grand front entrance of the house—an appearance with which their dimensions were equally consistent. In several instances I noticed that the interior of the rectangles was paved in square blocks, with a regularity, which would lead any one ignorant of the scientific means to suppose that the area had been flagged by human labor, and presented the appearance of some fortress court-yard. Nothing could be at once more characteristically sepulchral and Titanic than the spaces occupied by the tablets. Some of these were erect as I have described, but many lay on corner blocks, like the horizontal grave-stones of old-fashioned country church-yards. Here, stretched many a rood under the torrid sand, with prickly cactuses springing out of their brains, and wormwood out of their hearts, may lie the great warriors who fell on this same blasted heath in battle with Olympus. But they are no more silent than are the old lords of the palace who fell under the powdered ruins, the basement stones of which alone remain for witness, being lightened upon by Zeus Keraunios, and shot into the abyss, in the very ripeness of blasphemy, wassail, and defiance.

However forced this fancy may appear to the cool reader, it irresistibly suggested itself on the spot. The shapes and sizes of all the rocks within view contributed such consistent aid to this idea, that I travelled with a sense of delightful awe, as if I were exploring the gigantic remains of some dead civilization,—a Layard of the Titans. It would hardly have surprised me to find a hierographical inscription cut upon some corner-stone in letters a cubit deep.

About one P. M. we caught sight of a silvery streak in a valley about fifteen hundred feet below our present terrace. This we soon found to be the North Platte River, whose mature stream we had left at Latham, and whose upper waters we were now about to cross at no great distance from their source. By consulting a United States Survey map, it will be seen that this stream doubles on itself remarkably, rising just outside the southern wall of the mountain quadrilateral which incloses Laramie Plains, following the outer edge of the terraces which bound the level westerly, and reaching the Plains by an eastward return which brings it within a comparatively short distance northerly from the cradle where it sprung.

We now emerged from the gradually terraced dikes, and came to a place where the descent was so precipitous, that sitting on a coach-box one might well feel anxious about tumbling forward on the horses. Our road ran on bare cracked boulders of trap and altered sandstone; threaded black fissures; and slid, with the brake hard on, down slippery stone inclines, just over the edge of whose narrow shelf was a sheer precipice or overhanging wall of trachyte, two or three hundred feet high.

We marked the first appearance of the Platte, far to the south, in the fold of a system of round gray hills, which, as nearly as could be judged from their contour, belonged to that incoherent granite formation weathered into spherical forms, which I mentioned at Virginia Dale. The stream passed out of view to the northeastward, through a precipitous cañon of red sandstone, having frequent shelves and butments which projected several feet from the main wall, and averaging perhaps forty or fifty feet in height from the water-line. Its course traversed nearly the whole of our western horizon, being much of the way distinguishable from our elevation, by glimpses of silvery water or fringes of the always indicative cotton-wood. The round hills which close by at Virginia Dale had seemed, both in form and color, the convolutions of some petrified brain, now softened by distance, and having their gramma and sage-brush lighted by the intensest sun, looked like a flock of Cyclop sheep, whose woolly backs were rounded for slumber as they lay down beside the still waters of the Platte. Each glimpse of those waters the sun was now turning into a pool of silver fire.

Just as we rounded a steep jutting bastion of trap, which threw us a little further towards the outer precipice, I turned away from the beautiful valley view to look upward at those grim crags and terraces, by whose staircase we were descending to the Platte. I had looked just in time, for my point of view was exactly right for the recognition of one of the greatest mimetic wonders I ever saw, even in this most Titanic and Demoniacal country.

The terrace of the Giants' Graveyard, now left behind about five hundred feet above us, was perceived to have an extension far to the southward and westward of the point where we came down from it, until, a mile in front of our present niche, it projected a bold promontory into the valley, beyond the face of the entire remaining precipice, and at least a hundred feet higher. The lower and much the larger part of this promontory was perpendicular, or overhanging; but the upper end of it, for three hundred feet, was weathered into a colossal sculpture, a head and bust of such striking sharpness and vigor, that it seemed almost as impossible that no human artist had had a hand in the work as it was inconceivable how he could have accomplished it.

Behind this promontory, up to the occiput of the sculptured head, ran the wall of a principal trap dike; and further behind, overtopping the wall in a series of ascending towers and bastions, rose a vast pile of the same tremendous cubes, which constituted the foundations of the ruined palaces. It was an easy thing to imagine loopholes in that climbing city of strongholds; to see a spectral flag wave from the highest rampart; to wonder at the structure's grand, simple lines, as if we were criticising some splendid piece of military architecture; to delight in its idea as if Nature shared your humanity.

Braced against the westward wall of this Titanic fortress, and looking across the drowsy flock of hills shepherded by the silver crook of the Platte,—due west across the green oasis which, on the river margin, hundreds of feet below, awaited us with trees, grass, springs, and dinner,—solemn, stern, and saturnine, looked forth the face of *John Calvin*.

If a sculptor had undertaken to copy in stone the best known likenesses of this noted theologian, the result could not have been a more striking portrait. Any person familiar with the picture, would most instantly have seen it in this head and bust. Even to the traditional Genevese cap, this was the theologian's second self. If Presbyterians ever adopt the usage of a Mecca, this is the site for that Mecca. Here sits the Prophet, bearing witness forever; and his darkened, painful face shows that the Natural Depravity whereof he testified in Geneva, has not gone out of fashion since he left that pulpit. Looking westward, round the globe, he sees plenty to derange his moral liver; and because those rocky lips have no voice to utter warning, he sends it across the valley in a form of stone. From the point where I stood, I could see hardly a place on head, cap, or face, which could have been bettered, as likeness, by a more elaborate bringing out of details. The simulation was perfect, and for nearly half a mile continued so, with varying expressions of wrath or sternness, from every point of view.

Finally emerging from the terrace region, we came out upon the green and shady Platte bottom, which we had seen just below us for the last hour, and stopped at the ferry-station for our dinner.

BUFFALO CHARGE.

ATTACK OF PANTHER.

## CHAPTER VI.

# THE APPROACH TO SALT LAKE CITY.

WE crossed the North Platte by an ingenious contrivance which I here saw for the first time, though I cannot but think that some time or other it must have been employed upon many of our narrow Eastern streams, at places too deep and rapid for fording. This is a ferry-boat whose motive power was the current it had to cross. I venture to believe many of my readers as ignorant as I found myself, and endeavor to give some idea of this ingenious contrivance.

A stout post, square-hewn from an entire trunk, about eighteen inches in diameter, is driven firmly into each of the opposite bluffs, and between the two, tautened by a wind-lass, extends a heavy hempen cable, roven through a pair of lignum-vitæ double-blocks, of sufficient breadth of eye and depth of groove to run without friction and quite independent of each other, from post to post. The lowest sag of the cable, just over midstream, brings it within eight or ten feet of the water-level. So much for the locomotive apparatus.

The ferry-boat is a rough, strongly built scow, with standing room for a four-in-hand team and as many passengers as choose to wedge themselves in between horses and piles of baggage,—a craft apparently of ten or twelve tons burden. At each of its square ends an iron ring-bolt is securely screwed into the keelson, and to each ring a double pulley-block is attached by a hook. Through each of these blocks a stout line runs to the lower wheel of the corresponding block on the cable which spans the stream, reeves through it, and, returning inboard, passes around the second pulley of the block hooked to the ring-bolt to the hand of the ferryman, or a convenient cleat, where he fastens it with a half-hitch. By substituting the cable for a boom, a sloop's main-sheet may be made to give a correct idea of this apparatus and its *modus operandi*. When the two sheets are of equal length, the current strikes the side of the scow at right angles and it remains stationary. To set it in motion, it is only neces- sary to close-haul the sheet at that end of the scow which is intended for the bow *pro tempore*, and slacken the one at the other end. The current now performs the function dis- charged by a wind a-beam in the case of sailing vessels, and takes the ferry-boat across very cleverly.

The ferryman was a fine-looking solitary, who spent months at a time camped out under the cotton-woods of the margin without seeing a face except that of the emigrant or the traveller, yet lived in great comfort and contentedness in what might be called the most out-of-the-way spot on the Northern Continent. His calling was certainly of the most valuable character to his fellow-men, and equally so to himself; amounting to a monopoly of the entire transit busi- ness on the most important trail between the Missouri and California. He could not fail to make a fine income, charg- ing, I believe, two dollars a team for all ordinary ferriage, and having a private arrangement with Mr. Holladay.

I left this place with much regret, having a strong desire to explore the mountains south of us, from which the river issued, and between which for many miles, in the exquisitely clear atmosphere, we could catch glimpses of it in its silvery and sinuous course. Indeed, a month's stay there would not have been thrown away, either for purposes of art or science; the trap dikes, heretofore mentioned, being of the most interesting character, and the fauna and flora of the region tempting one by their marked individuality. I am not aware of a more favorable place for a depot camp of Rocky Mountain explorers than this ferriage. Among the attractions from which I broke in continuing my journey, were the "horned toads" of the rocky plateau, and a species of "fish with legs" which had been seen in the small streams emptying into the platte not far from here. I suffered the frequent fate of specimen gatherers in the Rocky Mountains, and lost every horned toad I had collected. The scientific student, after a few weeks' experience in a country where transportation is so difficult, learns to expect that much of his material will get destroyed or left behind, even where he has taken the most particular pains to collect and preserve it, and meets his disappointments with cool philosophy; but this particular case of my own was greatly aggravated by being not the result of chance but of a stupid retaliation on the part of a fellow-passenger, who secreted the box in which I had placed my specimens while we were ferrying across our luggage, and opened it on the west bank of the Platte, letting all my morning's collection escape. When it became too late to make the loss good, the stage having started, I was informed of the proceeding as a capital joke. If my toads shall establish a colony on the west bank, for the convenience of future collectors, I shall not so much regret my own disappointment. I regretted it at the time all the more, because one or two of the animals appeared to me a different species from any of the Phrynosomata I have ever seen described; in their general figure resembling *P. douglassii*, and their heads being decidedly like that of *P. cornutum*. At several places in the mountains I sought for the "fish with legs," which almost every old mountaineer has seen, but for none of which, as a matter of course, can anything be obtained like a scientific description. Whenever we stopped near a small stream to water or change horses, I spent all the available time in looking for him, but regret to say that fortune never favored me. I suppose the animal to be a species of Siredon. I need not explain to the student of natural history my anxiety to obtain a fresh specimen,—perhaps even a new species, of a genus thus far represented in cabinets by but two or three species and very few individuals, even these inadequate relics being imperfectly preserved.

The animal to which Baird has given the specific name of Lichenoides is one of the most beautiful and interesting of reptiles; having the head without the horns of the cat-fish, and a respiratory apparatus consisting of three branchial flaps on each side of the neck, fringed more delicately than the gills of any fish; and owing its special designation to the yellow spots distributed over the black or brown ground of its skin, like the variegations caused by lichens on the surface of a stone.

At Sage Creek, an inconsiderable but unfailing rivulet, fed from the snow-peaks, and about fourteen miles from the North Platte crossing, we met for the first time the bird most characteristic of the intra-montane levels and western slope of the Rocky Range—the Sage-cock.

This bird may well be called the king of the grouse tribe. His own average length is about thirty-two inches, and his hen's two feet; but I have seen specimens which exceed these measurements by several inches. When stalking erect through the sage, they seem as large as a good sized wild turkey. Their color and markings differ to some extent with age, sex, the season of the year, and the different individuals; but the prevailing appearance is that of a yellowish-brown, or a warm gray mottled with darker brown, shading from cinnamon to jet black, the dark spots laid on in longitudinal series of crescents. Their under parts are of a light gray,—sometimes of almost a pure white tint,—barred by slender longitudinal, streaks of brown,—the middle of the belly being pied with black patches. Their plumage is exquisitely smooth; the feathers of a handsome cock lying so close and kept in such perfect order, that under a bright sun he looks more like a bird encased in some beautifully grained and polished veneering than one in the usual cloak of feathers. The elegance of his figure exceeds that of any grouse on the Continent. He is slenderer and finer in his outlines than any allied bird, except the Chinese or golden pheasant. In recognition of his resemblance to these birds he gets one of his numerous aliases,—*Tetrao* (Bonaparte), or *Centrocercus* (Swainson) *Urophasiamus*. This last and specific title etymologists will recognize as Greek for "pheasant-tailed." This tail of his seems to have puzzled ornithologists somewhat as to the place where he belongs. It differs from that of the grouse family in general, by coming to a point instead of flaring in a fan; and some of his sponsors have made a new species for him, taking him out of the Tetraonidæ and calling him *Centrocercus* which, in connection with his specific title, certainly amounts to a pleonasm, the word being derived from the Greek χεντρον (a point) and χερχος (a tail), so that the translation of Swainson's nomenclature would be "The Pheasant-tailed Point-tail." The better view still keeps the bird a Tetrao. On each side of his neck he has a bare orange-colored spot, and near it a downy epaulet, which allies him as nearly to the ruffed grouse as his tail to the pheasant. His call is a rapid "cut-cut-cut," followed by a hollow blowing sound; he has the partridge's habit of drumming with his wings; his female knows the trick of misleading the enemy from her young brood; and although his curves are much longer and his figure less *stocky* than that of the grouse tribe in general, his affiliations on the whole seem stronger in that direction than in any other. He seldom rises from the ground, and his occasional flights are low, short, and labored; but he runs with rapidity, and in his favorite habitat, the sage brush, dodges and skulks with great dexterity, favored by the resemblance between his own and the bushes' neutral tints. His common title of sage-cock is derived from his favorite haunt. Another of his aliases is "Cock of the Plains," but I never knew him so called out of books, for the title is not descriptive. He is never seen on the Plains proper—the high mountain region, whether level or sloping, swarming with his family wherever sage is plenty, from the vicinity of the Rocky Mountain water-shed westerly to the Desert, and several hundred miles further west in the latitude of the South Pass, where be extends as far as the cataracts of the Columbia. In that region the sage brush has a much further westerly extension than further south,—and the bird peculiarly belongs to this growth of vegetation. Thus far, to my knowledge, he has never been found west of the Cascade Range or the Sierra Nevada. In the spring, or about the time of snow melting, which of course varies at diffident heights and in different latitudes, the sage-hen builds in the bush her nest of sticks and reeds, quite artistically matted together, and lays from a dozen to twenty eggs, a trifle larger than the average of the domestic fowl, of a tawny color, irregularly marked with chocolate blotches on the larger end. Her period of incubation does not, I believe, differ much from that of the domestic hen. When the brood is large enough to travel, its parents lead it into general society. In July and August the flocks begin assembling, and by fall it is not unusual to meet bands of two or three hundred. I reached and crossed their habitat during the last week in June, and between Sage Creek and Salt Lake daily encountered flocks of a score or over. I know scarcely any animal whose range is more sharply defined. It is a rare thing to meet with them on the eastern flanks of the ridges belonging to the Rocky Mountain system; though while I was in Denver, my friend, the indefatigable naturalist Dr. Wernigk, brought back from an expedition into the South Park very fine specimens of both cock and hen. This fact, however, hardly constitutes an exception to the general rule, since South Park is but little over a degree further east than Sage Creek and sheds a portion of its water to the west by small affluents of the Grand Fork of Colorado, though most of its drainage is by the South Platte.

I never saw tamer wild fowl than the little troop of sage-chickens which we encountered on striking Sage Creek. I could hardly realize they were what they were, though I had a vividly correct image of them in my mind from the stuffed specimens of Dr. Wernigk, and the admirable drawings of Baird's collection. As we wound along the brook margin, they strutted complacent between the gnarled trunks and ashen masses of foliage peculiar to the sage, paying scarcely more attention to us than a barn-yard drove of turkeys (whose motion theirs much resembles), the cocks now and then stopping to play the dandy before their more Quakerish little hens, inflating the yellow patches of skin on each side of their necks, by a peculiar air-syphon apparatus, until they globed out like the pouches of a pouter pigeon. As this was the first time I had seen them in their native haunts, and because their confidence quite disarmed me, I had no thought of shooting them, and had the driver slow his team to give our party a better opportunity of studying them. They continued dodging about the bushes not more than forty feet from us, until we thoroughly familiarized ourselves with their manners; and acknowledged that although some others of the grouse tribe rejoiced in richer colors than they, they certainly bore away the palm in the exquisite symmetry of their markings, and the grace of their figures as well as their movements. Wishing to get nearer them for the purpose of seeing if any young ones were concealed in the brush (whose trunks, consisting each of a number of smaller stems united in a spiral twisted as tight as any hawser, here measured everywhere the thickness of a man's thigh), I dismounted and quietly crept toward them. They did not take the alarm until I had got within twenty feet of them, and then went under cover with an air of dignified leisure. I suppose they knew by instinct that they had little to fear. Science and wantonness were their only enemies. I had their whole country before me, and would not burden myself with specimens prematurely; I was not fond of destroying life merely for murder's sake, and none of our party were starving. To kill a sage-hen for supper demands either this last condition, or the stomach of an Indian; for, with this handsome grouse, beauty is preeminently but skin deep,—the flesh of the bird, save in the youngest chickens, being a mess rather for the apothecary's shop than the kitchen. The sage-fowl not only live in the brush from which they get their name, but feed on it, as well as on the insects and smaller reptiles about its roots, thus acquiring a rank sage flavor which repeated par-boilings followed by roasting cannot entirely eradicate. The wild sage has no connection with our garden variety, except through its popular name and very unpopular taste, being, in fact, a wormwood (*Artemisia tridentata*), while our familiar pot-herb is the *Salvia officinalis*.

Sage Creek runs nearly due north and empties into a small nameless stream, which is the most westerly affluent of the North Platte, and which rises from the very summit of the water-shed penetrated by Bridger's Pass. After leaving Sage Creek we crossed two more anonymous rivulets which go to swell this affluent, on the way stopping at Pine Grove Station, twenty-four miles from the North Platte Crossing, to change horses.

Here we found, in the person of the station-keeper, one of the finest specimens of the American hunter and fearless pio-neer encountered in our whole journey. He was a splendidly built fellow, not more than twenty-two or three years old, six feet high, with an arm like a grizzly's paw, a fine, frank, fear-less face, full of ruddy health and quenchless cheerfulness. There was a look of capability and resource about him which made it easy to understand how the wilds of our country are settled, its rocky fastnesses made to roar with the blast of the forge, and echo to the sound of axe and hammer. Set him beside one of our pale, puny Metropolitan counter-jumpers, and ask the inhabitant of another planet to label the two for the shelves of some anthropological cabinet: ten to one they would not be included in the same species, perhaps not in the same genus of animal life. The young station-keeper told us that he had a partner, but it was very rare for both of them to be at home together. He had now been alone for several days, taking care of the stock, while the other man was trapping and shooting equally alone in the mountains. When we asked him what game he hunted, he invited us into his cabin and pointed us to the walls for the shortest answer. The skins hung so thick that we could not see the logs. Among them were a number of full-sized grizzly robes, and a few pretty little cub-skins, very soft and silky, belonging to the same species; a cinnamon bear-skin, besides gray and white wolf-skins, fox-skins, deer-hides, and smaller peltry without stint, including the wolverine, an exquisitely marked tiger-cat, and the robe of a mountain lion. His cabinet of deer and elk horns would have brought hundreds of dollars, if offered to an Eastern sportsman decorating his library. His taste in adornment was excellent; the lady-love of a prince might have envied him his *boudoir*. All his skins were in excellent preservation. The only one that he had never been able to preserve was that of the antelope; and that animal must forever baffle the cabinet collector, for his hair differs from that of every quadruped but the porcupine. It is stiff and spongy; the gentlest pull brings out a bunch of it in one's fingers, and this bunch looks and feels like a bundle of short threads of spun glass. Where it is thickest, on the breast and about the haunches, it stands out like bristles radiating from a centre in the brush form, with concentric rings of coarse, brittle fibre arranged round it. I have never seen anything exactly like it in any other animal, and never in the antelope anything like the other ruminants' wool or hair. The fibres of the antelope pelt are sometimes so brittle that they break across as easily as the spun glass which they resemble. The skin is thus valueless for the fur trade or the cabinet, a fact which I have often regretted; for its appearance upon the animal, with the sunlight striking its tawny ground and snow-white patches, as it goes glancing down a bluff in the arrow-flight of a stampede, is very beautiful.

Among other trophies which interested me greatly, were the horns and skin of a "Bighorn," or Rocky Mountain sheep (*Ovis montana*), an animal which even in the heart of this savage region is practically rare, since, like the chamois, it frequents the most inaccessible fastnesses, and is never seen save by the hunter who devotes himself entirely to its pursuit. The wariest Indian often lies in wait for it for days without seeing it, and when finally he does catch a glimpse of it, it only reveals itself on the brink of some snow-covered crag hundreds of feet above him, where neither ball nor arrow could strike, and no living being but its own kind could reach it without wings. Its color is a grayish-brown, like that of a ram in a dusty, droughty summer just before "sheep-washing" time, with a darker line down the spine, after the ass's fashion. Its horns (as one of the popular names indicates) are immense. Some of the old hunters told me that a pair, with the clean skull, sometimes weighed sixty pounds, but I have never found any actual authentic weight exceeding half that. The horns, like those of the antelope, are rooted so immediately above the orbital process that they seem to rise directly out of the eyes. They are almost close together at the base, where it is not unusual to find them measuring twenty inches in circumference. They curve gradually and evenly backward in an arc of about two hundred degrees, and to a length of thirty to forty inches, their tips being about half their length apart from each other. Their hoofs are generally black, and unlike the antelopes' are provided with the *dew-claw*, or upper and posterior rudimentary hoof common to the allied genera. Their hair is less brittle than the antelopes', and in winter is interspersed with a short, fine fleece, apparent on parting the straight fibres; but they have nothing that in the least approaches the wool of our domestic sheep. The animal is of immense size, the adults weighing between three and four hundred pounds. I have heard from old hunters and Indians, that when surprised upon a precipice where there is no room to turn, the bighorn will plunge headlong a distance of a hundred feet, and strike on his horns without breaking them or bruising himself, then bound to his feet by aid of their elastic spring, and run away as if nothing had happened. I cannot vouch for this story, since our party had no time to make a protracted halt at the great altitude which is the favorite and almost only habitat of the bighorn. Indeed, I must confess to never having seen him alive; but I have found the hunters of this country more strictly and conscientiously accurate in regard to *facts*, than any class of men from whom I have ever sought information. The theories by which they explain their facts have no more value than attaches to those of uneducated men anywhere, being, of course, frequently in diametrical opposition to established principles of science, and arising from a confusion of concomitant circumstances with the idea of cause and effect. But their report of matters lying wholly within experience is more trustworthy than that of the best educated savant, their eyes, ears, and all their senses being trained to a vigilant keenness which nothing escapes, and their freedom from superstition (a constant element of error in information given by the wildwoodsmen of other nations) securing them from the danger of mystical exaggeration. I believe I have before referred to an instance of this in the notion of prairie-dogs, owls, and snakes all inhabiting the same burrow. I was perpetually assured by plain, practical frontiersmen that the notion was a correct one, and after putting the question to repeated careful tests, discovered that they were right and the savant was wrong. So I can conceive it possible that the Rocky Mountain sheep does dive headlong from precipices and break his fall by a pair of horns for whose magnificent spiral curves and immense size there can scarcely be imagined any other, and certainly no better use. But it needs an enthusiast indeed to study an animal who keeps his admirers a week at the perpetual snow-line before vouchsafing them so much as a glimpse of him.

The young station-keeper's cabin was not far from that altitude. It was situated on a narrow shelf of one of the highest ranges, in a dense grove of firs and pines, and built of nicely hewn logs, cut close at hand. When we consider that, with the exception of this timber which made his dwelling, and the water which trickled from the adjacent snow-peaks for his drink, every necessary of life both for his horses, his partner, and himself, had to be brought to this solitary crest of the Continent all the way from the Missouri River (nine hundred and thirteen miles) by wagon, we may form some proximate idea of the indomitable energy required of the man, who, like Ben Holladay, could keep in steady running order a daily freight and passenger line across the entire Continent. A hitch in the machinery of this vast system, occurring in the stables or granaries of this station, packed

away as it is in the loneliest recesses of the world's topmost ridge,—the *furthest-off* place, so to speak, that mortal
can imagine,—anything awry here may throw out of gear
important interests and arrangements in St. Louis or San
Francisco. But things did *not* go awry; for one single tireless
man, with the finest talent for business combinations that
exists in America, was forever dropping into cabins under
the snow-peaks and *adobes* sweltering on the sand of the
desert; making the master's eye felt by the very horses; creating a belief in his omnipresence, and a sense that it was
worth while to be worthy of his confidence; he was found
in every part of the vast machinery whose steam lay in his
audacious force of character, and whose governor consisted
of his unrivaled business tact. Just before I left New York I
saw him at an artists' reception at Dodworth's. I ask the Pine
Grove hermit if he ever saw Mr. Holladay. "You bet!" replies
my hermit; "he was here day before yesterday."

With the exception of the abrupt descent made by us
from the plateau of the remarkable trap dikes, down the terraces where John Calvin frowns in eternal petrifaction to the
last crossing of the Platte, we had been climbing steadily to
this cabin, from the sunset which saw us over the lesser fork
of Laramie and the moonlight which made silver filagree
of the splash from our horses' hoofs as we forded Cooper's
Creek. We were now, by the most reasonable estimate, at
an altitude of more than ten thousand feet. Our calcula-
tions were corroborated by the character of the surrounding
vegetation. We had parted from cotton-woods on the western verge of Laramie Plains. Then the osiers left us, and the
dry Artemisia fringed the snow-cold rivulets that traversed
our trail—coming, with the greasewood, clear down to the

margin where at less elevations we might have looked for a swaying willowy fringe. Now, at Pine Grove, deciduous vegetation failed almost entirely. The hardiest of the succulent-leaved trees gave way to that sturdy growth which is separated only by the moss and the lichen from absolute barrenness. We saw no longer the "quaking-asp" (*Populus tremuloides*) nor the cañon maple (*Acer macrophyllum*, var. *Utahense?*). Here wan the kingdom of the Coniferæ, and even these were stinted. Around the young hunter's and station-keeper's cabin, the funereal foliage of spruce, and fir, and pine, attained a growth of but forty or fifty feet, though dense enough to add a strange solemnity to the obscure loneliness of this lofty mountain crest.

Emerging from the black shadows of the pines, we came into a tract whose colossal wildness of scenery stands apart in my recollection, by virtue of the same class of traits which isolate certain lonely and severe human characters.

In no one particular was it measured on so vast a scale as certain other savage landscapes I have visited. But its *toute ensemble* was that of utter, unbroken solitude. We hardly needed the information vouchsafed us by the driver, that we were now crossing the dividing ridge between the Atlantic and Pacific—the great water-shed of the Rocky Mountains.

Even after my long experience of the breadth of the range, I was not fully prepared to find this ridge so unostentatious of its true character. True, I had not expected when I reached it to see, as from the summit range of our narrow Alleghanies, the bird's-eye view of either slope and the plains below mottled with cloud and sunshine, and arabesqued in every direction by the silver threads of rivers belonging to the two systems of drainage; but neither, on the other band, had I looked for such a complete absence of all the distinctive traits proper to that idea of a mountain chain and water-shed which we get from maps and charts of physical geography.

We were completely shut in by a chaos of mountains. Our track kept the summit of a sinuous divide, for the most part narrow as a railway embankment, save where it inosculated with other like ridges, coming, seemingly without system of distribution, from every direction, and separated by deep gullies, pits, and trenches, bare of all vegetation, save here and there a scanty tuft of bunch grass, which seemed rather to have been calked into the dry seams of the soilless granite than to grow out of them. Our divide possibly varied from a few hundred to a thousand feet in height above the holes and chasms; while on either hand, looking in that crystal atmosphere of the upper world but a stone's cast off, and in reality at a distance to be measured by miles, the transverse convolutions of the range (those in fact which give propriety to its name of a "chain") rose two or three thousand feet higher still. These cross ranges were very precipitous, ascending, without regard to the irregular *glacis* of detritus at their base, at an angle of 60° to 70°, seamed with mighty scars where the frost had toppled over and slid off acre-large fragments of their battlements, furrowing their naked flanks all the way down—bare of all vegetation even in these channels—bare even of soil, until the eye paused just below their perpetual snow-line on a slender rim, green as emerald, fed by the meltings from above. It was almost midsummer,—a week after the solstice,—yet in many scars the snow lay uninterrupted from crest to base; and along the whole irregular line of the ridges it was the packed accumulation of numberless years, solidified to the consistency of a glacier, and wearing that peculiar pearl-blue or opalescent tint belonging to that formation. On the average the snow-line of these transverse ridges was drawn about a fifth of the distance downward from their crest, and the emerald band which ran almost exactly parallel, ranged half that distance further down the declivity. Below that, and in all directions around us, the congeries of mountains and lesser divides were bare as the pavemènt of a city, a quarry, or the driest thing known either to nature or to art. The prevailing color on the heights was a dull reddish-brown; in the pits and chasms, a leaden gray. Up in the emerald band was ice-cold water and succulent pasturage for the bighorn; thither must his hunter climb; there, freezing through long nights when the mercury fell to zero, must he wait patiently; there must he watch for days, with no food but a strip of jerked buffalo; thence might he never return at all, *his* hunter, the grizzly or the cougar, having "gobbled" him unaware; or returning, have nought to bring down with him but a set of frozen toes and the humiliating experience of a long-range shot at some Ulysses among rams, who had jumped a chasm with an ounce ball in his shoulder, and gained his inaccessible fastness in a peak a thousand feet higher yet.

Just beyond the water-shed this basin of mountains contracts into a narrow gallery, walled by noble precipices of red granite and metamorphic sandstone, rising directly from the traveller's side to the almost perpendicular height of from a thousand to twenty-five hundred feet. In some places this gallery appears scarcely more than a crevice of dislocation, a mere crack between stupendous naked rocks which would match joints exactly if slid back to their old position. In no part of it does the resemblance to a work of engineering art cease to strike one. Though the passage is in reality abundantly ample for an army, the vast height of its lateral walls makes it seem proportionally so narrow that it might be the rock-cut of some bygone race of road-builders. This American Simplon is Bridger's Pass. It is several miles in length and has a main westerly direction with a slope toward the same point of compass. It is quite sinuous, but nowhere turns so abruptly that its passage is difficult to a four-horse team, nor is its descent anywhere so sudden as to be liable to a like objection. I was astonished at finding the art of the engineer so far anticipated for the purpose of a convenient transit route between the two coasts of our country, as everywhere appears in Bridger's Pass. It is named after the celebrated explorer and trader, Major James Bridger, who was either its first white discoverer, or the first to make it widely known as a convenient means of access to the vast interior basin of the Continent. He came to this region nearly forty-five years ago, and during much of the period since then, remained in constant relation with the Indian tribes ranging between New Mexico and the Great South Pass—including those of the Upper Missouri, Green, and Columbia Rivers. He had established a trading post and an important depot and resting place for emigrants to California, at the fort which bears his name, long before it became a military station of the United States government.

Just at the western portal of this magnificent gallery, and at a depression of perhaps fifteen hundred feet below its eastern entrance, we emerged into another basin-shaped valley, walled by snow-crested ridges like those surrounding the watershed, but having a luxuriant green bottom, irrigated by rivulets from the meltings above. A large emigrant train had just made its halt there for the night. We felt an almost bovine sympathy for the cattle, who were eagerly browsing up to their bellies in the rank herbage of the stream-margins. It was half an hour after sunset, and the horizon toward which we were travelling was flushed with a clear salmon hue, which contrasted finely with the dark green of the valley-bottom, the lighter emerald of the band beneath the snows of the encircling precipice, and the third, almost black shade of the same color, manifested by the occasional groups of stinted evergreens, which marked the base of the slopes; while a still livelier tone was infused into the middle ground by the leaping jets of yellow flame which rose from the crackling sage and greasewood of the camp-fires where supper was cooking for three hundred men, women, and children, and, as it flickered, made the snow-white tilts of the great ox-wagons seem to dance and waver, go and come, like cheerful ghosts. The camp was full of farm-yard noises. Cows were lowing to be miked, and suckling calves were bleating to their mothers; a wandering, sniffing pack of curs were yelping at the welcome smell of supper and the thought of bones in reversion; and, from their coops slung to the backs of the wagons, side by side with that cooking stove and hickory-bottomed chair which are the emigrant's inevitable Lares, bewildered hens were clucking, and anachronistic cocks uttering a real break-o'-day crow,—their ideas utterly turned topsy-turvey by the inability to mark time with the proper roosting pole, and the mimicry of sunrise by the flash of camp-fires. We got cheerful nods and friendly greetings as we trundled through the camp, and came a few miles further on to our own supper at the Overland station of Sulphur Springs. This was the most elaborate meal we had enjoyed for some time. Sitting on the box with the driver, I had so fascinated that high authority's imagination by a description of the canned provisions in our "outfit," that he warmed to the proposition of stopping at Sulphur until I could prepare "a good square meal." The station-keeper at Sulphur had a wife and a baby. We expressed much delight at this joyful sight,—by no means a common one in the mountains or on the Desert, unless on an emigrant wagon *in transitu,*—and so won the family heart that we were admitted to all the rights and privileges of the cooking-stove. Getting out our provision box from under our feet in the wagon, we soon had employment provided for every utensil known to the Sulphur Springs cuisine. The sight of men cooking is no such portent in the Rocky Mountains as (unfortunately for health and good taste) it is in the rural districts of the East; and the mother beamed on us kindly as she tended the baby with one arm and handed us condiments with the other, all with such dispatch that we had to warn her against mistaking hands in her excitement, and throwing the baby into the stewed tomatoes while she dandled the pepper. It would do the hearts of our Eastern acquaintance good to see the skilled fingers which had composed a glacier and innumerable mountain tops equally glib in hotter preparations, where the spoon was substituted for the paint brush; laying in a background of prepared coffee, and gradually bringing up the high-lights with an inspired touch of condensed cream; while literary fingers, gambolling in long vacation from the pen, were preparing an article on the theme of Shaker sweet corn, another upon canned beef, and still another upon tomatoes, the whole edition of the work containing these to be absorbed eagerly as soon as published. The driver, who had travelled widely, and become conversant with the most elaborate cuisines of Denver and Salt Lake City, declared that even in those luxurious capitals this "outfit" was not to be surpassed.

After tea, while the fresh horses were getting attached, I wandered a few steps away from the back of the station to the springs which gave it its name. There were two of them, side by side—one, a white sulphur, of strength and flavor almost exactly resembling the Clifton water in Ontario County, State of New York; the other, more of the Kentucky Blue Lick type, but much more intense. The first I found very agreeable. I felt sorry that the rest of the party abhorred all such springs alike, for this was deliciously cold and limpid, beside being free from the saline and alkaline properties which were to make most of the springs henceforth, until we reached California, nauseous or wholly undrinkable. Though an epicure in the matter of mineral water, being very fond even of Blue Lick, I was obliged to confess that I could not drink the second spring. It was fairly saturated with sulphide of hydrogen, and had numerous other distinguishable flavors as badly intense, none of which I recognized save the chalybeate.

Shortly after we left Sulphur Springs, the moon rose, now near her full. As long as I could keep my eyes open, I sat on the box. The country was a congeries of bare round hills, receding and rising on either hand to mountain ranges, transverse to that which we had penetrated at Bridger's Pass. It was difficult to imagine that we were still in the very thick of the mountain system, and at an elevation at least as high as Laramie Plains. The stupendous scale upon which this system is constructed, constantly prevents the traveller from realizing where he is. Not till he has climbed over many ridges, and penetrated many passes, does he understand that his descent over the one or his emerging from the other is only equivalent to the entrance upon another lofty plateau,—a plain raised upon the very summit of the mountains themselves,—or into a basin formed by the inosculation of several separate mountain-crests. The ridges which bound the plateau or the basin recede so as to lose their prominence in the landscape; and until one reaches the spot where they curve together again, or encounters some new range which forms a boundary to the comparative level he has been travelling, he might easily suppose he had reached a low-land tract, and got out of the mountains altogether. There is no more appropriate name for the Rocky Mountain system than to call it a *chain*, and to no other mountain system is the term equally applicable. The traveller crossing one of its basins or plateaus is inside a link; a break in one of these links is a pass or cañon. As he goes through this break, he enters another link, belonging to another parallel and lower or higher series. Not until he descends to Salt Lake City through that tremendous system of connecting cañons which breaks through the Wahsatch, can he say that he has crossed the Rocky Mountains. In some places along the system one line of links, in some others all but one, disappear entirely; but anywhere on the United States line between New Mexico and the Great South Pass, the interoceanic traveller must cross a parallel series of them amounting to a score or more. One of these links is sometimes found to be constructed of a single line of upheaval, curving from its very origin; but the link oftenest seems to have been constructed by two separate sets of uplifts, operating at as many periods of disturbance: one, which we may call the primary, elevating the axial ranges of the Continent, whose principal trend is north and south; and the other, which we may call the secondary, operating subsequently between the parallel lines of the first uplift, with a general trend at right angles to it. The first upheaval produced a mountain region about six hundred miles wide at its widest part, with lofty valleys between its highest ranges. The second barred these valleys at intervals, turning them into the present plateaus or basins, and completing the link formation which we now see.

Though not entirely limited in its occurrence to the Rocky Mountains, this formation is strikingly characteristic of that system, and is nowhere else so constant a trait both of scenery and geology. Upon its existence depend the most important results to the future settlement of the interior. Wherever these transverse bars occur, it will instantly appear that the ease of irrigating the levels between the axial ranges is vastly enhanced. Many of them rise to a height as great as that of the longitudinal ranges; some of them are higher than those in their immediate neighborhood. They condense the moisture of the upper atmosphere currents, turn it into snow, and thus become reservoirs of irrigation—storehouses of fertility for the included levels below.

Any good map constructed after the latest surveys, but the maps of the War Department especially, will exhibit the link formation with peculiar clearness in many different portions of the range, but in none more strikingly than in the tract lying between 38° and 41° lat. N. and 105° and 107° lon. W. Within these boundaries lie three great links, whose interior basins possess a fertility of soil, a grandeur

and beauty of scenery, and a loveliness of climate which fascinated explorers long before the discovery of the precious
metals allured them to the interior of the Continent, and
which now cause them to be better known than almost any
part of the Rocky Mountain system, save that in the immediate vicinity of mines. These go by the titles of the North,
Middle, and South Parks. Their isolation from each other
is almost complete; the transverse ridge dividing the Middle from the South Park being quite impenetrable, while a
water-shed of gentler ascent and more broken lines separate
the former from the North Park. The resemblance which
these formations bear to the links of a chain strike one
instantly on looking at the map.

Not less striking is the amount of water shed into each
of the inclosed basins from the snow-ridges which form its
rim. The amount furnished by direct rain-falls is inconsiderable,—during some years almost literally nothing,—and may
be left out of the calculation. North Park will be observed to
possess a system of irrigation so complete and so bountiful
that art could scarcely improve it. Innumerable tributaries,
shed from its walls in every direction, unite to make the
North Fork of Platte, which was separated from us as we
crossed Laramie Plains only by the single range of black
hills on our left, and which, after flowing around the base
of that grand *mesa* on which the Laramie Plains lie, makes
another grand detour, and reaches the Great Plain at Fort
Laramie, a degree further north than where we left them.
Another system of tributaries combines to the southerly, and
sheds itself through a break in the southwest corner of the
link, under the name of the Blue River—contributing one
important affluent to that mysterious stream which, after

traversing one of the least known and most savage regions of the world, finally empties itself into the Gulf of California under the title of the Colorado River. A short inspection of the hydrography of this region will show us that the true division between the North and Middle Parks occurs in the line of the water-shed between the tributaries of the North Platte and those of the Blue. The latter river, it will also appear, receives the entire drainage of the Middle Park—an amount of water almost wholly derived from the snow-meltings of the tremendous ranges inclosing the park, yet equal to that of any tract of corresponding area under the moist sky of our Atlantic slope. The South Park gives birth to the South Platte and the Arkansas—both unfailing streams, though they receive no affluents of any size within a hundred miles of their source. The Cache la Poudre (through whose pass, it will be recollected, we ascended to the Laramie Plateau) is the first tributary of noticeable volume belonging to the South Platte; yet the latter stream is an abundant and rapid river long before it receives this increment, indeed in the immediate neighborhood of Denver.

Still further to the north than the Parks lie two examples of the link formation in Laramie Plains and the plateau of the Great South Pass. I have indicated, as it occurred in the order of our itinerary, the longitudinal and transverse ranges which environ the former. North of the Wind River Mountains, the transverse range which forms its lower boundary, lies an irregular plateau to which the South Pass furnishes its main western exit, of much vaster extent than those we have been considering, yet belonging equally with them to the link system. Within this link rise the Snake Fork of the Colombia (or, as we may properly say, the Columbia itself, the Snake deserving the honor of consideration as the main stream), the Yellowstone, and the Missouri. This link is the Delphi of our Continent's physical geography, the ομφαλος γης, since from it, as a nodal tract, flow the two chief streams of North America, the one sending its waters to the Gulf of Mexico, the other emptying into the North Pacific Ocean; their cradling fountains separated from each other by a narrow ridge, and their graves in the all-swallowing sea distant from each other 2,225 miles in an air line.

The link formation is exhibited everywhere in the Rocky Mountains. It is not only the type on which has been constructed every great tract of plateau or basin country like those just considered, but the traveller is constantly finding it repeated on a smaller or even a miniature scale. Thus, the famous gold-leads of Colorado lie environed on the north and south sides by walls belonging to the transverse system of uplifts; their west boundary is the giant wall of the Middle Park itself; from the west side of this wall flows a tributary to the Blue River, the Colorado, and the Gulf of California; from its eastern face comes Clear Creek, the famous stream that, after supplying the mines, runs to the Platte, and finally reaches the Gulf of Mexico: the springs of the two streams are divided by a single snow bank. "Ogden's Hole" is a tract lying in similar environment among uplifts of the Wahsatch, differing so much between themselves in point of geological period, that immediately adjoining the granite and sandstone of the main range are found much disturbed strata of the carboniferous series, which may become of immense value when the Pacific Railroad, with its locomotives, its machine-shops, and the increase of population following in its wake, shall demand and justify the development of Utah's internal resources.

In the mutual relations of the longitudinal and transverse systems of uplift lies a field of study no less important than interesting. Their relative ages; their conterminous points, or, where such cannot be made out, their tracts of transition into each other; the facts as to the existence of the precious metals in both or in one only, and if the latter, then in which one,—these are merely passing hints for a line of investigation which cannot fail to be fruitful of most valuable results.

This episode upon the link formation has its close connection with our itinerary, though I seemed to wander away from it just after leaving Sulphur Springs.

Descending from the water-shed, we had emerged through the magnificent gallery of Bridger's Pass into a tract which forms another link, not until now mentioned by me as such, of the same type as all the others, and nearly the same longitudinal system as that of the South Pass plateau. From that plateau we were now divided by the Wind River Mountains, and their continuation on a smaller scale along the Sweetwater. This transverse range formed the northern segment of our link. The Uintah range, and its continuations along the line of the Yampah, formed a corresponding segment on the south. With these the Wahsatch range inosculated on the west, and on the east the parallel longitudinal range which we had just penetrated by way of Bridger's Pass. The area thus bounded has but a single system of drainage: it contains the source of the Colorado, and every drop of its water goes to swell that stream.

Fremont's Peak may be called the western corner-stone of the wall formed by the Wind River Mountains along the south boundary of the South Pass Plateau. From the southern base of this corner-stone, and thus separated only by a single range from the drainage area which begets the Columbia, the Missouri, and the Yellowstone, springs another river, as remarkable as either of the former two, and, although lacking their commercial importance, destined to traverse an extent of country surpassed by the Missouri alone among all the rivers of North America. This stream is the Rio Colorado of the Californian Gulf, here at its fountain-head called the Green. From its springs to the mingling of its waters with the ocean, the distance measured in an air line is, for the Columbia, 650 miles; for the Colorado, 850; and for the Missouri, 1,750. We have seen that the shortest distance between the Columbia's and the Missouri's junction with the sea is 2,225 miles. By similar measurement the waters of the Green or Colorado reach the sea 1,520 miles from those of the Missouri, and 1,140 miles from those of the Columbia. Yet it is not improbable that in the neighborhood of Fremont's Peak (or about 44° lat. N. 112° lon. W.) there exist, upon an area no larger than an ordinary Eastern States' county, springs contributing to each one of these great rivers. It will be evident from the extreme tortuosity of all three, that a measurement made "as the crow flies" gives but a very inadequate idea of their length, or the vast surfaces which they lay under contribution. A juster conception of the Colorado may be acquired by observing that not only the entire area within this mighty link now surrounding us, but nearly the whole of the vast territory southward of us to the New Mexican line, and westward to the Sierra, contributes to this river all its water, with the exception of such streams as are swallowed out of sight by the "sinks" of the thirsty desert.

During the night, whenever I woke with a jerk from the feverish sleep of an Overland traveller, I could perceive the same features which characterized the landscape soon after we left the Sulphur Springs. The gray woolly-looking hills lay like the backs of a Cyclopean flock of sheep rounded in slumber and huddled as far as the eye could reach under a misty moonlight. Sometimes, though rarely, a wretched cedar, the victim of misplaced confidence, had established itself in a chink to struggle for life with sage brash and greasewood; but these latter and the gramma-grass ruled the arid region, dressing it out in one broad melancholy Quaker monotone which even the moon was not able to etherealize. The Florida moss is exquisitely beautiful in moonlight; indeed, when it festoons a circle of noble old live-oaks, it will make out of noonday a moonlight of its own for one inside the pavilion, by filtering the yellow glare through itself, and turning it to silver; but there one has at least some bright green for a contrast, and the moss, moreover, in its shape is graceful beyond all flattery. Fancy a world of moss and nothing else; fancy that moss formed like a dry haycock stuck raggedly on a gnarled stump three feet high; then you will have this sage brush, and a landscape which Genius itself could not beautify.

Fifty-one miles of rolling country, broken by nothing remarkable in the way either of scene or adventure, brought us about 8 A. M. to a station called La Clede. Upon consulting our itinerary we found that during the night we had passed our half-way mark between the Missouri and our California terminus at Placerville. For the benefit of future travellers I will state that this midway point occurred just half a mile west of the Duck Lake Station. We were now 983 miles from our journey's beginning, 930 from its end, and 272 from Salt Lake City.

While we were changing horses at La Clede, we loaded our fowling-pieces, and, after a walk of some forty rods into the sage brush, succeeded in starting up a flock of sage-fowl, and bagged three. They were in fine plump condition, but we had no desire to hazard the experiment of roast chicken with wormwood, even had there been time to stop and cook our game. Accordingly, we set about preserving the only part valuable to science, namely, the skins, leaving the meat for the coyotes. In this instance, as one among many, we had to return sincere thanks to Ben Holladay and Mr. Otis his superintendent, for the kindness shown us by an extension of courtesies in general, and an open letter in particular, calling on the drivers to halt half an hour at a time whenever we wished it to facilitate our scientific examinations and notes, the taking of sketches, and the collection and preparation of specimens. By the time our leave to halt was exhausted we had succeeded in getting a clean pair of skins (an adult cock and hen), without making a tear or losing a feather. Having rubbed them thoroughly with arsenical soap, we folded them as neatly as possible, tied them up in an India rubber bag, and stowed them under our seats, where they rode very comfortably to us as well as safely to themselves, until we reached California. The air of the Plains and Mountains is so dry and free from ozone that a nicely cleaned skin would run but little risk of becoming offensive even without the soap; but neither soap nor India rubber demand much room; and when a specimen is as rare as one of these birds, which it requires a journey into the very heart of a continent to get, every precaution should be taken. Before we left Denver, I had employed a rainy afternoon in the manufacture of bags for the preservation of delicate specimens, both botanical and zoölogical; using the India rubber cloth with which we had provided ourselves in New York, of a quality used for the lighter description of water-proof capes, and in quantity amounting to twelve yards. When I bought it, I feared that I was a little finical, and perhaps resembled those Cockney travellers who take marmalade and folding bath-tubs with them across the Sahara; but in fact it proved one of the most remunerative purchases of our outfit. It served us as many valuable turns as it does citizens who tarry at home. It rolled into very small compass, scarcely exceeding an umbrella in bulk, and was in constant requisition. It covered note-books and sketch-books when we were fording streams which splashed us from head to foot; it made excellent surtouts for leather rifle-covers; and it was invaluable as an air and water tight envelope to some plants which are equally ruined by soaking or desiccation. Negatively as well as affirmatively I afterward learned how to appreciate it, when it had all been used up, and I was compelled to expose one of the most gorgeous collections of Lepidoptera I ever saw in any cabinet to the searching, dry atmosphere of a California midsummer, with no protection but a cedar box; on opening which I found a few mummied bodies, minus legs, antennae, and siphons, together with a little heap of iridescent powder to represent what had once been rainbow banners, court-suits for the pages of Queen Titania; animated sweet-pea blossoms from Paradise: or if you *will* have the vernacular, butterflies' wings! Every collector of specimens in a wild country needs India rubber bags; and everybody with the least "gumption," and a pair of pocket-scissors or a penknife, can make them. I have made many a one whose adhesiveness proved perfectly satisfactory, simply by scraping away the cotton lining of the surface I wished to join, breathing on them and pressing them firmly together. A still closer and more artistic joint may be made with a special glue sold at the stores for that purpose, but which anybody can imitate by preparing a viscid solution (a little thicker than the thickest molasses) of pure gum caoutchouc in ether or sulphide of carbon. If you can carry this with the certainty of not having it spill out, it will prove very convenient It sticks like pitch, and, as its solvents are not always at hand, may make a dreadful mess of clothes, books, or papers; though I have carried it thousands of miles without an accident. It should be kept in a box with a screw cover.

During the day I had frequent occasion to regret the hurried rate at which our limited time compelled us to pass through this region. The area we traversed had evidently been the scene of frequent and varied geological disturbances. The strata which out-cropped among the round gray hills were of widely different lithological characters and widely separated periods. The hydrographic plan of the region was simple enough, having reference, as I have said, to the single drainage system of Colorado (Green) River. We passed, however, indications of a former entirely different distribution of the affluents; wide areas of water-rolled pebbles, sterile as a quarry, and precipitous cliffs guarding the plainly defined bed of a river which had once rolled at their base. Near the station of Rock Point, in a friable, ferruginous sandstone, I discovered well preserved casts and some fossil fragments of Ostracidæ which I referred to *Gryphæa*, and, in another bed of shaly texture, fragments of what I supposed to be an *Inoceramus*. I believe that a special survey of this entire link would abundantly repay the geologist. The precipitous line of river bluffs which marked the dry bottom had an extent of several miles, and were in some places as high as the Palisades of the Hudson. I much regretted having no time to go to them, but at the distance of about a mile and a half (our nearest approach) they appeared to belong to a sandstone period, probably of the cretaceous era. All day the same desolation marked the Flora of the landscape; greasewood, artemisia, and an occasional stinted cedar being the only shrubby vegetation.

On the levels strewn with water-worn pebbles I observed that the surface was changing almost hourly under the operation of the winds and sand. Within a few minutes I observed several sand dunes constructed, and several others removed,—both classes being cones of several feet in height. Several times we passed remarkable indications of the fact that at no very remote period, possibly since the commencement of white immigration to this region, the buffalo has existed on this side of the Rocky Mountain water-shed. At present his furthest range reaches only within the lower line of ridges on the eastern slope of the system,—individuals of the tribe being occasionally shot in the cañons of Colorado, but none having been known by the present inhabitants to pass the first snow-range. Several old hunters and trackers of large experience, whose acquaintance I formed in Colorado, believed in the existence of a separate species of bison, peculiar to the mountains, characterized by greater size than the Plains animal, and still further differing from those congeners in their stationary habits, remaining in the mountain fastnesses all the year round, instead of emigrating southward with the approach of winter. Furthermore, the habits of this supposed species were solitary. They were never met in herds, and in couples only during the marital season. At one time I was almost led by the accounts which I received into the belief that the animal described by hunters who had killed specimens in the range, was neither more nor less than a stray from that exceedingly interesting family which finds its usual habitat in the barrens of a much more northerly portion of our Continent; namely, that connecting link between the Bovidæ (already, as represented by the bison, manifesting a wide departure from the typical bull in this same direction) and the sheep (as compromised toward the bison in the "Bighorn"), the musk-ox, or *Ovibos moschatus*. Remains of this animal have been found in tertiary beds of the Continent much further south than Denver; but having no specimens, and only an unscientific report to proceed upon, I was obliged to abandon my hypothesis in view of the fact that no living individual has been found within the memory of man further south than 60° lat N. I know of no country where a given type of animals has its divisions shaded into each other by so complete a series of delicate gradations as prevails among the hollow-horned ruminants of North America, taking them in their order from the domestic sheep to the domestic cow, through the bighorn, the ovibos, and the bison. Indeed, either of these three suggests one type nearly as much as another.

The indications of the bison's former passage of the Rocky Mountains lie strewn over a wide area. In several places along our route within the Green River link, I observed skulls of this tribe in excellent preservation. In some instances the horns were as entire as on the day that the animal was killed; the apices being only slightly rounded. Some of them were in the argillaceous deposit of overflows from the tributaries of the Green; others projected out of sand dunes; and several lay entirely exposed to sight on the denuded and water-worn pebbles of the wide tract above referred to.

The fact of our gradual approach to Salt Lake was now indicated increasingly at every stage of our progress. We found in every spring the evidence of a former submersion of this entire tract beneath the waters of a stagnant inland sea. Salt Lake remains as the last vestige of a period when the vast estuary which set northwesterly from the present boundaries of the Gulf of Mexico to the plateau of Snake River, was caught by a sudden upheaval of transverse ranges which forever shut it up from its connection with tide-water, and cut it up, by a series of colossal walls or dams, into a number of minor saline lakes, in all respects but size exactly corresponding to the present Great Salt Lake of Utah. The theory of this formation, fortunately for the student, has a perfect paradigm in that remarkable reservoir; and in the proper place I shall show how admirably, yet minutely, it explains itself and many neighboring tracts, which, but for its survival from the period when it was only one of many, might prove obstinate problems to the geologist and physical geographer.

At Rock Point we encountered, for the first time since leaving the Nebraska Plains, what in this region and at this season was an unusual phenomenon, a drenching shower of rain. I would have been glad to have caught some of the sky's bounty, had any receptacle been at hand, for the spring water found at long intervals on our route was exceedingly nauseous. The alkaline water on the eastern side of the mountains was bad enough, but this was many grades beyond. Much of the soda and potash in the former was drawn from vast beds of feldspar, a mineral which seems in this climate peculiarly susceptible to decomposition, and in many places may be seen rotting out of the granite formations into an impalpable powder. The mineral constituents of the springs we now encountered were much more varied and abundant, embracing chloride of sodium, sulphur and sulphide of hydrogen, iron in the form of chromate and peroxide, carbonates of potash and soda, sometimes associated with bromine and iodine. The source of these was no contemporary decomposition, but the beds deposited through an unmeasured period by stagnant bodies of salt water, cut off from all means of escape save evaporation and a gradual deposit from a super-saturated solution.

The night after leaving Rock Point was the wildest in which I ever travelled. The heavens were pitchy black, except in patches where now and then the moon succeeded in struggling through a thinner layer of clouds to flash on us an instantaneous view of our horrible surroundings, drowning in the midnight sea directly after, and leaving us to a worse mystery and dread. The wind blew from every point in the compass, and would have howled had there been anything to howl in, but trees there were none. Our way wound over a succession of bare, rocky ridges, like the perilous reefs of a sea suddenly drained dry. Some of these were two or three hundred feet above the general level, and as nearly perpendicular as they could be consistently with offering any possible foothold and passage to our horses. This part of the Overland road abundantly deserves its reputation of being the worst between the Missouri and Washoe. Like the boy in the song, I did not dare to sleep, and went, metaphorically, to walk the deck with the pilot. Bracing my feet against the dash-board, I saw that remarkable man at my side put his six-horse team (we were obliged to take an extra pair for this part of the route) over precipices where I should as soon have thought of driving over a well-curb. Quintus Curtius at $50 a month! Even he acknowledged that he never drove this stage without expecting to break his neck. Frequently the valleys into which we dove were so narrow and abrupt (I say "valleys," though they were mere crevices of dislocation in perfectly bare rock) that our leaders were clawing their way up the slippery sandstone ledges, while ourselves, our wheelers, and the middle team were rushing headlong with the weight of the wagon almost tumbling on them bodily. In one such place the descent was full sixty feet, with a 45° incline; and the road up the opposite wall of the chasm instead of lying in line with that we were descending, turned abruptly to one side nearly a full quadrant to avoid a precipice tenfold worse than that down which we were plunging. Talk of steeple-chases! A good horseman on his own trusty horse knows only the name of fear before any leap short of the eaves of a house; but cooped up with six in a box, he might well turn pale and be no coward. Save me henceforth from a steeple-chase in a wagon!

Soon after daylight broke we reached the Green River. The approach to it was through a picturesque cañon walled by perpendicular crags of red sandstone five or six hundred feet high. This formation was several miles in length, and abutted boldly upon the river, where its face was weathered into remarkable imitations of sculpture similar to that of the Stone-Calvin Terrace, down whose giant staircase we had carefully crept to the last crossing of the Platte. At every turn some colossal profile of Indian, sphinx, helmeted warrior, or frowning Afrite projected from an outstanding vertical ledge. Often as I have had to refer to these strange mimicries of Nature's own carving, I cannot refrain from saying here that they always took us by surprise; and that for variety and number of profiles, no formation which we anywhere found marked by these strange freaks surpassed the present one.

A moment's glance at the Green River reveals the reason of its name, although its tinge tends rather toward the olive than to that intense beryl shade which characterizes the waters of the Niagara and Columbia Rivers. We intersected it at a distance from its source (following its sinuosities) of about 125 miles; and, although we had no means of measuring it accurately, I think that its breadth at this point cannot much exceed eighty yards. Its banks were from twenty-five to forty feet higher than its present water level, so that its bed cannot vary laterally to any great extent with drought or snow-melting.

We were ferried across here by the same ingenious apparatus as that which passed us over the Platte, though the current is rather more sluggish than that stream's, and the trips necessarily longer. The river at this season apparently averages ten feet in depth at mid-stream, though its bottom is very irregular, abounding in sliding clay and quicksand, which vary the depth from time to time. While the horses were changing, I had a chance to test the character of its bed. As the gastronomer and commissary of the party, I had measured out our rations of canned sweet corn and tomatoes, and intrusted them for preparation to a woman at the station-house who had gained my confidence by her wholesome tidy look, no less than the assertion that she had just arrived here from the *East*, (Fort Leavenworth!) and was well acquainted with that kind of victuals. While breakfast was preparing under her auspices, I strolled a short distance down the river in search of any specimens that might offer. Scrambling down the bank in one place, I saw what seemed a firm promontory of hard-baked clay stretching out several feet from the base of the bolder river wall, and just beyond its point a lizard-like reptile, which might be the very new Siredon by whose discovery I was waiting to distinguish myself. Fortunately fame has not so much fascination for me as a dry skin, to say nothing of a live one, so I felt my ground with one foot fast. The promontory proved to be of the consistency of soft soap, my mere experimental pressure bogging my boot in it nearly up to the knee; and when for the sake of future travellers possibly with less experience, together with a just vengeance for the dirty trick it had well-nigh played me, I gave it a few vigorous kicks at its junction with the bank, it fell of, and dissolved away into a sort of milky emulsion, which went down with the current like so much suds. It was the finest argillaceous silt I ever saw assuming coherency, and I saw several other instances of the same formation on tributaries of the same stream. Emigrants lose many cattle every year in this deceitful ooze, the poor creatures running into it mad with thirst after a long day's drive over a springless tract, or, what is still worse, a tract whose springs are alkaline and saline. Even the more experienced cattle of permanent settlers along the banks of similar streams are frequently betrayed by the substantial look of the slough; and the boldness of the true margin, together with the rapidity of the current, renders it almost an impossibility to save them. I found here an excellent illustration of the process which has preserved for us so many elephants of the tertiary and earlier

Adamic ages. I have no doubt that an industrious overhauling of all the plainly marked river beds which exist in this region at the foot of palisades whose base has not been wet for centuries would abundantly repay the palæontologist, furnish to cabinets the finest collections in the word, not only of duplicates to the extinct specimens already known, but possibly of species entirely new to science, and settle the now very uncertain original boundaries of the entire tribe of American ruminants. Yet more: it might throw much light on the very curious fact yearly receiving new illustrations, that the American Fauna is chronologically far in the rear of that belonging to the Old World. The eminent entomologist. Dr. Loew of Meseritz, in Prussia, has discovered that a number of very singular and interesting insects belonging to the palæontology of Europe, and immemorially extinct there, exist as living species in our North American forests. It may not be straining the analogy too far to conjecture that higher tribes than the Diptera found in amber, existed on this Continent long after they had become obsolete in the other; even, for example, that the gigantic saurians of the Jurassic survived into our tertiary, and that tertiary pachyderms of Europe, or yet undiscovered congeners of theirs, roved the emerging lacustrine beds, and got bogged in the treacherous fluviatile silt of our earlier Adamic period. The unavoidable rapidity of my journey through this most interesting tract, and my consequent inability to offer anything better than hints for the thorough workman who shall come after me when a Pacific Railroad insures the safe transport of specimens, and puts the time of explorers entirely at their own disposal, must save from scientific contempt these crude and unsupported suggestions.

Getting back to breakfast, I found that my confidence had not been misplaced. The nice, tidy Eastern woman from Leavenworth had done full justice to our provisions, and added further blessedness to the repast by the first bowl of rich fresh milk and dish of new-laid eggs we had tasted since leaving Denver. While we were breakfasting with a relish, one of our fellow-passengers at the same board vouchsafed a remark about the Mormons, to the effect that we were rapidly nearing their kingdom, with a little half-jocose warning against the danger of having one's throat cut. A sunburnt, taciturn young man, who apparently belonged at the station as a "herder," or stable-helper, looked up furtively from under a pair of shaggy black eyebrows, took the speaker in with a quick but comprehensive glance, and, without having been noticed by more than one besides myself, proceeded impassively with his ham and eggs. After we rose from the table, and paid our dollar a head for our really excellent breakfast (the price invariably charged us since we entered the Mountains, without regard to the large portion of every meal furnished from our own private stores, and not exorbitant considering the immense distance which every staple article has to be hauled by the Overland supply wagons) we strolled out to the corral, and got into conversation with our next driver. Our jocular fellow-passenger was nearer "the kingdom" than he knew. We were *in* Utah. Our maps had not indicated the last few miles of the route by which we had come to Green River, and we had crossed the stream at a point different from our previous calculation; in other words, near the point of its intersection with the one hundred and tenth parallel, where it coincides with the eastern boundary line of Utah. I had not expected to recognize Utah

by any unerring sign; to know when I came to it by a polygamistic flavor in the atmosphere; but I own that the sensation
of entering Mormondom without knowing it was somewhat singular. My own party were all too old travellers to
have been in any danger of making such an unguarded self-
committal as that of our fellow-passenger at the breakfast
table, but for many reasons we felt securer for the knowledge
where we were.

"Never been in Utah afore, I reckon?" said the driver half
interrogatively.

"No nearer than the Wind River Mountains."

"They don't have many o' them fellows up there?"

"What fellows?"

"Why, these here Mormons."

There was a slighting tone in his voice which we could not
fail to recognize as an assumption. If he had meant to speak
disparagingly out of a sincere heart, he was too old a hand to
select such entire strangers for his confidants. Fortunately we
were no younger, and "*smoked*" him at once without showing
that we did. He was throwing out feelers.

"You don't seem to like them much, judging from your
tone," said I. "That's unfortunate, seeing you have to drive
thirty or forty miles every day in their country. But you just
use them well, and go you own way quietly,—you'll never
get anything but good treatment from them. If you're a new
hand here, as I should judge you are, take an old traveller's
advice, and always think half a dozen times before you speak
once. If you should happen to be overheard talking about
Mormons in such a tone by that that young man with the
bushy eyebrows who sat opposite me at breakfast, you'd
be spotted at once, and it might make no end of trouble

for you all along the road. You know whom I mean—that brown-complexioned young Mormon: what's his name?"

We looked him in the face without flinching; he looked at both of us with undisguised perplexity, and, as I put the question, answered involuntarily,—

"Cowperthwaite! Well—why—why—how did you know he was a Mormon?"

"D'ye remember how the girl knew her father? Jest as *easy!* How do I know *you* are one? The same way."

"Well, *that's* so! No use o' concealin' on it as I know. I ain't ashamed o't—, *you* bet! But d—d if you ain't a queer 'un? You beat my time, anyhow. Wall, I'm glad to see you're so friendly—give us yer hand."

"We're friends to everybody that's civil and obliging—that goes straight ahead minding his own business well, and letting other people mind theirs. That's the only way to get on in this world, driver."

This colloquy not only afforded us the amusement of beating a man at his own game, but resulted in the greatest convenience to us practically. Without duplicity or the need of insuring ourselves against all risk by exaggerated professions of good-will to every new acquaintance we were brought into contact with, we were immediately crossed off the list of *suspects*, and had no further anxiety regarding jealous misconstruction or disagreeable espionage. We took an early occasion to warn our incautious fellow-passenger, a little Swiss, who was going out to Washoe to form a watchmaking partnership with a brother who had preceded him to this country by several years. When he heard he had got into Utah without knowing it, his knees smote together at the memory of the morning's indiscretion; his jolly round face paled to the hue of the Jungfrau summit; his broken English deserted him entirely, and he fell back on his French.

"Mon Dieu! ce n'était qu'une de mes petites plaisanteries! seulement ça,—seulement, *seulement*—parole d'honneur! Je n'ai point de prejugés, moi! Toute ma famille, nous sommes francs-penseurs—mon frère ainé est Voltairien. Ventrebleu! un des plus preéminens! Je suis Philosophe,—je ne crois rien de tout. Adolphe (c'est notre cadet là), il n'a que vingt ans et ses liaisons montent jusqu'à deux fois ce numerò! il est vrai libertin—vrai Don Giovanni! Moi je n'ai point de prejugés—quant aux Mormons, de mon enfance j'ai éprouvé, pour ces braves gens des sentimens les plus respec- teuses, les plus affectionées. Que voulez-vous? Une femme, deux femmes, trois, quatre, cinq, cent, mil—c'est égal! Mais quoi! Si je resterais à Sâlt-Lac—je ne me gênerais pas par l'arithmetique—je me marierais, je vous le jure! deux fois par mois—régulièr-r-r-ement!"

I now had to caution him against error in the opposite direction, lest, in singing the praises of polygamy, he should rush into such burlesque as to bring himself into worse sus- picion. I could see, at succeeding stations along the road, that the beetle-browed young man had not failed to send his "charàcter" ahead of him. He was eyed sharply; but as we took him to a certain extent under the wing of our party, he escaped trouble,—the excuse that he was a Frenchman, and ignorant of our free institutions (from bigamy upward), also procuring him a certain amount of clemency. A more thor- oughly frightened man I never saw in my life. His idea of a Mormon was Dantesque in its horror—an elaborate incarna- tion of all the choicest varieties of atrocious cruelty, ingenious dishonesty, blasphemous impiety, satyrian immodesty, and quintessential wickedness, loved, sought after, practiced for its own dear, radical, and unassisted sake; a compound of three parts Balfour of Burley, a dozen of some bandit chieftain of the Abruzzi, ten of Autolycus, fifty of Caligula, five hundred of Silenus, and the remaining equivalents in a scale of thousands belonging to the old original Sathanas himself. Seven hundred miles of horse-travel through ninety-six thousand monsters compounded after formula! fancy the agony of a poor little Swiss who had that before him, with half his worldly fortune in French Louis-d'or galling his ribs in a sort of India rubber pack-saddle (Paris patent), and the other half in San Francisco credits, covered with sheets also of rubber, and sewed up within the lining of his coat! I may forget him if I leave his conclusion to fall into its proper chronology; so I will skip ahead with him, and give him his definite dismissal in a few words.

Having come to regard our protection as his only salvation, he altered his original plan of going on to Washoe night and day, *sans arrête*, and stayed over with us during the time we spent in Brigham's capital.

We resumed our journey at the peril of our lives, the whole Desert at that time reeking with massacre. Here our horrors began. For three hundred miles we rode expecting death in every cañon. But the Indian had no terrors for poor little Foiedelis. The stoutest hearts that beat in *our* breasts were heavy as lead, and we thought a great deal of our mothers and sisters and wives. But the face of Foiedelis, with every league that put Salt Lake further behind, grew more and more like a wilted pippin under an exhausted receiver. We reached Ruby Valley one afternoon at sundown. We climbed from the military post at that point through Hastings' Pass, up the tremendous eastern slope of the first range of the Humboldt Mountains. It was after midnight when our last panting relay stopped to breathe on the summit round of that wonderful scaling ladder of the Titans. Under the unflickering stars of that vaporless upper firmament we seemed unbosomed, purged of all care,— so close to them that their measureless quiet and endurance looked clear down into us, read us, knew us, soothed us like children who had come home to them from prodigal wanderings in the desert of the world below. Set the White Mountains there! the flattered, the boasted of the East. The star-shadows of our lower ridge would eclipse them; taken into the shelter of a sublimity which merged them with its flanking foot-hills, they would be obliterated as independent existences, yet have glory enough in swelling a grandeur by which it is no shame to be conquered. From this height of vision we seemed to see half a world—the globe around and down to its very girdle. It was the grandest night-sight I ever saw in nature. We had well-nigh forgotten the horrors out of which we had now climbed forever. Our hearts seemed to beat close against the everlasting youth of the heavens; we could not think of the imminent slaughter skulking with us three days ago through steppes of dazzling, blistering sand and gnarled, funereal wormwood; probable slaughter yesterday; possible slaughter all day long to-day. Life, life, everlasting life, fresh distilled for our first breathing, right out of the loving heaven itself; dew from the nectaries of amaranth and asphodel, to wipe from the anxious wrinkles of heart and brow the dust which the sirocco had powdered on us from the leaves of the wormwood.

But, lest we should forget devout thanksgiving in the levity of mere selfish safety and boastful joy, sudden reminders of the greatness of our salvation catch our eyes as we bend them eastward over the night-empurpled immensity of the far-down desert. Not meant as such reminders—ah, no! though the grateful heart turns all evilest things out of their evilest purpose into goodness and blessing, as the sun melts the very offal of the world into mother liquor for precious crystals and life-blood for flowers of Eden. The Goshoot devils, who have been dogging our steps with the arrow and tomahawk, are lighting up their signal fires on the black porphyry crags which rise from the floor of the desert. Like eyes of baffled fiends, they wink up at us out of the dark, opening, one after the other, till more than a score gleam balefully between our mighty mountain citadel and the far horizon. But we are forever out of the demons' clutches. We have passed the hostile boundary, we have climbed the tremendous barrier, and the key to our stronghold is held by a sturdy garrison of Californians, thousands of feet below in the Ruby Valley post. Each man rejoices after his temperament: one thanks God quietly; another utters a deep sigh of relief as for the first time in days he slings his rifle over his head, and shuts his eyes to sleep; another whirls his slouch about his head, breaking into cheers and song. Only Foiedelis remains stolid amid the general joy. Somebody has told him that he is not yet out of Utah, though he is out of the Goshoots. He will not halloo till he gets out of the woods. So he waits. When the day dawns,—when we cross the second ridge, go through Chokup Pass, are at once over the 116th parallel and the Nevada line,—then our little Switzer has his own private jubilee in his own original way. While we stop to change horses he dances a *pas-seul*, which fills a family of Digger Indians, pensioning on the station-keeper, with admiration and dismay; he snaps his fingers; he shakes his fist to the eastward in sublime menace to a whole Territory at once; and finally, having expended the bottled feelings of the last three weeks, he rejoins us, wiping the perspiration from his face with a handkerchief.

The fact of meeting Mormons on the instant of stepping foot into the Territory did not surprise us, for we had by no means waited so long as this to make their first acquaintance on the Overland road. They are strewn all along from the Missouri River to San Francisco. Some of them are avowed, others known only to the initiated, others, undoubtedly not known at all. A Mormon and his wife formerly kept the station at Liberty Farm, one hundred and ninety-three miles west of Atchison. Several of them I have known among drivers, numbers among stable-helpers and stock-tenders. They are, so far as I know, unblamable in the discharge of their duties; in fact, they must attend to their business as well as anybody obtainable for their places, or they would not be kept twenty-four hours under the strict regime of Ben Holladay. None of them are out of Utah in disgrace; they keep up their relations with the Church government as closely as ever. They are detailed to duty on the Church's behalf. Their enemies call them by the invidious name of spies. It is certainly the case, that, by some means or other, nothing happens along the great avenues to Salt Lake, of which Brigham Young does not get the earliest advices. He is never surprised at the arrival of any person in his capital. Long before your arrival is announced in the "Deseret News," he has a memorandum of your name, your residence, your appearance, your circumstances, your purpose in coming to Utah, your intended length of stay there, and (unless you are enough of an old traveller to know "a pump" at first sight,

and keep your likes and dislikes to yourself in all promiscuous companies) your animus towards Mormonism, your
value as an ally, and the importance of providing against you,
or propitiating you if you are a foe. The secret police system
of France was never more efficient than Brigham Young's;
and, considering the much vaster territory that lies under
his organized espionage, I might be justified in saying that
in efficiency none ever equaled his. As a ruler of men, I think
the earth has scarcely had his peer. The "one-man power"
system is hastening towards its final extinction, but its last
days are its greatest. It dies giving birth to two of its grandest
examplars in a single age—Louis Napoleon and Brigham
Young. I do not think the grandson of the Creole a match
for the Ontario County ploughboy. Brigham Young is a religious fanatic; Napoleon has no enthusiasm of any sort; but
I believe that the fanatic has the cooler business head. He
would never have sent an expedition to Mexico. He may
commit crimes, but he does not "do what is worse, make
blunders."

After leaving Green River, we continued our way across a
country of the same sterile aspect as that described the day
before. The occurrence of extensive level tracts, covered with
water-worn pebbles, still testified to the former existence of
much larger bodies of water that are now compressed into
the numerous but narrow tributaries of the Green. The temperature was truly delightful, standing not far from 70° F.
all day long, with a light breeze from the northwest which
we found very pleasant, except in the vicinity of sand dunes,
where its addition of powder to our toilet could have been
spared. We saw numerous sage-fowl during the day, as tame
as barnyard turkeys; but having secured all the specimens

we needed, and having no idea of adding them to our larder, had no motive for shooting them. I deeply regret the impossibility of having taken a number of them alive to the States with me on my return. They would make a most valuable addition to our poultry yards, and I can see not the slightest obstacle to their domestication.

About four o'clock in the afternoon we suddenly came upon one of the grandest marvels which Nature has given to human admiration on this Continent. This is "The Church Buttes."

I have had frequent occasion in these pages to refer to that remarkable class of formations which, though not entirely absent from the scenery of our Atlantic slope, exist in so few instances (as the Catskill, Franconia, and Niagara Profile Rocks) that they have never attracted more than passing attention; while, throughout the savage interior of the Continent, they have attained the same neglect by the opposite reason of their very frequency. We go out of our way to lavish raptures upon the temples of Yucatan, the mausolea of Dongola, Nubia, and Petrea, the Sphinx, and the Cave of Elephanta, while through-out our own mountain fastnesses and trackless plains exist ruins of architecture and statuary not one whit behind the foreign remains of forty centuries in power of execution, and far vaster in respect to age and sixe. At every change of position as we came through the sandstone cañon to the Green River this same morning, the giant buttresses of red sandstone at one side showed some new sculpture which lacked nothing to compete with the half-reliefs of the kings whose slumber was broken by Layard, or the front-faced colossi carved on the African ruins. Strong, stern, characteristic faces were there; no feature was missing;

no imagination was needed to eke out their details. Rather was there needed an imagination of the means by which nature mimicked art after such faithful fashion, or indeed, at first glance, of the possibility that it could be unassisted nature at all.

The Church Buttes surpass all natural feats of this order which I have ever seen in my life, even that wonderful succession of palaces, temples, and cemeteries between Monument Creek and the foot of Pike's Peak. I have often been asked why they had never been spoken of in such extravagant terms before I wrote of them. The reasons are: because the hardy pioneers who live among the wonders of this Continent get hardened to them by familiarity; because, even if they remained impressible, they have too much stern matter of fact in their existence (and for a generation to come will have) to give them time for the cultivation of the æsthetic; because this class does not, as a usual thing, correspond with magazines and journals; because the trail which runs by Church Buttes is not the one followed by the vast majority of travellers; and because most of those who do pass them are night-and-day men, who spend most of their time in sleeping between the Missouri and Washoe.

Twenty-one miles east of Fort Bridger, a line of sand and sandstone bluffs which for the last hour had been seen skirting our southern horizon at the distance of a league, suddenly curved toward us, sending out in a nearly due-north direction a narrow spur, at whose extremity, and abutting upon our tracks rose the mighty mass of which, with a foregoing sense of inadequacy, I must now try to convey some idea. The impression produced by the Church Buttes upon one standing about fifty yards from their façade (the best

THE HEART OF THE CONTINENT

distance for attaining the perfect harmony of their effect) is
that of a stupendous cathedral or basilica, admirable for the
breadth and dignity of its design, and the absolute symmetry
of its proportions, built after a new style of architecture, as
justly deserving a place among the most strongly individualized orders of the art and science as the pure Greek of
the Parthenon or the Gothic of Salisbury Cathedral. Almost
simultaneously we exclaimed, "O that all our American
architects could see this marvelous model!" for we irresistibly felt that here were the suggestions for an order as fresh
and original as comported with the virgin fields and forests,
life and energy, spirit and material of the New World. Were
I an architect, I should to-morrow be on my way to spend
a year, if need be, in the study of the Church Buttes; not
coming away till I had made myself master of every line in
the structure, and arrived at the method of repeating it in
accordance with the limitations of stone and mortar and the
principles conditioning habitable structure. The first temple
of art, science, or religion which I constructed upon this plan
in New York would be that city's greatest ornament, and
the guarantee of my immortality on the roll of the civilized
world's artistic benefactors. If this assertion seem vainglori-
ous, let it be remembered that it is also hypothetical; for in
the great temple, at whose holiest holy minister Vaux, and
Mould, and Wight, and Gambrill, I worship in the Gentiles'
court,—loving the art dearly, but afar; also that were I an
architect, and successful as my hypotheses, the praise would
belong not to me, but to the nature I had humbly studied.
With these explanations I shall be granted the mere amateur's license to commit purely technical blunders, and make
an occasional misuse of names.

The ground-plan of the Church Buttes Cathedral deviates in a slight degree from the circular contour, being a quatre-foil whose four component curves differ very little in their elements, but meet each other at internal angles sufficiently acute to give an impression of the cruciform outline proper to Christian architecture. The nave and transept find their places here, though the curved have been substituted for the right-lined exterior.

Upon this base-line the body of the Cathedral rises to a height of about three hundred feet (I give the dimensions approximately, for the reason that the half-hour conceded to our halt was necessarily consumed, as indeed a hundred times that period might have been, in familiarizing ourselves with the artistic proportions and scientific composition of the magnificent mass. A few hasty sketches, or memoranda of its impression on us at different elevations, were all that we had time for, anything like an accurate trigonometrical observation being quite out of the question. I have taken care that my estimates understate the facts where they err at all.) The body of the structure consists of a perpendicular wall following (in cross sections) the curves of the base-line, braced at intervals of astonishing equality by massive buttresses of the same altitude as itself. At the proper distance for a comprehensive view, these buttresses apparently differ from each other in size and shape scarcely more than if they had been erected upon one single and uniform plan. The space between the buttresses further carries out the minute resemblance to the planned offspring of a human intellect, by exhibiting in several places the appearance of deep, arched recesses, which it needs but little imagination to regard as windows or niches for the reception of statuary.

I hardly dare to add the assertion that in several of these niches the statues for which they seem the intended receptacles actually exist, and are by no means the least startling elements in a mimicry which descends to the minutest details of its working pattern. Had not my travelling companions (some of whom never in their lives rode a fantasy without curb and snaffle) noticed these images, and called my attention to their striking enhancement of the *vraisemblance* of the structure,—this, too, long before I could make up my mind to speak of them at the risk of having my lively imagination cast in my teeth,—I should hesitate to refer to them in these pages, lest the incredulous reader, whose prosecution of acquaintance with mouldy European ruins has denied him the time to visit nature's immortal temples in the heart of his own Continent, should say, "Well! *this* is going a little too far." Let me hasten to save my credit by recording one break in the continuity of the imitation. The figures, which at the proper focal distance for a harmonious view of the *tout-ensemeble* appear absolutely statuesque, are in no case entirely detached from the wall, but, on close approach, are perceived to be irregular knobs and projections from its surface. Fortunately for the Church Buttes! If they could be moved, some American Turk would have long ago split them in pieces to make commemorative paper-weights when he returned from his journey; some Lord Elgin or Barnum would have long ere this had them labeled on the shelves of his museum. As a further concession to incredulity, let me add that although their statue-like appearance at the proper point of view is most wonderful, Nature does not tax our astonishment by the still more elaborate consistency of making them religious in their sentiment like the temple

which they adorn. She acts as if her mighty effort of architecture (as happens so sadly often in other fields worked by
genius) had toppled down her reason just as she came to the
final adornment of her nobly realized conception. Her over-
strained intellect became ungeared just as she grasped the
chisel which was to people her niches with patriarchs and
saints, prophets, apostles, martyrs, cherubim, and grown-up
angels.

To return to the architectural part of the subject. The superstructure resting on the buttresses consisted of two domes,
one superimposed upon the other; the upper inclosing the
crown of the lower, and descending over it to the extent of
about one third its height. Each of these domes was surrounded by a series of butments proportioned to their size,
and seeming the diminished continuations of those about
the body of the edifice below. The school of architects which
makes truth rather than beauty the guide of the builder, and
introduces conscience into the arena of art, will cavil at the
proposal to imitate any such arrangement, on the ground that
these buttresses could have no necessary office in sustaining
the domes, and are therefore false. I am not going to introduce any discussion of this subject into these pages. They
are too limited to hold one of the widest quarrels of modern
times. I can only say that the effect of breaking up the domes
by these obviously unnecessary buttress-like projections was
very beautiful. Together the domes were somewhat higher
than the lower structure, and made a total altitude of about
seven hundred feet.

I have been thus minute, because in no other way could I
convey to my readers the effect produced by this wonderful
structure. It is not intended, I hardly need say, to convey the

impression that a man with a microscope would discover the absolute mathematical lines of a structure such as I have described, should he attempt to verify me by passing his face over the entire surface of the Church Buttes. What I assert is that at the distance of from fifty to a hundred yards, the effect of such a structure is produced, with very little assistance from imagination.

Coming upon the formation in the wild heart of the Continent, no human society near you save nomads like yourself, your irresistible feeling (if any feeling you have for either nature or art) must be one of silent, awe-struck wonder. The imitation of man's work by nature always arouses such a feeling. Before reaching here, you will have felt it, roving the green bottoms of the Republican, and suddenly coming upon lovely parks whose floor of fresh turf seem newly dismissed from the lawn-shears of the gardener; whose stately elms, pecans, and cotton-woods were disposed in such graceful groups and leaf-arched avenues that but for their age Downing himself might have set them; whose well defined paths, entirely free from undergrowth, so symmetrical and so convenient in their direction and arrangement, you can hardly credit to the water-seeking elk and buffalo. At every step of your way among the Colorado foot-hills, the same feeling will be awakened in you by natural ruins, statues, castles, temples, monuments; it will follow you through the grim defiles and up the snow-crowned ridges of the Rocky Mountain system, excited by the ruins of Titanic cities scattered over areas of many grassless, soilless leagues. It never lost its freshness with me; it was always a source of child-like terror and delight; to this day I cannot analyze it, unless on the principle of its affording a certain momentary argument for the supernatural, which, ere you can recover your cold literalism and *modernity,* your logical balance, and your grasp of philosophical explorations, sets you back in your childhood's or your ancestors' marvel-world—shows you how the baby feels, how the ancients felt. It is as if the kobold, the elf, the cyclops, and the afrite had suddenly confronted you, barring the way through some awful fastness of a scarcely trodden world, and, catching you all alone there in the gloom, said to you,—

"You have abjured us; you laugh at us; you deny us. Look at our proofs: there are the sculptures we carved, the cities we built!"

About nightfall we reached Fort Bridger. This, like every military post in the mountains, is a plain stockade work, incapable of resisting civilized siege, but quite sufficient for the protection of its inmates against any force which could be brought against it by its only enemies, the Indians. The inclosure contains several barrack-buildings and a dépôt for government supplies as well as a large store furnishing all the necessary equipments for a settler's outfit. We found the fort garrisoned by detachments from several Nebraska, Kansas, and Colorado regiments, whose officers extended very cordial invitations to our party to lie over for a few days, enjoy the fine hunting and scenery in the neighborhood, and become better acquainted with a mess whose courtesy gave us assurance of a very agreeable time, had we not felt it necessary to reach California as soon as possible.

Here, too, we found one of the most noted of Overland characters, Slade, formerly one of the road-agents of the line we were now travelling, on his way to Virginia City in Idaho. I had an interesting talk with him, and asked him for an account of his celebrated fights with Old Jule, as well as the terrible vengeance which he wreaked upon him. Our time being limited, of his own accord he promised to write me what I asked, and forward it to me for use in this or any future work I might write, introducing characters or scenes from the Plains and the Mountains. Without any appearance of self-conceit, he still seemed pleased when I told him what was very true,— that his adventures in the wilds would afford materials for an intensely interesting romance of adventure. Poor fellow! The next time I heard of him was in conversation with an Idaho man who had been present at his death. During the reign of terror, which is one of the invariable stages of a new mining settlement, and may be called its "teething" period, Slade was an efficient member of the Virginia City vigilance committee, and took part in the execution of many terrible desperadoes. But bloody revolution, like France's earliest and typical one, generally "return to plague the inventor"; and Slade, becoming a terror to his compeers, was in April, 1864, himself put to death without even being granted the privilege of a parting farewell to his wife. When the news reached her, she had no tears to shed, but "spotted" the members of the committee, and registered a fearful oath, that before she died her husband should be avenged on them to the full. I should hate to be one of that committee; for not only is Mrs. Slade one of the finest pistol-shots in the West (without any allowance for her sex), but a woman of long memory, and in reckless courage the perfect match and compeer of her late husband. She is a magnificent woman in appearance, and I thought Slade himself a model of manly beauty.

Much as we regretted missing an Indian powwow that was to have taken place the day after, and would have supplied much valuable *genre* material to pencil and pen, we bade good-by to our kind would-be entertainers, with a promise to stop with them if we returned from California overland.

Black's Fork of the Green River is a small stream affording good water privileges to the Fort, and puzzles the traveller by running north from the spot where he now crosses it, until his map shows him its remarkable sinuosity. Having crossed this and Muddy Fork, about twelve miles further on, he is out of the Green River basin, and almost immediately enters a tract tributary to that of the Great Salt Lake. A series of tremendously heavy grades lead him into the Wahsatch, the last and westernmost range of the Rocky Mountains.

Immediately about Fort Bridger a small surface had been put under cultivation for the partial supply of residents at the Post, and in some directions evergreen wood was plenty; but on entering the Wahsatch, we again came into a region of gray round hills having no vegetation but the artemisia and greasewood. The night was a magnificent one. The full moon was in a cloudless sky; the air was perfectly still, and although abundantly cold, to show us that we were still at a mountainous altitude, not to compare in this respect with that of the ridges we had hitherto passed at night. I had by this time acquired the habit of going without sleep (one much easier than that of sleeping bent into an ampersand); so I abandoned the inside to companions accomplished in that performance, and, having lost at some stage-changing station the guy-rope apparatus by which I had lashed myself to the wagon-top in former times of miserable sleepiness, at once selected the one practicable method of entertaining myself and got into conversation with the driver. The only scenery was that congeries of ashen-hued hills I have mentioned, whose formation could be accounted for by a lively imagination on the hypothesis that when this part of the world was in a liquid, or, more strictly, in a lathery condition, some Titan school-boy had put his pipe-bowl into the basin, and blown the contents up into a mass of contiguous bubbles. If these bubbles had been iridescent like those of our childhood, the reflection of that gorgeous full moon on them to-night would have been worth seeing; but their gray monotone and constantly repeated figure made this landscape the drowsiest on our journey.

The sun was well up when we reached Bear River (the first of the Salt Lake tributaries), striking it about thirty miles north of its head, where it is a substantial stream of forty or fifty yards in breadth, with less than the average rapidity of mountain currents, of a somewhat muddy tinge, and cradled by the same round hills of gray sage as those which we had been threading all night. Here we took breakfast. I long ago concluded not to bore my readers with gastronomic comments, unless the subject deserved animadversion by unusual excellence or absolute atrocity. The Bear River breakfast does not belong to the first class of subjects; a recent good dinner has made me magnanimous toward the errors of my race, so I spare Bear River.

We were now ninety-two miles from Salt Lake City. Bear River, at this point, lies in the trough between the first and second ridges of the Wahsatch Range. Immediately after crossing the river by a substantial wooden bridge, we began to ascend a bald mountain, which rose, as I estimated, from twelve to fifteen hundred feet above the bed of the stream, and which compelled us, for the horses' sake, to dismount and walk. I must not omit to say that our load had been increased at Bear River by three soldiers of a California regiment stationed at Salt Lake City. These constituted part of the detail for Overland Mail protection, furnished by General Connor, commandant at the Mormon city, and afterwards, as he well deserved, and as an instance of unusual government perspicuity, at the head of the expedition sent out for a final ending of all our Indian troubles. Our gallant preservers were a noble set of men, but (I say it neither in sorrow nor in anger) they took up room. We knew that although the present area of greatest peril to our scalps lay on the other side of Salt Lake City, extending over a little less than three hundred miles of desert; there *had* been, at various times, terrible massacres on this side of the Wahsatch also; yet our intellects, prevented by long cramping and distortion of their fleshly receptacle, lacked the equanimity for a just striking of the balance between death by scalping and the same disaster more slowly effected by squeezing. I fear we were not grateful. I know that I myself wished the detail belonged to the Cavalry arm of our service. But the brave fellows were very patient with us, and sat as nearly sideways as could be expected of the class whose prime aphorism is "Eyes front!"

In a state of semi-somnambulism we all got out, and effected the ascent of the first grade from Bear River on foot. Even the sleepiest of us was rewarded when he reached the top, and stood still to wait for the panting beasts we had distanced, and was obliged in candor to own that the view from this height to the opposite ridge and along the slender creeping line of the Bear was abundantly worth the fatigue of walking to obtain it.

About noon we entered that famous gallery of the Wahsatch, the first of an intercommunicating series which lead by easy grades entirely through the range and down to Salt Lake City—*Echo Cañon*. The series is one of the most magnificent avenues by which Nature has ever supplemented human art or challenged it to hopeless contest. To wring from Nature such an avenue and right of way between two tracts divided in their physical geography by a heaven-high barrier a hundred miles thick, would have cost man at least a century of the most enlightened skill and the most industrious labor. Therefore, as if she felt sympathy with those social and commercial currents which seek to mingle grandly over the whole world, she gives man the pass of the Wahsatch, free as air.

The Echo Cañon is a cleft through the range, about ten miles long and of varying width, sometimes opening laterally into valleys or recesses a mile broad, often contracting to a mere alley-way of twenty or thirty yards across. It has a main southwesterly trend, and at its bottom runs the little creek named after it, a small mountain rivulet fed partly by springs and partly by such slender tricklings as reach it from the distant snows. The walls of the cañon are everywhere precipitous, and in the narrowest defiles quite perpendicular, frequently rising to a height of ten or twelve hundred feet. These are mostly of a brilliant red sandstone, and their effect on a sunshiny day is like that of masses of carbuncle.

Echo Cañon must obviously have received its name from an echo, though neither by experiment nor asking could I discover one sufficiently remarkable to have given its name to such a magnificent work of Nature. Its grandeur fortunately makes it of no importance whether this subsidiary clap-trap be well based or not. Another source of its reputation exists in Brigham's preparation to fortify it, several years ago, when, to appease a sudden access of anti-Mormonism at the East, Government (or rumor for it) proposed to send an expedition against Salt Lake City, and break up the entire Mormon settlement. Fortunately that act of folly was not committed, although a still worse one was. The Mormons were not attacked, but a body of United States troops were subsisted at enormous expense at Camp Floyd (well named after a thief and spendthrift of the people's money), a place thirty-nine miles from the Mormon city, and having no single advantage as a strategic or commercial post, except its possession of a well not too brackish to drink of. These unfortunate troops were called an army of observation, probably because they must have built an observatory, and used a telescope, to see any Mormons at all. The distance was not, however, too great for the interchange of courtesies on the part of the chief men of either side, nor for the daily visit of enterprising commercial saints with something to sell. General Johnson, in accordance with the orders of the venerable imbecile at the head of affairs, acted as the leader of a nice, well-behaved little army should, and never gave the saints any offense. To revive a joke invented for the benefit of another military quietist: It seems a shame to attack him; he never attacked anybody. So he stayed there, until from being an eye-sore to the more irritable Mormons, he became a laughing-stock to all of them. He is a good joke among them to this day. The crows laugh at a scare-crow they have detected; how much heartier would they laugh if they could sell him his own grain at one hundred per cent. over the market, or, to stretch the metaphor, his own beeves at the same rate!

The narrow defile which Brigham selected to fortify before he knew his invaders, is a very Thermopylæ. Its bare red walls rise to a height of fifteen hundred feet in a sheer perpendicular. An army of the size of Johnson's could have been decoyed into this defile (its narrowest part is no wider than Broadway at Union Square), and there put to death at the pleasure of their foes. Brigham's idea was to shower them with grape and shrapnel from declined guns facing over the edge of the precipice, and sweep them with similar missiles from each end of the defile; but an ambuscade of sharp-shooters at the top of the precipice, and a body of men with crow-bars to topple down loose fragments of the crag on the invaders' heads, would have been all sufficient for the bloody work.

Early in the afternoon we reached another small affluent of the Great Salt Lake known as Weber River, and thenceforward our course lay through a region very different from any we had been travelling since we left Denver, indeed, since we left the Missouri itself.

We had entered the area of Mormon conquests. Thus far this strange people had crowded back against the mountains, desolation, sterility, and poverty. With a delight no words can paint, no heart can feel save that of a traveller who for a thousand miles has seen the earth beneath his feet an almost unbroken ashen gray, or burnt brown, did we look out upon a boundless scope of living green—green grass, green grain-fields, green gardens—cool, fresh, and tender as New England meadow-land in June. The great sleek oxen and the mild-eyed cows were browsing lazily, up to their bellies in verdure. The rye and wheat were so packed by their luxuriance, that to us, looking down on them from a crag of the defile, their tops seemed almost like a solid turf, but for the faint wind that sent waves of shadow over them, chasing waves of light. Five minutes had sufficed to bring about the greatest visual contrast of our lives. Sterility, savage gloom, death, or the even deeper death of never having yet been born,—these were the burden of Nature's chant among the crags not a mile behind us; now she reveled like a Bacchante singing the joys of corn, and wine, and oil, or better yet, crowned with plumes of harvest, came as the matronly Ceres, leading by her little berry-stained fingers the young Pomona, with prophetic orchard blossoms wreathed about her sunny hair, both singing with the stately bard of old, "The wilderness and the solitary place shall be glad for them; and the desert shall rejoice and blossom as the rose."

The beneficent cause of all this luxuriance was as silent about itself as divine charity. But we knew, here and there we could see, the canals with their innumerable smaller channels of irrigation which ramified over the whole field, hiding their bounty under the stalwart stalks, and juicy blades, and plump ripening ears whose roots they nourished. To the unstudied observer, him to whom all sand is the same, the witness of his eyes seems incredible. The soil of that wonderful harvest field must be like this which blows in our faces from the shifting dunes at our side; yet this is sand. True, but it is also one of the richest soils in the world; for it is the detritus of rocks which, without exaggeration, the scientific man might choose to call *baked fertilizers*. We have made our soup, our stove-polish, even our fuel, into blocks; so we may have blocks of condensed soil. Piled up into crags till we want them, they make excellent scenery; the weather grinds them down, and spreads them over our grain fields and kitchen gardens; by and by they are as good dinner as they were scenery. There is no *bad* soil in the world. There are incomplete soils,—soils that say, "I'll advance all the silex you want, all the lime, or all the potash, only you must get the aluminum." But Utah soil need hardly be defended in this category. As yet it needs no manure, scarcely any top-dressing, unless as a mulch to guard against excessive evaporation. All it needs is water, and how to get that is the plain problem which engages the Mormon farmer day and night; not so complicated a problem as presents itself to many a New England agriculturist, but making up for its slight draft on skill by a tremendous call on industry. The Utah farmer must woo the very snow-peaks, and through them the clear, unanswering heavens, which smile on his starvation, until he makes the mountain-top his mediator, and builds a channel from the edge of the eternal ice to his own acres, that the bounty of the sky may not pay too large a commission to his sub-lime go-between by leakage on the way. None but the Mormon himself can tell you what miles of patiently constructed troughing, and piping, and ditching are expressed in those glorious green acres which, like the finest things in a picture, seem the easiest done because the artist spent his sweat, and blood, and very soul in giving them the look which hides his great struggles forever.

It was nearly sundown when we stopped to change horses at Kimball's, twenty-nine miles from Salt Lake City, and the last station but one between us and the capital of the Saints. Hitherto during the afternoon I had found the beauty of the world's newly recovered green somewhat marred by the absence of the highest element in life's comfort, and the dearest stimulus to, as well as resting-place from, life's industries. I looked for it steadily, yet found it never. The chickens had coops; the stock had its corrals, and stables, and pens;

the very grass and grain were coming in at last from the heat and burden of their day, to rest and shelter in substantial barns. But for them who toiled that these might thrive, for whom these lived, and moved, and had their being,—the men, the women, and the children,—what had they to come to? I looked about me over the green fields, carefully, wonderingly, everywhere, and found *houses* in plenty, but *no home*.

Not that the material was lacking. Some of the houses were excellent snug specimens of the adobe; others were neat structures of wood; scarcely any gave outward sign of poverty, shiftlessness, or un-neatness in their occupants. The dejection which they produced in me, their utter un-home-likeness, proceeded almost wholly from negative causes. They looked like mere sleeping and eating places. The spirit which raises the human habitation above the grade of the marmot's burrow, the fox's cover, or the bear's den—the spirit without which a palace is no better than these—was utterly absent,—not *gone*, for it never had been.

When the quantity of houses within the same inclosure increased, the quality decreased proportionally. I saw little red-headed, tow-headed, black-haired children tumbling together in promiscuous heaps, rolling on the unsodded ground of the same door-yard, while a couple of women were sitting listlessly on different porches, watching their play, calling to them in shrill accents, yet seeming to ignore each other entirely. No house had its pretty little garden-patch in front of it. No flower-beds testified to the pride which wifely hands took in making the house, whither a lover brought them home, the delightful and longed-for nest which means earthly heaven to the matured husband. There was no indication anywhere of keeping the marriage wine, yielded by the clusters of maidenhood, from turning into the vinegar of that wretched self-deception, "the steady old married people's" condition. No climbing rose stretched its arms over the gable to fling bouquets and perfumed dew into the second-story window. Around the porch-pillars, where such there were, nestled no honey-suckle, no columbine, no Wisteria, nor cypress, nor morning glory, nor madeira, nor trumpet vine. What unvarying betrayal of the house's inside is always given, clear as speech, by these lovely dumb outsiders! While you listen and assent to them, there she stands, turning their tendrils about her finger, with as delicate lovingness as if they were her own soft curls, and she standing before a toilet whose true tale makes her modesty blush with joy because it is almost tea-time, and *he* is coming. There is no need she should be here with her tender little prunings, her dexterous persuasions of the wayward shoot, her fond help of the right twisting one; for the caress she gave her pets yesterday is still gratefully remembered by them, and they tell of her in ways unmistakable. The very bees, for whom she has made an emerald spiral stair up to a seventh heaven of blessedness among the nectaries, croon about her as they drink honey from goblets of alabaster, and gold, and ruby, and empurpled crystal, saying, "There's a woman within! there's a woman within!" Yes, indeed! who else? The husband puts *his* name on a silvered copper-plate—great, gross, mechanical, purchasable thing, which you might melt down to make pennies, or stair-rods, or andirons; the wife writes hers in God's live letters that grow, not get shaved and jointed into sentences, on the lattice of a shady veranda. And when she is gone,—look at the vines and the flower-beds,— then there is no need of crape on the door-knob. As they wilt, the bees come again: "There's no woman within—no woman—no woman within any more."

The nearest approach to the New England standard which I saw in Utah, was Kimball's, the next station but one, as I have said, to Salt Lake City. The driver promised to be as long as possible in changing horses, that I might seek admission to the house—a cozy white cottage, low, broad, and roomy, with those architectural after-thoughts, known as wings and lean-tos, which mark the increase of family and prosperity as the growth of a tree has its memorandum in the rings of its bark. This admission I sought, not from any desire to take Time by the forelock in my exploration of the Mormon's domestic concerns, but because the house looked like one where I could get bread and milk. Its outside had a promise of scoured white-oak shelves within; of dazzling pans, golden cream, and snowy loaves.

My knock at the door was answered with an immediate "Come in!" I found myself in a sunny, low-ceiled sitting-room, where a fine-looking matron, somewhere in her well-preserved fifties, sat talking to a pair of very tidy and prepossessing young women, both under twenty-five, and each holding a healthy baby.

I frankly stated my case at once. I was an Over-land traveller who had lived on cured provisions and hard-tack so long that a slice of fresh bread and butter, with a bowl of sweet "morning's milk," undenuded of the cream, would not only insure my gratitude, but the regular-market price, left to their own quotation.

The matronly lady instantly arose and went to the dairy closet. The material for my satisfaction was before me in a few seconds, with the snowiest of damask towels beneath it.

I felt new life with every bite and table-spoonful. I felt the dust washed out of me, body and soul. A still further freshening occurred to me as I looked at these pretty young mothers and their babies. I made up a pretty little idyl about them. The mothers were former school acquaintances—cousins—something of that sort. They had been married about the same time; by a pleasant turn of Fortune's wheel they had been brought to be near neighbors in the same settlement; and now, as I had seen at the East so often, one of the pretty young mothers had run in to match babies with the other, and prattle out their hearts' sweet foolishness without risk of being misunderstood—talking lovely rigmaroles of baby-talk to their "*ittle pessus tittens,*" with fullest sympathy from each other and benignant grandma.

The sight of them, after six hundred miles of sterile ice and stone, exhilarated me like a generous ladleful of punch. "Those are very pretty babies!" said I, addressing the matron in all sincerity of heart.

"Yes, I think so," she replied; "but you must allow for a grandmother's partiality."

I replied that no such allowance was necessary to me, and continued, "These young ladies are your daughters, then?"

"They are my daughters-in-law, sir," returned the fine-looking matron.

"So you have both your sons and their wives with you? Indeed, you are to be envied, with such a delightful home about you in other respects."

"These babies, sir," answered the matron gravely, "are the children of my *son,* now abroad on the Lord's business—my son, Mr. Kimball, after whom this place is called. These young ladies are his wives, and I am the first wife of one you have often ere this heard of in the States,—Heber Kimball, second President, and next to our prophet Brigham Young in the government of Utah."

Why should I blush? Nobody else did. The babies crowed as they were tossed ceiling-ward in the maternal fashion, not even paying the Gentile intruder the compliment of getting scared by him. The young mothers had heard the whole conversation; yet Eve before the fall could not have been more innocent of shame. Mrs. Heber Kimball showed no sign of knowing that I could be surprised by anything she told me. Yet I, a cosmopolitan, a man of the world, liberal to other people's habits and opinions to a degree which had often subjected me to censure among strictarians in the Eastern States, blushed to my very temples, and had to retire into the privacy of my tipped milk-bowl to screen the struggle by which I restored my moral equipoise. I was beyond measure provoked at myself. Ever since we left Green River I had known I was in Utah. I had been thinking about Mormon peculiarities all day long; yet the first apparition to my senses of that which had absorbed my intellect, took me entirely aback!

If the three observed my confusion, they had sufficient tact not to show it. I think that Mrs. Heber Kimball the first must undoubtedly have understood my position, and that the plain straightforward statement which she made, was for the purpose of landing me at one throw in the midst of polygamic ideas. She did not ask my name; made no inquiries regarding my companions, who were stretching their legs outside of the cottage gate, rejecting all invitations on my part to come in and share my bread and milk with me. She was kind and pleasantly interested in my well-being to the extent of this provision, but as nonchalant of whatever spirit I might cherish toward Utah as one can well imagine. Without the least braggadocio or offensive protrusion of our mutual and radical differences, she nevertheless set me at once upon the true basis, and let me know that polygamy was the law of the land where I now trod, and she and her own as firm in the faith as I in monogamy, without anything more to be ashamed of in her creed than the Vicar of Wakefield or Horace Greeley in theirs.

Had I never seen anything more of polygamy than I met here, I should have gone my way feeling puzzled as to whether the system might not have possessed a certain advantage for people arrived at one particular stage of civilization, akin to that which it bestowed upon the Old Testament Jews. I had no doubt that it would be a frightfully retrograde step for the society whence I came, but that decided nothing in regard to these Mormons. On the ladder of civilization, round number two would be degradation to the foot planted on number three; but it would be as great an elevation to the stander on number one.

Mrs. Heber Kimball the first, though rapidly nearing her grand climacteric, was the finest-looking woman whom I saw in Utah. In the Highlands of Scotland she might have been Helen McGregor; in Palmyra, Zenobia; in France, Joan of Arc. She was considerably above woman's middle size; her hair, slightly grizzled, was dressed neatly back beneath a plain, snow-white cap; her figure was erect, and the embodiment of strength and endurance; her eyes, which seemed a bluish gray, were fearless, and looked straightforward; her mouth was almost masculine in its firmness; her nose a finely cut aristocratic Roman; her manner perfectly self-poised, replete with influential and winning dignity, and expressive

of a powerful will, strong for the control of her own faculties, as well as the whole nature of other people; her voice
pleasant, yet commanding; her general expression that of
pride without self-consciousness, and courage untainted by
braggadocio. She was a woman to make you stop and look
back after her in a crowded thoroughfare; she would have
arrested your attention anywhere, on Broadway, the Strand,
or the most thronged portion of the Parisian Boulevards. I
did not wonder when, days afterwards, in talking with her
husband, who knew nothing of my previous meeting with
her,—since she was only visiting her daughters-in-law at
the time I saw her,—Heber Kimball told me that not only
in time, but in ability, she was the very first of his wives—
the wife to whom he most deferred, and in whose wisdom
he had the most implicit confidence. I was fully prepared
for that assertion; but I confess that my credulity was at first
nearly staggered, when I heard that her conversion to Mormonism was prior to her husband's, and that, in plain terms,
*he* was *her* convert to all the tenets of Joe Smith and the
later dogma of polygamy—last of all conceivable doctrines
for whose championship you would think of looking to a
wife! Paradoxical as this assertion may be, I have repeatedly
heard it made among Mormons, yet never with the faintest
hint at a denial. Indeed, the style of her few short sentences
addressed to me seemed to show that she gloried in it.

After my recovery behind the charitable shelter of the
milk-bowl, I could not succeed in disciplining my mind as
thoroughly as I had my face. That poor monogamic brain of
mine kept pondering and dreaming as if it were dazed. How
could those pretty young women sit and look at each other's
babies—both of nearly the same age; hear the matron talk

of the youthful apostle to the Gentiles now gathering in the elect from foreign parts; see, each in the opposite infant, the plain apostolic seal stamped on its little countenance,—yet rock away so cheerfully and talk baby Latin so blithely; be-sister each other, and give mutual advice about the cut of long clothes, or the management of teething? Heavens! What strange unsexing operation must their souls have gone through to keep them from frenzy—murder—suicide? I afterward put this question to their father-in-law, Heber the first, and his terse, all-conclusive explanation was, "Triumph o' grace."

I know that conscience is mostly custom, that taste is training, and shame the sense of being singular. Still I confess that my imagination's utmost stretch falls short of realizing how that double pair, baby and mother, can sit *vis-á-vis* all day long, and not feel hate, horror, hell itself striving somewhere in their depths! I ache as I look at them; for it seems as if those breasts which suckle the babies, must suffer such frightful tension as sometimes, instead of wholesome human milk, to yield gall and blood!

I should have felt relieved if those two pretty young girls of a sudden had leaped up and fired their babies at each other's heads, pounced upon each other with a tigrine spring, seamed each other's faces with relentless nails, tore hair, gouged eyes, bit, maimed, killed! Then would they have shown decidedly less *grace*, but considerably more humanity. The *saints* would have evaporated, but in their places would be *women*.

I meant to say just what I have written; so I felt glad that these charming, kindly, self-crucifying creatures offered not the slightest objection to my paying a quarter for my bowl of milk and buttered slice. I never belonged to that class who believe a good dinner equivalent to a contract to lie for the flattery of one's host. Truth always, on my time-table, has the right of way over turbot.

After leaving Kimball's, we rode a distance of twenty-nine miles through a continuation of the widening gallery which had hitherto led us through the Wahsatch, stopping about midway at Mountain Dell, where a beautiful stream ran crystal-clear to unite its waters with the Salt Lake Basin, and where I had time to take the first invigorating plunge which I had enjoyed since leaving Denver. This description of the refreshing bath is perhaps rather too conventional and rhapsodic; for my action was a much sedater one, and consisted in lying down and having the dust washed from my parched body by a flow of deliciously pure water, two or three feet deep above the pebbly bottom.

I found the effect of the bath so sedative that I enjoyed, after returning to my seat, the first unbroken sleep I had known in several days.

I was awakened by my companions to enjoy the weird picturesqueness of a fire kindled by camping emigrants, and flashing its spectral light upon a fine perpendicular precipice of white granite, just as we broke through the western face of the Wahsatch, and came to the head of the foot-hills from which the vast basin of the Lake is for the first time visible, with the embowered City of the Saints sleeping at the bottom of its vast cradle.

Under a vague mysterious moonlight we whirled of a sudden among the adobe houses and the shadowy streets of Brigham's capital. Going at once to the only hotel of the town, in fifteen minutes, and with our piles of Eastern letters unread, we were, for the first time in six days and nights, as soundly asleep as Epimenides.

CHAPTER VII.

## THE NEW JERUSALEM.

THE original sense in which I use the title to this chapter will be defended as I proceed. I certainly do not bestow the name of New Jerusalem upon the Mormon capital because of its bearing any resemblance to the city of the disembodied saints.

Among the many courtesies extended our party by Mr. Holladay and others connected with the Overland road was a letter from Mr. Center, commending us to the attention of Mr. Rumfield, representative of the Wells-Fargo interest at Salt Lake City. Through this gentleman we made the acquaintance of Mr. Stein, then Mr. Holladay's agent at the same place, and since occupying an important position as manager of one of that great stage-man's new lines, for which he is eminently fitted by a grade of business talents and indefatigable industry seldom met with at the East or West.

These gentlemen formed the capital of acquaintanceship upon which we began business in Utah. To them we owe innumerable and peculiar facilities for the study of Salt Lake City, its scenery, its people, and its usages, though they are responsible for none of my opinions.

The Salt Lake Hotel, where we stopped, is the only one frequented by Gentiles; indeed, the only one which claims any position corresponding to the hotels at the East. It is a good-sized house of two stories in height, with broad verandas on its façade. Our rooms opened upon the upper one, and thence we had a fine view of the principal street.

The peculiarities of Mormonism are not external; and a traveller merely seeing the city *in transitu*, must be disappointed of the keen, fresh sensation which people expect in visiting the centre of the most remarkable social system in Christendom.

The hotel we found to differ in no important respect from the well kept, homely tavern of any quiet Eastern village. Tourists fortunate enough to have received their first impressions of Green Mountain scenery before Vermont began to be crossed by its net-work of iron rails, used to see a very similar tavern on their way over the magnificent stage road from Troy to Rutland, when they halted for dinner the first day out at "Love's," in Bennington. Townsend, who keeps the Salt Lake Hotel, is a gruff but obliging man, between fifty and sixty. It never occurred to me that he was a Saint until Heber Kimball called him "brother"; and the unobtrusiveness of polygamy at its very head-quarters may be inferred from the fact that a week elapsed before it occurred to me that the industrious old lady who gave us such nice little dishes of hot scrambled eggs, and made us fresh coffee when we came down late to breakfast was one Mrs. Townsend, and a younger woman who took such good care of our rooms was another.

The only peculiarity of the hotel was its lack of a bar-room; and with this few people obliged to make any protracted stay at a Western hotel will be disposed to quarrel. The deficiency was a guarantee of quiet nights and orderly days. From sunrise till sunset the long line of tie-posts in front of Townsend's was studded with hardy little mustangs, whose sun-browned riders were refreshing themselves within, or transacting business without; and until a late hour of the night (always till the Overland stage arrived from the East), the verandas were occupied by gentlemen smoking and chatting in their easy-chairs; but never was the seemly order of the establishment broken by any approach to a row, or even by vociferous discussion.

The dining-room was lively and bustling for a couple of hours from the bell-ringing of each meal, fresh relays of guests occupying vacated seats as fast as one battalion of dishes could be cleared from the field, and a fresh one brought into position. Townsend was largely patronized by both ladies and gentlemen; but neither among permanent nor transient guests was there anything to suggest the existence of peculiar social customs, had we not already been aware of it.

The main street, which ran in front of the hotel, was splendidly broad,—in this respect not surpassed by the widest portion of Pennsylvania Avenue. Its architecture was nothing to boast of, being that of a town whose citizens are still in the first stage of doing, and have not yet reached the second one of considering how to do. The shops were consistent with the hotel, and like it might have been transported from the principal street of any prosperous Eastern village. There were some brick, some wooden, and numerous adobe houses, generally two stories in height, and without decoration. The commercial fronts displayed their wares through no ambitious plates of French glass, but announced them on shingles or handbills, and by the still more straightforward method of samples at the door-way. All the ordinary trades were represented, but there seemed to be the usual country fondness for miscellaneous traffic within one inclosure; the house-furnishing business, inclusive of groceries, shoes, hardware, all, indeed, that one would look for in the "country store" *par exellence*, being a favorite and well patronized kind of commerce. The milliner and dress-maker had their separate sanctuaries, as one finds all over the civilized world, but possessed no such prominence as they might naturally be supposed to occupy in Utah. It was evident that polygamy and gynocracy are terms by no means convertible. The vast scale of shopping prevalent in Gentile communities is the grand guarantee and safeguard of monogamy. Brigham Young is undoubtedly the richest man in the Western Hemisphere, even richer perhaps than any single member of the Rothschild family; but were his milliner's and mantua-maker's bills to be calculated on the basis of a single-wived establishment at the East, even his exchequer might be excused for coming to bankruptcy. From my observation of Mormon sumptuary habits, I should suppose that the budget of a polygamic household was made up on the principle of dividing one normal and Eastern wife's allowance among a multitude, instead of multiplying it by the number of the harem. The philosopher acquainted with the underlying motive of most marriages in society will find no insuperable difficulty in understanding how a given number of wives can consent to receive the fraction of a man apiece; but when it comes to dividing the pin-money, he beholds an eternal obstacle to the spread of polygamic ideas among the higher classes of society.

I was struck by the rarity of doctors' and lawyers' shingles in the principal street of Salt Lake City. The former deficiency is easily accounted for. There are few more healthful localities on the Continent than this. In the immediate neighborhood of the Great Salt Lake, fogs are frequent and obstinate. The only escape of such a vast body of water being air-ward, the evaporation constantly going on beneath an unclouded sun necessarily keeps the atmosphere overladen with moisture. But the shores of the lake are almost as unsettled as when the Mormons first came to the Territory. The nearest point of the shore (Black Rock) is twenty miles distant from the city; and although the temperature of the latter must be to a certain extent modified by the lake fogs, during the summer at least, they do not manifest themselves in the city as unpleasantly perceptible moisture. The outskirts of the city along the river Jordan are in some places overflowed and boggy; within five miles of it are a number of large thermal springs; yet the people seem troubled by no malaria, nor by the endemic diseases which arise from it.

The vital intertexture of social, religious, and civil polity resulting from the Mormon system, would well-nigh do away altogether with the profession of the attorney and counselor, but for the fact that the United States Government still claims territorial jurisdiction in Utah. The Federal authority is nominally paramount, but one fact must always operate to nullify it for all practical purposes. The United States courts may get their judges from any portion of the Union at our Chief Magistrate's discretion, but their juries must always be impaneled from among the Mormons themselves. The Gentile, resident in or travelling through Utah, gains nothing by getting his cause into the United States courts. Human ingenuity can fashion no oath comprehensive enough in its form or terrible enough in its sanction to bind a Mormon juryman to the prejudice of his coreligionist, or of the vast autocracy (*theocracy* he calls it) by whose favor he holds all that is most precious to him, not only for the life which now is, but for that which is to come. Where the matter in dispute is indifferent to "*the Church*" or to any Mormon in it, the citizen of Utah is as just as another man. Under the same circumstances, the Gentile litigant may be sure of justice at Brigham Young's own hands. Were I anxious for speedy adjustment of a cause between myself and any other Gentile, and confident of the justice of my own side, I do not know the referee in whose hands I would more gladly leave my interests than Brigham Young's. Outside the arena of his fanaticism, he is not surpassed in honesty of purpose, clear-headedness, purity of motive, and justice of feeling, by any man I ever met. But rare indeed must be the case in which "the Church" has not some little fibre of interest, some trifling stake sufficient to partialize the referee, in a community the boast of whose religious polity is that it interpenetrates every relation of life, and ramifies through every interest of the proprietor, the citizen, and the man. The result of this state of things is to remove the whole amenability of private conscience, not only from the United States tribunal which frames the oath, but from the Gentile's God whose power forms its sanction, to the Church of the Latter-day Saints and the incarnation of its divine authority in the apostle, prophet, autocrat, and vicar of the true God, Brigham Young.

So long as our Government respects Magna Charta privaliges, and deals with Mormonism upon common-law principles and a peace *status*, so long will its courts in Utah remain mere scarecrows, known by the people to be made of rags and bean-poles. No order of court has the slightest

validity; no gubernatorial proclamation even the poor privilege of a right to be published and circulated, without the
indorsement of Brigham Young. There is but one remedy to
this condition of Federal powerlessness—the declaration of
martial law throughout the Territory. Military command-
ers stationed in Utah have repeatedly urged this course on
the Washington Executive. There has been at least one case
in which I think the prayer must have been indorsed by
the most rigorous theorist upon popular rights and constitutional measures. But it has never been granted. The past
few years have greatly modified men's views regarding the
safety and propriety of a recourse, in extreme exigencies, to
abnormal methods. We have seen the rights of jury trial and
*habeas corpus* suspended in emergencies far less imperative
than several which have called for that action in Utah. Still,
the reaction of feeling following our late war's necessary
laxities will operate strongly against any future attempt at
interference with the course of civil law; and in any case, the
Executive which declares martial law in Utah must occupy
a position of most weighty and delicate responsibility. At
the same time, it is beyond peradventure that whenever the
United States Government finds it vital to make its power
felt as paramount above that of Mormonism, and to do more
than preserve the mere semblance of royalty in Utah, the
only possible path to such a result is through the court-martial. But I did not mean to begin political discussion so early
in my acquaintance with Salt Lake.

The traveller, coming into the Saints' City, either from the
mountain or the desert side, finds much to expand his mind
and rest his eyes. The breadth of the streets is delightful to
him after squeezing his way through the narrow defiles of

the Wahsatch,—for we judge of all things relatively,—and
the Mormon Boulevards are as broad for a street, as the
cañons are narrow for a mountain pass. By survey, all the
streets of Salt Lake City are one hundred and thirty-two
feet wide between fence lines. Twenty feet of this width, on
each side, belong to the sidewalk. The blocks, in the thickly
settled part of the city, contain eight lots apiece; each of
these lots measuring one and a quarter acres—a most generous apportionment for any city proprietor. The blocks front
alternately upon the streets running north and south, and
those running east and west. For instance, suppose us entering the city by the "Emigration road,"—our faces directed
due westward,—the lots belonging to the first block on our
right front our street; those on our left offer us their sides;
we cross the first transverse street, and the lots of the block
on the left front us, while we flank the lots of the block
on our right. An inconsiderable portion of the city, some
distance to the northward of the Emigration road, contains
blocks of four lots measuring two and one-half acres, and
five-acre lots exist in some other blocks to the southward.
The dwelling-houses, like the stores, are principally of adobe,
with here and there a brick or wooden one, and an occasional building, belonging to some more opulent Saint, of
the gray sandstone or granite from the cañons. By a municipal regulation the builder is obliged to set his house at least
twenty feet back from the front fence of his lot, and to plant
shade-trees along his street line. The effect of this arrangement, and the lateral isolation of all dwelling-houses which
seems as strictly enjoined, is to give the streets a dignity and
generosity of appearance quite independent of architecture.
It is but twenty-three years since the advance guard of the

first Mormon expedition camped down in the brush upon the site of the present flourishing and growing city, yet the wonderful industry and undaunted faith of this remarkable people have seemed to infuse their spirit into the very trees, for the sidewalks along the front of their courts-yards are densely roofed avenues of living green; the maple, the cotton-wood, the poplar, a species acacia like our honey-locust, seeming to have thriven apace wherever the settler's hand has planted them, and at a more rapid rate than is anywhere witnessed in the East.

Along the principal streets of the city exist some such pleasant exceptions to the dejected unhomelikeness which I have heretofore mentioned, as characterizing the grounds around Mormon houses, that I hasten with delight to give them their due. Even these exceptions are the mere external symbolizations of that higher grade of wealth and luxury distinguishing all cities; the gardener's paid work, not the wife's and daughter's sweet pastime, save in one or two cases (those the best) where a true marital love had kept a household, though Mormon, still monogamic.

The space between the house and the front fence is managed according to the means and taste of the proprietor. In some instances, the utilitarian element, being in the ascendant, has boldly brought the vegetable garden forward into public notice. I like the sturdy self-assertion of those potatoes, cabbages, and string-beans. Why should they, the preservers and sustainers of mankind, slink away into back lots, behind a high board fence, and leave the land-holder to be represented by a set of lazy bouncing-bets and stiff-mannered hollyhocks, who do nothing but prink and dawdle for their living,—the deportment Turvey-drops of the vegetable kingdom? Other front yards are variegated in pretty patterns with naturalized flowers—children of seed brought from many countries: here a Riga pink, which minds the Scandinavian wife of that far off door-way around which its ancestors blossomed in the short Northern summer of the Baltic; here a haw or a holly, which speaks to the English wife of yule and spring-time, when she got kissed under the one or followed her father clipping hedge-rows of the other; shamrock and daisies for the Irish wife; fennel—the real old "meetin'-seed" fennel—for the American wife; and in some places where tact, ingenuity, originality, and love of science have blessed a house, curious little alpine flowers of flaming scarlet or royal purple, brought down from the green dells and lofty terraces of the snow-range, to be adopted and improved by culture. Of all I liked best a third class of front courts, given up to moist, home-looking turf-grass, of that deep green which rests the soul as it cools the eyes—grass, that febrifuge of the imagination, which, coming after the woolly gramma and the measureless stretches of ashen-gray sage brush through which the traveller reaches Salt Lake City, almost makes him go to sleep singing; grass, that silent ballad of Nature, whereof the dying babble dimly caught snatches, because of all created things it best blends in with the Eden meadows dawning on their inner eyes as the outer glaze slowly on this world.

Brigham Young, Heber Kimball, and Porter Rockwell, beside many other Mormons of less celebrity, have told me that when they first came to the present site of Salt Lake City, it was as arid a sand and sage barren as can be found anywhere in the plateaus of the Rocky Mountain chain. Their assertion is corroborated to the traveller reaching Salt Lake

City from any point of the compass, by the sharply drawn boundary between fields fairly packed with harvest, smiling gardens, and orchards where the branches crack under their wealth on the one hand; and on the other, tracts where no living thing breaks the monotony of sand and alkali but the ashen artemisia, the cactus, greasewood, or salicorm.

I asked the Mormon leaders how, under the circumstances, they could ever have decided to found a nation here. Twenty years ago, the theory of soils, physical geography, organic chemistry, and the entire tribe of sciences embracing these, were inadequately understood, even by technical people, professors and the like, whose business they were. As to our best practical farmers, in comparison with many boys at this day in the higher classes of our scientific schools, they were so ignorant that they would have turned in dismay from the project of bringing the Salt Lake Basin under profitable culture. Among the Mormon leaders were none who possessed the advantages which we express by the comprehensive term of "a liberal education." Most of them were the plainest of plain farmers. Yet, without hesitation, they undertook to reclaim, for the support of man, a tract whose latent possibilities of cultivation, even at this day, would fail to present themselves by any external indication to ninety-nine hundredths of the best-read and keenest-minded men of their class. This soil is tractable. Indeed, its fertility is wonderful. But how could *they* know it? Or was it possible that the chiefs of the enterprise felt contented with the mere fact of putting between their people and their persecutors twelve hundred miles of unsettled wilderness, half of it a succession of giant mountain walls, with a coping of eternal snow?

What a frightful responsibility must theirs have been who founded the future of all those women, children, and old men (not to mention the able-bodied men) upon a guess!

But Brigham Young solemnly assured me that it was no guess. His contemporaries among the leaders indorse that statement. Their answer is that God bade them stop here. To the north of the city, along the Wahsatch range, they point out for the curious stranger a peak where Brigham Young, like Jacob, passed the night in wrestling with an angel. Going up alone into this mountain to pray at the close of the day when the people with him reached the first ridge whence an outlook could be obtained across the valley now cradling the Saints' metropolis, he fell into a trance of revelation. A certain shining one came to him direct from God and the martyred prophet, and telling him that the base of the range was his nation's goal, finished by a command to lead the people down into the plain, and there to found the city whereof the Lord had promised aforetime, "All men shall flow unto it, and be saved." By obedience to those heavenly instructions, the Mormons have made "the wilderness like Eden, the desert like the garden of the Lord." Thus, the establishment of the Salt Lake colony is without a precedent in the history of fanaticism; for it is not only the grandest in its faith against all apparently rational likelihood, but the most fully justified by its success. After this, it can be no matter of astonishment to any reflecting mind that the Mormons unreservedly believe in a man and a system vindicated by results so imprevisible on the ordinary basis of human experience. As a direct corollary from this statement flows the irresistible conviction, that, of whatever else they may be guilty, the great majority of Mormons, from Brigham Young down, believe in themselves and their fanaticism as sincerely as the devoutest Christian believes in the Gospel of Christ. In view of all I have seen and heard, I could no more find room for the accusation of these men as *hypocrites* than for a suspicion of the sincerity of the most illustrious martyr in the Christian Church.

The truth, which they could not have known scientifically, because as yet Science scarcely knew it herself, was that the only element lacking to the utilization of the Utah soil was water. Irrigation of course had been understood from the earliest antiquity; but that this was the only need of a soil like that of the Great Basin, no one knew, for the fact was contrary to all external indications.

In applying the process of irrigation to their city site, the Mormons performed an incredible amount of labor. Much of this, from their inexperience and their want of scientific education, was merely thrown away, or, more accurately speaking, useful only as "practice." They had to begin studying the problem of hydraulics and engineering where their ancestors began. When we see the blunders frequently made by nations building on that aggregation of past experiments and generalizations known as science, we shall not wonder that one painfully constructed conduit intended to supply the Saints with water, refused to fall in with its builders' wishes, from the fact that it sloped up toward the city instead of down. The successful portion of their result remains. It is ample for their present purposes, and is one of the earliest novelties which strike a purely American traveller passing through their streets.

On each side of the highway one is surprised to see a small, but rapid and unfailing stream, running in what we

should call the gutter. No artificial means are taken to protect it. It is not piped, nor tiled, nor sluiced; the utmost that
is anywhere done for it is to pave its channel, two or three
feet in breadth, with uncemented cobble-stones. But this is
the aqueduct. From this open gutter, the inhabitants of Salt
Lake City, now numbering between seventeen and eighteen
thousand people, draw their entire supply of water for all
purposes whatsoever. To be sure a few wells have been sunk
in different portions of the city; Townsend, our landlord, has
one of them in his back yard; but the supply which they
afford is only a drop in the bucket compared with that running along the curbs, and even to the taste of a new-comer
altogether inferior to the latter.

All the earlier associations of an Eastern man connect the
gutter with ideas of sewerage; and a day or two must pass
before he can accustom himself to the sight of his waiter
dipping up from the street the pitcher of drinking water for
which he has rung, or the pailful which is going into the
kitchen to boil his dinner, and into the laundry to wash his
clothes. The novelty of the sensation, however, soon disap-
pears when he pushes his investigations from street to street,
and nowhere finds impurity of any kind mingling with the
rivulet which runs clear and pellucid before his own door.
Dead leaves and sand, the same foreign matters as the wind
drifts into any forest spring, are necessarily found in such an
open conduit; but no garbage, nothing offensive of any kind,
disturbs its purity.

Though there must needs be some unmanifested legislation upon the subject, the water seems to take care of itself;
there are no regulations posted for its protection; the gutters
are under the surveillance of no visible police. A Mormon

citizen need hardly be forbidden to throw ashes, or slops, or swill into the water on which he and his neighbors depend for comfort, cleanliness, and even life itself I never saw anything done to mar the purity of this paragon of gutters by the littlest child or most ignorant stranger.

But this gutter has an agricultural as well as a domestic function to perform. Across the sidewalk in front of every citizen's inclosure runs a narrow channel, sometimes tiled over, sometimes a mere open depression such as might be scratched with a hoe, leading from the outer and public stream to the inner and private domain. The simplest of sluice-gates, a smooth board, a mere shingle, shuts the curb end of this channel. It seems an easy matter to pull it up. A baby could lift it, speaking after the manner of muscles and tendons. But the late lamented Windship could not stir it, speaking "*in foro conscientiæ.*" Starr King used to tell with great gusto the story of a New England official, small, unusually small, in the respect of avoirdupois, but great in soul, who, on being threatened with personal violence by the malcontent whom he was sent to arrest, replied, "*Shake* me? Shake *me?* When you shake *me,* you shake the State of Massachusetts!" Similarly, the person who inconsiderately lifts that shingle, lifts the Church of the Latter-day Saints; and that, as my old pioneer Comstock would say, "is a pretty hefty pull for any man."

The water of Mormondom, like everything else vital, except the contumacious air which has not yet been brought to its bearings, is the property and the concern of the Church. The Church therefore appoints a water-warden, whose business it is to see that the supply gets apportioned on principles of equity to every man's close, so far as he has reduced it to cultivation. Sometimes, when the previous winter's snow has been comparatively scanty on the mountain-tops (as was the case during the winter precedent to this particular summer of which I speak), great discretion is necessary in the allotment of the shares devoted to irrigation. A scheme is carefully laid out by the water-warden, calculated for the portion of the common territory which each land-holder owns, and showing as delicately as possible, by the necessarily rude means of measurement, just how much water *per diem* falls to the share of each cultivated lot in the city. With this scheme in hand, the water-warden daily goes his rounds, and lifts the sluice-gates accordingly. Thus, for instance, Brother Brown's lot is twice the area of Brother Perkins's immediately adjoining; therefore the warden lifts Brother Brown's gate from 9 until 11 o'clock A. M., Brother Perkins's gate meanwhile remaining shut. At 11 o'clock Brother Brown's gate is shut, and from that time till noon Brother Perkins has his gate "histed." This system accords with a state of society patriarchally simple; and the existence of such a state of society among the Mormons is sufficiently indicated by the fact that the misdemeanor of "histing" one's own gate is almost, if not entirely, unknown to the calendar of the ecclesiastical court.

Inside the land-holder's fence the apparatus for the distribution of his share to the thirsty soil is no less simple than effective. Across the land which he cultivates runs a net-work of shallow furrows or scratches connected with the channel coming under his fence from the gutter. As the water is let in to him it finds its way through this right-angled system of channels, and is rapidly drunk up by the planted squares between them. If he is an enthusiast in horticulture, and has particular beds or single plants which are his favorites, he leads a private *tidbit* (if I may be allowed that term for anything fluid) to the roots of his pet, by opening a temporary channel from the main furrow with his cane or the toe of his boot. The associations of Palestine throng everywhere throughout Mormondom, and with special cogency they came upon me here. I remembered the declaration of the Psalmist, "Thou turnest men's hearts as the rivers of water are turned," in connection with another scriptural expression: "When a man's ways please the Lord, he maketh even his enemies to be at peace with him." Nowhere on this side of the Holy Land could the preacher find such an illustration for the first text. The proprietor's foot made a little scratch toward the root of a Lawton blackberry he was trying; the activity he put forth was nearly unconscious, but the longed-for moisture crept toward the delicate thirsty spongioles, and by one slight contraction of a human muscle, the prosperity of that strange orphan, that banished scion among shrubs, was permanently secured. How much of the Bible's poetry we lose through our ignorance of physical geography! Henceforth to the Lawton blackberry, the cloudless sun, which had shone but to wilt it before, was a guide luring it upward with a golden finger. So the proprietor's furrow, scratched with a mere boot-tip, had instantly changed a curse into a blessing; and the wilting, parching, blasting enemy was in an instant converted to the best of friends. The poor little spindling thorny canes found the sunlight "at peace with them," as the rivulets of water were turned to give them drink. This is but one of the multitudinous, even constant illustrations of some Old Testament statement found among the Mormons, whether they be citizens or agriculturists. Indeed, the whole Mormon polity is only a fresh realization of the elder and original Jewish life.

The freshly arrived Gentile is surprised at the paucity of women in the streets of Salt Lake City, and still more so by the appearance of the few who do manifest themselves. I had expected to find the feminine element largely predominating on the side-walks of a nation whose essential characteristic is disproportion of the sexes on the woman's side. But the settlements of Colorado (a Territory in which the disproportion in the opposite direction is something quite appalling) are gay with the ornamental portion of the race, compared with the thoroughfares of Mormondom. Any sunshiny day in Denver or Central City brings out on the promenade a greater number of women than can be found under the most favorable circumstances in the streets of Salt Lake City. I could only account for this fact by supposing that the institution of the harem, no matter where trans- planted nor by what race adopted, inevitably brings with it the jealousies and the rigors of Stamboul; that polygamy and the seclusion of women are fundamentally inseparable.

Such women as appear are a further surprise to the Gentile, by their unobtrusive, unconscious demeanor. Not unnaturally, one expects to find the Mormoness either shamefaced or brazen. I looked for dejected faces, faces that knew, felt, and showed their owners' degradation; or hard, defiant faces, glorying boldly in their shame. Nothing of the kind appeared. My mistake arose through forgetfulness that the social moralities are manufactured; artificial, not natural; man's temporary expediency, not God's eternal law; that shame is merely the regret one feels, discovering himself ridiculously at variance with the usages of the surrounding majority. The poet is right by the lofty ideal standard (which nobody observes); entirely wrong by the practical standard (on which the whole world shapes itself), for, whenever the high ideal man gets grouped with others into a community, there "honor and shame" *do* "from condition rise," and, indeed, rise from nothing else. A public opinion, isolated from all others on one hand by a mountain system six hundred miles wide, and on the other hand by a desert of equal width, accepts of polygamy as the normal state of the race. Thus, on all principles of social morality, I, who had been looking to see Mormon women blush and drop their veils as they passed me, should have stayed in my room at Townsend's, with my cheeks crimsoned by the thought that I was a degraded monogamist! In fact, the women appeared like the respectable class of seamstresses common in any Eastern city, conscious not only of no degradation, but of no singularity. A person ignorant of the system under which they lived, would never have looked at them a second time.

After getting thoroughly rested from our sleepless ride of six hundred miles, we gladly accepted the guidance of one of our newly acquired acquaintances, and went out to overhaul the lions of Salt Lake City.

One of the first places which we visited was the Theatre, or Opera-house. This was a comparatively recent building, but engaged our earliest attention from the fact that its interior was at the present moment lively with preparations for the coming Independence Ball to be given by the President. We were now at the end of June or early in July. My diary does not tell me the exact date, but it could not have been later than the first day of the latter month.

The building was situated on one of the streets running parallel to that Main (or *vulgariter* "Whiskey") Street on which Townsend's fronted. It was situated at a trifling distance from the presidential mansions, and belonged to Brigham Young, who had erected it not only with a view to furnishing accommodation for the amusements of his people as a state expediency, but as a business speculation. I am far enough from any inclination to state this fact as a slur. Brigham Young has no less right to make money than any private citizen; and it is creditable to his tact and foresight to have initiated an enterprise which abundantly conduces to the welfare of the Church, while it acts for his own emolument. Here, once for all, I desire to record my conviction, that if, instead of harmonizing, as in the present instance, the two interests of church advancement and selfish aggrandizement happened to clash, Brigham Young would not hesitate the fraction of a second after perceiving the fact to put his own interests under foot, and conserve those of abstract Mormonism.

Without any such knowledge of the classics as might have informed Brigham Young how the Roman ruler kept his people good-natured by bread and circus acting, the remarkable master of this remarkable nation, by his own shrewd sense and clear intuitions, from the beginning understood the vast efficiency of amusements as an element in the enginery of a rigorous government. While the "Social Hall" (a small saloon like those devoted to concerts and lectures at the East) seemed sufficient for popular accommodation, the head of the "Latter-day Saints" gave not only the prestige of his approval and monetary aid to the institution which provided his people with innocent recreation, but contributed his actual presence to their sports, and (what was a still more perilous experiment, but abundantly justified by the result) personally joined in these sports, leading the dance, like Napoleon at the Tuileries.

When the rapid growth of the population demanded a wider area for the hours of its unbending, the President, taking the initiative as in all other popular movements, condescended to become the builder and proprietor of the first nominally constituted theatre or opera-house erected within the Mormon dominions. The accounts of this enterprise belong to his personal ledger, and its use is granted to any organization calculated to further its purpose, at a rate merely equivalent to the interest on his expenditure in building and keeping it in repair. I have spoken of it as tending to his aggrandizement, but in justice I should substitute for that statement the assertion that it does not tend to his loss.

We found the building a very plain one. Its façade was covered with a neutral-tinted stucco, and entirely without ornamentation, unless a surface broken by simple pilasters be considered as such.

The front doors were closed. It was still early in the afternoon, and we visited the theatre quite as much for the sake of becoming acquainted with the people whom we were likely to find engaged in the overseeing or handiwork of its preparation for the approaching festival, as for a good view of itself. We passed by a narrow side-alley to the rear, and entered through a dark, tortuous passage, such as leads through the hinder part of any theatre at the East.

We found the stage finely commodious, less so than that of the New York Academy of Music, but a trifle larger than that of Niblo's. Its area was not so well distributed as that of the latter theatre, the breadth to a certain extent being sacrificed to the depth; but the happy calculation or chance which made Niblo's stage as nearly perfect in its proportions as any in the world, cannot be expected everywhere,—even among an inspired race like the Modern Theocracy. No Mormon doubts the fact that the plan of the Tabernacle and the Temple have been revealed to Brigham Young, as was the pattern of the former edifice among the Jews to Moses; but I suppose that even the most enthusiastic theocrat does not expect to have Heaven make out all the specifications for a Mormon Winter Garden.

The air was busy with the sound of the carpenter's hammer, putting down the last planks of the temporary floor flush with the stage, and covering the entire parquet; and between the strokes rose a hum of women's voices, or above them every now and then a shrill call or a ringing laugh. The talk was polyglot; for among the sisters who were dressing the theatre were not only the elder comers and experienced Saints, but recent arrivals from numerous nationalities. I noticed in the bustling little groups that sat binding the ropes with evergreens after the manner of an Eastern Christmas church-dressing, or supplied the binders with culled cedar sprigs from the big fragrant heaps, a number of fresh Scandinavians, and many more of those unmistakable German *bauerinnen*, whose short blue petticoats and elephantine ankles make such a large portion of the picture presented by every station platform in the West where an emigrant train lies by on the switch. The Kätchens and Gretchens had not lost a single one of those distinctive peculiarities which mark them anywhere between Castle Garden and St. Louis, except that their big, honest, glass-blue eyes looked a trifle less dolly and wondering. Well might this be, after their bumps of the marvelous had been calloused by such tremendous thumps of impression as even a Yankee gets from twelve hundred miles of Plains and Rocky Mountain travelling, to say nothing of the peculiar and special blow which must have been inflicted on candidates for female saintship by the realities of Mormondom itself. Otherwise they were the same sturdy, stumpy little peasants as huddle about the Battery on the arrival of a Bremen bark, with the same linty locks straggling from under their caps over full-moon faces of that curious color produced by *tan* upon a blonde complexion. The sun which had flooded them throughout their Overland journey, had only intensified the photography of Bavarian harvest-fields and Prussian turnip-patches. Intermingling, or rather forming interspersed groups, with these (for as yet they had learned no common tongue) were Kent and Surrey hop-pickers; sprightly Welsh shepherdesses, brightest-eyed, sturdiest-calved, blackest-haired of all; Irishwomen (the smallest lot, as belonging to a race preoccupied by other than the Mormon despotism) and a few Americans, who, wherever they appeared, were the dominant sisters of the circle. I wandered among them, and universally found cheerful, contented faces, except where middle age, attained before the peasant left Europe, had made indelible the traces of servile labor and hardship. Nowhere, however, could I find a countenance which even so much as once in its lifetime had been enlivened by the higher class of thoughts and emotions. The better brute faculties were represented everywhere. Industrious patience, good nature, dog fidelity, sullen strength,—these were ubiquitous; and I could well believe that in many cases the emancipation of such elements from the hopeless servility of peasant life in Europe had been a true improvement and elevation, even though the change had been from a professed Christianity into a real Mormonism. Certainly the monogamy of a Staffordshire potter's hovel, or of a den in the mining districts of England, on the gauge of progressive civilization is several notches below the polygamy of Utah. Certain apes are monogamic, but their females would be bettered by becoming women, though the transformation involved their participation in a Tartar harem. Thus, despite our view of it in the absolute, Mormonism may prove, *in transitu*, a valuable ascending step to many wretched slaves among the laboring classes of Europe, who now are women but in name, bearing all the pangs and insults of the man, with an addition of maternal throes and wearinesses. I felt glad to think thus as I went looking about me among the new-come women dressing the Salt Lake Theatre. Here they were not doing field labor, hoeing, carrying asses' burdens. Many of them, in twining these pretty cedar wreaths and making these ropes of fragrant greenery, had the first womanly work of their lives, the first work to be sung or smiled over, to call out the higher faculties of soul or fingers. Some of them *were* singing, many smiling, and I felt a mixture of pain and pleasure as I saw how awkward their features were at it. It was as if the facial muscles were taking an apprenticeship at expressing happy thoughts, and their hearts had a furlough to be glad for the first time. What struck me most strangely was the entire absence of representatives from the upper ranks of Mormon woman society, for comparatively, at any rate, there are such ranks. At the East, even among the monogamists of a society so full of imperfections as our own, such like festival preparation rallies all the squires' and lawyers' wives, the ladies from the first village families, those who are conspicuous at the quiltings, those who lead in the Dorcas and sewing societies. No women corresponding to those who make vestry-rooms and school-houses cheery throughout the week before an Eastern Christmas were anywhere visible among the ever-greens of the Salt Lake Theatre.

On the stage I was introduced to several prominent men of the Territory who were superintending the work. They were capable, intelligent-looking people, and so well dressed that they might easily have passed for Gentile visitors. The day of religious costuming seems to have gone by everywhere. The "great human average" runs through sects as well as nationalities; in cities at least, Quakers manifest their adherence to the meeting by their primness in the clothes of the world, rather than by the assumption of any uniform garb of their own. Similarly among the ruling Mormons, singularity of dress or hair-cut has fallen out of favor, on the very admirable principle of Goethe (I quote "Wilhelm Meister" from memory) that he who differs from his fellows in some chief particular should be all the more careful to conform to them in non-essentials. Thus a very influential Mormon then standing on the stage, and a son-in-law of Prophet-President Brigham, was really a surprise to me when I discovered his belonging to the Saints, since on Broadway he would have passed for a thriving Boston merchant or a Lowell manufacturer. He had the clean-shaven, keen-featured face of a New England business man still clinging to the habitudes of twenty years ago. (I set the chronological limit to save the former epithet, "*clean-shaven*" which is distinctive of no class of sensible men at the present day, though occasional individuals of sense, through eccentricity or misfortune, are still found beardless.) The governing classes on the stage (there *were* several of that denomination) were as un-mistakable in the crowd of workmen and work-women as they are everywhere else.

Out of all present, I recognized one man as the ruling spirit the moment I set my eyes on him, and it required but small discrimination of character to do so. He more fully met my preconceived ideal than any of the Saints I saw on that or any other time. He might have stood for a full-length statue of "The Mormon." Perhaps because my mind felt flattered to find its preconceptions so fully realized, even where some of them were not entirely just to the Saints in general, my attention had become pleasurably riveted upon him several minutes before our cicerone had an opportunity to introduce us to his apostolic notice. He was a man apparently somewhat over sixty, but showing none of the infirmity of years. He was erect, portly, full-chested, broad-shouldered, powerfully made, about six feet high, and weighed two hundred pounds. Perhaps he was originally a blacksmith, as they say; he may have combined that employment with the agricultural calling, which he afterward told me occupied his youth. He was built like a cyclops, at any rate. Everything about him spoke of rude animal vigor. His face was very striking: a compound of keen wit, finesse, insight into character, with native sensuality enough to furnish the basis for a Vitellius. Perhaps it was the latter half of his face which made him satisfy my ideal of "The Mormon," and there I was unjust; for on close study I did not find that the basis of this remarkable people's fanaticism was laid in sensuality,— however much the fact of polygamy might superficially point to that conclusion. Neither would it be just to call sensuality this particular Mormon's governing trait.

His bright black eyes were small and twinkling; his well proportioned nose regular, but coarse. His cheeks encroached on the orbital cavities above them, and in common with his whole face were pluffy and blonde, with a glaze of sunburn from apostolic summer tours. His lips were very full, and the expression of the whole mouth lickerish as Falstaff's; his chin was double and shiny, from the twin effect of good living and close-shaving. His *tout ensemble* spoke a man who, to the utmost, relished and possessed the seventh heaven of bodily bliss, unalloyed by the slightest complication with poetic fantasies, undisturbed by the least intrusion of metaphysical obstacles or problems. I am only as uncomplimentary as a photograph,—moreover, I can heal the wounds of visual truth, as a photograph cannot, by saying that, no matter how he *looked*, the man who had climbed to the second place in a nation of one hundred thousand people, was one of the most energetic apostles of the Latter-day faith, and shared Brigham Young's most intimate friendship, must have possessed very strong qualities whereby to accomplish these things in addition and counterpoise to mere sensuality. Let me finish the statue before I engrave its name on the pedestal. This powerful figure is an exception to my recent assertion, that among the Mormons singularity of dress has become obsolete. His dress is not a sectarian uniform, nor is it absolutely eccentric; still it is curious. One would not like to dress in such fashion anywhere out of Salt Lake City, nor even there, unless he were an apostle. The costume consists (beginning as is proper from the base), *imprimis*, of a pair of plain but well blacked and polished cowskin shoes, with simple galloon strings running through two holes each in flaps and upper; next, a pair of pantaloons, fashioned out of the identical buff and apparently cotton fabric, which twenty-five years ago was worn in the nursery by the author's contemporaries, under the agreeably Shemitic-sounding name of *nankeen* (and which he may say, fascinated by its clean look, no less than its cool and pleasant memory, he has often sought for in the shops of adult experience); thirdly, of a vest identical in material with the pantaloons; next, of an alpaca coat, whose pattern, though ecclesiastical, the ungodly call "shadbelly," but which, to unconverted ears, will be familiar as a "cutaway" or "claw-hammer jacket." Certain persons may wonder why I do not call the upper garment a dress-coat at once; but the dress-coat varies, having no eternal principle about it, save the absence of front skirts. Its tails may be of *any* cut, but the exact curve of the apostolic skirts is expressed to any American mind, familiar with camp-meetings, by the term "shadbelly." The aperture of the nankeen vest is cut to a medium depth, and discloses a faultless frill of delicately hand-stitched linen, white as a snow-flake fresh caught on the apostolic bosom. A narrow black stock, of silk, loosely holds the turn-down collar about a throbbing, manly throat; while, last of all exterior embellishments, a sugar-loaf hat, of the finest yellow Leghorn, puts the top finish on my statue of Heber Kimball. We were presented to him by the President's favorite son-in-law, Mr. Clawson.

"Travellers are ye, heh?" said Heber Kimball, after he had taken us in at the front of those alert little sparkling black eyes, and remanded us over to their tail for further consideration. "York?"

"Yes! What made you think so?"

"Don't know; kinder tell a man from York, *allers*. Came from there m'self. Didn't ye know that?"

"Indeed! Is that so?"

"*Cer*-tin! Joseph Smith, Brigham Young, 'n I, were all neighbors when we were boys. Lived right 'n the same school-deestrict, Ontario County. Our parents came there 'n settled when we weren't more 'n so high" (the apostle flattened his broad brown hand about three feet from the ground).

"I've spent months in Ontario County myself."

"Where's that?"

"At Clifton, where they have the Water Cure."

"Don't say? That's clos't' the Sulphur Springs! *Tew* be sure! I know where *that* is, perfectly. They used to have a ta-ar-vern there where the boys 'n gals went out a sleigh-ridin', 'n wound up with a dance. Ever out to the hill where Joseph Smith dug up the plates?"

"No, I've often heard of the place, but never had a chance to go to it"—

"Yes, to be sure, that's in another direction. Well, I know all that country. Been in Canandaigua lots of times; used to be our market; there, in fact, we lived till they drove us out, when the persecution first began, ye know. We never had no fair chance there. But there the prophet of the Lord begun, and now—well, *don't* it seem a kinder cur'us ?" (turning to the President's son-in-law) "when I think o' all the way the Lord's led us, it seems like a dream! There I was down in Lake City yesterday, and Provo the day afore, and Payson and Nephi the week afore that, and the Lord was with us, and we had big meetin's, and the brethren and sisters all came in from a-gettin' in the harvest, and the grain was all ripe for the sickle (turning again half unconsciously to the saintly son-in-law), and we had a *blessed* time! O, Brother Brigham spoke with power. We must a had a thousand each time, and though it was a putty busy season with crops, the work o' the Lord was gay-lo-rious! Right into the midst o' my talk about the valleys and the mountains whereunto them as is blessed o' the Lord is all a-flowin' to be saved, I thought of that old Ontario County and the deestrict school, where we all sot together afore the Lord called Joseph—seemed's if the old place stood right afore my face: wall, I suppose the old county ain't much changed; 'twas a kinder slow old neighborhood, anyhow."

"No, I don't suppose that many changes have taken place since you saw it last. It's still a quiet farming country. Nothing, except the town of Canandaigua, seems to keep it alive, unless it's the Sulphur Springs at Clifton, where there is a pretty steady flow of sick people as well as sulphur,—the one coming to get cured by the other."

"That al'ays used to be a steady business. They reckoned it was good for the cattle before folks that had suthin' a matter o' them went there. The people that didn't like it said it biled right out o' hell. When the first trains were a-comin' over, before the Lord pitched our tents down here in the valley, we used to hear a good deal o' the same kind o' talk talked by the people. It used to seem kind o' familiar to me, and I said to 'em there was no use o' judgin' a matter before they heerd it, for I remembered those very Sulphur Springs of Ontario County; and here, right among the selfsame kind o' waters, springs the streams that is for the healing o' the nations. How long h'ye been here?"

"Only a couple of days."

"Well, you must stay and get better acquainted. Look around here! What d'ye think o' this? Some o' these women ha' only been here since the last tram got in. *There's* 'similation! We work the material right in at once! There's every kind here; some o' them can't speak a word o' English."

"Yes, so I hear. They seem very contented."

"Contented? Yes. Their hearts are ready to leap for joy! These are they of whom it was spoken, 'All flesh shall flow unto it and be saved!' You must go around among us. It's a wonder to all who will behold. Why, sixteen years ago this very plot we're standin' on was the barrenest sage brush you ever see. Now, lo and behold! the Lord is covering with his chosen all the face thereof and the country round about. Where 'r ye stayin'?"

"At Townsend's."

"Good man, Brother Townsend. Does a smashing business. I'll come and see you."

"We shall be very happy, I'm sure."

Thenceforth Heber took a vivid interest in our eternal welfare. He quite laid himself out for our conversion, coming to sit with us at breakfast in the black shadbelly, the nankeen vest and breeches, and the truncate cone of Leghorn, which made him look like an Italian mountebank physician of the seventeenth century.

I have heard men who could misquote Scripture to suit their purpose, and talk a long time without saying anything; but in both these particulars Heber Kimball so far surpassed the loftiest efforts within my previous experience, that I could think of no comparison for him but Jack Bunsby converted by Stiggins, and taken to exhorting. Witness a sample:—

"Seven women shall take a hold o' one man! There!" (with a slap on the back of the nearest subject for regeneration.) "What d'ye think o' that? Shall! *Shall* take a hold on him! That don't mean they *shan't*, does it? No! God's word means what it says, and therefore means no otherwise—not in no way, shape, nor manner. Not in no Way, for He saith, 'I am the *way*, and the truth, and the life.' Not in no *shape*, for 'a man beholdeth his nat'r'l shape in a glass;' nor in no *manner*, for 'he straight-way forgetteth what manner of man he was.' Seven women shall catch a hold on him. And ef they *shall*, then they *will!* For everything shall come to pass, and not one good word shall fall to the ground. You who try to explain away the Scriptur' would make it fig'rative. But don't come to me with none o' yer spiritooalizers! Not *one* good word shall fall. Therefore *seven* shall not fall. And ef seven shall catch a hold on him,—and, as I jist proved, seven *will* catch a hold on him,—then seven *ought*; and in the latter-day glory, *seven*, yea, as our Lord said un-tew Peter, 'Verily I say un-tew you, not seven but seventy times seven,' these seventy times seven shall catch a hold and cleave. Blessed day! For the end shall be even as the beginning, and seventy-fold more abundantly. Come over into my garden."

This invitation always wound up the homily. We gladly accepted it; and I must confess that if there ever could be any hope of our conversion, it was just about the time we stood in Brother Heber's fine orchard, eating apples and apricots between exhortations, and having sound doctrine poked down our throats, with gooseberries as big as plums, to take the taste out of our mouths, like jam after castor-oil.

Mr. Kimball's city establishment (he is a large property holder elsewhere) is situated on a rise of ground but a few rods from the Temple corner and the President's inclosure. Dr. Bernhisel, a former Congressional delegate from the Territory, and a man possessing much influence as well as five or six wives, has a place in the same neighborhood, on the opposite side of the street. The houses of both are neat and commodious, but unostentatious, like the residence of some principal selectman in a New England village. Utah has not yet had time to grow the noble elms which shade such a residence; but everything which money, keen business tact and indomitable energy can do has been done by Heber Kimball at least, to make his place a paradise of luxuriant vegetation. In picturesquely selected places he has contrived to create pretty little groves of maple, poplar, acacia, and box elder, transplanting the young trees from the Wahsatch cañons, and by plentiful irrigation making them grow so rapidly that they had already attained the respectable height of twenty-five or thirty feet. In this matter of irrigation I noticed that both Brothers Brigham and Heber seemed to be "not under the law, but under grace." The chief water supplies of the Mormon city may without metaphor be said to run through each apostle's back yard, and no hand but their own shuts the gate on their trenches. The lower level of Heber Kimball's place, toward the city, is a garden laid out under its owner's supervision by an old Mormon gardener (Irish or English, if I recollect right) in whom he feels great pride, and to whom he evidently seems the greatest man in Christendom, or "*paritibus Gentium.*" (I add the "or," not knowing precisely with which class to pigeon-hole Mormondom.) The plan of the garden is as simple and natural as a path through the woods, the walks wandering hither and thither among intersecting rivulets, and under green arches of apricot, apple, peach, plum, and nectarine, whose pleasant-scented fruit, ripe already or mellowing to ripeness, bowed their over-weighted branches together above our heads. Heber's melons and cucumbers were very thrifty; indeed, the soil and climate of Utah are finely suited to the cultivation of all gourd fruit. It was a week too late for strawberries, or, Heber told me, I should have seen a sight,— Brother Brigham's crop had amounted to over eighty bushels, and he had gathered an almighty lot himself. Heber was cultivating a kind of currant which he had introduced from the cañons, and which by high science had been so far domesticated and improved that its fruit was very pleasant, having an abundant juice, less acid, and a flavor no less pronounced, than our own large white currants at the East; furthermore, attaining the weight of a good-sized gooseberry.

We visited upon the same grounds, on the bank of one of those streams heretofore mentioned as traversing apostolic back yards, a cider-mill, a grist-mill, a feed-grinder, a workshop with lathes, belts, and shafting, and almost every conceivable mechanism for economizing human power in the management of a large estate demanding constant supplies and repairs. Indeed, in both Brigham Young's and Heber Kimball's establishments one sees not the mere *ferme ornée* of a proprietor living within hail of all the luxuries of civilization. Such a man can afford to neglect domestic manufactures,—all that he wants, from a tooth-pick to a steam saw-mill, being manufactured within a hundred miles, and sold within a hundred rods of his park gate. Not so one of the Mormon Presidents. He must have his resources within his walls; any day he may be in a state of siege. He has had to stand on guard all his life. From Ontario County to the Wahsatch cañon, the Mormon's only motion has been a sullen retreat, facing the foe that drove him backward; his only rest, to stand at bay or lie in wait for the same foe. He is the Manfred among nationalities—spurned by his mother, Judaism, and by the children of Christendom alike. By dint of exquisite craft and perpetual presents, he has reduced the savage tribes of the Desert to allies of his strange religious scheme. But he remembers the time when his "Lamanite brother," as he now calls him, had a disagreeable way of attacking Mormon trains, and making descent on Mormon ranches, and trusts him as one trusts a cat, though making use of him freely. He remembers Nauvoo, Missouri, and Johnson's army lying at Camp Floyd, inactive but insulting. Nor need he go back to Buchanan's time; for there this moment, just across the valley, he sees white tents pitched on the hither face of his guarding ridges; and over the cannon which command his harem floats the flag of a mother who has spurned him from her door, and whom he hates with all the heart-burning of a deformed and outcast child. Those iron throats that threaten to bellow at him, would not plead for him when his Prophet lay dying by the shot of the assassin, and his home was sacked by a delirious mob. He shakes his fist at them across the valley, and bides his time.

Well if the thought of Johnston past, of Connor present, were all that the apostles had to disturb them that sunny day I stood by the water-wheel of Heber's versatile factory! They had also to remember foes within their body politic,— the revolution, partly religious, partly political, which so few years ago Brigham was obliged to quell with cannon; the burrowing discontents and treacherous schisms of the Legitimists, who look upon Joe Smith's son as the true heir to the Presidency, and more or less openly, as they dare, insinuate that the powers regnant are usurping a divine right; and, last but not least, the miserable jealousy and discontent, existing to an extent betrayed by the very pains taken to conceal it, among the wives of polygamistic marriages. They always tell how happy the women are, but it is the rarest possible occurrence for a Gentile to receive an invitation to any home or public festivity where he has an opportunity to examine this happiness for himself. You also hear it asserted that the Smith faction never had any existence, or is perfectly appeased. George Smith, Joe the Prophet's cousin, occupies high official positions, and is one of the most influential men in the Church. This fact is pointed out as a proof that his family are friendly to Brigham's administration; but the feeling in favor of the Smith succession is such a fanaticism among a large class, that no man of less ability and popularity than Young could keep it down for a week; and were the administration overthrown Joe's son, or some Perkin Warbeck in place of him, would ascend the throne if only for a day and in the city. I think the Smith faction would worship anybody that looked as if his name might be Smith. There are other minor factions whose existence hourly threatens the stability of the government. The Mormon Presidents may well live within walls, and have their materials for independent subsistence close at hand.

Among other apparatus operated by Heber's water-wheel I observed a carding-machine, and was told by the proprietor that he had the entire gear of a woolen factory on a small scale, and when it was set, could manufacture from the fleece excellent yarn and durable cloth, sufficient at least for all household uses.

Already (about July 1st) some apples were ripe enough in Salt Lake City to make good cider, as we tested. Specimens of the fruit we found quite spicy, resembling the wine-apple of New York State in size, shape, and flavor. One day, coming out of the vegetable garden on our return to the hotel, we were accompanied to the gate by Heber Kimball. A cow was eating the bark of a young shade-tree planted in front of his property, having burglariously broken the tree-box to get at it. Heber naturally waxed wroth, and cudgeled the cow away. Just then a keeper of the Church cattle passed on horseback, with a small drove in front of him. Brother Heber hailed him, and wished to know whose cow this was that had gnawed his tree,—was it the herder's, for instance? "It was not; it belonged to Brother What-d'ye-call'um, up the next street a piece; he had a way of letting his cattle run loose." "Well!" said Heber, "this is the third time his cussed cow hez eaten a tree of mine, with the tree-box for seasonin'. Here, herder! Take this critter, put her in your drove, and this afternoon drive her down to Church Island with the rest. If anybody asks your authority, say *I* told you to."

Without a moment's demur the herder obeyed the second President. I did not ask whether Brother What-d'ye-call-'um had more than one cow, and could get along without serious diminution to his milk-porridge from the loss of this one. But that was of no consequence; *dictum est.* That afternoon the cow went down to Church Island, and was henceforth as sacred as among the Brahmins, though in a different sense. She belonged to the Church herd—to give milk in life, beef, horn, and hide in death, for the advancement upon earth of the Saints' latter-day kingdom. Before I leave Salt Lake City I shall say more *in extenso* what relation "The Church" bears, not only to such waifs of emolument as this cow, but to every Mormon's entire property.

During our stay at Townsend's, we were one morning sitting on the veranda, when our landlord, a portly, kindly man, brought up a friend of his to introduce to us. It was Porter

Rockwell, the Destroying Angel and chief of the Danites. Apart from his cause, I felt an abstract interest in this old fighter, and was glad to become acquainted with him. He welcomed us very cordially to Utah, and told us we ought to stay: our only bad taste was exhibited in merely going through. We could not avoid telling him, with a smile, that Utah had a reputation for stopping people who showed such taste, to take a permanent residence. He answered good-humoredly that he had heard the rumor, and intended so far to verify it that he should halt us on our way past his door, when we started to cross the desert, put our horses in his own stable, carry us to his table, and inflict on us the penalty of a real Mormon dinner—after which (if our horses had got through their feed) we should be let off with an admonition never to try to pass *his* door if we came that way again. "Bless yer soul, but we're savage!" said Porter Rockwell. "Once drew a sassige on a Yankee Gentile myself—crammed it right down his throat with scalding hot gravy and pancakes. We Mormons torture 'em awful. The Gentile I drew the sassige on bore it like a man, and is livin' yet. Well, I'll soon see ye agin." So he shook hands with us, jumped on his mustang, and ambled away as gently as if, instead of being a destroying angel, he were a colporteur of peace tracts, or a peddler of Winslow's Soothing Syrup.

He kept his word to us, seeing us soon and frequently. Next to Brigham Young, he was the most interesting man and problem that I encountered in Utah. His personal appearance in itself was very striking. His figure was of the middle height, and very strongly made; broad across the shoulders, and set squarely on the legs. His arm was of large girth, his chest round as a barrel, and his hand looked as powerful as a grizzly bear's. His face was of the mastiff type, and its expression, fidelity, fearlessness, ferocity. A man with his massive lower jaw, firm mouth, and good-humored but steady and searching eyes of steel-blue, if his fanaticism takes the Mormon form, must infallibly become like Porter Rockwell. Organization and circumstances combine to make any such man a destroying angel. Having always felt the most vivid interest in supernatural characters of that species, I was familiar with most of them from the biblical examples of those who smote Egypt, Sodom, and Sennacherib, to the more modern Arab, Azrael, and that famous one who descended, all white-bearded and in shining raiment from the Judges' Cave, to lead the van of Quinnipiack's forlorn hope and smite the red-skinned Philistines. Out of this mass of conflicting and particular angels I had abstracted an ideal and general angel; but when I suddenly came on a real one, in Porter Rockwell, I was surprised at his unlikeness to my thought. His hair, black and iron-gray in streaks, was gathered into a cue, just behind the apex of the skull, and twisted into a hard round bunch, confined with a comb—in nearly the same fashion as was everywhere prevalent among Eastern ladies twenty years ago. He was very obliging in his manners; placable, jocose, never extravagant when he conversed, save in burlesque. If he had been converted to Methodism in its early times, instead of Mormonism, he might have been a second Peter Cartwright, preaching and pummeling his enemies into the Kingdom instead of shooting them to Kingdom Come. No one ignorant of his career would take him on sight for a man of bad disposition in any sense. But he was that most terrible instrument which can be handled by fanaticism; a powerful physical nature welded to a mind of very narrow perceptions, intense convictions, and changeless tenacity. In his build he was a gladiator; in his humor, a Yankee lumberman; in his memory, a Bourbon; in his vengeance, an Indian. A strange mixture, only to be found on the American Continent.

In the forenoon of the Fourth of July, Porter called at our hotel to invite us to take a drive with him. His carriage was a large coach of the most ancient Overland fashion, with a boot; room for nine inside (using the swing strap in the middle), six on top, and three on the box. He had bought this vehicle at the auction of a deceased stage company's effects. It used to run from Salt Lake City to Nephi, or some other Mormon settlement, and upon its emancipation from these diurnal labors struck the eye of the angel, he told me, as the fair thing to air the angelic "ole wimmen" and the little destroying angels in. It still bore its original coat of flaming vermilion, and the name of the company, if I recollect, which used to employ its services. It was just the chariot for a large family of angelic beings, whose wings had not been sent home yet. You could have piled all the old masters' cherubim, plus the supplementary legs, into the cavern of Porter's vast coach, without their troubling each other more than the souls in the old scholastic thesis who dance on the point of a needle, besides leaving room for the parental destroyers on top and box.

Porter, in his desire to do the hospitalities of the occasion in the most graceful manner, proposed to mount the box, and take the reins himself. But we represented, as was true, that we should feel much more pleased and honored if he gave us his company inside the stage. We wished to converse with and see this interesting man,—not to ride behind him,—and so persuaded him to let a stable-boy drive for us.

I do not know if I have stated that we had been rejoined by our two companions, who had preceded us on our way from Denver to Utah as far as Virginia Dale. These gentlemen, with Porter, our artist, and myself, composed the party that rode out to visit the Springs.

These art situated at a distance of two or three miles from the northern border of the city. The road thither leads along the base of a peculiar series of hills skirting the higher ranges in all directions about the city; a formation principally limestone, and terraced in planes accurately corresponding, across valleys of upheaval and erosion that intervene. These mark the successive periods of depression for the level of that great sea which once filled the whole tract between the Uintah Range and the Snake Plateau, the Wahsatch and the Humboldt Mountains. Every sedimentary rock stands the self-registering tide-mark of an ocean which man never saw till it had shrunk to its last puddle in the present Great Salt Lake, which knew no floods, and had long eras of rest, followed by ebbs comparatively short and sudden, but outlasting a thousand generations of those pelicans, who, sole Smithsonians of the period, made meteorological investigations from the porphyritic pinnacles of their observatories across the sullen and solitary sea. In coming to speak of Salt Lake itself, I may give its geologic history more *in extenso*.

Behind the terraced hills which bounded the north road and rose above it to a height of from two to four hundred feet, Ensign Peak, a lofty projection of the Wahsatch, came in view at frequent intervals. This is the Sinai of Mormonism, for it was on this peak that the Saints' Moses, Brigham, met the spirit of Joe Smith, and received his orders for the disposition of the people. This occurred in a vision, very shortly, if not the first night, after the tents of the faithful were pitched in sight of the valley. Near the foot of this peak gush another set of thermal waters besides those we came to visit; and Porter showed us from the window of the coach the superannuated remains of an arrangement which had formerly been made to bring it nearer the Salt Lake citizens by conduits and a bath-house. The Springs we sought were reached by a ride of about three miles from Townsend's, and the day being unusually hot, betrayed themselves as far as we could see by copious evaporations, like the steam of a large laundry; hanging in the sultry air like an idle cloud over a mass of ragged rocks, on the right hand of our road. Reaching them, we alighted and spent more than an hour in their examination.

The rock from which they emerge is a limestone, belonging to the terrace formation, and stands at the foot of one of the bare gray hills which rise abruptly from the road. It is honeycombed and tunneled for yards, in all directions, by vents and channels.

We were told that some of the vents eject water hot enough to cook an egg in. I suppose that this statement is true, meaning a soft egg. I explored all the basins as far as I could get under the rocks which overhang them, and found several crevices where the jets scalded on instant contact, as well as several deep pools in which I could not bear my hand more than a second. But water actually boiling at the surface was nowhere visible.

Even in the hottest pools I was deeply interested to find fresh-water algæ growing abundantly. I had snatched up the nearest pitcher as I left the Fourth of July confusion of the hotel, intending to bring back a sample of the waters. This I now found convenient for the collection of the algæ, and I nearly blistered my hands in fishing from the basins all the prettiest specimens within reach. They were very frail—more like a mucus or a jelly than a plant—yet, even to the naked eye, distinctly organized. Their cellular structure is even more visible, now that they are dried and lying before me in the book where I pressed them, than it was in the water which bore them. I much regretted having no good blotting-book in so much of our dunnage as we had detained at Salt Lake, but, on getting back with my algæ to the hotel, made shift to use an old edition of Comstock's Mineralogy, arranging the specimens on note paper, putting them between the book-leaves, and setting the foot of my heavy fore-poster on the whole, till such time as we should "break camp" for the Desert. The method of treating these algæ was similar in other respects to that observed at the sea-side in collecting their marine cousins, by lady enthusiasts at the East.

On reaching home with my pitcher, I emptied it into a pail of water. When I saw an alga floating naturally, I dipped my sheet of note paper under it (card-board, which is better, not being at hand), and slowly lifted it, arranging the forms with a pin, as nearly as I could in the way they swam. Some of them were a string of inflated globules, in shape like the bladder-weed of our sea-shore, but the brightest transparent emerald in color. Others were only a viscous mass like "frog-spittle," with covered but certain traces of organization. Still others were tapes and coils of a tissue simulating fibre,—the former resembling eel-grass, the latter a fine moss or lichen. Several amorphous masses, which I poked asunder, broke up into distinct and evident organisms, coming under one or another of the forms described. Even more than the absence of our albums do I regret that of the microscope, which might have enabled us to examine these specimens in their fresh state. I have nearly a hundred of the dried algæ, and hope some time to have them thoroughly treated. Their hues in nature were the emerald green I have mentioned, a delicate pink of the shade sometimes called French gray, a lilac, an ashen, an ultramarine blue, and a brown. Some of my specimens still keep their color very well.

The average temperature of the water in the larger pools is 128° F. It is much higher than that under some of the jets in whose basins the algæ grow. In midwinter the brook which runs from these springs is said to heat the air for many rods along the road, so that benighted people have often camped there as around a fire-place. Even on such a hot day as the Fourth of July in Salt Lake Valley, the air was perceptibly cooler after leaving the springs' vicinity. No other plant than the algæ grew within reach of its waters, nor was any higher organization than the vegetable perceptible in them. That they do not contain animal life no one can positively assert,—the Great Salt Lake itself, as I myself have tested, not being devoid of such life, though its azoic character was once universally believed. Nothing of the kind, however, has yet been found in the springs. In the winter, ducks, geese, and an occasional crane or pelican, over from their cold side of the school-house at Salt Lake, with leave to stand up by the stove, huddle in the genial steam of the reedy level which drinks the springs' overflow. We now had only a few solitary magpies to cheer our way home through the hot dust.

Porter Rockwell studiously avoided referring to Mormonism seriously, though he seemed willing enough to talk

about it in a playful manner if any one else broached the subject. He was rough, but kind and conciliatory, in everything
he said, and sometimes very amusing. A description he gave,
accompanied by pantomime, of the way in which he had
seen a Goshoot family sitting in a circle on their haunches
when the grasshoppers were plenty, using their palms as
scoops and "paying" the insects into their mouths with a
windlass motion as fast as their hands could fly, was irresistibly laughable. It seemed strange to be riding in the carriage
and by the side of a man, who, if universal report among the
Gentiles were correct, would not hesitate to cut my throat
at the Church's orders. It was like an Assyrian taking an airing in the chariot of the Angel of Death. I was not likely to
become obnoxious to the Church: I certainly did not mean
to be if I could help it. Knowing I had been very careful
along the way from the Missouri never to express myself
before anybody who might be a Mormon spy, I felt pretty
tranquil upon the subject of any change in Porter Rockwell
from his present agreeable relation of entertainer to the less
pleasant one of executioner, though an hour's study of him
enabled me to say that though, if he had it to perform, less
heart might be in his execution of the latter than of the former function, there would be at any rate no less efficiency
and sureness. He had the reputation of having killed many
men—forty, report said; and there are not lacking those who
suspect him of still more. From an eye-witness I received,
while in Utah, the following account of one of his *ven-
dette*. A Gentile doing business in Salt Lake City during
Johnston's occupation of Camp Floyd, suffered oppressive
exaction from the Church authorities; and after failing, as
might have been expected, to get a decision in his favor from

a local Mormon judge and jury before whom he brought his petition for relief, he retired in a most exasperated state of mind to the United States encampment,—partly with a view to obtaining redress through Johnston, and partly for self-protection from the Danites, with whom his prosecution of the Church had made him a marked man. One day Porter Rockwell rode into Camp Floyd. At no time during Johnston's occupation was there anything but the merest farcical show of hostilities. Invader and invaded hobnobbed together at officers' quarters, over fiery glasses of "Valley Tan" (the demoniacal whiskey of the region); Saints and Gentiles winked at each other from the jury-box to the dock; the matters in dispute between Brigham Young and Buchanan were treated by all classes as a mere technical squabble, in which nobody was hurt. Yet, though the familiarity was on both sides, all the confidence was on that of the army, which got regularly plucked in every transaction, from the disgraceful treaty not to approach within forty miles of the city, to the buying of adobes, feed, and lumber. At no time during the burlesque of invasion was intercourse suspended between the Mormons and the camp. They drove a thriving business in huckstering commissariat supplies of all kinds, skins, clothes, and moccasins, horse-trading, and every other branch of traffic which can be transacted between the shrewdest of camp-followers and a petty force of soldiery, hundreds of hostile miles from their basis of supplies. The Mormons spoiled the Egyptians they despised; and the only results of the Johnston expedition were an engorgement of the Saints' exchequer, the passing of a pretty additional sum to the already overloaded side of Buchanan's account with the American people, and the exacerbation of the whole

Mormon body. Buchanan, through Johnson, simply pinched the ears and filliped the noses of the Saints, whereas a private man, or a ruler of any brains, always gives his enemy a wide berth or a thrashing such as he never will forget, on the maxim (whose wiser Shakespeare never wrote),—

"Beware
Of entrance to a quarrel; but, being in,
Bear it that the opposed may beware of thee."

In accordance with habitual usage, Porter Rockwell, on the occasion mentioned, rode up to head-quarters at Camp Floyd, and was sitting undismounted in conversation with one of the officers at the door, when the aggrieved plaintiff in the late suit espied him, and approached in a violent passion.

For several minutes this man publicly addressed Porter Rockwell in every term of vituperation and insult which an outraged nature could suggest, furthermore characterizing Brigham as a swindling old scoundrel, and the entire Church as his nice little game of thimble-rig. Not a muscle of Porter's face moved till this harangue was finished. Then he very quietly replied, "O! you shoot your mouth at *me*, do ye? Well, I'll remember you some time," and rode away.

A few days after that some officers came up to Salt Lake City on all night's leave, and, thinking himself amply protected by their escort, the exiled trader accompanied them. During the evening he separated from his party, and went alone into a side street to call on a Gentile friend. The officers never saw him again till he lay in their presence with a revolver hole from temple to temple, having been picked up dead a little while after he left them. Of whose pistol killed him, there is no eyewitness, and as little doubt.

I have somewhat violated the successions of time, that I might bring into my picture of Utah one of the most prominent figures of the Territory. Before our ride with Rockwell, we received notes of invitation to certain festivities in the Mormon Academy of Music, intended for the commemoration of our national independence.

These festivities took the form of a ball, and afforded such an opportunity for studying Mormon sociology as three months' ordinary stay in Salt Lake might not have given me. Though Mormondom is disloyal to the core, it still patronizes the Fourth of July, at least in its phase of *high-jinks*, omitting the patriotism, but keeping the fireworks of our Eastern celebration, substituting "Utah" for "Union" in the Buncombe speeches, and having a dance instead of the Declaration of Independence. All the Saints within half a day's ride of the city come flocking into it to spend the Fourth. A well-to-do Mormon at the head of his wives and children, all of whom are probably eating candy as they march through the metropolitan streets in solid column, looks, to the uninitiated, like the principal of a female seminary taking out his charge for an airing.

That Fourth of July fell on a Saturday. In their ambition to reproduce ancient Judaism (and this ambition is a key to most of their puzzles), the Mormons are Sabbatarians of a strictness which would delight Lord Shaftesbury. Accordingly, in order that their festivities might not encroach on the early hours of Sunday (or "Sabbath" as it is noticeably called by all sects who have the Jewish idea of the day), they had the ball on Forth of July eve instead of the night of the Fourth. I could not realize the risk of such an encroachment when I read the following sentence printed upon my billet of invitation:—

"Dancing to commence at 4 P. M."

Our party, and a friend whose position as agent of Wells & Fargo ministered unto him an abundant entrance everywhere in Utah, were the only Gentiles whom I found invited by President Young to meet in the neighborhood of three thousand Saints.

We repaired to the Opera-house at 8 o'clock, feeling a certain degree of remorse at seeming so "stuck up" as the lateness of our arrival must make us in the eyes of people who had been cutting pigeon-wings since 4 P. M.

On entering the theatre, we were surprised to see how remarkably it had been improved since we stood on the stage in daylight, listening to Heber Kimball, and seeing the women busy in the preparation of the festive trimmings. Fragrant ropes of evergreen hung in symmetrical festoons from the cornice and the edge of the galleries; others wound spirally about the pillars, and wreathed the capitals. A great central chandelier was similarly ornamented, while interspersed among the pine and cedar were immense garlands and bunches of natural flowers, native and exotic, freshly plucked that day to lay upon Brigham's shrine. The lights were so abundant that in the galleries the heat was oppressive, and the whole house was illuminated nearly as well as could have been accomplished by gas. The boundary between stage and parquet having been obliterated by planking over the seats flush with the former, the whole area of both was thrown open to the dancers, making as commodious a ball-room as could be desired by any pleasure-seekers in the world. A Mormon band gave vent to the music of the occasion. As they did not pretend to be Dodworths, Thomases, Koenigs, or anything of the sort, it would be unfair to criticize them closely; but I will say that I could better understand that immemorial usage which has restricted Saints to the use of the harp, after hearing their performance on other instruments. They played, however, quite as well as the ball-room bands of most Eastern towns no larger than Salt Lake City, if we except those whose population has become somewhat Teutonized: and what they lacked in quality, they made up in quantity. The Mormon principle of devoting to the Church one tenth of all a man is and has, was fully exemplified by the violins who gave it in the form of elbow, and by the trombones who blew that proportion of their annual increase into the ears of the Saints during the first four contra-dances. The merry-makers at any rate enjoyed the music as much as if it had been Musard's, which, after all, was the only matter of consequence.

We sought out our entertainer, Brigham Young, to thank him for the flattering exception made in our Gentile favor. He was standing in the dress-circle of the theatre, looking down on the dancers with an air of mingled hearty kindness and feudal ownership. I could excuse the latter, for Utah belongs to him of right. He may justly say of it, "Is not this great Babylon which I have built?" Like any Eastern party-goer, he was habited in the "customary suit of solemn black," and looked very distinguished in this dress, though his daily homespun detracts nothing from the feeling, when in his presence, that you are beholding a most remarkable man. He is nearly seventy years old, but appears very little over forty. His height is about

"five feet ten.
The height of Lord Chesterfield's gentlemen";

his figure very well made, and slightly inclining to portliness. His hair is a rich curly chestnut, formerly worn long, in supposed imitation of the apostolic coiffure, but now cut in our practical Eastern fashion, as accords with the man of business whose *métier* he has added to apostleship, with the growing temporal prosperity of Zion. Indeed, he is the greatest business man on the Continent,—the head and cashier of a firm of one hundred thousand silent partners, and the only auditor of that cashier besides. Brigham Young's eyes are a clear blue-gray, frank and straightforward in their look; his nose a finely chiseled aquiline; his mouth exceedingly firm, and fortified in that expression by a chin almost as protrusive beyond the rest of the profile as Charlotte Cushman's, though less noticeably so, being longer than hers; and he wears a narrow ribbon of brown whiskers meeting on the throat. But for his chin, he would greatly resemble the best portraits of Sidney Smith, the humorist. I think I have heard Captain Burton say that he had irregular teeth, which made his smile unpleasant. Shortly after the Captain's visits our benevolent President altered all that, sending out as Territorial Secretary Mr. Fuller, who, besides being a successful politician, was an excellent dentist. He secured Brigham's everlasting favor by making him a very handsome false set, and performing the same service for all of his favorite but edentate wives. Several other apostles of the Lord owe to Mr. Fuller their ability to gnash their teeth against the Gentiles. The result was, that he became the most popular Federal officer (who didn't turn Mormon) ever sent to Utah. The man who obtains ascendency over the mouths of the authorities cannot fail ere long to get their ears.

Brigham's manners astonish any one who knows that his only education was a few quarters of such common-school education as could be had in Ontario County, Central New York, during the early part of the century. There are few courtlier men living. His address is a fine combination of dignity with the desire to confer happiness, of perfect deference to the feelings of others with absolute certainty of himself and his own opinions. He is a remarkable example of the educating influence of tactful perception wedded to entire singleness of aim, without regard to its moral character. His early life was passed among the uncouth and illiterate; any tow-headed boy coming into the Clifton Water-cure to sell Ontario County maple-sugar has, to all external appearance, a better chance of reaching supreme command than Brigham had in his childhood; his daily associations since he embraced Mormonism have been with the least cultivated grades of human society, a heterogenous horde, looking to him for its erection into a nation; yet he has so clearly seen what is requisite in the man who would be respected in the Presidency, and has so unreservedly devoted his life to its attainment, that in protracted conversation with him, I heard only a single solecism ("ain't you" for "aren't you"), and saw not one instance of breeding which would be inconsistent with noble lineage.

I say this good of him frankly, disregarding any slur which may be cast on me as his defender by those broad-effect artists who always paint the Devil black; for I think it high time that the Mormon enemies of our American idea should be plainly understood as far more dangerous antagonists than hypocrites or idiots can ever hope to be. Let us not twice commit the blunder of underrating our foes.

Brigham began our conversation at the theatre by telling me I was late—it was after 9 o'clock. I replied that this was

CHO-LOOKE, THE YO-SEMITE FALL.

the time we usually set about dressing for an evening party in Boston or New York.

"Yes," said he, "you find us an old-fashioned people; we are trying to return to the healthy habits of the patriarchal age."

"Need you go back so far as that for your parallel?" suggested I. "It strikes me that we might have found four o'clock balls among the *early* Christians."

He smiled, without that offensive affectation of some great men, the air of taking another's joke under their gracious patronage, and went on to remark that there were, unfortunately, multitudinous differences between the Mormons and Americans at the East besides the hours they kept.

"You find us," said he, "trying to live peaceably. A sojourn with people thus minded must be a great relief to you, who come from a land where brother hath lifted hand against brother, and you hear the confused noise of the warrior perpetually ringing in your ears."

Despite the courtly deference and scriptural dignity of this speech, I detected in it a latent crow over that "perished Union" which, up to the time of Lee's surrender was the favorite theme of every Saint one met in Utah, and hastened to assure the President that I had no desire for relief from sympathy with my country's struggle for honor and existence.

The Opera-house was a subject which Brigham and I could agree upon. I was greatly astonished to find in the desert heart of the Continent a place of public amusement which, regarding comfort, capacity, and beauty, has but two or three superiors in the United States. It is internally constructed somewhat like the New York Academy of Music, seats twenty-five hundred, and commodiously receives five hundred more when, as in the present instance, the stage is thrown into the parquet. My greatest surprise was excited by the remarkable artistic beauty of the gilt and painted decorations on the great arch over the stage, the cornices, and the moulding about the proscenium boxes. President Young, with a proper pride, assured me that every particle of the ornamental work was by indigenous and Saintly hands.

"But you don't know yet," he added, "how independent we are of you in the East. Where do you think we got that central chandelier, and what d'ye suppose we paid for it?"

It was a piece of work which would have been creditable to any New York firm, apparently a richly carven circle, twined with gilt vines, leaves, and tendrils, blossoming all over with flaming wax-lights, and suspended by a massive chain of golden lustre. So I replied that he probably paid a thousand dollars for it in New York.

"Capital!" exclaimed Brigham; "*I* made it myself!" That circle is a *cart*-wheel, the wheel of one of our common Utah ox-carts. I had it washed, and gilded it with my own hands. It hangs by a pair of ox-chains, which I also gilded; and the gilt ornaments of the candlesticks were all cut after my patterns out of sheet tin!"

This is but one among a thousand illustrations of the versatility which characterizes this truly remarkable man. They are familiar to every Mormon; you can go nowhere in the Territory without hearing them admiringly recounted by the people. As I have said, in the society sense of the word, Brigham is far from being an educated man. He knows neither Latin, Greek, nor, so far as I am aware, any modern foreign language, unless, perhaps, like several prominent men among his subordinates, he has acquired sufficient acquaintance with the dialects of Shoshone, Ute, and other neighboring Indian tribes, to help in their reduction to the condition of tools and emissaries of the Church. I am not at all sure that he possesses even this slight lingual accomplishment, for, as I may hereafter show, the division of labor has been so clearly systematized, that even the business of learning Indian is apportioned chiefly to a class of Mormons who, when occasion demands, can assume all the other characteristics of red-deviltry, as well as the use of those incoherent grunts which constitute its language. Brigham's knowledge of mathematics stops at a moderate practical acquaintance with surveying, and the ability to keep books with a particularly cheerful credit side. Every deficiency in the matter of polite education which his enemies can lay to his charge, Brigham acknowledges with a simple-hearted frankness and an evident appreciation of the advantages denied his youth, challenging the admiration of all fair minds far more than any mere accomplishment could. In hearing him, one naturally feels that Brigham must possess some compensatory gifts and acquirements, in whose presence ordinary attainments become a matter of trifling moment, and that the man able to confess his weak places with such modest dignity has elements of strength within him sufficient to brace them, even in the most trying exigencies of his life. Among such elements, his versatility is by no means the least. The great American talent of *un-cornerableness*; the habit of always striking on one's feet; that Promethean faculty which in the grand passage where Zeus sends his blacksmiths to rivet the Titan down on Caucasus, Æschylus through the mouth of Force calls the ability to break away—

"Ἐκ των αμήχανων κακων"

"out of unengineerable evils,"—this, Brigham Young enjoys
to a degree which I have never seen surpassed in any great
man of any nation. He cannot be put into a position where
he is at the end of his resources; earthly circumstances never
take to him the form of a *cul de sac*. He has been at a college
whose president is Multiform Experience, whose matron is
Inexorable Necessity. If he were obliged to support himself
by farming, he understands soils, stock, tools, rotation, irrigation, manures, and all the agricultural economies so well
that he would speedily have the best crops within a hundred
miles' radius. With his own hands he would put the best
house in the settlement over the heads of himself and his
family, while other Desert Islanders in a ship-load of Cru-
soes were bewailing the loss of their carpenter. On Sundays
he can preach sermons cogent and full of common sense, if
not elegant or always free from indelicacy. On week-days he
sits in the Church office, managing a whole nation's temporalities with such secular astuteness that Talleyrand or
Richelieu would find him a match should the morning's
game be diplomatic, and the Rothschild family could not
get ahead of him if the stake were a financial advantage. On
the perilous and untried road to Utah, he was faith, wisdom,
energy, patience, expedients, courage, enthusiasm, veritable life and soul to all the fainting Saints; they never would
have reached the Rocky Mountain watershed, much less the
Great Salt Basin, without him; he was the grand incarnate
will and purpose of the Mormons' fiercely tried fanaticism;
and though he naively said to me, in speaking of the height of
Ensign Peak, "I got Brother Pratt, who had the book-learn-
ing, to take the observations, not knowing enough about
such things to do it myself," there was not a "slewed" ox-cart

on the way to that peak's base, at whose wheel his was not the first and sturdiest shoulder; and after wrestling with angels or remaining instant in prayer all night, he could yoke up his team, and trudge along by its travel-chafed necks, urging it on with ge-haws as cheerful and getting out of his black-snake cracks as resonant as the lightest-hearted bumpkin in a smock frock. In a new country and an infant civilization, specific gravities take care of such a man's position; he infallibly determines to the top of things, and will though he hide himself, less like Brigham than Saul the son of Kish, among the stuff. He *must* govern, because he is the only one of his lot who is necessary to everybody; he is not elected, but he *is*; not because he is fortunate, an heir of the past, but because among men he is the manliest, and thus what Homer meant, not the king of lands and coffers, but "αναξ ανδρών"—the king of *men!* I believe that Brigham Young was brought out by Mormonism; but I believe that if any other cause with which he might have identified himself had taken as strong possession of his nature, it would have developed him as fully, and that with the usual Christian creed and training, he would have made another Beecher in the pulpit, another Webster in the Senate, and a Sherman in the army unsurpassed by Tecumseh.

I excused myself from numerous kind invitations by the ball-room committee to be introduced to a partner and join in the dances, because (though I did not give my reason then) I wished to make a circuit of the ball-room for the purpose of thorough physiognomical study of Utah good society.

There was very little taste in dressing displayed at the ball, but there was also as little ostentation. Patrician silks and broadcloths were the rare exception, but these cordially associated with the great mass of plebeian tweed and calico. Few ladies wore jewelry, feathers, or artificial flowers; and these adornments, when I saw them, seemed to have been drawn from trunks which had crossed the Plains and the Mountains, perhaps also the Atlantic previously to either— the breast-pins, and ear-rings being of that red gold and slender workmanship which delighted our revolutionary ancestors; the head-gear of an exuberance so ancient that it has just completed its cycle, and become the mode again in this age of top-heavy belles with bushel-baskets of finery dumped on their heads and left to stay there higgledy-pig-gledy—just as a toy-watch, by standing still forever, once a day tells the time as truly as the sun. There were some pretty girls, like those who came to Brigham, swimming about in tasteful whip-syllabub of puffed tarlatan. Where saintly gentlemen came with several wives, the oldest generally seemed the most elaborately dressed, and acted much like an Eastern chaperon toward her younger sisters. (Wives of the same man habitually be-sister each other in Utah. This is what Heber Kimball would call another "triumph of grace.") Among the men, I saw some very strong, capable faces, but the majority had not much character in their looks; indeed, in that regard differed little from any average crowd of men anywhere. To my surprise, I found among the women no really degraded faces, though many stolid ones, many impas-sive ones; but only a single face expressive of deep dejection, and this belonged to the wife of a hitherto monogamic hus-band who had left her alone in the dress circle, while he was dancing with a chubby young Mormoness likely to be added to the family in a month or two. Though I saw multitudes of kindly, good-tempered countenances, and at least a score which would be called pretty anywhere, I was obliged, after a most impartial and anxious search, to confess that I had not met a single woman who looked high-toned, first-class, capable of poetic enthusiasm or heroic self-devotion; not a single woman whom an artist would dream of, and ask to sit for a study; not one to whom a finely organized intellectual man could come for companionship in his pursuits or sympathy in his yearnings. Because I knew that such a verdict would be received at the East with a "Just as you might have expected," I cast aside everything like prejudice, and forgot that I was in Utah, as I threaded that great throng.

CHAPTER VIII.

## THE DEAD SEA.—THE PHYSICAL GEOGRAPHY AND HISTORY OF ITS BASIN.

WE were distributed into two hacks of an ancient yet comfortable build, and carried a hamper of provisions to provide against the occasioned leanness which is found in the larders of the only human dwelling at Black Rock. The day was bright and breezy, the ponies in good spirits, and the road in nice condition.

The nearest point from Salt Lake City at which one may strike the lake by following a straight line, is only about ten miles in a northerly direction from the suburbs. The River Jordan pursues nearly this direction from the city to its mouth; but the shore of the Dead Sea, where it discharges, is low, swampy, and uninteresting. The most favorable place to strike the lake is nearly twenty miles west of the city, the scenery there being beautiful and unique beyond description.

This point is called "Black Rock," from a weathered boulder of peculiar shape, projecting boldly into the lake at the extremity of a low reach of shingle, and may be regarded as the farthest northern extremity of the Oquirrh Mountains, that lofty ridge to the westward of the city, which, with the loftier snow-range of the Wahsatch running parallel on the east, forms the cradle of the Mormon capital, and the more or less fertile valley of the Jordan. It would be nearer correct to call Black Rock the most northerly main-land extremity of the Oquirrh; for Church and Fremont Islands take up the broken line of the range, and carry it nearly across to the great promontory which juts many miles into the lake from the northern shore to form Bear River Bay.

Just after leaving the eastern edge of the city, our road crossed the Jordan, here a sluggish stream, eight or ten rods wide, with low fenny shores steaming under the sun, and exhibiting no signs of life or cultivation. From the low wooden bridge straight west-ward to the Oquirrh, the land is an alluvial flat, boggy and reedy wherever it can be reached by the overflow of the Jordan, covered with a loose soil on the surface of the terraces marking those successive levels of elevation to which I have referred in speaking of the hot springs and their vicinity. On this ascending series of plains, no trees or large shrubs are anywhere visible. The vegetation of the moister portions chiefly consists of various sedges, rushes, and grasses: comprising an *Equisetum*, or scouring rush; a species of *Juncus* (the *Balticus*, qu.=*Bulbosus?*); the blue-eyed, feather, hedgehog, and squirrel-tail grasses (*Sisy-rinchium, Eriocoma,* or *Stipa, Elymus*, and *Hordeum*); with a variety of *Scirpus*, or club-rush, and of the *Chara*, or feath-er-bed plant, in the pools and marshes. On the higher levels, our old comrade, the sage, appears again, and a plant some-what resembling it in fetid pungency, the hemlock geranium (*Erodium cicutarium*). The yarrow (*Achilleaa millefolia*) exists here, as, indeed, it seems to exist over the whole Conti-nent, having followed us through every change of climate and physical condition over mountain and plain, from the Atlantic side. The same may be said of the *Asclepius*, or milk-weed family, which, in the Rocky Mountains as well as here, appears in much greater profusion and number of varieties than at the far East. Here, too, are those other cosmopolites of the flora, the fleabane (*Erigeron*); the golden-rod, the mouse-ear, a variety of the evening primrose; one or more of the asters; a gentian; the *Argemone*, or "horn-poppy"; the veined dock (*Rumex venosus*); the true and the bastard toad-flax (*Antirrhinum* and *Cemandra*) a hogweed (*Ambrosia*); many leguminous tribes; a species of thistle, a clematis, and the wild rose. These reveal themselves to minute research; in a single afternoon, and without going two miles from the road, a botanist, with well trained powers of observation, might discover them all, and many more possessing considerable beauty and marked interest, from the fact that they are peculiar to the region. But the country in its general view, as taken from the road, possesses no salient features. It is a dreary waste of sun-scorched brown, excepting in the spots, few and far between, where the stinginess of the heavens has been supplemented by human industry, and the melted largess of the snow-range brought down to nourish vegetable life by irrigating apparatus in the form of conduits, where that is possible; by windmills, pumps, reservoirs, and ditches, where the mountains are too far off to afford the quantity and force of water requisite for a steady current through the thirsty fields, or where the Jordan and its tributaries run in the immediate neighborhood. In the month of July the cereals are ripe for the sickle; and Brigham Young himself told me that on a tract which he had seen, and belonging, if I remember rightly, to himself, eighty bushels of wheat had been raised to the single acre. Astonishing as this crop appears in comparison with the best results of our Eastern farming, it did not surprise me after I had seen the standing grain upon vast fields, on whose irrigation no expense had been spared, and whose product was like a solid vegetable plush or green velvet, the threads in whose pile were six feet high, and so closely packed together that they had scarcely room to bend under the wind, and the field seemed to ripple merely on its surface in chasing waves of sun and shadow. Nor does it astonish any one who compares the soil of Utah with the analysis of those inorganic substances which wheat must derive from the soil. Sprengel's analysis gives the following result for the 11.77 lbs. of ash left after the combustion of 1,000 lbs. of grain wheat, and the 35.18 lbs. remaining from an equal weight of similarly treated wheat straw:—

*The results are expressed in pounds and decimals of pounds.*

|  | GRAIN | STRAW |
|---|---|---|
| Potash | 2.25 | 0.20 |
| Soda | 2.40 | 0.29 |
| Lime | 0.96 | 2.40 |
| Magnesia | 0.90 | 0.82 |
| Alumina (with a trace of iron) | 0.26 | 0.90 |
| Silica | 4.00 | 28.70 |
| Sulphuric acid | 0.50 | 0.87 |
| Phosphoric acid | 0.40 | 1.70 |
| Chlorine | 0.10 | 0.30 |

The decomposed feldspar and limestone which constitute the soil of the terraces, consist as follows: The feldspar, of silica, 64.8; alumina, 18.4; potash, 16.8 per cent.; or, silica, 68.7; alumina, 19.5; soda, 11.8; and in some cases of 20 per cent. of lime replacing the other alkalies, with a nearly equal division of the remaining 80 per cent. between silica and alumina: the limestone, of sulphates, phosphates, and carbonates in various proportions, the last frequently associated in the form of dolomite with carbonate of magnesia to the extent of nearly half the weight. Chlorine necessarily abounds in a soil which at one time was covered by a solution of its product with sodium; and were not sulphur plentifully supplied by the decomposition of gypsum, enough of it exists in the virgin state throughout Utah to furnish material for crops demanding it. In the sesquioxide, the sulphide, the chloride, and numerous other combinations, iron is found throughout the detritus of all rocks which have formed portions of the ancient lake border. A soil could scarcely be prepared in the laboratory by artificial synthesis, better adapted for the growth of the cereals. The only desideratum which gives the Mormon farmer any anxiety is water. Even on the desert, the lack of this element is the only obstacle to a successful cultivation of wheat, rye, oats, and barley. In the vicinity of the springs, of artesian wells, or of the little rivulets born on the summits of the independent peaks (the "lost mountains" as the natives poetically express their isolation), and managing to reach the level without entire absorption by the hot sands, the luxuriant green which marks the oasis proves how rich the desert is in every solid element of fertility. Before leaving Utah, I shall endeavor to show that a large, if not the greater, proportion of all the barren tract now called "desert," as legitimately to all appearance as that of Sahara, may be converted by the outlay of comparatively small labor and capital, under the guidance of scientific enlightenment, into a district no less productive of all vegetable food demanded by the necessities of human life than the areas most famous for fertility in the Genesee, Ohio, and Mississippi Valleys. At present let us return to our road.

The dull, tawny hue of the bare ground, and the brown monotony of the withered vegetation, was strangely contrasted with the vapory gold of the atmosphere, where it floated over the fens of the Jordan in a languid dream of mid-summer and midnoon, with the intense blue of the cloudless sky, and the rosy surfaces of the Wahsatch behind us, the Oquirrh in front. Both ranges looked close by; the broken lights and shades seemed laid in as distinctly as by some delicate pencil, and the terraces or "benches" of the slope which faced us on the west, were as clean-cut as the steps of a temple. Nothing on the palette of Nature is lovelier, more incapable of rendition by mere words, than the rose-pink hue of the mountains in that rainless climate, unmodified by any such filtering of the reflected light through lenses of forest verdure as tones down and cools to a neutral tint the color of all our Eastern mountains, even though their local tint be the reddest sandstone. The Oquirrh has hues which in full daylight are as positive ruby, coral, garnet, and carne-lian,—at sunset and in twilight as positive amethyst, jacinth, topaz, and opal,—as the stones which go by those names themselves. No amount of positive color which an artist may put into his brush can ever do justice to the reality of the Rocky Mountains, the Oquirrh, the Humboldt, in noon or at sundown.

The road was in good condition, and we reached the base of the Oquirrh in about three hours. Passing around a low spur of the mountains jutting northerly, we descended among bold limestone crags and masses of debris, scantily patched with artemisia, squab cactus, and the thistly *Cirsium*, to the level of the great basin. A mile or two further, and we got our first blue glimpse of the lake. A fifteen minutes' ride, and Black Rock rose grim and ugly, like the foundation of some ruined round tower, across the end of our road, seeming to shut it in. The beetling precipices of limestone, rent with innumerable clefts and fissures, came down close upon our left hand, and we stopped just where they crowded us to the brink of the sea.

We had expected a grim and desolate landscape; a sullen waste of brine, stagnating along low reedy shores, black as Acheron, gloomy as the sepulchre of Sodom. Never had Nature a greater surprise for us. The view was one of the most charming which could be imagined. Its elements of sublimity were many, but *beauty* was its most impressive characteristic, and the word "lovely" occurred to us instantly as its fittest description.

On our left and western side, as we faced the sea, the lateral ranges of the Oquirrh decreased in height until they melted into vapory streaks of pale turquoise on the far horizon, their northward terminations forming bold headlands, or long, low promontories, with dreamy bays setting back into the indentations of the coast between them. The coast line in that direction had a southwesterly trend for about thirty miles from Black Rock, at which distance occurs the farthest point to which the lake extends southerly. All the headlands within sight—some of them apparently possessing an elevation of fifteen hundred or two thousand feet—exhibited that gorgeous variety and brilliancy of tints which we remarked on the faces of the Wahsatch and Oquirrh; the lime-stone rock, in many places crystalline, shining in the sun like chased silver, or iron at a white heat; the conglomerates, the metamorphic and the volcanic strata, here and there striated with bands of the same silvery lustre, but mainly characterized by different shades of red, graded from the nearest positive carmine to the most distant flushed with a faint hint of pink almost evanescent, exquisitely delicate and tender, like the merest glaze of rose-madder over a ground of cream. To the northeast the shore was comparatively low and uninteresting, possessing the characteristics of that plain whose edge it was, the level on which Salt Lake City lies, and on which we had spent the three hours between the city and the Oquirrh. From our feet to the northwestern horizon stretched the sea like a pavement of pure sapphire, flecked here and there with drifting whirls of marble dust. It may have been imagination, but I could not help thinking that the excessive specific gravity of the lake-brine, even had we never heard of it, must have revealed itself in the heavy swing of the waves like that of quicksilver rather than of water, and the scanty, powdery character of the spray, like the fine dry grains of an unusually cold snow-storm. Directly before us, to the northward, the southern end of Church (or Antelope) Island rose from the lake—shaped like a lofty pair of pyramids, whose surface below the sky-line was broken into many smaller peaks of the same configuration, projecting from the main pyramids like the forms of a secondary crystallization. Those of our party who enjoyed reminiscences of the Mediterranean found much in Church Island to remind them of Capri. Singularly enough, the Mormons report a cave in a bold precipice on the former's coast-line which may carry the distant relationship a step nearer by doing duty for a Blue Grotto. Certainly the most ravishing May-noon that ever shone on the Italian prototype never warmed its cliffs into a lovelier dream of color. At the distance of six miles from our stand-point, and seen through the screen of mellowing vapors which insensibly tinged the atmosphere above the lake, the whole vast mass of tufa, hornblende-rock, conglomerate, mica-schist, talcose and other metamorphic slates, gneiss, and limestone, seemed soft as a sunset cloud in tone of both of feeling and color, or might have been taken for a luxurious bank of roses set adrift to sway lazily on the long swells of some hasheesh-eater's Lotos Bay. Directly behind us, to the height of ten or twelve hundred feet, rose several successive "benches" or terraced planes of elevation—conglomerate near the base, but limestone a little higher, the sides nearly or quite perpendicular, in many places even overhanging, and threatening at no distant day to follow the example and share the fate of the great masses of debris at their feet, varying in the comminution of their fragments from whole detached blocks as large as a moderately sized house to the finest dust, sometimes the accumulation of so long and undisturbed a period as entirely to obliterate the line of demarcation between the successive benches. Here and there, in the finer detritus, a stinted maple, a quaking aspen, or a dwarf willow, belonging to some one of the many species found in this region, had taken root; but with the exception of secluded spots sheltered from the direct force of sun and wind, the crags were bare of any vegetation more ambitious than the artemisiaceæ and certain little lanigerous plants. Far up the face of one precipice we were pointed out the entrance to a remarkable cave. Accompanied by a couple of my friends, I had the recklessness to clamber up the slippery tablets and tottlish boulders which lay strewn upon the glacis of detritus intervening between us and the lofty hole, but lost all confidence in caverns when I discovered this particular one to be merely a shallow recess in the limeestone, nowhere reëntrant to a distance of over forty feet, of the general proportions of a tin oven, and transacting an immense business of mystery (or what they call, as far west as this, "*Shenandigan*" and "*Scullduggery*") with those who gape at it from below, on the capital of a dark, overgrown portal, as big as the cave itself. I could extemporize as good a cave anywhere in the country by knocking one side out of a medium-sized cow-stable. On reaching terra firma (a distinction unusually but properly applied, as any one who has ever broken his shins on one of those stones which gather no moss and show no remorse will testify) we had the further satisfaction of learning that we had not been to the right cave at all. The discoverer of the right cave, an orphan cowherd named Smith, who "ran" the Black Rock Ranch, in the absence of proprietors still keeping Fourth of July in that vortex of brilliant revelry, "the city," told us that he had explored it for about forty rods, and seemed to like it as far as he had gone, though his descriptive powers rather failed him when he was called on for particulars. The cave had no name, he said; so, after hesitating in view of a question whether it bettered the matter, we advised him to give it his own; but, with the modesty of all great discoverers he replied that this had never struck him. One or two of the party, who had not already broken their shins for the fraudulent cavern, set out under his guidance to visit Smith's Cave, but came back unsatisfied, having omitted to take candles. The locality is a very likely one for such *lusus naturæ*, or would be, were there more running water in the neighborhood to produce the phenomena of erosion. The rock in which Smith found his cave is a limestone, similar to that capping the conglomerate and metamorphic slates everywhere on the lofty benches about the lake basin; a favorite stratum for Nature's operations in the line of subterranean architecture, and, in the abundance of sulphur associated with it under various forms, showing a probability of sufficient gypsum for the extensive manufacture of stalactites. The limestone stratum is distinctly carboniferous, and affords numerous indications of the former existence of superimposed coal-beds, now destroyed by long exposure to the weather, or those volcanic agencies which have contributed heat to the metamorphose of the talcs, schists, gneiss, and other rocks in the vicinity still preserving their planes of stratification. In several portions of Utah—the valleys of Bear and Weber Rivers, of Silver and Sulphur Creeks—coal has been found; also on the Green (or Main Fork of the Colorado) River, and in the Little Salt Lake Valley. The latter coals are believed to be altogether bituminous; but none of them seem to belong, like those of the Platte and head-waters of the Arkansas, to the tertiary and cretaceous. I have mentioned in its place the coal which I examined on the Platte, not far from Denver, as belonging to a very recent period; retaining perfectly distinct impressions of the cotton-wood, ash, willow, and poplar leaves, to whose deposit under heat and moisture its existence seems due, and of such imperfect compactness that it was impossible to coke it, its residuum after combustion being only a light ash, like that of burnt straw. Tertiary and cretaceous coal may very likely be found in the lowlands of the Mormon Territory, but the limestone benches of the Great Basin and its affluents possess a true carboniferous character, as marked as any strata in Pennsylvania. I felt amply repaid for my barked shins and misplaced confidence when, on my way down from the bogus cave, I came upon a fragment of limestone whose face was stamped all over with the delicate daisy-like cells of the *Lithostrotion*. Near the same place I found another piece of limestone marked, in cross sections, with beautifully preserved stems of some crinoid. Stansbury's Island (with the exception of Church Island, the largest in the lake, lying southwest of it and out of sight as we look from Black Rock) possesses a summit of the same limestone as this by the lake-shore, and in it the expedition of the captain who gave his name to the island found the same corals that I found here—a fact which seems to corroborate the view that the Oquirrh ranges are continued through the lake. The variety of conditions under which, within a small area, I found the limestone existing on the cliffs above Black Rock, was very curious and interesting. I found an isolated piece of cretaceous lime-rock so soft as to be scratched by the finger-nail; close by it a fossiliferous fragment; and not far away a block so much altered by heat as to approximate the constitution of marble, while everywhere were to be seen masses of fine-grained blue limestone, unaltered, but traversed in all directions by infiltrated veins of beautifully lustrous and crystalline calc-spar, as finely pearly as aragonite, crossed and reticulated in such strange patterns that a polished slab of it would make as rich a mantel or a table as Carrara marble.

Desiring to repeat mere arbitrary geographical names and measures as little as possible, I will dismiss that portion of my Salt Lake material in a few sentences, quoting as far as possible from the report of Captain Stansbury. The circumference of Salt Lake is 291 miles. Its greatest length in a nearly north-northwest direction from Black Rock to the shore of Spring Bay is 75 miles. Its maximum width, measured along the forty-first parallel, is 35 miles. It contains six islands, the sum of whose circumference amounts to 96 miles. Church Island, the largest, received its name from the fact that all the stock belonging to the Church, especially the beeves and milch cattle, are sent there through the temperate season of the year to graze in charge of a herder. Whence it received its alternate, perhaps its original designation of Antelope Island I cannot tell, as I have never heard of any antelope inhabiting it within the memory of Mormons or aborigines. It ranges nearly north and south; has a maximum length of about sixteen miles, a maximum breadth of five, and rises in its loftiest peak to a height of three thousand feet above the lake, or more than seven thousand above the sea level. Far to the eastward of Black Rock, a shoal of compact sand connects the island with the mainland. In the summer this strip is left bare by the recession of the lake, and it is seldom flooded to a greater depth than three or four feet. Its surface is hard enough for the passage of every description of animal or vehicle, and it thus affords a convenient bridge or ford for the transit of the Church herds which pasture on the island. The island vegetation, like that of the main-land, is short and withered in appearance, but succulent and wholesome, as the condition of the ecclesiastical cattle testify.

About ten miles to the northward of Church Island lies Fremont Island, about fourteen miles in circumference and rising to the height of a thousand feet from the lake, or more than five thousand feet above the sea level. Its shape was quaintly but not inaccurately expressed by an old hunter who told me that it was like a kidney potato with a good big bite taken out of one side. The bitten side lies to the southwest, and the whole circumference of the island is from fourteen to sixteen miles, according to whether one counts the undulations of the coast-line or not. Neither trees nor fresh water exist there; but grass, the wild onion, a palatable bulb about the size of a plover's egg, called the sego (*Calochortus luteus*), and the wild parsnip abound on it. In the spring this vegetation is so luxuriant as to cover the steep sides of the island with a verdure delightfully contrasting with the barren crags and burnt-looking wastes seen elsewhere about the lake. Stansbury gave it its present name in honor of its first explorer, who had named it Disappointment Island, from the fact that he had expected, from the vague report of the old voyageurs, a perfect tropical paradise of thick forest, luxuriant shrubbery, and wild game, but discovered only the small vegetation we have mentioned, and no animal life at all, except the colonies of wild fowl which frequent the sheltered nooks along the craggy coast-line of every island in the lake. I only follow the example of every traveller who has preceded me in preserving the tradition that here also, on the very summit, Fremont lost the cover to the object-glass of his telescope, and that Stansbury sought for it in vain; an additional reason for Fremont's designation, since in this vapory region the cover of a telescope is not its least valuable part. The island rises steeply from the water, in some places with an ascent of more than forty-five degrees, with outlying reefs here and there of mica-schist and green hornblende. The composition of its rocky mass is variable, comprising tufa derived from the feldspathic detritus of the older strata, conglomerate formed of water-worn quartzose and granitic fragments imbedded in a sedimentary matrix, and many metamorphic forms in which the clay schists predominate, these last often containing an abundance of iron pyrites, entire or in minute decomposition. This island does not rise high enough to reach the level at which the sub-carboniferous limestone would be likely to occur in a band continuous with that which caps Church Island and the main-land ranges to the south, but the lower and metamor-phic strata which exist on it are sufficiently correspondent and cognate with those of the range to prove it a contin-uation of the Oquirrh. Near the summit is a very curious mass of schistose rock, perforated by three immense win-dows, two of which are separated by a ragged mullion, and through them a splendid view of the lake may be obtained. From the highest table-land projects a castellated fragment which has led the Mormons to give the island a third name, so that one now has his choice between "Castle," "Fremont," and "Disappointment" Island. The suggestion of Stansbury, that good water might be obtained here by boring, has not thus far been acted on. Thus, although the vegetation of the island is more luxuriant and varied than that of Antelope, it still remains tenantless, and, so far as I know, unvisited. The absence of such springs upon it as water Antelope, is easily accounted for by its less height, and its consequent deficiency in capacity and area for congelation, all the springs of the former island coming from beds which have received the percolations of higher levels, in winter covered with vast masses of snow and ice. Boring would undoubt-edly reach water, but of what kind may be questioned; the strata through which it would be necessary to pass in order to strike the impervious stratum dipping under the bed of the lake from the Oquirrh, and forming the natural water-bed and conduit from the latter's summits, being largely saliferous themselves, and so friable as possibly to admit of transudations from the surrounding brine. At a sufficient distance from the lake shore to obviate the latter difficulty, the increased height of the island would largely add to the labor and expense of boring; but it is certainly worth while to make the experiment, as the present abundance of small vegetation, and the richness of the rapidly decomposing rock in all the solid elements of fertility, prove that irrigation would make the island one of the finest cattle ranges between the Mississippi and the west slope of the Sierra Nevada. The "benches," chronicling successive periods of the lake's recession, are very prominent around the coast of this island everywhere.

About fifteen miles from Fremont's Island and, nearly the same distance from Black Rock, across that bay lying on our westward hand, whose deepest indentation is the furthest southerly point of the lake's extent lies a lune-shaped mass called Stansbury Island, although its insular character is part of the year entirely obliterated by the emergence of a sand-flat which connects it with the main-land not merely at one point, like the isthmus between Church Island and the lake shore, but along its entire breadth. It is the second of the islands in size, having a length of twelve miles, a circumference of thirty, and a peak near its centre, about three thousand feet above the level of the lake. As Antelope is the continuation of the Oquirrh, so Stanbury's Island seems to be the reappearance of a range running parallel to the Oquirrh, and separated from it by the Tuilla Valley about as far as that is separated from the Wahsatch. This valley is a basin corresponding to that in which Salt Lake City lies, though it differs from the latter in cradling no stream like the Jordan. As the Oquirrh dips at Black Rock to rise again in Antelope and Fremont Islands, so does this westward and parallel chain sink at a point exactly due west of the dip of the Oquirrh to reappear in Stansbury and Carrington Islands. Stansbury Island shows that it is the outlier and continuation of a distinct range from those of the Oquirrh system, by the difference in its geological formations. Its capping stratum is a black and gray limestone, like that of the Oquirrh, containing multitudes of fossils belonging to the carboniferous period, both coralline and crinoidal; but immediately beneath this the jumbled strata of conglomerate and metamorphic rocks found on Antelope and Fremont are replaced by deposits of a fine white sandstone, having in places an uninterrupted thickness of two hundred feet, even along the edges where they crop out. On the eastern shore springs of water are abundant, and vegetation is luxuriant. Above the springs, the fine silicious rock rises in magnificent cliffs, whose shining white wall and castellated cornice, contrasted with the rich verdure around the clear, fresh streamlets at their base, in sunlight and full-moonlight present a picture of inconceivable beauty. Still higher the island rises toward the central dome in noble masses of barren rock, piled step on step in that singular imitation of basalt which we sometimes find in limestone, amounting almost to a deception concerning its lithological character; huge foursquare pillars and cleanly beveled battlements, vast towers and frowning fortresses, with salient and, reëntrant angles succeeding each other, as if by the plan of some Titanic military engineer; great *culs-de-sac* and deep recesses cut into the precipitous face of the coast wall; all these making the grandest effects of chiaroscuro as the light plays with their vast bulks and hollows, until the weather-rounded summit is reached at a height as great as the monarch of the Catskills, and a view breaks on the adventurous climber, comparing for rugged sublimity with any but the grandest of the two Sierras. The rich vegetation and abundant water on the lower levels of Stansbury Island make it the finest cattle range in the neighborhood of Salt Lake; and it would doubtless receive the preference of the Saints over Antelope as a pasturage for the sacred herds, were it not at so great a distance from the city. Time out of mind it has been frequented by the Indians; its easy means of transit from the main-land make it a favorite retreat and browsing-place for antelope and other wild animals; while the settlers of the Tuilla Valley herd their cattle there habitually.

Carrington Island, named after Captain Stansbury's assistant in the survey, is a mass shaped somewhat like a thick and clumsy fish-hook, with its heel placed southerly and about four miles from the northern promontory of Stansbury Island, about eight miles long from heel to point, six miles from heel to top of shank, and five miles in width, measuring from outside to outside across the deep bay on the north which separates the two members. It is separated from the eastern shore of the lake about as far as it is from Stansbury, by a shoal of hard, tufaceous rock which never becomes entirely uncovered; indeed, reefs of tufa and sand-flats under water surround it on almost every side, covering an area larger than the island itself. It is without springs, but abounds in plants, many of them interesting both from their novelty and for their intrinsic beauty. The sego, before referred to, is very plenty; and Stansbury, who saw it on the 17th of June, when it was in full blossom, describes it as bearing lovely, lily-like flowers, which enlivened all the gentle slopes of the island. Its inner sepals are a delicate white, soft and creamy like the calla's, with a golden-yellow claw. "A large number of other plants were collected here, among which *Cleome lutea, Sidalcia neo-mexicana, Malvastrum coccineum, Stephanomeria minor*, a new species of *Malacothrix*, and *Grayia spinosa* were the most prominent." Limestone of numerous varieties belonging to the carboniferous seems the predominant formation on this island, suggesting the theory that the summit of the range has here dipped to the lake level; as the island, though possessing an acuminated form like the rest, does not rise to any great height above the water.

Hat Island is a bare rock, rising from the lake five miles north of Carrington, and so called from its fancied resemblance to an old beaver. About thirty miles to the north-northwest of this is Gunnison's Island, named after one of the officers in Stansbury's expedition. It really consists of two islands, the smaller of the two, a mere outlying knob of rock, rising about a hundred yards to the northward of the larger, and once, as Stansbury thinks, forming a part of it. The main island consists of an irregular ridge of compact limestone, like the cap of the range, and the great mass of Carrington Island. Its indented coast is peopled with countless hosts of cormorants, herons, gulls, and pelicans. Its northward face rises almost perpendicularly from the water's edge to the height of six hundred feet; a wall of limestone showing strata of both the black and gray varieties. Stansbury reports that the space between this precipice and the outlying islet is occupied by a beautiful and romantic little bay, with deep-blue waters so crystal-clear that the bar connecting the islands is distinctly visible beneath the water. Ten miles further to the north-northwest, and about two miles from the west shore of the lake, lies a small mass of emergent conglomerate, about seventy feet high at its loftiest point, and continued under water in a shoal about knee-deep, for a mile or more northerly. From the shape of its ridge, it has received the name of Dolphin Island. Beside these, there are in the lake several small banks and rocks just large enough to moor a boat to, but insignificant and bare of vegetation. So far as I know, the only ones which have received any name, are Egg and Mud Island.

Having discharged my conscience of all duties due the geography and hydrography of the lake, I return to my party, who have by this time finished their cave-hunting excursions, unpacked from the vehicles the hampers of eatables, and set the discoverer Smith at work preparing for our dinner. Though the proprietors of Black Rock Ranch are still Fourth-of-Julying it at "the city", the cows are at home, carrying on their important part of the business with a week-day steady-mindedness as prosaic as if nobody ever had a holiday or flung a torpedo the whole year round. Smith, the discoverer, has acquired something of their business regularity by association; and the dairy of Black Rock Ranch groans through all its clean-scrubbed shelves and bright-scoured pans, with the rich yellow produce of his herd. There are plenty of active partners in the ranch, too, to be found among the denizens of its poultry-yard; so that we are going to have the royalest of lunches, on fresh country cream, butter, and eggs, beside a big kettleful of that savory prepared coffee, whose solid basis, to the extent of two tin boxes full, we had brought with us from our own travelling stores, and whose invaluable assistance in getting up hasty camp breakfasts we have had occasion so often to acknowledge in crossing the Plains and the mountains, and bivouacking on the hunting grounds of our Western country. Besides these luxuries werae a quantity of cold broiled chicken, some loaves of sweet home-made bread constructed from Utah wheat, a boiled ham, half a dozen boxes of sardines, a jar of Crosse & Blackwell's chow-chow, another of Shaker apple-butter, and still another of hermetically sealed tomatoes,—some of these articles drawn from our own commissariat, and a part packed into our hamper by one of the Mesdames Townsend. While the discoverer was busy setting the tables and building a roaring fire in the kitchen to prepare our grub, we found a spare quarter of an hour on our hands, which it was decided, by a unanimous vote, could be no better spent than in making the better acquaintance of Salt Lake by a plunge into its bosom.

We undressed in the kitchen of the ranch, and had only about half a dozen rods to walk to the water's edge. The beach was very disagreeable, consisting of flinty rock fragments, sharp as a razor, from one to eighteen inches long, and all seeming to lie edge and point upward. At every step some cut or bruised foot came up with a jerk and a yell from its indignant owner, and self-gratulations were profuse when we reached the water. But our rejoicing was short-lived. The exchange was, if possible, of bad for worse. The water deepened very gradually; and after wetting our feet, we had to walk further to reach a swimming depth than we had previously come from the kitchen. The mangling chunks of stone were no longer visible, but they were still there, and tangible as ever. Worse yet, it was not sand which covered them out of sight, but a layer of black mud six inches thick, through which the foot sank to its torture bed of spikes below, as through the fine silt of a sewer, or a compost-heap. No words can do justice to the filthiness of this Stygian mire. Every sense to which it appealed, recoiled in loathing. It felt like a clammy paste of rottenness, much colder than the water above, and sent a chilly shudder of horror crawling up one's spinal marrow, as one foot came up with a disgusting *thlupp*, and the other sank deeper with the vile stuff oozing up between its toes; it dyed the clear blue brine, wherever it was disturbed, a black like foul ink diffusing itself in clouds for two yards round; and its smell,—what word-perfumer can do justice to that? It was rottenness itself. The worst odor of putrefaction that ever sickened me elsewhere, was night-blooming cereus compared with it; it would have turned the stomach of a turkey-buzzard or a ghoul. I had the hardihood to examine it, and found that it consisted of the decomposed larvæ of some insect like the mosquito. But where had the tenants of these cast-off dwellings gone? We were never troubled with mosquitos or gnats at Salt Lake, either in the city or any other portion of the region; yet the larvæ present along a rod of that shore represented a host of those midnight assassins large enough to have driven all Utah Territory stark mad, and sucked every Saint in it dry as parchment, though its population were as densely packed as that of China. At that time I had read nothing written by other explorers, and having only heard the commonly received report that Salt Lake, like the Dead Sea, is an absolutely azoic body of water, supposed I had made a new discovery in ascertaining the existence of insect remains there. Since then I learn, through Captain Stansbury, that the foul mass was examined by Mr. T. R. Peale, who pronounced it to consist, nine tenths of larvæ and exuviæ of *Chironomus*, or some species of mosquito probably undescribed; the remainder of fragments of other aquatic diptera and hymenoptera, both in the pupa and the mature state. Deposits similar to this at Black Rock are found in all the shallow bays of the lake, extending in layers a foot deep over areas of many hundred acres in extent, and always horrible in their fetor, blackening the water like cuttle-fish fluid, and producing an overwhelming nausea wherever they were stirred up. Neither Mr. Peale nor Captain Stansbury could arrive at any theory adequate for the explanation of the vast quantity in which the exuviæ appeared. The latter, on page 177 of his most interesting report, says: "The question where these larvæ originated, presents a curious subject of inquiry. Nothing living has yet been detected in the lake, and only a few large insects in the brackish springs, which do not at all resemble these either in shape or size." I have seen no observations since his which throw any light upon the subject, unless my own be deemed thus successful. *I* did detect something living in the lake water, though whether its connection with the larvæ be capable of making out I am not prepared to say. I brought back from the lake to Townsend's a quart-bottle of the water, gathered near the shore, but without disturbing the filthy deposit, and placed it in a west window, where it had the sun for the last five hours of the afternoon. For the first day or two the water remained perfectly clear. About the third day I observed small vermicular animals in it. I then neglected it until I came to pack the bottle the night before leaving,—it may have been a week from the time of my visit to Salt Lake. Then for the first time I discovered a number of minute diptera floating in it dead. They resembled, in all but size, our common house-fly, or the Platte River buffalo-gnat, rather than a mosquito.

It then struck me as possible that the great number of these larvæ deposited on the lake bottom may be accounted for by supposing a species whose rapidity of transit through their various stages of existence was as great as that of the insects found in my bottle, and whose mature life in the winged state was merely ephemeral. I think my experiment, in spite of its rudeness, still free from most of the sources of error. The water was so clear when I bottled it that I certainly should have seen any object as large as the dead flies I finally found there; and as the bottle was never for a moment uncorked, their eventual existence in it could not be accounted for by their having entered in their winged state at the hotel, and perished there. I am therefore compelled to believe that the microscopic ova of some aquatic dipterous species were suspended in the lake water when I bottled it; that they hatched into the grub state in the sunlight at my window, appearing as the worms I first noticed; and the flies were their matured form (the sediment at the bottom containing their pupæ), dead when I found them, either because they had no means of escape into the air, or because they were ephemeral, and had run their full cycle. I cannot account for the existence of such vast masses of exuviæ in the lake on the ground that they are the sloughs of an extinct race or of an extant one accumulated through many ages, as the preservation of their forms, and the still active putrefaction at whose expense the terrible stench is kept up, necessitate a comparatively recent origin. It seems strange how such putrefaction can go on anyhow in a pickle as strong as that of Salt Lake; but the probable truth is that it is commenced in the open air and hot sun, where the exuviæ are cast up by the waves on the beach.

I leave a subject which would be wholly unpleasant but for its bearings on the interesting scientific question whether or not Salt Lake is uninhabited, with a passing reference to the fact that Governor Cummings mentioned to Captain Burton his having seen in the lake a reddish vermicular animal, about as long as the top joint of his little finger, who had spun himself a sheltering web inside of a curled leaf a few inches long. This may be some new variety of the caddis-worm, and it would be an interesting subject for examination.

After wading this sty of concentrated nastiness (which nothing ever pushed me through but scientific enthusiasm, and the reflection how ashamed I should hereafter be if compelled to acknowledge that I had stood on the Salt Lake margin, without having breasted its waters), I came, nearly a hundred feet from shore, into a depth where I could comfortably swim. Once fairly in, I found the water very exhilarating. It was as cold to the feel as the ocean at Long Branch in the bathing season, and from this cause, with its intense brininess in addition, gave me a tonic sensation like a brisk shower-bath. I felt none of the acidity and burning with which the lake affects some skins—only a pleasant pungent sense of being in pickle, such as a self-conscious gherkin might experience in Cross & Blackwell's aristocratic bath of condiments, after he had set his mind at rest about copper by reading the assurance on the label, and intrusted himself with full abandon to his luxurious immersion. I swam out about twenty rods into the lake, and supposed I must certainly be a long way beyond my depth, so stopped to tread water and look about me. As I threw my feet down, to my utter surprise they touched bottom again; and the way that I put out for the open sea, remembering the horrible pit and miry clay was a caution! I had to get some distance beyond the line of Black Rock before I found water over my head. At that time I had no idea of what a shallow puddle the Great Salt Lake was. I thought, as I suppose most people do, that it was at least a thousand feet deep in the middle, and shelved off rapidly from the bold limestone precipices which wall it at Black Rock. Instead of that, it is almost everywhere bordered by shallows, reaching from a hundred rods to several miles from the shore; and the very deepest place found by that most minute and painstaking of hydrographers, Captain Stansbury, after innumerable soundings in every direction throughout the lake, was only thirty-five feet! In some portions of the lake, many miles from either shore, I might have swam for half a day without getting beyond my depth.

In common with all travellers, I experienced the most curious sensations of over-buoyancy. Without special effort, it was impossible to keep myself under sufficiently to have it feel like swimming, and not like lying on a sort of India rubber bed, where I made no break, but only a dent in some elastic substance which sprung under me. When I trod water, my bust emerged to considerably below the armpits; when I lay prone or on my back, so much of the uppermost surface was exposed that I had to change my position frequently, in order to keep myself uniformly wet, so as not to be scorched by the perpendicular rays of the midsummer sun. It would be a splendid place for a swimming-school. No confidence need be taught there—nothing but the motions. And a more delightful gamboling-place cannot be imagined. I was always passionately fond of swimming; and after my long, dry, dusty ride across the plains and mountains, where I had enjoyed no bath with ample room to disport myself, or indeed any swim at all since I ducked in the crystal flood of the "Fonten-kee-boo-yeh" at the base of Pike's Peak, it may be conceived that I rioted in the bracing blue brine of Utah with a perfect boyish delight. I could scarcely bear to leave it, even to the dinner for which my clamber and my swim had procured me an appetite as boyish. I stayed in till all the rest of my party had gone out, then, lying flat on my back, with my head to the land and perfectly motionless, abandoned myself to the cradling motion of the long ground-swells, trusting to a breeze which blew directly on shore to waft me gently thitherward. The breeze did as I expected. I drifted in very rapidly and so comfortably that I could have lain on my soft couch and slept all day. Presently I put down my hand to turn over, intending to swim the rest of the way ashore face forward. My palm instantly touched bottom, and I found that I had floated so far land-ward that I was in water only six inches deep! The fact that a craft of a full-grown man's draught of water no more touched bottom in a shoal like that than in mid-ocean, is the best illustration I can give of the remarkable density and lifting power of the Salt Lake water. Glad to have been saved the greater part of my return journey through the dumping-ground of dead gallinippers, I scrambled to my feet, and picked my way over the daggery beach to the kitchen with no worse result than a heel-bruise. I had from hearsay some idea of the incrustations of salt which appear on every bather in Salt Lake when he comes out, but was not at all prepared for the reality. The evaporation taking place while I walked the trifling distance across the beach to the house, was sufficient to turn me into a pillar of salt, or, as an old Mormon called it, to "Lotswificate" me. From head to foot, almost without a break, I was covered with a crystalline film, white as leprosy, and the thickness of ordinary stove-door isinglass. I had been a Nazarene ever since leaving New York; and the effect of my long hair and full beard with the salt dried into them was very like that of the grasses which country ladies amuse themselves by vitrifying with saturated solutions of alum, giving me the appearance of a shaggy Triton wreathed with sea-weed and crystals. In the kitchen I found that very necessary conclusion to a Salt Lake swim, a wash-tub full of fresh water, and, jumping into that, divested myself of my acrid *exuviæ*. The sensation of getting off the salt was very grateful, for, as I got drier, it made my skin feel absolutely thirsty like a tongue; indeed, a smarting, burning sensation lingered in my pores to a greater or less degree all day; and I could not help fancying that it made my fauces dry as well as my skin, producing by absorption an internal thirst corresponding to the outer one. This is not to be wondered at when we consider the great affinity of salt for the fluids of the body, the activity of all the absorbent surfaces in summer, and the intense brininess of the lake as revealed by the analyses made during Stansbury's expedition. The brine of Salt Lake, in point of density, has but one known superior on the globe—the waters of the Dead Sea. In a hundred parts by weight, the latter contain 24.580 of solid contents, and the former 22.422. The solid contents were constituted in the following proportions:—

| | |
|---|---|
| Chloride of sodium | 20.196 |
| Sulphate of soda | 1.834 |
| Chloride of magnesium | 0.252 |
| Chloride of calcium (a trace) and waste | 0.140 |
| | 22.422 |

(The specimen brought home by Captain Stansbury to be subjected to Dr. Gale's analysis was too small to be examined with reference to any other components than those here stated, and omits consideration of all gaseous matters held in solution by the Salt Lake waters, which are likely to be considerable, especially along the shore, where decay of organic bodies is constantly going on, and sulphide of hydrogen may naturally be looked for. Still, for all practical purpose, the analysis is abundantly precise.)

The waters of the Dead Sea are much weaker in chloride of sodium, and much stronger in chloride of magnesium; containing in their 24.580 of solid contents only 10.360 of the former, but 10.246 of the latter, while their chloride of calcium amounts to 8.920 parts, and their sulphate of soda to 0.054. The Salina salt wells are the strongest in the States, and the maximum yield of their brine is about 17⅓ per cent. in solid salt. That of the Salt Lake brine is about 20 per cent. It will be seen that although the density of the Dead Sea water is about two per cent. greater, its per cent. of chloride of sodium is only about one half and thus the waters of Salt Lake are by nearly three per cent the strongest natural brine in the world. The Mormons avail themselves of it for domestic purposes by the crudest possible processes of manufacture,—or frequently without manufacture of any kind,—collecting it from the rocks, which it incrusts in large quantities, and bringing it to the city by cart-loads. I noticed that on Townsend's table it often seemed singularly damp, considering the dry climate. Dr. Gale explains this fact by the presence of the chlorides of magnesium and calcium, both of which are very deliquescent, and in dissolving extend their deliquative action to the common salt. In any but a new country, where people have enough to do without attending to the extreme refinements of domestic life, the lake salt would be refined, instead of used in its crude state, as it now so generally is. Dr. Gale's method for this purpose is beautifully simple and easy. It consists merely in pouring lake water, either just as it is bailed up or concentrated by boiling, upon a heap of the drying incrustations laid on a blanket or other porous bottom. This water being already a saturated solution of chloride of sodium, or nearly so, will dissolve little or none of that component, but takes up and leaches away all the other chlorides present. After repeating this process three or four times, and allowing the residuary mass to crystallize in the sun, the result is pure enough for all practical purposes. If absolute purity is desired, another filtration, this time fresh water at a temperature of $91\frac{1}{2}°$ F. being employed instead of salt, will remove the small per cent of Glauber-salts still remaining, though its quantity is not sufficient, if left in the table salt, to produce any cathartic effect.

The road which we had come is one of the emigrant routes to California, leading from Salt Lake City round the northern promontory of the Oquirrh into the Tuilla Valley, past the range forming that valley's western wall, which sinks to the level of the lake at a considerable distance from its shore, instead of dipping boldly into its waters like the Oquirrh or the Wahsatch, and leaves a broad plain for the passage of the road further west, thence striking across the desert and the Humboldt Mountains to the Sierra Nevada, and climbing over the latter into the great Gold State of the Pacific. The other principal road, and the one which we took on leaving Salt Lake City for good, strikes southerly from the city up the valley of the Jordan to Utah Lake and Camp Floyd (now "Fort Crittenden"), and traverses a more southerly portion of the Great Desert to California. The former route is taken by many, indeed, by most of the emigrant trains, the pasturage and springs along its course being plentier and more excellent. On our way back to the city we encountered a long train of forty or fifty wagons drawn by mules and oxen, and followed by herds of milch cattle, oxen, and yearlings, and flocks of sheep. The drivers were a fine-looking set of men, unmistakably Scandinavian in their features, dress, and language; muscular, well knit, large-framed, and bronzed by long exposure over the mountains and plains which they had travelled for twelve hundred miles between the Missouri and Mormondom. The women were apparently a better grade than those who visit Salt Lake from Sweden without going further, and sat knitting, singing, and tending their babies as if they had not spurned the gospel offers, and were not now, with every turn of their heavy wagon-tires, putting further behind them the invitation to stay and go to heaven with a fractional husband. Everybody looked contented except the poor draught animals, who lolled painfully, their big pleading eyes telling of a thirst which could be but poorly slaked at the scanty and brackish springs where they stopped just as we met them, and which would be only intensified as they proceeded over the broad desert area between here and the Humboldt. I felt thirsty myself and got out of our wagon to drink at the well where the herdsmen were supplying their need. The water was a warm, nauseous solution of minerals, which betrayed the existence of sulphur in the soil as well as the near neighborhood of the lake. I drank as much of it as I could, hoping that it would moisten my throat sufficiently to last till I could get a draught from the city conduits; but its effect was only to sicken even my far from fastidious stomach, and increase my thirst to such a miserable degree that Townsend's was doubly welcome when we arrived shortly after sundown. The effect of the snow lying in the lofty valleys between the mountain-tops of the Wahsatch and the pure red lustre of the Wahsatch itself, in the twilight reflections from the brilliant heaven over the Oquirrh, behind which the sun had just gone down, was a sight of such magical beauty as no pen or brush can hope to paint, no heart which it has filled with ecstasy can ever forget. Nine thousand feet above the Jordan, twelve thousand above the sea, inaccessible in many places to any climbing, and accessible nowhere short of forty or fifty miles' difficult, devious, and dangerous climb,—those spotless abysses of pearl and rose-tinted opal, of marble and clear onyx, contrasted with vast masses of bare mountain that were all one auroral blush, looked to our enamored eyes like part of the heaven itself— the very gates and foundations of the city of God.

CHAPTER IX.

## Seven Weeks In The Great Yo-Semite.

It is as hard to leave San Francisco as to get there. To a traveller paying his first visit it has the interest of a new planet. It ignores the meteorological laws which govern the rest of the world. There is no snow there. There are no summer showers. The tailor recognizes no aphelion or perihelion in his custom: the thin woolen suit which his patron had made in April is comfortably worn until April again. The only change of stockings there is from wet to dry, or from soiled to clean. Save that in so-called winter frequent rainfalls alternate with spotless intervals of amber weather, and that soi-disant summer is one entire amber mass, its unbroken divine days concrete in it, there is no inequality on which to forbid the bans between May and December. In San Francisco there is no work for the scene-shifter of Nature: the wealth of that great dramatist, the year, resulting in the same manner as the poverty of dabblers in private theatricals,—a single flat doing service for the entire play. Thus, save for the purpose of notes of hand, the almanac of San Francisco might replace its mutable months and seasons with one great kindly, constant, sumptuous All the Year Round.

Out of this benignant sameness what glorious fruits are produced! Fruit enough metaphorical: for the scientific man or artist who cannot make hay while such a sun shines from April to November must be a slothful laborer indeed.

But fruit also literal: for what joy of vegetation is lacking to the man who every month in the year can look through his study-window on a green lawn, and have strawberries and cream for his breakfast,—who can sit down to this royal fruit, and at the same time to apricots, peaches, nectarines, blackberries, raspberries, melons, figs both yellow and purple, early apples, and grapes of three kinds?

Another delightful fact of San Francisco is the Occidental Hotel. Its comfort is like that of a royal home. There is nothing inn-ish about it. Remembering the chief hotels of many places, I am constrained to say that I have never, even in New York, seen its equal for elegance of appointment, attentiveness of servants, or excellence of *cuisine*. Having come to this extreme of civilization from the extreme of barbarism, we found that it actually needed an exertion to leap from the lap of luxury, after a fortnight's pleasaunce, and take to the woods again in flannel and corduroys.

But far more seductive than the beautiful bay, the heavenly climate, the paradisaical fruits, and the royal hotel of San Francisco, were the old friends whom we found, and the new ones we made there. With but one exception (and that an express-company, not a man), we were received by all our San Francisco acquaintance in a kind and helpful manner, with a welcome and a cheer as delightful to ourselves as it was honorable to them. Need I say whose brotherly hands were among the very first outstretched to us, in whose happy home we found our sweetest rest, by whose radiant face and golden speech we were most lovingly detained evening after evening and far into the night? A few days after our return to the East, when we read that dreadful message, "*Starr King is dead*," the lightning that carried it seemed to end in our hearts. We withered under it; California had lost its soul for us; at noon or in dreams that balmy land would nevermore be the paradise it once was to us. The last hand that pressed our own, when we sailed for the Isthmus on our way home, was the same that had been first to give us our California welcome. Just before the lines were cast off, Starr King stood at the door of our state-room, and said,—

"I could not bear to have you go away without one more good-by. Here are the *cartes-de-visite* I promised. They look hard-worked, but they look like me. Good-by! God bless you! I hope to make a visit to the East next summer, and then we will get together somewhere by the sea. Good-by!"

He went down the ladder. When the steamer glided off, his bright face sent benedictions after us as far as we could see; and then, for the last time on earth, that great, that good, that beloved man faded from our sight,—but, O! never from our hearts, either in the here or the hereafter. "We shall see him, but not now." We shall be together with him "in the summer by the sea"; but that summer shall have other glory than the sun to lighten it, and the sea shall be of crystal.

King was to have joined us in our Yo-Semite trip. We little knew that we were losing, for this world, our last opportunity of close daily intercourse with his sweet spirit, though we were grievously disappointed when he told us, on the eve of our setting out, that work for the nation must detain him in San Francisco, after all.

If report was true, we were going to the original site of the Garden of Eden,—into a region which out-Bendemered Bendemere, out-valleyed the valley of Rasselas, surpassed the Alps in its waterfalls, and the Himmal'yeh in its precipices. As for the two former subjects of comparison, we never met any tourist who could adjust the question from his own experience; but the superiority of the Yo-Semite to the Alpine cataracts was a matter put beyond doubt by repeated judgments; and a couple of English officers who had explored the wildest Himmal'yeh scenery told Starr King that there was no precipice in Asia to be compared for height or grandeur with Tu-toch-anula and Tis-sa-ack.

We were going into the vale whose giant domes and battlements had months before thrown their photographic shadow through Watkins's camera across the mysterious wide Continent, causing exclamations of awe at Goupil's window, and ecstasy in Dr. Holmes's study. At Goupil's counter and in Starr King's drawing-room we had gazed on them by the hour already,—I, let me confess it, half a Thomas-a Didymus to Nature, unwilling to believe the utmost true of her till I could put my finger in her very prints. Now we were going to test her reported largess for ourselves.

No Saratoga affair, this! A total lack of tall trunks, frills, and curling-kids. Driven by the œstrum of a Yo-Semite pilgrimage, the San Francisco belle forsakes (the Western vernacular is "goes back on") her back hair, abandons her capillary "waterfalls" for those of the Sierra, and, like John Phoenix's old lady, who had her whole osseous system removed by the patent tooth-puller, departs, leaving her "skeleton" behind her. The bachelor who cares to see un-hooped womanhood once more before he dies, should go to the Yo-Semite. The scene was three or four times presented to us during our seven weeks' camp there,—though the trip is one which might well cost a feeble woman her life.

Our male preparations were of the most pioneer description. One wintry day since my return I was riding in a train on the New York Central, when an undaunted herdsman, returning Westward, flushed with the sale of beeves, accosted me with the question, "Friend, yeou've travelled consid'able, and believe in the religion of Natur', don't ye?" "Why so?" I responded. "*Them boots*," replied my new acquaintance, pointing at a pair with high knee-caps, like those our party wore to the Yo-Semite. Otherwise, we took the oldest clothes we had,—and it is not difficult to find that variety in the trunk of a recent Overland stager. We were armed with Ballard rifles, shot-guns, and Colt's revolvers which had come with us across the Continent; our ammunition we got in San Francisco, together with all such commissariat luxuries as were worth transportation: our necessaries we left to be purchased at that jumping-off place of civilization, Mariposa, whence we were to start our pack-mules into the wilderness. Let me recommend tourists like ourselves to include in the former catalogue plenty of canned fruits, sardines, and apple-butter,—in the latter, a jug of sirup for the inevitable camp slapjacks. No woodsman, as will presently appear in our narrative, can tell when a slapjack may be the last plank between him and starvation; and to this plank how powerfully sirup enables him to stick!

The only portion of our outfit which would have pleased an exquisite (and he must be rather of the Count Devereux than the Foppington Flutter school) was our horseflesh. That greatest of luxuries, a really good saddle-animal, is readily and reasonably attainable in California. Everybody rides there; if you wish to create a sensation with your horsemanship in the streets of San Francisco, you must ride ill, not well: everybody does this last. Even since the horse-railroad has begun to clutter Montgomery Street (the San Franciscan

Boulevards) with its cars, it is a daily matter to see capitalists and statesmen charging through that thoroughfare on a gallop, which, if repeated in Broadway by Henry G. Stebbins, would cost him his reputation on 'Change and his seat in Congress. The nation of beggars on horseback which first colonized California has left behind it many traditions unworthy of conservation, and multitudinous fleas not at all traditional, but even less keepworthy; but all honor be to the Spaniards, Greasers, and mixed breeds for having rooted the noble idea of horsemanship so firmly in the country that even street-railroads cannot uproot it, and that Americans who never sat even so little as an Atlantic State's pony, on coming here presently take to the saddle with all their hearts. In most of the smaller California towns, a very serviceable half or quarter-breed saddle-horse is to be had for forty dollars,—the "breed" portion of his blood being drawn from an Eastern stallion, the remaining fraction being native or Mustang stock. This animal, if need be, will live on roadside croppings nearly as well as a mule,—travel all day long on an easy "lope," never offering to stop till fatigue makes him fall,—and, if you let him, will take you through *chaparrals*, and up and down precipices at whose bare suggestion an Eastern horse would break his legs. Our party, seeking rather more ambitious mounts, supplied itself, after a tour through the San Francisco stables, with saddle-animals at an average of seventy dollars apiece. This, payable in gold, then amounted to one hundred dollars in notes; but the New York market could not have furnished us with such horses for three hundred dollars.

It may seem as if, like most cavalcades, we should never get started, but I must linger a moment to do justice to our

accoutrements. If there be a more perfect saddle than the Californian, I would ride bare-back a good way to get it. Anything
more unlike the slippery little pad on which we of the East
amble about parks and suburban roads cannot be imagined.
It is not for a day, but for all time, and for those who spend
nearly the latter in it. Its wooden skeleton is as scientifically
fitted to the rider's form as an old "*incroyable's*" pair of pantaloons. There is no such thing as getting tired in or of it. Rising
to the lower lumbar vertebræ behind, and in front terminating gracefully in a broad-topped pommel, it enables one to
lean back in descending, forward in climbing, the great ridges
on the path of California travel,—thus affording capital relief
both to one's self and one's horse, and bringing in both from a
fifty miles' march comparatively unjaded.

The stirrups of this saddle are broad hickory hoops,
shaped nearly like an Omega upside-down ($\Omega$), left unpol-
ished so as to afford the most unshakable footing, covered
with a half-shoe of the stoutest leather, which renders it
impossible for the toe to slip through or the ankle to foul
under any circumstances. Attached to the straps from which
these swing is a wide and neatly ornamented stirrup-leather,
which effectually prevents the grazing of the rider's leg. The
surcingle, or, *Californicè*, the *cinch*, is a broad strip of hair-
cloth with a padded ring at either end, through which you
reeve and fasten with a half-hitch stout straps sewed to other
rings under the saddle flaps. This arrangement is not only far
securer than our Eastern buckle, but enables you to graduate
the tightness of your girth much more delicately, and make
a far snugger fit.

The only particular in which I could not commend and
adopt the native practice was the Mexican bit. It is a dreadful

instrument of torture, putting immense leverage in the rider's hands, and enabling him at will to tear the mouth of his horse to pieces; indeed, the horse on which it is used is guided entirely by pressure on the opposite side of the neck from that in which one seeks to turn him. Our Eastern way of drawing his head around would so lift the bit as to drive him frantic. There are very few horses of any breed, even the mustang, that *never* stumble; and as I prefer lifting my horse to letting him break his knees or neck, I want a bridle I can pull upon without tearing his mouth. So, in spite of its handsome appearance and the very manageable single white cord into which its two reins are braided, I eschewed the Mexican head-gear, and took the ordinary Eastern snaffle and curb. Immense spurs completed our accoutrement,— whips being here unknown.

I may as well make a word-map of our route before going farther. Pilgrims to the Yo-Semite ship themselves and their horses from San Francisco by steamer to Stockton. This town is on the San Joaquin, the most northerly of a series of rivers fed directly from the Sierra Nevada watershed,—a series, indeed, continued through much of the still lower Pacific coast to the Isthmus of Nicaragua. The Sacramento drains quite a different region, that of the broad plains between the Sierra and the Coast range, occupying the northern portion of the State,—resembling in its physical features, much more than any of the Pacific streams beside, the large isolated trunks which drain the east slope of the Alleghanies. The Colorado is almost the only other large river created from many tributaries, which debouches between the Columbia and the Isthmus,—and that rises east of the mathematical axis of the Rocky Mountains. The

Yo-Semite Valley is one of the cradles through which the short Sierra-draining rivers reach the ocean; its threading stream is the Merced; and if on any good United States Survey map you will please to follow that river back to the mountains, when your finger-nail touches the Sierra it will be (or would, were the maps somewhat correcter) in the Great Yo-Semite. You will then see that our course led us across three streams, after leaving the San Joaquin at Stockton *en route* for Mariposa,—the Stanislaus, the Tuolomne, and the main Merced. The distance from Stockton to Mariposa is about one hundred miles, a small part of the way between fenced ranches, a much greater part on wide, open, rolling plains, somewhat like those of Nebraska, embraced between the two great ranges of the State. Here and there you find an isolated herdsman or a small settlement dropped down in this not unfruitful waste, and thrice you come to a hybrid town, with a Spanish *plaza*, and Yankee notions sold around it. We went the distance leisurely, consuming four days to Mariposa, for we stopped here and there to sketch, "peep, and botanize"; besides, we were dragging with us a Jersey wagon, bought second-hand in Stockton, in which we carried our heavier outfit till we should get our extra pack-beasts at Mariposa, and to which we had harnessed for their first time an implacable white mule with an incapable white horse, to neither of which each other's society or their own new trade was congenial.

I shall not linger here as we did there. To an ornithologist the whole road is interesting,—especially to one making a specialty of owls. The only game within easy reach is the dove and the California ground-squirrel,—a big fellow, much like our Northeastern gray, barring the former's subterranean habits. On the plains threaded by the road the pasture is good, save in the extremest drought of summer, when the great herds which usually feed at large on and between the river bottoms are driven to the rich green grass in the high valleys of the Sierra,—or ought to be: many cattle die along the San Joaquin every summer for want of this care. Occasionally the road winds through the refreshing shadow of a grove of live-oaks, standing far from any water on a sandy knoll. But the most magnificent trees of the oak family that I ever beheld were growing on the banks of the Tuolomne River, where we forded it at Roberts's Ferry. They were not merely in dimension superior to the finest white-oaks of the East, but surpassed in beauty every tradition of their genus. Their vast gnarled branches followed as exquisite curves as belong to any elm on a New England meadow, and wept at the extremities like those of that else matchless tree,—possessing, moreover, a sumptuous affluence of leafage, an arboreal *embonpoint*, unknown to their graceful sister of our low-lands.

At Princeton, a thriving suburb of Mariposa, we completed our cavalcade of pack-animals, transferred our wagon-load to their backs (the average mule-pack weighs from two hundred and fifty to three hundred pounds), roped it there in the most approved *muletero* fashion, and started into the wilderness.

Let us call the roll. Beside the three gentlemen who with myself had formed the original Overland party, we numbered two young artists of great merit then sojourning for a short time in California,—Williams, an old Roman, and Perry, an ancient Düsseldorf friend,—also a highly scientific metallurgist and physicist generally, Dr. John Hewston of San Francisco.

To serve the party, we secured a man and a boy. Regarding the former, perhaps the more truthful assertion would be that he secured us; for, as will shortly appear, though we bought his services, he sold us in return. We picked him up in a San Francisco employment office, after looking all over the city for a respectable groom and camp-cook, and finding that in a scarce-labor country like California even fifty gold dollars per month, with keep and expenses, were no sufficient bait for the catch we wanted. He was a meagre, wiry fellow, with sandy hair, serviceable-looking hands, and no end to self-recommendations; but then it was impossible to ask after him at his "last place," that having been General Johnston's camp during Buchanan's forcible-feeble occupation of Utah. As he said he had been a teamster, and knew that soup-meat went into cold water, we rushed blindly into an engagement with him, marriage-service fashion, and took him for better or worse. The thing which I think finally "fired our Northern hearts" and clinched the matter was his assertion of nephewship to the Secession Governor Vance, whose name he bore, combined with unswerving personal loyalty. Lest by some future D'Israeli this be written down among the traditional greennesses of learned men, let me say that he was our *pis-aller*,—we finding ourselves within two hours of the Stockton boat, with nobody to help pack our mules or care for them and the horses.

The boy we obtained near Mariposa: He was an independent squire to the man of whom we got the extra animals, and accompanied them as a sort of trustee and *prochain ami* to an orphan family of mules. At fifteen years and in jackets, he was one of the keenest speculators in firearms I ever saw; could swap horses or play poker with anybody; and, take him all in all, in the Eastern States, at least, I shall never look upon his like again.

Thus manned, and leading, turn-about, four or five pack-beasts by as many tow-lines, we struck up into the well-wooded Sierra foot-hills, commencing our climb at the very outset from Mariposa. The whole distance to the Valley was fifty miles. For twelve of these we pursued a road in some degree practicable to carts, and leading to one of those inevitable steam saw-mills with which a Yankee always cuts his first swath into the tall grass of Barbarism. Passing the saw-mill in the very act of astonishing the wilderness with a dinner-whistle, we struck a trail and fell into single file. Thenceforward our way was almost a continuous alternation of descent and climb over outlying ridges of the Sierra. Our raw-recruited mules, and the elementary condition of our intellects in the science of professional packing, spun out this portion of our journey to three days,—though allowance is to be made for the fact of our stopping at noon of the second day and not resuming our trail till the morning of the third. This interim we spent in visiting the Big Trees, which are situated four or five miles off the Yo-Semite track.

"Clark's," where tourists stop for this purpose, is just half-way between Mariposa and the great Valley. "Clark" himself is one of the best-informed men, one of the very best guides, I ever met in the Californian or any other wilderness. He is a fine-looking, stalwart old grizzly-hunter and miner of the '49 days, wears a noble full beard hued like his favorite game, but no head-covering of any kind since recovered from a fever which left his head intolerant of even a slouch. He lives among folk, near Mariposa, in the winter, and in summer occupies a hermitage built by himself in one of the loveliest lofty valleys of the Sierra. Here he gives travellers a surprise by the nicest poached eggs and rashers of bacon, home-made bread and wild-strawberry sweetmeats, which they will find in the State.

Before reaching Clark's, we had been astonished at the dimensions of the ordinary pines and firs,—our trail for miles at a time running through forests where trees one hundred and fifty feet high were very common, and trees of two hundred feet by no means rare, while some of the very largest must have considerably surpassed the latter measurement.

But these were in their turn dwarfed by the Big Trees proper, as thoroughly as themselves would have dwarfed a common Green Mountain forest. I find no one on this side the Continent who believes the literal truth which travellers tell about these marvelous giants. People sometimes think they do, but that is only because they fail to realize the proposition. They have no concrete idea of how the asserted proportions look. Tell a carpenter, or any other man at home with the look of dimensions, what you have seen in the Mariposa County groves, and his eye grows incredulous in a moment. I freely confess, that, though I always thought I *had* believed travellers in their recitals on this subject, when I saw the trees I found I had bargained to credit no such story as that, and for a moment felt half-reproachful toward the friends who had cheated me of my faith under a misapprehension.

Take the dry statistics of the matter. Out of one hundred and thirty-two trees which have been measured, not one underruns twenty-eight feet in circumference; five range between thirty-two and thirty-six feet; fifty-eight between forty and fifty feet; thirty-four between fifty and sixty; fourteen between sixty and seventy; thirteen between seventy and eighty; two between eighty and ninety; two between ninety and one hundred; two are just one hundred; and one is one hundred and two. This last, before the storms truncated it, had a height of four hundred feet. I found a rough ladder laid against its trunk,—for it is prostrate,—and climbed upon its side by that and steps cut in the bark. I mounted the swell of the trunk to the butt, and there made the measurement which ascertained its diameter as thirty-four feet,—its circumference one hundred and two feet *plus* a fraction. Of course the thickness of its bark is various; but I cut off some of it to a foot in depth, and there was evidently plenty more below that.

To make some rough attempt at a conception of what these figures amount to, suppose the tree fallen at the gable of an ordinary two-story house. You propose to cross by a plank laid from your roof to the upper side of the tree. That plank would perceptibly slope *up* from your roof-peak. Through another tree, lying prostrate also, and hollow from end to end, our whole cavalcade charged at the full trot for a distance of one hundred and fifty feet. The entire length of this tree before truncation had been about three hundred and fifty feet. In the hollow bases of trees still standing we easily sheltered ourselves and horses. We tried throwing to the top of some of them with ludicrous unsuccess, and finally came to the monarch of them all, a glorious monster not included in the above table of dimensions, as most of those measured are still living, and all have the bark upon them still, while *the* tree is to some extent barked and charred. When it stood erect in its live wrappings, it measured forty feet in diameter,—over one hundred and twenty in circumference!

Estimates, grounded on the well-known principle of yearly cortical increase, indisputably throw back the birth of these largest giants as far as 1200 B.C. Thus their tender saplings were running up just as the gates of Troy were tumbling down, and some of them had fulfilled the lifetime of the late Hartford Charter Oak when Solomon called his master-masons to refreshment from the building of the Temple. We cannot realize time-images as we can those of space by a reference to dimensions within experience, so that the age of these marvelous trees still remains to me an incomprehensible fact, though with my mind's eye I continue to see how mountain-massy they look, and how dwarfed is the man who leans against them. We lingered among them half a day, the artists making color-studies of the most picturesque, the rest of us *izing* away at something scientific,—Botany, Entomology, or Statistics. In Geology and Mineralogy there is nothing to do here or in the Valley,—the formation all being typical Sierra Nevada granite, with no specimens to keep or problems to solve. Of course our artists neither made nor expected to make anything like a realizing picture of the groves. The marvelous of size does not go into gilt frames. You paint a Big Tree, and it only looks like a common tree in a cramped coffin. To be sure, you can put a live figure against the butt for comparison; but, unless you take a canvas of the size of Haydon's, your picture is quite as likely to resemble Homunculus against an average timber-tree as a large man against *Sequoia gigantea*. What our artists did was to get a capital transcript of the Big Trees' color,—a beautifully bright cinnamon-brown, which gives peculiar gayety to the forest, "making sunshine in the shady place"; also, their typical figure, which is a very lofty, straight, and branchless trunk, crowned almost at the summit by a mass of colossal gnarled boughs, slender plumy fronds, delicate thin leaves, and smooth cones scarce larger than a plover's egg. Perhaps the best idea of their figure may be obtained by fancying an Italian stone-pine grown out of recollection.

Between all the ridges we had hitherto crossed, silvery streams leaped down intensely cold through the granite chasms,—all of them fed from the snow-peaks, and charmingly picturesque,—most of them good trout-brooks, had we possessed time to try a throw; and now, on leaving Clark's, we crossed the largest of these, a fork of the Merced which flows through this valley. For twelve miles further a series of tremendous climbs tasked us and our beasts to the utmost, but brought us quite *apropos* at dinner-time to a lovely green meadow walled in on one side by near snow-peaks. A small brook running through it speedily furnished us with frogs enough for an *entrée*. Between two and three in the afternoon we set out upon the last stage of our pilgrimage. We were now nearly on a plane with the top of the mighty precipices which wall the Yo-Semite Valley, and for two hours longer found the trail easy, save where it crossed the bogs of summit-level springs.

Immediately after leaving the meadow where we dined, we plunged again into the thick forest, where every now and then some splendid grouse or the beautiful plume-crowned California quail went whirring away from before our horses. Here and there a broad grizzly "sign" intersected our trail. The tall purple deer-weed, a magnificent scarlet flower of name unknown to me, and another blossom like the laburnum, endlessly varied in its shades of roseate, blue, or the compromised tints, made the hill-sides gorgeous beyond human gardening. All these were scentless; but one other flower, much rarer, made fragrance enough for all. This was the "Lady Washington," and much resembled a snowy day-lily with an odor of tuberoses. Our dense leafy surrounding hid us from the fact of our approach to the Valley's tremendous battlement, till our trail turned at a sharp angle, and we stood on "Inspiration Point."

That name had appeared pedantic, but we found it only the spontaneous expression of our own feelings on the spot. We did not so much seem to be seeing from that crag of vision a new scene on the old familiar globe, as a new heaven and a new earth into which the creative spirit had just been breathed. I hesitate now, as I did then, at the attempt to give my vision utterance. Never were words so beggared for an abridged translation of any Scripture of Nature.

We stood on the verge of a precipice more than three thousand feet in height,—a sheer granite wall, whose terrible perpendicular distance baffled all visual computation. Its foot was hidden among hazy green *spiculæ*,—they might be tender spears of grass catching the slant sun on upheld aprons of cobweb, or giant pines whose tops that sun first gilt before he made gold of all the Valley.

There faced us another wall like our own. How far off it might be we could only guess. When Nature's lightning hits a man fair and square, it splits his yardstick. On recovering from this stroke, mathematicians have ascertained the width of the Valley to vary between half a mile and five miles. Where we stood, the width is about two.

I said a wall like our own; but as yet we could not know that certainly, for of our own we saw nothing. Our eyes seemed spell-bound to the tremendous precipice which stood smiling, not frowning at us, in all the serene radiance of a snow-white granite Boodh,—broadly burning, rather than glistening, in the white-hot splendors of the setting sun. From that sun, clear back to the first *avant-courier* trace of purple twilight flushing the eastern sky-rim—yes, as if it were the very butment of the eternally blue Californian heaven—ran that wall, always sheer as the plummet, without a visible break through which squirrel might climb or sparrow fly,—so broad that it was just faint-lined like the paper on which I write by the loftiest waterfall in the world,—so lofty that its very breadth could not dwarf it, while the mighty pines and Douglas firs which grew all along its edge seemed like mere lashes on the granite lid of the Great Valley's upgazing eye. In the first astonishment of the view, we took the whole battlement at a sweep, and seemed to see an unbroken sky-line; but as ecstasy gave way to examination, we discovered how greatly some portions of the precipice surpassed our immediate *vis-à-vis* in height.

First, a little east of our off-look, there projected boldly into the Valley from the dominant line of the base a square stupendous tower that might have been hewn by the diamond adzes of the Genii for a second Babel experiment, in expectance of the wrath of Allah. Here and there the tools had left a faint scratch, only deep as the width of Broadway and a bagatelle of five hundred feet in length; but that detracted no more from the unblemished foursquare contour of the entire mass than pin-mark from the symmetry of a door-post. A city might have been built on its grand flat top. And O! the gorgeous masses of light and shadow which the falling sun cast on it,—the shadows like great waves, the lights like their spumy tops and flying mist, thrown up from the heaving breast of a golden sea! In California, at this season, the dome of heaven is cloudless; but I still dream of what must be done for the bringing out of Tu-toch-anula's coronation day majesties by the broken winter sky of fleece and fire. The height of his precipice is four thousand feet perpendicular; his name is supposed to be that of the Valley's tutelar deity. He also rejoices in a Spanish *alias*—some Mission Indian having attempted to translate by "*El Capitan*" the idea of divine authority implied in Tu-toch-anula.

Far up the Valley to the eastward there rose high above the rest of the sky-line, and nearly five thousand feet above the Valley, a hemisphere of granite, capping the sheer wall, without an apparent tree or shrub to hide its vast proportions. This we immediately recognized as the famous To-coy-ee, better known through Watkins's photographs as the Great North Dome. I am ignorant of the meaning of the former name, but the latter is certainly appropriate. Between Tu-toch-anula and the Dome, the wall rose here and there into great pinnacles and towers, but its sky-line is far more regular than that of the southern side, where we were standing.

We drew close to the edge of the precipice and looked along over our own wall up the Valley. Its contour was a rough curve from our stand-point to a station opposite the North Dome, where the Valley dwindles to its least width, so that all the intermediate crests and pinnacles which topped the perpendicular wall stood within our vision like the teeth of a saw, clear and sharp-cut against the blue sky. There is the same plumb-line uprightness in these mighty precipices as in those of the opposite side; but their front is much more broken by bold promontories, and their tabular tops, instead of lying horizontal, slope up at an angle of forty-five degrees or more from the spot where we were standing, and make a succession of oblique prism-sections whose upper edges are between three and four thousand feet in height. But the glory of this southern wall comes at the termination of our view opposite the North Dome. Here the precipice rises to the height of nearly one sheer mile with a parabolic sky-line, and its posterior surface is as elegantly rounded as an acorn cup. From this contour results a naked semi-cone of polished granite, whose face would cover one of our smaller Eastern counties, though its exquisite proportions make it seem a thing to hold in the hollow of the hand. A small pine-covered *glacis* of detritus lies at its foot, but every yard above that is bare of all life save the palæozoic memories which have wrinkled the granite Colossus from the earliest seethings of the fire-time. I never could call a Yo-Semite crag *inorganic*, as I used to speak of everything not strictly animal or vegetal. In the presence of the Great South Dome that utterance became blasphemous. Not living was it? Who knew but the *débris* at its foot was merely the cast-off sweat and *exuviæ* of a stone life's great work-day? Who knew but the vital changes which were going on within its gritty cel-lular tissue were only imperceptible to us because silent and vastly secular? What was he who stood up before Tis-sa-ack, and said, "Thou art dead rock!" save a momentary sojourner in the bosom of a cyclic period whose clock his race had never yet lived long enough to hear strike? What, too, if Tis-sa-ack himself were but one of the atoms in a grand organism where we could see only by monads at a time,—if he, and the sun, and the sea were but cells or organs of some one small being in the fenceless *vivarium* of the Universe?

Let not the ephemeron that lights on a baby's hand generalize too rashly upon the non-growing of organisms! As we thought on these things, we bared our heads to the barer forehead of Tis-sa-ack.

I have spoken of the Great South Dome in the masculine gender, but the native tradition makes it feminine. Nowhere is there a more beautiful Indian legend than that of Tis-sa-ack. I will condense it into a few short sentences from the long report of an old Yo-Semite brave. Tis-sa-ack was the tutelar goddess of the Valley, as Tu-toch-anula was its fostering god,—the former a radiant maiden, the latter an ever-young immortal,—

"amorous as the month of May."

Becoming desperately fascinated with his fair colleague, Tu-toch-anula spent in her arms all the divine long days of the California summer, kissing, dallying, and lingering, until the Valley tribes began to starve for lack of the crops which his supervision should have ripened, and a deputation of venerable men came from the dying people to prostrate themselves at the foot of Tis-sa-ack. Full of anguish at her nation's woes, she rose from her lover's arms, and cried for succor to the Great Spirit. Then, with a terrible noise of thunder, the mighty cone split from heaven to earth,—its frontal half falling down to dam the snow-waters back into a lake, whence to this day the beautiful Valley stream takes one of its loveliest branches,—its other segment remaining erect till this present, to be the Great South Dome under the *in memoriam* title of Tis-sa-ack. But the divine maiden who died to save her people appeared on earth no more, ad in his agony Tu-toch-anula carved her image on the face of the mile-high wall, as he had carved his own on the surface of El Capitan,—where a lively faith and good glasses may make out the effigies unto this day.

Sometimes these Indian traditions, being translated according to the doctrine of correspondences, are of great use to the scientific man,—in the present instance, as embalming with sweet spices a geological fact, and the reason of a water-course which else might become obscured by time. You may lose a rough fact because everybody is handling it and passing it around with the sense of liberty to present it next in his own way; but a fact with its facets cut—otherwise a poem—is unchangeable, imperditable. Seeing it has been manufactured once, nobody tries to make it over again. The fact is regarded subject to liberal translation; poems circulate virgin and *verbatim*. In another chapter I may recur to this topic with reference to the Columbia River, and the capital light afforded to delvers in its wondrous trap-rock by the lantern of Indian legend.

Let us leave the walls of the Valley to speak of the Valley itself, as seen from this great altitude. There lies a sweep of emerald grass turned to chrysoprase by the slant-beamed sun,—chrysoprase beautiful enough to have been the tenth foundation-stone of John's apocalyptic heaven. Broad and fair just beneath us, it narrows to a little strait of green between the butments that uplift the giant domes. Far to the westward, widening more and more, it opens into the bosom of great mountain-ranges,—into a field of perfect light, misty by its own excess,—into an unspeakable suffusion of glory created from the phœnix-pile of the dying sun. Here it lies almost as treeless as some rich old clover-mead; yonder, its luxuriant smooth grasses give way to a dense wood of cedars, oaks, and pines. Not a living creature, either man or beast, breaks the visible silence of this inmost paradise; but for ourselves, standing at the precipice, petrified, as it were, rock on rock, the great world might well be running back in stone-and-grassy dreams to the hour when God had given him as yet but two daughters, the crag and the clover. We were breaking into the sacred closet of Nature's self-examination. What if, on considering herself, she should of a sudden, and us-ward unawares, determine to begin the throes of a new cycle,—spout up remorseful lavas from her long-hardened conscience, and hurl us all skyward in a hot concrete with her unbosomed sins? Earth below was as motionless as the ancient heavens above, save for the shining serpent of the Merced, which silently to our ears threaded the middle of the grass, and twinkled his burnished back in the sunset wherever for a space he glided out of the shadow of woods.

To behold this Promised Land proved quite a different thing from possessing it. Only the *silleros* of the Andes, our mules, horses, and selves, can understand how much like a nightmare of endless roof-walking was the descent down the face of the precipice. A painful and most circuitous dug-way, where our animals had constantly to stop, lest their impetus should tumble them headlong, all the way past steeps where the mere thought of a side-fall was terror, brought us in the twilight to a green meadow, ringed by woods, on the banks of the Merced.

Here we pitched our first Yo-Semite camp,—calling it "Camp Rattlesnake" after a pestilent little beast of that tribe which insinuated itself into my blankets, but was disposed of by my artist comrade before it had inflicted its fatal wound upon me. Removing our packs and saddles, we dismissed

their weary bearers to the deep green meadow, with no farther qualification to their license than might be found in
ropes seventy feet long fastened to deep-driven pickets. We
soon got together dead wood and pitchy boughs enough to
kindle a roaring fire,—made a kitchen table by wedging logs
between the trunks of a three-forked tree, and thatching
these with smaller sticks,—selected a cedar-canopied piece
of flat sward near the fire for our bed-room, and as high up
as we could reach despoiled our fragrant *baldacchini* for the
mattresses. I need not praise to any woodsman the quality of
a sleep on evergreen-strewings.

During our whole stay in the Valley, most of us made it
our practice to rise with the dawn, and, immediately after a
bath in the ice-cold Merced, take a breakfast which might
sometimes fail in the game department, but was an invariable success, considered as slapjacks and coffee. Then the
loyal nephew of the Secesh Governor and the testamen-
tary guardian of the orphan mules brought our horses up
from picket; then the artists with their camp-stools and color-boxes, the sages with their goggles, nets, botany-boxes,
and bug-holders, the gentlemen of elegant leisure with their
naked eyes and a fish-rod or a gun, all rode away whither
they listed, firing back Parthian shots of injunction about
the dumpling in the grouse-fricassee.

Sitting in their divine workshop, by a little after sunrise
our artists began labor in that only method which can ever
make a true painter or a living landscape,—*color*-studies on
the spot; and though I can not here speak of their results, I
will assert that during their seven weeks' camp in the Valley they learned more and gained greater material for future
triumphs than they had gotten in all their lives before at

the feet of the greatest masters. Meanwhile the other two vaguely divided orders of gentlemen and sages were sight-seeing, whipping the covert or the pool with various success for our next day's dinner, or hunting specimens of all kinds,— *Agassizing*, so to speak.

I cannot praise the Merced to that vulgar, yet extensive class of sportsmen with whom fishing means nothing but catching fish. To that select minority of *illuminati* who go trouting for intellectual culture, because they cannot hear Booth or a *sonata* of Beethoven's,—who write rhapsodies of much fire and many pages on the divine superiority of the curve of an hyperbola over that of a parabola in the cast of a fly,—who call three little troutlings "*a splendid day's sport, me boy!*" because those rash and ill-advised infants have been deceived by a feather-bug which never would have been of any use to them, instead of a real worm which would—let me say that we, who can make prettier curves and deceive larger game in a dancing-party at home, did not go to the Yo-Semite for that kind of sport. When I found that the best bait or fly caught only half a dozen trout in an after-noon,—and these the dull, black, California kind, with lined sides, but no spots,—I gave over bothering the unambitious burghers of the flood with invitations to a rise in life, and took to the meadows with a butterfly-net.

My experience teaches that no sage (or gentleman) should chase the butterfly on horseback. You are liable to put your net over your horse's head instead of the butterfly's. The butterfly keeps rather ahead of the horse. You may throw your horse when you mean to throw the net. The idea is a romantic one; it carries you back to the days of chivalry, when court butterflies *were* said to have been netted from the saddle,—but it carries you nowhere else in particular, unless perhaps into a small branch of the Merced, where you don't want to go. Then, too, if you slip down and leave your horse standing while you steal on a giant *Papilio* which is sucking the deer-weed in *such* a sweet spot for a cast, your horse (perhaps he has heard of the French general who said, "Asses and *savans* to the centre!") may discover that he also is a sage, and retire to botanize while you are butterflying,—a contingency which entails your wading the Merced after him five several times, and finally going back to camp in wet disgust to procure another horse and a lariat. An experience faintly hinted at in the above suggestions soon convinced me that the great arm of the service in butterfly warfare is infantry. After I had turned myself into a modest Retiarius, I had no end to success. Mariposa County is rightly named. The honey of its groves and meadows is sucked by some of the largest, the most magnificent, and most widely varied butterflies in the world.

At noon those of us who came back to camp had a substantial dinner out of our abundant stores, reinforced occasionally with grouse, quail, or pigeons, contributed by the sportsmen. The artists mostly dined *à la fourchette*, in their workshop,—something in a pail being carried out to them at noon by our Infant Phenomenon. He was a skeleton of thinness, and an incredibly gaunt mustang was the one which invariably carried the lunch; so we used to call the boy, when we saw him coming, "Death on the Pail-horse." At evening, when the artists returned, half an hour was passed in a "private view" of their day's studies; then came another dinner, called a supper; then the tea-kettle was emptied into a pan, and brush-washing with talk and pipes led the rest of the genial way to bed-time.

In his charming "Peculiar," Epes Sargent has given us an episode called the "Story of Estelle." It is the greatest of compliments to him that I could get thoroughly interested in her lover, when he bore the name of one of the most audacious and *picaresque* mortals I ever knew,—our hired man, who sold us—our—But hear my episode: it is

## THE STORY OF VANCE

Vance. The cognomen of the loyal nephew with the Secesh uncle. I will be brief. Our stores began to fail. One morning we equipped Vance with a horse, a pack-mule to lead behind him, a list of purchases, and eighty golden dollars, bidding him good-speed on the trail to Mariposa. He was to return laden with all the modern equivalents for corn, wine, and oil, on the fifth or sixth day from his departure. Seven days glided by, and the material for more slap-jacks with them. We grew perilously nigh our bag-bottoms.

One morning I determined to save the party from starvation, and with a fresh supply of the currency set out for Mariposa. At Clark's I learned that our man had camped there about noon on the day he left us, turned his horse and mule loose, instead of picketing them, and spent the rest of the sunlight in a *siesta*. When he arose, his animals were undiscoverable. He accordingly borrowed Clark's only horse to go in search of them, and the generous hermit had not seen him since.

Carrying these pleasant bits of intelligence, I resumed my way toward the settlements. Coming by the steam saw-mill, I recognized Vance's steed grazing by the way-side, threw my lariat over his head, and led him in triumph to Mariposa. There I arrived at eight in the evening of the day I left the Valley,—having performed fifty miles of the hardest mountain trail that was ever travelled in a little less than twelve hours, making allowance for our halt and noon-feed at Clark's. If ever a California horse was tried, it was mine on that occasion; and he came into Mariposa on the full gallop, scarcely wet, and not galled or jaded in the least.

Here I found our mule, whose obstinate memory had carried him home to his old stable,—also the remaining events in Vance's brief, but brilliant career. That ornament of the Utah and Yo-Semite expeditions had entered Mariposa on Clark's horse,—lost our eighty golden dollars at a single session of bluff, departed gayly for Coulterville, where he sold Clark's horse at auction for forty dollars, including saddle and bridle, and immediately at another game of bluff lost the entire purchase-money to the happy buyer (Clark got his horse again on proving title),—and finally vanished for parts unknown, with nothing in his pocket but buttons, or in his memory but villainies. Nowhere out of California or old Spain can there exist such a modern survivor of the days of Gil Blas!

Too happy in the recovery of Clark's and our own animals to waste time in hue and cry, I loaded my two reclaimed pack-beasts with all that our commissariat needed,—nooned at Clark's, on my way back, the third day after leaving the Valley for Mariposa, and that same night was among my rejoicing comrades at the head of the great Yo-Semite. That afternoon they had come to the bottom of the flour- bag, after living for three days on unleavened slap-jacks without either butter or sirup. I have seen people who professed to relish the Jewish Passover-bread; but, after such an experience as our party's, I venture to say they would have regarded it worthy of a place among the other abolished types of the

Mosaic dispensation. As for me and the mule, we felt our hearts swell within us as if we had come to raise the siege of Leyden. In that same enthusiasm shared our artists, *savans*, and gentlemen, embracing the shaggy neck of the mule as he had been a brother what time they realized that his panniers were full. Can any one wonder at my early words, "A slapjack may be the last plank between the woodsman and starvation?"

Just before I started after supplies, our party moved its camp to a position five miles up the Valley beyond Camp Rattlesnake, in a beautiful grove of oaks and cedars, close upon the most sinuous part of the Merced margin, with rich pasture for our animals immediately across the stream, and the loftiest cataract in the world roaring over the bleak precipice opposite. This is the Yo-Semite Fall proper, or, in the Indian, "Cho-looke." By the most recent geological surveys this fall is credited with the astounding height of twenty-eight hundred feet. At an early period the entire mass of water must have plunged that distance without break. At this day a single ledge of slant projection changes the headlong flood from cataract to rapids for about four hundred feet; but the unbroken upper fall is fifteen hundred feet, and the lower thirteen hundred. In the spring and early summer no more magnificent sight can be imagined than the tourist obtains from a stand-point right in the midst of the spray, driven, as by a wind blowing thirty miles an hour, from the thundering basin of the lower fall. At all seasons Cho-looke is the grandest mountain-waterfall in the known world.

While I am speaking of waterfalls, let me not omit "Po-ho-nó," or "The Bridal Veil," which was passed on the southern side in our way to the second and about a mile above the first camp. As Tis-sa-ack was a good, so is Po-ho-nó an evil spirit of the Indian mythology. This tradition is scientifically accounted for, in the fact that many Indians have been carried over the fall by the tremendous current both of wind and water forever rushing down a cañon through which the stream breaks from its feeding-lake twelve or fifteen miles before it falls. The savage lowers his voice to a whisper and crouches trembling past Po-ho-nó; while the very utterance of the name is so dreaded by him that the discoverers of the Valley obtained it with great difficulty. This fall drops on a heap of giant boulders in one unbroken sheet of a thousand feet perpendicular, thus being the next in height among all the Valley cataracts to the Yo-semite itself and having a width of fifty feet. Its name of "The Bridal Veil" is one of the few successes in fantastic nomenclature; for, to one viewing it in profile, its snowy sheet, broken into the filmy silver lace of spray, and falling quite free of the brow of the precipice, might well seem the veil worn by the earth at her granite wedding,—no commemorator of any fifty years' bagatelle like the golden one, but crowning the one millionth anniversary of her nuptials.

On either side of Po-ho-nó the sky-line of the precipice is magnificently varied. The fall itself cuts a deep gorge into the crown of the battlement. On the southwest border of the fall stands a nobly bold, but nameless rock, three thousand feet in height. Near by is Sentinel Rock, a solitary truncate pinnacle, towering to thirty-three hundred feet. A little further are "Eleachas," or "The Three Brothers," flush with the front surface of the precipice, but their upper posterior bounding-planes tilted in three tiers, which reach a height of thirty-four hundred and fifty feet.

One of the loveliest places in the Valley is the shore of Lake Ah-wi-yah,—a crystal pond of several acres in extent, fed by the north fork of the valley stream, and lying right at the mouth of the narrow strait between the North and South Domes. By this tranquil water we pitched our third camp, and when the rising sun began to shine through the mighty cleft before us, the play of color and *chiaroscuro* on its rugged walls was something for which an artist apt to over-sleep himself might well have sat up all the night. No such precaution was needed by ourselves. Painters, sages, and gentlemen at large, all turned out by dawn; for the studies were grander, the grouse and quail plentier, and the butter-flies more gorgeous than we found in any other portion of the Valley. After passing the great cleft eastward, I found the river more enchanting at every step. I was obliged to penetrate in this direction entirely on foot,—clambering between squared blocks of granite dislodged from the wall beneath the North Dome, any one of which might have been excavated into a commodious church, and discovering, for the pains cost by a reconnoissance of five miles, some of the loveliest shady stretches of singing water and some of the finest minor waterfalls in our American scenery.

Our last camp was pitched among the crags and for-ests behind the South Dome,—where the Middle Fork descends through two successive waterfalls, which, in appar-ent breadth and volume, far surpass Cho-looke, while the loftiest is nearly as high as Po-ho-nó. About three miles west of the Domes, the south wall of the Valley is interrupted by a deep cañon leading in a nearly southeast direction. Through this canon comes the Middle Fork, and along its banks lies our course to the great "Pi-wi-ack" (senselessly Englished as "Vernal") and the Nevada Falls. For three miles from our camp, opposite the Yo-Semite Fall, the cañon is threaded by a trail practicable for horses. At its termination we dismounted, sent back our animals, and, strapping their loads upon our own shoulders, struck nearly eastward by a path only less rugged than the trackless crags around us. In some places we were compelled to squeeze sideways through a narrow crevice in the rocks, at imminent danger to our burden of blankets and camp-kettles; in others we became quadrupedal, scrambling up acclivities with which the bald main precipice had made but slight compromise. But for our light marching order,—our only dress being knee-boots, hunting-shirt, and trousers,—it would have been next to impossible to reach our goal at all.

But none of us regretted pouring sweat or strained sinews, when, at the end of our last terrible climb, we stood upon the oozy sod which is brightened into eternal emerald by the spray of Pi-wi-ack. Far below our slippery standing steeply sloped the walls of the ragged chasm down which the snowy river charges roaring after its first headlong plunge; an eternal rainbow flung its shimmering arch across the mighty cauldron at the base of the fall; and straight before us in one unbroken leap came down Pi-wi-ack from a granite shelf nearly four hundred feet in height and sixty feet in perfectly horizontal width. Some enterprising speculator, who has since ceased to take the original seventy-five cents' toll, a few years ago built a substantial set of rude ladders against the perpendicular wall over which Pi-wi-ack rushes. We found it still standing, and climbed the dizzy height in a shower of spray, so close to the edge of the fall that we could almost wet our hands in its rim. Once at the top, we found that Nature had been as accommodating to the sight-seer as man himself; for the ledge we landed on was a perfect breastwork, built from the receding precipices on either side of the cañon to the very crown of the cataract. The weakest nerves need not have trembled, when once within the parapet, on the smooth, flat rampart, and looking down into the tremendous boiling chasm whence we had just climbed.

Above Pi-wi-ack the river runs for a mile at the bottom of a granite cradle, sloping upward from it on each side at an angle of about forty-five degrees, in great tabular masses slippery as ice, without a crevice in them for thirty yards at a stretch where even the scraggiest *manzanita* may catch hold and grow. This tilted formation, broken here and there by spots of scanty alluvium and stunted pines, continues upward till it intersects the posterior cone of the South Dome on one side and a colossal castellated precipice on the other,—creating thus the very typical landscape of sublime desolation. The shining barrenness of these rocks, and the utter nakedness of that vast glittering dome which hollows the heavens beyond them, cannot be conveyed by any metaphor to a reader knowing only the wood-crowned slopes of the Alleghany chain.

Climbing between the stunted pines and giant blocks along the stream's immediate margin,—getting glimpses here and there of the snowy fretwork of churned water which laced the higher rocks, and the black whirls which spun in the deep pits of the roaring bed beneath us,—we came at last to the base of "Yo-wi-ye," or Nevada Fall.

This is the most voluminous, and next to Pi-wi-ack, perhaps, the most beautiful of the Yo-Semite cataracts. Its beauty is partly owing to the surrounding rugged grandeur which contrasts it, partly to its great height (eight hundred feet) and surpassing volume, but mainly to its exquisite and unusual shape. It falls from a precipice the highest portion of whose face is as smoothly perpendicular as the wall over-leapt by Pi-wi-ack; but invisibly beneath its snowy flood a ledge slants sideways from the cliff about a hundred feet below the crown of the fall, and at an angle of about thirty degrees from the plumb-line. Over this ledge the water is deflected upon one side, and spread like a half-open fan to the width of nearly two hundred feet.

At the base of Yo-wi-ye we seem standing in a *cul-de-sac* of Nature's grandest labyrinth. Look where we will, impreg-nable battlements hem us in. We gaze at the sky from the bottom of a savage granite *barathrum*, whence there is no escape but return through the chinks and over the crags of an old-world convulsion. We are at the end of the stupen-dous series of Yo-Semite *effects*; eight hundred feet above us, could we climb there, we should find the silent causes of power. There lie the broad, still pools that hold the reserved affluence of the snow-peaks; thence might we see, glitter-ing like diamond lances in the sun, the eternal snow-peaks themselves. But these would still be as far above us as we stood below Yo-wi-ye on the lowest valley bottom whence we came. Even from Inspiration Point, where our trail first struck the battlement, we could see far beyond the Valley to the rising sun, towering mightily above Tis-sa-ack herself, the everlasting snow fore-head of Castle Rock, his crown's serrated edge cutting the sky at the topmost height of the Sierra. We had spoken of reaching him,—of holding con-verse with the King of all the Giants. This whole weary way have we toiled since then,—and we know better now. Have we endured all these pains only to learn still deeper life's saddest lesson,—"Climb forever, and there is still an Inaccessible?"

Wetting our faces with the melted treasure of Nature's topmost treasure-house, Yo-wi-ye answers us, ere we turn back from the Yo-Semite's last precipice toward the haunts of men:—

"Ye who cannot go to the Highest, lo, the Highest comes down to you!"

CHAPTER X.

## ON HORSEBACK INTO OREGON.

AFTER my return from the Yo-Semite Valley, I remained in San Francisco, or its delightful neighborhood, making short excursions around and across the bay, for more than a fortnight. But this lotus-eating life soon palled. I burned to see the giant Shasta, and grew thirsty for the eternal snows of the Cascade Peaks still further north. So much of a horseback ride to the Columbia as brought us into Oregon I here propose to sketch in brief.

With the exception of one artist companion and myself, our party had become sated with travel, and gone home. One glorious September day we two took our saddle-bags, note-books, and color-boxes, put our horses on board the Sacramento steamer, and, without other baggage or company of any sort, set out for the Columbia River and Vancouver's Island.

At Sacramento, on the next morning after leaving San Francisco, we shifted our quarters to a smaller and light-draught boat which was to take us up the shallow river to its head of navigation. This arrangement was a great economy of time. The country bordering the Upper Sacramento, for two hundred miles from the Californian capital, is level and comparatively tame, so that no artistic advantage would have resulted from following the bank on horseback. From the little steamer the view became a perpetual pleasure. About twenty miles above Sacramento we passed the mouth of

Feather River, disgorging coffee-colored mud from the innumerable gold diggings along its course, and came into lovely blue water, pure as the cradling snow-ridges between which it issued. The immediate margin began to be thickly wooded with overhanging willows, oaks, and sycamores. These were alive with birds of every aquatic description. The shag, a large fowl of black and dingy-white plumage, apparently belonging to the cormorant family, peopled every dead tree with a live fruit whose weight nearly cracked its branches; every snag projecting from the river-bed was studded with a row of the same creatures at mathematically equal intervals, each possessing just room enough for his favorite pastime of slowly opening his wings to the utmost, and then shutting them again in solemn rhythm, like a pupil of Dr. Dio Lewis's, or a patient in the Swedish Movement-cure. The quiet embayed pools and eddies swarmed with ducks; every sunny bar or level beach was a stalking-ground for stately cranes, both white and sand-hill; and garrulous crows kept the air lively, in company with big California magpies, above our heads.

The course of the river grew more and more sinuous as we ascended; it was near the close of the dry season, and there remained none of those cut-offs which economize distance during the prevalence of the rains. The Upper Sacramento, especially when softened and rendered illusory by such a full moon as it was our good fortune to travel under, perpetually recalls that loveliest of fairy streams, the higher St. John's, in Florida. Nothing out of dreams is more peacefully enchanting than the embowered stretches of clear water rippled into silver arabesque through a long moonlight night, or the hazy vistas, impurpled by twilight, into which one swings around the short curves of the Sacramento, amid a silence that would be absolute but for his own motion, while beyond either woody margin the great plains spread away untenanted, a waving wilderness of wild grass and *tulé*.

Enjoying *far-niente* of a life of such sweet monotone all the more because it was such a contrast to our rough riding, past and future, we spent two golden days, as many mezzotint twilights, and a pair of silver nights upon our steamer. On the morning of the third day we reached Tehama, a dead-and-alive little settlement, seven hours' journey by the river-windings from Red Bluffs, the head of navigation, but only ten miles by land. We had now got in sight of mountains; the ethereal blue of Lassen's Buttes, rimmed with the opal of perpetual snow, bounded our view northerly; and as every motive for taking to the saddle now consisted with our desire for economizing time, we here began our horseback ride, reaching Red Bluffs several hours before the steamer.

Just out of Tehama we struck into a country whose features reminded us of the wooded tracts between Stockton and Mariposa. After two days of *tulé* and wild grass, Nature grew suddenly ennobled in our eyes by thick and frequent groves of the royal California oak. There was a feeling of luxury in the change, which none can know who have not had a surfeit of boundless plains. We bathed our hearts and heads in shadow; the fever of unbroken light went out of us; our very horses shared in the relief and gave themselves up to a sweet somnambulism with which we had too much sympathy to break it by spurs.

Red Bluffs we found a place of more apparent stir and enterprise than any Californian town we had seen, except San Francisco and Sacramento. There was quite a New England air about the main street,—so much so that I have forgotten to call it *Plaza*, as I ought. This place is the starting-point for all Overland supplies sent between the Sacramento and Portland. Immense wagons—shaped like the Eastern charcoal-vehicle, but dwarfing it into insignificance by a size not much inferior to that of a Mississippi flat-boat—are perpetually leaving the town, drawn by twelve mules or horses, and in charge of drivers whose magnificent isolation has individualized them to a degree not exceeded in the most characteristic coachman of the Weller tribe, or the typical skipper of the Yankee fishing-smack. There are few finer places to study *genre* than the California ranches frequented by the captains of these "prairie schooners." At convenient distances for noon halts and nightly turnings-in, the main freighting-roads of the State are adorned with gigantic caravanserais offering every accommodation for man and beast, provided with arcades straddling nearly across the road, under which all passing wagoners not only may, but must, shelter themselves from the rigors of rain or sun, and billeted along their fronts with seductive descriptions of the paradise within, to which few hearts prove obdurate after being softened by the compulsory magnanimity of the arcade.

In time there must be a railroad all the way from Sacramento to Portland. There is not a mile of the distance between Bed Bluffs and the Oregon metropolis where it is not greatly needed already. Nearly the whole intervening region is exhaustlessly fertile,—one of the finest fruit countries in the world,—but so entirely without an economical avenue for its supplies or outlet for its productions, that many of the ranchmen who have settled in it feel despondent in the midst of abundance, and leave hundreds of magnificent orchard acres paved with rotting apples which would command a "bit" a pound in the San Francisco market, if the freight did not more than consume the profit, and the length of the journey render the fruit unsalable.

The first day out from Tehama we made a distance of nearly forty miles,—part of the way through oak-groves and part over fine breezy plains, with the noble mountain chain out of which Lassen's Buttes rise into the perpetual-snow region continually in sight on the right hand. The only incident that occurred to us this day, in any other key than that of pure sensuous delight in the fact of life and motion under such a spotless sky and in an air that was such breathable elixir, together with the artistic happiness which flowed down on us from the noble neighboring mountains, was our discovery early in the afternoon of a cloud of dust about half a mile ahead, with the forms of a hundred horsemen dimly looming through it. Such a sight sets an old Overlander instinctively fumbling at his holsters; fresh as we were from the horrors of the desert, we felt our scalps begin to detach themselves slightly from the cranium. But we rode straight ahead, as our only method of safety was to wear a bold front, if the cavaliers were, as we half suspected, a party of Humboldt Indians, who had lately taken the war-path between Lassen's Buttes and the coast. I don't recollect ever having been better pleased with the look of Uncle Sam's cavalry uniform than we were, upon coming up with the squad and finding it a detachment of our own men sent out to chastise the savages.

That night we reached a ranch called the "American,"— and certainly its title was none too ambitious, for it had the whole horizon to itself, and to all appearance might have

been the only house on the Continent. It was a place unvisited of fresh meat and ignorant of gridirons; but we were
tired enough, after the first day of our return to the saddle,
to sleep soundly in a bed of tea-tray dimensions, and under
what appeared to be a casual selection from a hamper of
soiled pocket handkerchiefs, when we had dispatched the
first of that long series of suppers on fried pork and green-
serpentine saleratus-biscuits which stretched between us
and the northern edge of Oregon.

Though the month was September, the heat in the middle of the day upon the broad, rolling plains we now had to
traverse was as oppressive as an Eastern July. During our
whole horseback journey, therefore, we made it our custom
to rise as soon after dawn as possible, breakfast, travel a stage
of fifteen or twenty miles, make a long midday halt in some
pleasant nook, and push on twenty miles further before we
unsaddled for the night. We were just now enabled to make
this second stage the most leisurely and the longest of the
two,—for the moon was still in all the glory of its California brightness and plenitude, and to have travelled by
moonlight between the Sacramento and Mount Shasta is
one of the prominent memories of a life-time. No patriotic
attachment is demanded to make the Californian say with
the Irish-man, that his country's full moon is twice as large
and splendid as any other's. Phenomenally, at least, the bare
facts support him.

At noon of the day on which we left the American Ranch,
we came up a rugged hill into the settlement of Shasta.
This town is a mining depot of some importance, chiefly
memorable to us for some excellent pie, made out of the California apple-melon, in wonderful imitation of the Eastern

green-apple tart, and a charge of five dollars and a half in gold made by the great Californian Express Company for bringing a color-box (heavy as a small valise) from Red Bluffs, whither we had let it go on by boat. Why this should have left a memorable impression on our minds it would be hard to say; for, although the demand was somewhat more than the stage employed by the Express Company would have charged to take either one of us the same distance, accompanied by a heavy trunk, we should by this time have acquired sufficient familiarity with extortion from the Company's officials to have paid very quietly a bill of fifty dollars for the same service, and then dismissed the trifling matter from our minds. But indignation at swindles is sometimes cumulative.

At the town of Shasta we left the main wagon road,—finding that it passed a long way from the most important point on our itinerary, the base of Shasta Peak. By striking across the country six miles to the small settlement of Buckeye, we intersected a route little travelled, but far more picturesque, and leading directly to the great object of our longings. On the way to Buckeye we again encountered the Sacramento, here dwindled to a narrow mountain stream, with bold, precipitous banks and a rock bottom, a smooth and deep, but rapid current, and full of trout and salmon. We crossed it on a rope-ferry, and climbed the steeps on the other side, but did not leave it. Thenceforward to Shasta Peak we were never out of its neighborhood.

By this *détour* of ours we came into a country better wooded and watered than any through which we had been travelling. When the sun left us, we found the moonlight so seductive that we pushed on late into the evening,—making our all-night halt at a ranchman's whose name had been given us by some passing native, who praised his accommodations un-boundedly, but proved much more of a friend to him than to ourselves. It is a duty to visit the afflicted. It is a misfortune, not a crime, to have a wife and six children, the latter all under twelve years of age. It is a still greater and no less irresponsive calamity to have them all prostrated by chills-and-fever, yet forbidden to yield to its depressing influence by the stimulus of several million healthy fleas. Ignorance, not willfulness, may be at the causal bottom of a batch of bread which is half saleratus, and a stew of venerable hens which is one third feathers. Nor can we regard it as other than a beneficent arrangement in the grand scheme of Nature's laws, that a pack of noble hounds should pass the hours of slumber around our humble casement in die free indulgence of a liberty distinctly authorized by the sacred Watts, as follows:—

"*LET* DOGS DELIGHT TO BARK," ETC.

Still, I think public opinion will sustain me in the view that the much afflicted family were not agreeable to pass the night with.

This is the place for a useful financial statement. Everything on our present trip cost a dollar. Bed for one, *i.e.* one's share of a bed for two,—supper,—each horse's forage,—breakfast,—every several item, a dollar. No matter how afflicted the family, saleratusy the bread, loud the dogs,—nothing was furnished under the dollar. When people happen to have enough dollars, this becomes comic. It reminded us of the Catskill Mountain House, where in specie times everything (after hotel bills) was twenty-five cents,—from getting a waiter to look at you, to having the Falls tipped up for you and spilt over.

The day's journey between the afflicted family and Dog Creek, where we stopped the third night, is such an afflu- ent remembrance of beauty that I feel glad while I write about it. We started under circumstances somewhat tedious. Nobody was going toward Mount Shasta with so much as a pack-mule. The father of the afflicted family labored under the blight of his surroundings, and after severe thought gave up the task of attempting to recall when anybody *had* been going toward Mount Shasta. It was also too much for him to calculate when anybody would be going. We paid him his dollars,—wished that his shadow might never be less, which it couldn't very well, unless the ague can dance on a mathematical line,—and set out with the color-box carried alternately before us on our pommels. It had been our *bête noire* from the time five dollars and fifty cents ransomed it at Shasta. We now began to wonder whether the Express Company also had carried it on a pommel,—in which case we thought we could forgive the Express Company. The morning was sultry, and as we started our horses forth upon a walk,—for the box could not stand jolting,—we looked forward to a tiresome day.

As we went on, Nature seemed determined to kiss us out of the sulks. Just as we broke into fresh grumbles, which we wanted to indulge, and our horses into fresh trots, which we desired, but could not tolerate, we entered some lovely glen, musical with tinkling springs, its walling banks tapestried with the richest velvet of deep-green grass, brocaded with spots of leaf-filtered sunshine. When we began to swelter, we came into the dense shadow of great oaks, or caught the balmiest wind in the world through aromatic pine and cedar vistas along the crown of some lofty ridge. It was impossible to be vexed with the stepmother, Fate, when the fingers of our mother, Nature, were straying through our hair. To drive away the last elf of ill-humor, and make us thenceforth agree to regard the box as an ornamental appendage which we were good-natured enough to let each other enjoy by turns, Pitt River, the last fork of the Upper Sacramento, came glancing into our landscape, the very perfection of fluent freedom and gladness. Every rod of the journey along its west bank disclosed a new picture. The misty blue mountains of the range toward Shasta Peak formed the abiding background of every view. Steep, fir-battlemented banks of one generic form, but endless variety in the beauty of the tree forms and groups which rose from their *glacis*, mile after mile, framed in some new loveliness of light-and-shadow flecked bend, deep sepia-dark pool, singing shallow, or brawling rapid of the clear stream. Eagles were sailing, like a placid thought in a large heart, far over our heads in the intimacy of a spotless sky; the great ground-squirrel flashed like a gray gleam over the gnarled mossy roots at the side of our narrow dug -way; and in brilliant blots or darting shafts of Magenta fire, we recognized among the tree-tops that loveliest bird of the North American forest, the great crested woodpecker. Here and there, to introduce a human element, came cleared spaces by the river's brink, where pointed wands stood impaling flakes of red salmon-flesh,—the open-air curing-house and outdoor store-room of the Pitt River Indians. Once in the course of the day we lighted on a picturesque ragged hut, where the purveyors of this meat were soaking themselves in full side-hill sunlight,—where little savages of every degree of gauntness in their limbs, ochriness on their cheeks, shockiness in their heads, and protuberance in their abdomens, were gorging themselves to still more hideous ventral *embonpoint*,—where white men, lower than the lowest Diggers they herded with, had forgotten the little they ever knew of civilization, and stood glaring at us like half-sated satyrs as we passed. Other bits of *genre* hourly came into the picture with papoose-carrying squaws who hunted yew-berries along the road-side fringe of woods, youngsters wearing no attire but a parti-colored acorn basket of deft finger-work, which they carried loaded on their shoulders, or listlessly trailed empty at their sides. Dr. Prichard has some hideous pictures of Papuans and Australians; but if Ethnology were a match game, we could give him those two points, and beat him easily by playing a few of the Digger women whom we saw that day. They reached the ugliness of aboriginal specimens which we had encountered on the west verge of the Goshoot country; and if any earthly pilgrimage, short of the mountains of Nightmare, can reveal *their* rivals, I should like to get into a prime state of health, and be allowed a peep at them through a spy-glass.

The condition of the white men who live and make alliances with these poor creatures is too heart-sickening to print. The law that governs all associations of culture with barbarism, where the latter is in dynamic excess, holds rigorously true in California. The higher race recollects only the cultivated evil of the state whence it fell,—and carrying to its savage mates subtler means of accomplishing vice than they knew before, presently gives rise to a combination from which all the simplicity of the low race is eliminated, and into which enter all the devils of mature civilization.

Nor do these devils come accompanied by a single grace or angel which softened or restrained crime in the developed community. The attachment of this region's older settlers for their savage comrades is something incredible. To enjoy their society, they cheerfully embrace a life as impure, uncleanly, free from all humanizing influences, as that of the lowest Digger with whom they consort. Sometimes a strange incongruous romance, like moonlight on a puddle, lights up these mongrel *liaisons*, and infuses into them a burlesque of sentiment. We found one old hunter whose squaw ran away from him into the mountains at regular six months' intervals, and who invariably spent hundreds of dollars and no end to hardships in hunting her up and restoring her to his wigwam. Another, who had kept an Indian seraglio from the time of the earliest gold discoveries, had repeatedly been to the nearest legal officer (two or three days' journey off), and besought him, without effect, to marry him to one of his squaws in Christian fashion. It certainly did seem hard that the poor fellow should be forbidden to make the only reparation in his power for wrongs of twelve years' standing; but the æsthetic, naturally enough to those who have seen Diggers, predominated over the legal and moral in the judicial mind, and he was finally sent away with an injunction never to show his face again while "this court continued to know herself" in the Shasta region.

As often happens in the discipline of human life, the thorn in the flesh was withdrawn as soon as we had learned the lesson of bearing it resignedly. At the last crossing of the Sacramento, we learned from the ferryman that a providential wagoner was just ahead of us, going certainly to Dog Creek, and presumably, if we made it an object, all the way to Strawberry Valley, at the foot of Shasta. The one whose turn it was not to carry the color-box galloped ahead, and detained the wagoner until the heavy dragoon had time to come up. With a deep sigh of relief, we stowed our box in the "prairie schooner,"—made a contract to have it packed on mule-back from Dog Creek to Shasta, in consideration of one among a gross of cheap watches which we had brought for trade with Indians and Trappers,—and, relieving our horses by the first canter they had enjoyed that day, sped away with the deep conviction at the man who first called chrome and white lead *light* colors must have been indulging the subtile irony of a diseased mind.

The seven miles of our journey from the last Sacramento crossing to Dog Creek were even grander in their scenery than our morning stage. The road was a dug-way from one to seven hundred feet above the base of a winding castellated cliff, here and there cut in rugged sandstone, but often both walled and buttressed with steep slopes of virgin turf kept emerald by innumerable trickling springs, ice-cold and crystal-clear, while here and there it passed through woods as dark as twilight. The slope on which we travelled formed one side of a valley, green at its bottom as a New England meadow, and watered by a picturesque affluent of the Sacramento. About dark we came to the Dog Creek Ranch, where we had such a delicious supper of trout, cooked in the good old Green Mountain fashion with an Indian meal night-gown on, as made us "forget the steps already trod," followed by a really nice *pair* of beds, wherein we took long and ample preparation to "onward urge our way" upon the morrow.

At Dog Creek we were encamped round about by the largest and most prosperous Indian tribe that we had seen on our trip. Their bows and arrows were elegant in shape and color: the former stained in a variety of patterns, sometimes carved, and wrapped as well as strung with deer sinews; the latter headed with nicely cut pieces of a black obsidian which abounds in the vicinity of Shasta Peak, and which of itself is an unerring test of the original volcanic character of the mountain. The quivers of this Dog Creek tribe were the most beautiful preparations of whole mink, otter, and sable skins, which I have seen in Indian hands anywhere on the Continent. One of the men had a great cap made out of an entire grizzly cub-skin, the claws very nicely preserved and dangling behind, while the head curved forward on top like the crest of an old Greek helmet. Nowhere did we find neater, more ornamental berry baskets, or more carefully worked dishes and basins, than those woven or scooped and stained by this tribe. In wandering through their stick-and-bark lodges, we found some tolerably good-looking men, far above the average brutality of the Diggers, with simple, pleasant expressions, and not afraid to look one in the eye. In one lodge crouched a man and woman who without exception were the oldest-looking people I ever saw. The husband was blind, the wife palsied; but they had been left in charge of a sprawling family of their fifth generation, which haste and the warm weather forbade our counting. I gave the old lady a plug of tobacco, and watched, as she put it up against her husband's face, to see which of the wrinkles was his mouth; while, on her filling a pipe and smoking with grunts of evident approbation directed to myself, I felt pleasant and biblical, as if I had been doing a good turn to Methuselah's aunt.

Only forty miles more stretched between us and Shasta Peak. We had now reached an elevation where it was visible to us in its full majesty from the southwestern side. All day, after our leaving Dog Creek, its giant cone, snow-wrapt half way to the base, kept surprising us through clefts in the surrounding crags at the end of long wooded vistas, or on some clear, treeless height to which we had climbed, forgetting the mountain in our heat and labor. The country about us was becoming wilder and wilder: our road was sometimes a mere trail, half obliterated by springs or traversing rivulets. We now rode in the woods most of the time, and found the shadow, stillness, and fragrance all delicious. Beside all the springs we discovered the southernwood of our Eastern gardens growing wild, its strawberry-scented and maroon-colored buds much larger than those of our variety, and, though a trifle less intense in their perfume, still sufficiently sweet to make every nook in which they grew delicious for yards around. Here and there the woods showed some symptoms of autumnal change; there were hectic spots now and then on the maple leaves; but nothing approaching in loveliness the forest euthanasia of our Eastern fall appeared until we had crossed the boundary of Oregon. Shasta Peak is, by the track, nearly eighty miles from that line. To-day, just as the sun got down to the tree-tops, the wooded slope suddenly receded from our left, and towered into one of those noble crags which all over the Continent go by the name of "Castle Rock," but which include no instance more truly deserving the name than this bold mass of pinnacles and bastions, bare as a Yo-Semite precipice, which lifted itself apparently about a thousand feet above the green *glacis* of the slope, stern and gray at the base, but etherealized along its crest and battlement by sunset splendors of red and gold. Simultaneously with the Castle's appearance, our leafy covert parted before us, and disclosed in level light, which made its snow opalescent, and bathed its vast, rugged masses of stone and earth in one inclusive winy glow, the glorious giant of California which had drawn us hither through the wilderness. The height of Shasta is variously stated. It is certainly over sixteen thousand feet, and may likely be nearer eighteen thousand. One geological survey pronounces it the highest mountain in the Nevada Range,—a statement taking into account Mount Hood and the other great peaks of the Cascade system, which itself is but an Oregon reappearance of the Sierra Nevada. The distance from which Hood, Saint Helen's, and Ranier could be seen with the naked eye led us afterward to regard this statement with some doubt; but certainly no peak which we met in all our large experience of the mountains of this Continent ever compared with Shasta in producing the effect of vast height. All the others which we have seen, with the exception of Lander's Peak, whether in the Rocky, the Nevada, the Cascade, or the Pacific Coast Range, have suffered, visually, from modulation through their gradually ascending tiers of foot-hills, or by the blending of their outlines with the neighboring peaks. This is especially so with Pike's Peak, which, despite its being one of the loftiest mountains in America, has its proportions most dissatisfyingly disguised, in all but a single point of view in the cañon of the Fontaine-qui-Bouille. Shasta is a mountain without mediations. It sits on the verge of a plain, broken for a hundred miles to the northward only by pigmy volcanic cones heaped around extinct *solfataras*. We approached it in the only direction where there were anything like foot-hills to climb; but even upon us, on reaching Strawberry Valley, at its southwestern foot, the wonderful peak broke with as little feeling of gradual approach as if we had not seen its head glowing grander and more real out of the blue distance repeatedly during the last three days. When we first saw the whole of it distinctly, it seemed to make no compromise with surrounding plains or ridges, but rose in naked majesty, alone and simple from the grass of our valley to its own topmost iridescent ice.

That view was not accorded to us on our first day out from Dog Creek. It was nearly dark when we reached the Soda Springs, nine miles south of Strawberry,—took a draught of the most delicious mineral water I ever drank, more piquant than Kissingen, and cold as ice,—resisted the seductions of a small, premature boy of eight, who issued from the Springs Ranch to dilate agedly on the tonic properties of the water, the relaxing virtues of the beds, and the terrors of the grim forest which lay for us in the black night between there and Strawberry,—and, clapping spurs to our tired horses, pushed forward with stern determination to reach Sisson's that evening.

I think that a darker night than presently lapped us among the thick evergreens was never travelled in. There were some streaks of blackness a mile long, in which, literally, I could not see my horse's head. But we had learned confidence in our animals' sagacity, and walked them, cheerily whistling to keep each other informed of our whereabouts, through at least six miles of road utterly unknown to and unseen by us. It was what Eastern people call very "poky"; but the language addressed to us by the premature boy had made it a matter of personal self-respect for us to get to Sisson's that night. With a certain sense of triumph over that unpleasant and dissuasive child, we saw a lantern gleam from a corral about ten P. M., and had our interrogative hail of "Sisson's?" answered in welcome affirmative by Sisson himself.

At Sisson's, or exploring with him in the neighborhood of Shasta, we passed one of the most delightful weeks in our diary of travel through any land. His house was a low, two-story building, which had run like a verbena in all directions over a grassy level,—putting out a fresh arm at every new suggestion of domestic convenience, until it had become at once the most amorphous and the most comfortable dwelling in the California wilds. His herds were populous and prosperous; only the merest pretence of fences broke their dream, without affecting their reality, of limitless pasture. His ranch ostensibly consisted of a few hundred acres; but old Shasta was his only surveyor of landmarks, and his base of supplies was coextensive with the base of the mountain. His family consisted of an admirably energetic and thrifty wife, who had accompanied him from Illinois, where he used to be a school-master, and one pretty little baby-girl indigenous to Strawberry Valley. The presence of this mother and child in a wilderness which otherwise howled chiefly with rough sporadic men and equally rough ubiquitous bears, was a perpetual delight to us, so far from our domestic communications. We admired Shasta all the more for looking at it over a little, gentle, pink-and-white baby who lay asleep in its shadow, like a cherub pressed to the bosom of one of the Djinn. Escaping from the poetical ground, I may observe that between the chief French *restaurant* of Sacramento City and the Dennison House in Portland, Oregon, no family whom we encountered lived in such wholesome and homelike luxury as Sisson's. If a Society for the Diffusion of Gastronomic Intelligence among the Heathen is ever founded in California and Oregon (and how bitterly such a philanthropic enterprise is needed my diary, spotted with the abominable grease of universal *frying*, bears abundant witness), I hope that the first tract which it publishes will be a biography of Mrs. Sisson; the first point insisted on by that tract, "This excellent and devoted woman used a gridiron." Bless her! how she could broil things! No man who has not built up his system during a long expedition with brick after brick of pork fried hard in its own ooze,— who has not turned all his brain's active phosphorus into phosphate of soda by alkali biscuits drawn from the oven in the hot-dough stage,—who has not drunk his pease-coffee "straight" at the tables of repeated Pike settlers too shiftless to milk one of their fifty kine,—who has not slept myriads in a bed with *Climex lectularius* and his livelier congener of the saltatory habits,—can imagine what a blissful bay, in the iron-bound coast of bad living, Sisson's seemed to us both in fruition and retrospection. We occasionally had beef, when Sisson, or some near neighbor ten miles off, "killed a critter," and distributed it around; excellent mountain mutton, flavorous as the Welsh, was not lacking in its turn; but the great stand-by of our table was venison,—roast, broiled, made into pasties, treated with every variety of preparation save an oil-soak in the pagan frying-pan of the country. As for chickens and eggs, it "snewe in Sisson's house" of that sort of "mete and drinke,"—he was Chaucer's Franklin transported to Shasta. Cream flowed in upon us like a river; potatoes were stewed in it; it was the base of chicken-sauce; the sirupy baked pears, whose secret Mrs. Sisson had inherited from some dim religious ancestor in the New England past, were drowned in it; and we took a glass of it with magical shiny rusk for nine o'clock supper, just to oil our joints before we relaxed them in innocent repose. Our rooms were ample, our beds luxurious, our surroundings the grandest within Nature's bestowal. Our capital host and hostess became our personal friends; and all that they did for us was so heartily kind and so cheerily comfortable, that, if we were asked where, on the whole, we passed the pleasantest, as distinct from the grandest, week in California, I think we should answer, "At Sisson's, in Strawberry Valley."

Sisson was, without exception, the best rifle-shot I ever saw. I have seen him bring down an eagle soaring as high as I could see it. Before a target, at any distance usual for such experiments, his aim was practically unerring. He possessed, in addition, two other prime qualities of a first-class woodsman,—keen sight for game in covert, and soft-footedness in stealing on it,—to a degree so unequaled in my acquaintance that I feel justified in calling him, not only the best shot, but the best hunter I ever knew. We spent three days in exploring, sketching, and deer-stalking with him, during all which time he was never once taken by surprise, but invariably saw his game before it scented him, and as invariably cracked it over before ourselves, or another old huntsman with us, had time to say, "Where is it?" Our main excursion led us about a dozen miles from the house to a lofty ridge, populous with game, thickly wooded with evergreens, and on its bold prominences giving us splendid views of Shasta. No height that we could attain dwarfed the grandeur of the mountain by sinking its base, and no lateral variation of our standing-points produced any change in its shape. New delicacies of rock and snow net-work came out as we shifted, and the sunlight produced different beauties of color and chiaroscuro in the glacier-like cradles of its upper ice; but so far as height and form were concerned, it seemed to have no more parallax than a fixed star. This fact is of course partly due to its being a nearly regular cone, but much of it depends on the intrinsic grandeur of a mountain standing lonely on the plain, full sixty miles in cincture, and in stature nearly eighteen thousand feet.

We came back from our expedition with an abundance of venison, a number of interesting color-studies, and memories of California scenery surpassed only by the Yo-Semite. We had struggled through miles of *chaparral*, after which no abatis that I ever saw on the Potomac would have been any discouragement to us, provided only we had the same wonderful horses. To get some idea of this peculiarly Californian institution as we encountered it, imagine a side-hill which would have given the best horse a hard pull, even had it been bare of undergrowth, and set this hill as thick as it will hold with *manzanita* and burr-oak: the former, as its name implies, like a little apple-tree, only more viciously gnarled, leathery, and complicated in its boughs than the most picturesque old russet in a New England orchard, and ramifying at once from the root without any main trunk; the latter, an oak-bush of the same general characteristics, having its swarming acorn-cups covered with spikes like the chestnut. When these have interlocked with each other till the earth is invisible and the whole tract has become a lattice of springes and pitfalls, push a horse through it three miles up a slope of forty-five degrees, the breast-high twigs scourging him at every step; and if you get out, as we did, without a fall or a broken leg to either man or beast, you will not only have acquired a just idea of the California *chaparral*, but an admiration for the California horse which will last you to your dying day. To repay us for this struggle, we had found one lake lying in a picturesque gorge, only twice before visited by white men; while my artist comrade, always the most indefatigable explorer of every party we were in together, climbed with his color-box to still another lake, of which he was the first discoverer, and whose lovely lineaments he preserved in one of the best studies of our trip. Besides these results of our expedition, we brought away the satisfaction of having leaped our horses across the Sacramento River. Where it flowed at the bottom of one deep ravine we had to traverse, it was a foot deep and ten feet wide. The twig which cracked under my horse's hoof, and fell into the stream as he sprang over, a month hence might be dashing about in the scud under the foot of some Pacific whaler, or, still further off in time, drift into the harbor of Hong Kong. Rivers always seem to me like the nerves of Nature: there is no conductor of thought and impression like that little silver thread which leads out from the ganglion of a deep forest spring, to spread, many leagues off, upon the sensory surface of the Oceanic World. In an earlier chapter I spoke of the mighty emotions which came thronging on me at the heads of the Platte and the Colorado: I felt them only less powerfully when my horse jumped across the Sacramento's birthplace.

After a good day's rest at Sisson's, we bade the capital fellow and his excellent wife a good-by which had more regret in it than we ever felt before for comrades of a single week's standing, and resumed our northward journey.

The country continued thickly wooded for nearly twenty miles from Strawberry, and the forest trail was every now and then drowned out of sight by streams rushing from the snow

of Shasta. When we emerged from the timber, we found ourselves on a plain opening widely to the north between diverging
ridges, and scattered here and there with black *scoriæ* like the
slag of a furnace. In some places an attempt had been made to
mend the road with lava; and as it crunched under our horses'
hoofs we could almost imagine ourselves making the circuit
of Vesuvius, so evident was it from the look and feel of things
that Pluto has at no very remote period boiled his dinner-pot
on the hob of Shasta Peak.

The day was fine,—the air more bracing than we had found
since leaving the Yo-Semite. Our week of comparative rest
at Sisson's had brought our horses into splendid condition
for the road; both we and they were boiling over with animal
spirits; and it was still early in the afternoon when we rode
the fortieth mile of our way into Yreka, on the full gallop. I
need not say that we had made other arrangements than our
pommels for the transportation of our heavy baggage to the
next place where we should need it. Sisson, always full of
resources, had taken good care of that for us both.

Neither to the traveller nor the *raconteur* is Yreka a place
to linger in. It consists of one long street, with a tolerable
brick hotel at one end, and a kennel of straggling houses
swarming with Chinese of ill odor and worse repute at the
other,—intersected by half a dozen lanes, devoted principally to stables, gambling-shops, and liquor dens. I only
quote the language of all the inhabitants whom I conversed
with, when I say that such glory as it once held among the
northern mining-towns has entirely departed from it. The
discovery of the Boisé and John-Day mines to the far northeast has attracted away all the principal gold seekers who
once dug and panned in the vicinity; and if there ever was

a place which had nothing intrinsic to fall back upon, it is Yreka. We were glad to leave it after one night's rest.

The day we evacuated it was atmospherically the most glorious that we enjoyed upon our whole trip. The air had a golden look, as if it not merely transmitted, but were stained with sunshine. The sky was spotless, the weather as warm as our mid-June, but without the least languor. The landscape was that broad plain I have mentioned, with Shasta on its verge, intersected by low rolling ridges, and broken by the cones of extinct volcanic spiracles, sometimes grouped, but oftener isolated. Shasta himself seemed to have gained rather than lost in majesty by our forty and now steadily increasing miles of distance. Either from atmospheric effect, or because we now saw a new and more irregular portion of his crown, the snow upon it became opalescent to a degree which I have never seen surpassed by any such effect. The light reflected from it seemed to gleam like a softened flame deep down beneath some pearly medium, rather than any rebound of sunlight from a surface.

The rugged hillocks between which we rode were bare and craggy at their tops, but all about their base, and far down into the plain, grew abundance of a plant wonderfully like the heather in its size as well as in the shape and color of its blossoms. Broad, exquisitely claret-tinted streaks and patches of this lovely thing softened the landscape everywhere. We seemed to be travelling in a beautiful confusion of Nature, where the Scottish Highlands had got together under a California sky with the Roman Campagna. Throughout this sweet desolation reigned a visible and audible quiet which made our horses' hoofs seem noisy. Between Yreka and the Klamath River—a narrow, rapid stream, recalling some portions of the Housatonic, which we intersected about noon, and along which we rode for an hour—we met only two or three silent horsemen and as many eremetic wood-choppers.

Turning north from the Klamath, we dined at a miserable settlement called Cottonwood, around which for miles in every direction departed gold hunters had burrowed till the ground was a honey-comb, or more properly a last year's hornets' nest, since there was no sign of honey in the cells, and, from what a most dejected native told us of the yield, never had been any to speak of.

Leaving dreary Cottonwood with even greater pleasure than we had felt in abandoning Yreka, we began ascending the slope toward the Oregon line. At every mile the country grew lovelier. California seemed determined to make our last impressions of her tender. The bare, brown rocks became densely wooded with oaks and evergreens. Late in the afternoon we came to broad meadows of such refreshing deep-green grass as we had not seen before since we left the rich farming lands of the Atlantic side, and the level golden bars which lay on them between forest edges made us homesick with memories of peaceful Eastern lawns at sunset. After crossing several miles of such meadows, and the quiet brooks which ran through them, we traversed a number of strange low ridges, undulating in systematic rhythm, like a mountain-chain making a series of false starts prior to the word "go," reached the true base of the Siskiyou Mountains, and began our final climb out of the Golden State.

The road was very uneven, rocky, cut up by rivulets from the higher ridges, and in most places only a rude dug-way, with a rocky wall on one side, and a butment of thickly wooded *débris* steeply descending to a black, brawling torrent on the other. But we did not trouble ourselves with the road. The wild beauty of the forest absorbed us on either hand; and we were astonished at the rapid transition which the leaves suddenly took on, from the dry, burnt look, characteristic of the end of the California dry season, to autumnal splendors of red and yellow, hardly rivaled by the numberless varieties of tint in our own October woods. Just as the sun sank out of sight, we reached a lofty commanding ridge, stopped to rest, turned around and saw Shasta looming grandly up out of the valley twilight, his icy forehead all one mass of gold and ruby fire. It was one of the grandest mountain sights I ever looked on: such a purple hush over the vast level below us; such colossal broad shadows on the giant's foot; such a wonderful flame on that noble, solitary head, which, but for the unbroken outlines leading up to it out of the twilight, might have been only some loftier cloud catching good-night sun-glimpses at half-way up the firmament. Good-night from Shasta! Alas, not only to the sun, but to us! We felt a real pang, as we confessed to ourselves that we were now looking upon this noblest and serenest, if not loftiest of all the mountains in our travel, for the last time in years,—perhaps the last forever. We gazed wistfully till admonished by the deepening twilight; then, as Shasta became a shadow on the horizon, plunged silently into the dense woods again, climbed to the Siskiyou summit, and, descending through almost jetty darkness, were in Oregon.

# CHAPTER XI.

## On The Columbia River.

I HAVE never known, nor seen any person who did know, why Portland, the metropolis of Oregon, was founded on the Willamette River. I am unaware why the accent is on the penult, and not on the ultimate of Willamette. These thoughts perplexed me more than a well man would have suffered them, all the way from the Callapooya Mountains to Portland. I had been laid up in the backwoods of Oregon, in a district known as the Long-Tom Country—(and certainly a longer or more tedious Tom never existed since the days of him additionally hight Aquinas),—by a violent attack of pneumonia, which came near terminating my earthly with my Oregon pilgrimage. I had been saved by the indefatigable nursing of the friend I travelled with,—by wet compresses, and the impossibility of sending for any doctor in the region. I had lived to pay San Francisco hotel prices for squatter-cabin accommodations in the rural residence of an Oregon landholder, whose tender mercies I fell into from my saddle when the disease had reached its height, and who explained his unusual charges on the ground that his wife had felt for me like a mother. In the Long-Tom Country maternal tenderness is a highly estimated virtue. It cost my comrade and myself sixty dollars, besides the reasonable charge for five days' board and attendance to a man who ate nothing and was not waited on, with the same amount against his well companion. We had suffered enough extortion before that to exhaust all our native grumblery. So we paid the bill, and entered on our note-books the following *Mem.* "In stopping with anybody in the Long-Tom Country, make a special contract for maternal tenderness, as it will invariably be included in the bill."

I had ridden on a straw bed in the wagon of the man whose wife cultivated the maternal virtues, until I was once more able to go along by myself—paying, you may be sure, maternal-virtue fare for my carriage. During the period that I jolted on the straw, I diversified the intervals between pulmonary spasms with a sick glance at the pages of Bulwer's "Devereux" and Lever's "Day's Ride." The nature of these works did not fail to attract the attention of my driver. It aroused in him serious concern for my spiritual welfare. He addressed me with gentle firmness:—

"D'ye think it's exackly the way for an immortal creatur' to be spendin' his time, to read them *novels?*"

"Why is it particularly out of the way for an immortal creature?"

"Because his higher enterests don't give him no time for sich follies."

"How can an immortal creature be pressed for time?"

"Wal, you'll find out some day. G'lang, Jennie."

I thought I had left this excellent man in a metaphysical bog. But he had not discharged his duty, so he scrambled out and took new ground.

"Now say,—d'*you* think it's exackly a Christian way of spendin' time, yourself?"

"I know a worse way."

"Eh? What's that?"

"In the house of a Long-Tom settler who charges five dollars a day extra because his wife feels like a mother."

He did not continue the conversation. I myself did not close it in anger, but solely to avoid an extra charge, which in the light of experience seemed imminent, for concern about my spiritual welfare. On the maternal-tenderness scale of prices, an indulgence in this luxury would have cleaned me out before I effected junction with my drawers of exchange, and I was discourteous as a matter of economy.

We had enjoyed, from the summit of a hill twenty miles south of Salem, one of the most magnificent views in all earthly scenery. Within a single sweep of vision were seven snow-peaks,—the Three Sisters, Mount Jefferson, Mount Hood, Mount Adams, and Mount St. Helen's,—with the dim suggestion of an eighth colossal mass, which might be Rainier. All these rose along an arc of not quite half the horizon, measured between ten and eighteen thousand feet in height, were nearly conical, and absolutely covered with snow from base to pinnacle. The Three Sisters, a triplet of sharp, close-set needles, and the grand masses of Hood and Jefferson, showed mountainesque and earthly; it was at least possible to imagine them of us, and anchored to the ground we trod on. Not so with the others. They were beautiful, yet awful ghosts,—spirits of dead mountains buried in old-world cataclysms, returning to make, on the brilliant azure of noonday, blots of still more brilliant white. I cannot express their vague, yet vast and intense splendor by any other word than incandescence. It was as if the sky had suddenly grown white-hot in patches. When we first looked, we thought St. Helen's an illusion,—an aurora, or a purer kind of cloud. Presently we detected the luminous chromatic border,—a band of refracted light with a predominant orange tint, which outlines the higher snow-peaks seen at long range,—traced it down, and grasped the entire conception of the mighty cone. No man of enthusiasm, who reflects what this whole sight must have been, will wonder that my friend and I clasped each other's hands before it, and thanked God we had lived to this day.

We had followed down the beautiful valley of the Willamette to Portland, finding everywhere glimpses of autumnal scenery as delicious as the hills and meadows of the Housatonic. Putting up in Portland at the Dennison House, we found the comforts of civilization for the first time since leaving Sisson's, and a great many kind friends warmly interested in furthering our enterprise. I have said that I do not know why Portland was built on the Willamette. The point of the promontory between the Willamette and the Columbia seems the proper place for the chief commercial city of the State; and Portland is a dozen miles south of this, up the tributary stream. But Portland does very well as it is,—growing rapidly in business importance, and destined, when the proper railway communications are established, to be a sort of Glasgow to the London of San Francisco. When we were there, there was crying need of a telegraph to the latter place. That need has now been supplied, and the construction of the no less desirable railroad must follow speedily. The country between Shasta Peak and Salem is at present virtually without an outlet to market. No richer fruit and grain region exists on the Pacific slope of the Continent. No one who has not travelled through it can imagine the exhaustless fertility which will be stimulated, and the results which will be brought forth, when a continuous line of railroad unites Sacramento, or even Tehama, with the metropolis of Oregon.

Among the friends who welcomed us to Portland were Messrs. Ainsworth and Thompson, of the Oregon Steamship Company. By their courtesy we were afforded a trip up the Columbia River, in the pleasantest quarters and under the most favorable circumstances.

We left Portland the evening before their steamer sailed, taking a boat belonging to a different line, that we might pass a night at Fort Vancouver, and board the Company's boat when it touched at that place the next morning. We recognized our return from rudimentary society to civilized surroundings and a cultivated interest in art and literature, when the captain of the little steamer Vancouver refused to let either of us buy a ticket, because he had seen

my companion on the upper deck at work with his sketchbook, and me by his side engaged with my journal.

The banks of the Willamette below Portland are low, and cut up by small tributaries or communicating lagoons, which divide them into islands. The largest of these, measuring its longest border, has an extent of twenty miles, and is called Sauveur's. Another, called "Nigger Tom's," was famous as the seigniory of a blind African nobleman so named, living in great affluence of salmon and whiskey with three or four devoted Indian wives, who had with equal fervor embraced the doctrine of Mormonism and the profession of day's washing to keep their liege in luxury due his rank. The land along the shore of the river was usually well timbered, and in the level openings looked as fertile as might be expected of an alluvial first bottom frequently overflowed. At its junction with the Columbia the Willamette is about three quarters of a mile in width, and the Columbia may be half a mile wider, though at first sight the difference seems more than that from the tributary's entering the main river at an acute angle, and giving a diagonal view to the opposite shore. Before we passed into the Columbia, we had from the upper deck a magnificent glimpse to the eastward of Hood's spotless snow-cone rosied with the reflection of the dying sunset. Short and hurried as it was, this view of Mount Hood was unsurpassed for beauty by any which we got in its close vicinity and afterward, though nearness added rugged grandeur to the sight.

Six miles' sail between low and uninteresting shores brought us from the mouth of the Willamette to Fort Vancouver, on the Washington Territory side of the river. Here we debarked for the night, making our way in an ambulance sent for us from the post, a distance of two minutes' ride, to the quarters of General Alvord, the commandant. Under his hospitable roof we experienced, for the first time in several months and many hundred miles, the delicious sensation of a family dinner, with a refined lady at the head of the table and well-bred children about the sides. A very interesting guest of General Alvord's was Major Lugenbeel, who had spent his life in the topographical service of the United States, and combined the culture of a student with an amount of information concerning the wildest portions of our Continent which I have never seen surpassed nor heard communicated in style more fascinating. He had lately come from the John Day, Boisé, and Snake River Mines, where the Government was surveying routes of emigration, and pronounced the wealth of the region exhaustless.

After a pleasant evening and a good night's rest, we took the Oregon Company's steamer, "Wilson G. Hunt," and proceeded up the river, leaving Fort Vancouver about seven

A. M. To our surprise, the "Hunt" proved an old acquaintance. She will be remembered by most people who during the last twelve years have been familiar with the steamers hailing from New York Bay. Though originally built for river service such as now employs her, she came around from the Hudson to the Columbia by way of Cape Horn. By lessening her top-hamper and getting new stanchions for her perilous voyage, she performed it without accident.

Such a vivid souvenir of the Hudson reminded me of an assertion I had often heard, that the Columbia resembles it. There is some ground for the comparison. Each of the rivers breaks through a noble mountain-system in its passage to the sea, and the walls of its avenue are correspondingly grand. In point of variety the banks of the Hudson far surpass those of the Columbia,—trap, sandstone, granite, limestone, and slate succeeding each other with a rapidity which presents ever new outlines to the eye of the tourist. The scenery of the Columbia, between Fort Vancouver and the Dalles, is a sublime monotone. Its banks are basaltic crags or mist-wrapt domes, averaging below the cataract from twelve to fifteen hundred feet in height, and thence decreasing to the Dalles, where the escarpments, washed by the river, are low trap bluffs on a level with the steamer's walking-beam, and the mountains have retired, bare and brown, like those of the great continental basin further south, toward Mount Hood in that direction, and Mount Adams on the north. If the Palisades were quintupled in height, domed instead of level on their upper surfaces, extended up the whole navigable course of the Hudson, and were thickly clad with evergreens wherever they were not absolutely precipitous, the Hudson would much more closely resemble the Columbia.

I was reminded of another Eastern river, which I had never heard mentioned in the same company. As we ascended toward the cataract, the Columbia water assumed a green tint as deep and positive as that of the Niagara between the falls and Lake Ontario. Save that its surface was not so perturbed with eddies and marbled with foam, it resembled the Niagara perfectly.

We boarded the "Hunt" in a dense fog, and went immediately to breakfast. With our last cup of coffee the fog cleared away and showed us a sunny vista up the river, bordered by the columnar and mural trap formations above mentioned, with an occasional bold promontory jutting out beyond the general face of the precipice, its shaggy fell of pines and firs all aflood with sunshine to the very crown. The finest of these promontories was called Cape Horn, the river bending around it to the northeast. The channel kept mid-stream with considerable uniformity,—but now and then, as in the highland region of the Hudson, made a *détour* to avoid some bare, rocky island. Several of these islands were quite columnar,—being evidently the emerged capitals of basaltic prisms, like the other uplifts on the banks. A fine instance of this formation was the stately and perpendicular "Rooster Rock" on the Oregon side, but not far from Cape Horn. Still another was called "Lone Rock," and rose from the middle of the river. These came upon our view within the first hour after breakfast, in company with a slender, but graceful stream, which fell into the river over a sheer wall of basalt seven hundred feet in height. This little cascade reminded us of Po-ho-nó, or The Bridal Veil, near the lower entrance of the Great Yo-Semite.

As the steamer rounded a point into each new stretch of silent, green, and sunny river, we sent a flock of geese or ducks hurrying cloudward or shoreward. Here, too, for the first time in a state of absolute Nature, I saw that royal bird, the swan, escorting his mate and cygnets on an airing or a luncheon-tour. It was a beautiful sight, though I must confess that his Majesty and all the royal family are improved by civilization. One of the great benefits of civilization is, that it restricts its subjects to doing what they can do best. Park-swans seldom fly,—and flying is something that swans should never attempt, unless they wish to be taken for geese. I felt actually *désillusionné*, when a princely *cortége*, which had been rippling their snowy necks in the sunshine, clumsily lifted themselves out of the water and slanted into the clouds, stretching those necks straight as a gun-barrel. Every line of grace seemed wire-drawn out of them in a moment. Song is as little their forte as flight,—barring the poetic license open to moribund members of their family,—and I must confess, that, if this privilege indicate approaching dissolution, the most intimate friends of the specimens we heard have no cause for apprehension. An Adirondack loon fortifying his utterance by a cracked fish-horn is the nearest approach to a healthy swan-song. On the whole, the wild swan cannot afford to "pause in his cloud" for all the encomiums of Mr. Tennyson, and had better come down immediately to the dreamy water-level, where he floats dream within dream, like a stable vapor in a tangible sky. Anywhere else he seems a court-beauty wandering into metaphysics.

Alternating with these swimmers came occasional flocks of shag, a bird belonging to the cormorant tribe, and here and there a gull, though these last grew rarer as we increased our distance from the sea. I was surprised to notice a fine seal playing in the channel, twenty miles above Fort Vancouver, but learned that it was not unusual for these animals to ascend nearly to the cataract. Both the whites and Indians scattered along the river banks kill them for their skin and blubber,— going out in boats for the purpose. My informant's boat had on one occasion taken an old seal nursing her calf. When the dam was towed to shore, the young one followed her, occasionally putting its fore-flippers on the gunwale to rest, like a Newfoundland dog, and behaving with such inno- cent familiarity that malice was disarmed. It came ashore with the boat's-crew and the body of its parent; no one had the heart to drive it away; so it stayed and was a pet of the camp from that time forward. After a while the party moved its position a distance of several miles while Jack was away in the river on a fishing excursion, but there was no elud- ing him. The morning after the shift he came wagging into camp, a faithful and much over-joyed, but exceedingly bat- tered and used-up seal. He had evidently sought his friends by rock and flood the entire night preceding.

Occasionally the lonely river-stretches caught a sudden human interest in some gracefully modeled canoe gliding out with a crew of Chinook Indians from the shadow of a giant promontory, propelled by a square sail learned of the whites. Knowing the natural, ingrained laziness of Indians, one can imagine the delight with which they comprehended that substitute for the paddle. After all, this may perhaps be an ill-natured thing to say. Who does like to drudge when he can help it? Is not this very "Wilson G. Hunt" a triumph of human laziness, vindicating its claim to be the lord of matter by an ingenuity doing labor's utmost without sweat? After all, nobody but a fool drudges for other reason than that he may presently stop drudging.

At short intervals along the narrow strip of shore under the more gradual steeps, on the lower ledges of the basaltic precipices, and on little rock-islands in the river, appeared rude-looking stacks and scaffoldings where the Indians had packed their salmon. They left it in the open air without guard, as fearless of robbers as if the fish did not constitute their almost entire subsistence for the winter. And within their own tribes they have justification for this fearlessness. Their standard of honor is in most respects curiously adjustable,—but here virtue is defended by the necessities of life.

In the immediate vicinity of the cured article (I say "cured," though the process is a mere drying without smoke or salt) may be seen the apparatus contrived for getting it in the fresh state. This is the scaffolding from which the salmon are caught. It is a horizontal platform shaped like a capital A, erected upon a similarly framed, but perpendicular set of braces, with a projection of several feet over the river brink at a place where the water runs rapidly close in-shore. If practicable, the constructor modifies his current artificially, banking it inward with large stones, so as to form a sort of sluice in which passing fish will be more completely at his mercy. At the season of their periodic ascent, salmon swarm in all the rivers of our Pacific coast; the Columbia and Willamette are alive with them for a long distance above the cascades of the one and the Oregon City Fall of the other. The fisherman stands, nearly or quite naked, at the edge of his scaffolding, armed with a net extended at the end of a long pole, and so ingeniously contrived that the weight of the salmon and a little dexterous management draw its mouth shut on the captive like a purse as soon as he has entered. A helper stands behind the fisherman to assist in raising the haul,—to give the fish a tap on the nose, which kills him instantly,—and finally to carry him ashore to be split and dried, without any danger of his throwing himself back into the water from the hands of his captors, as might easily happen by omitting the *coup-de-grace*. Another method of catching salmon, much in vogue among the Sacramento and Pitt River tribes, but apparently less employed by the Indians of the Columbia, is harpooning with a very clever instrument constructed after this wise. A hard wood shaft is neatly, but not tightly, fitted into the socket of a sharp-barbed spear-head carved from bone. Through a hole drilled in the spear-head a stout cord of deer-sinew is fastened by one end, its other being secured to the shaft near its insertion. The salmon is struck by this weapon in the manner of the ordinary fish-spear; the head slips off the shaft as soon as the barbs lodge, and the harpoon virtually becomes a fishing-rod, with the sinew for a line. This arrangement is much more manageable than the common spear, as it greatly diminishes the chances of losing fish and breaking shafts.

There can scarcely be a more sculpturesque sight than that of a finely formed, well-grown young Indian struggling on his scaffold with an unusually powerful fish. Every muscle of his wiry frame stands out in its turn in unveiled relief, and you see in him attitudes of grace and power which will not let you regret the "Apollo Belvedere" or the "Gladiator." The only pity is that this ideal Indian is a rare being. The Indians of this coast and river are divided into two broad classes,—the Fish Indians, and the Meat Indians. The latter, *ceteris paribus*, are much the finer race, derive the greater portion of their subsistence from the chase, and possess the athletic mind and body which result from active methods of winning a livelihood. The former are, to a great extent, victims of that generic and hereditary *tabes mesenterica* which produces the peculiar pot-bellied and spindle-shanked type of savage; their manners are milder; their virtues and vices are done in water-color, as comports with their source of supply. There are some tribes which partake of the habits of both classes, living in mountain-fastnesses part of the year by the bow and arrow, but coming down to the river in the salmon-season for an addition to their winter bill-of-fare. Anywhere other than among the pure Fish Indians is the place to look for savage beauty. Still these tribes have fortified their feebleness by such a cultivation of their ingenuity as surprises one seeing for the first time their well-adapted tools, comfortable lodges, and, in some cases, really beautiful canoes. In the last respect, however, the Indians nearer the coast surpass those up the Columbia,—some of their carved and painted canoes equaling the "crackest" of shell-boats in elegance of line and beauty of ornament.

In a former chapter devoted to the Great Yo-Semite I had occasion to remark that Indian legend, like all ancient poetry, often contains a scientific truth embalmed in the spices of metaphor,—or, to vary the figure, that Mudjekeewis stands holding the lantern for Agassiz and Dana to dig by.

Coming to the Falls of the Columbia, we find a case in point. Nearly equidistant from the longitudes of Fort Vancouver and Mount Hood, the entire Columbia River falls twenty feet over a perpendicular wall of basalt, extending, with minor deviations from the right angle, entirely between-shores, a breadth of about a mile. The height of Niagara and the close compression of its vast volume make it a grander sight than the Falls of the Columbia,—but no other cataract known to me on this Continent rivals it for an instant. The great American Falls of Snake are much loftier and more savage than either, but their volume is so much less as to counterbalance those advantages. Taking the Falls of the Columbia all in all,—including their upper and lower rapids,—it must be confessed that they exhibit every phase of tormented water in its beauty of color or grace of form, its wrath or its whim.

The Indians have a tradition that the river once followed a uniform level from the Dalles to the sea. This tradition states that Mounts Hood and St Helen's are husband and wife,—whereby is intended that their tutelar divinities stand in that mutual relation; that in comparatively recent times there existed a rocky bridge across the Columbia at the present site of the cataract, and that across this bridge Hood and St. Helen's were wont to pass for interchange of visits; that, while this bridge existed, there was a free subterraneous passage under it for the river and the canoes of the tribes (indeed, this tradition is so universally credited as to stagger the skeptic by a mere calculation of chances); that, on a certain occasion, the mountainous pair, like others not mountainous, came to high words, and during their altercation broke the bridge down; falling into the river, this colossal Rialto became a dam, and ever since that day the upper river has been backed to its present level, submerging vast tracts of country far above its original bed.

I notice that excellent geological authorities are willing to treat this legend respectfully, as containing in symbols the probable key to the natural phenomena. Whether the original course of the Columbia at this place was through a narrow cañon or under an actual roof of rock, the adjacent material has been at no very remote date toppled into it to make the cataract, and alter the bed to its present level. Both Hood and St. Helen's are volcanic cones. The latter has been seen to smoke within the last twelve years. It is not unlikely that during the last few centuries some intestine disturbance may have occurred along the axis between the two, sufficient to account for the precipitation of that mass of rock which now forms the dam. That we cannot refer the cataclysm to a very ancient date seems to be argued by the state of preservation in which we still find the stumps of the celebrated "submerged forest" extending a long distance up the river above the Falls.

At the foot of the cataract we landed from the steamer on the Washington side of the river, and found a railroad train waiting to do our portage. It was a strange feeling, that of whirling along by steam where so few years before the Indian and the trader had toiled through the virgin forest, bending under the weight of their canoes. And this is one of the characteristic surprises of American scenery everywhere. You cannot isolate yourself from the national civilization. In a Swiss *châlet* you may escape from all memories of Geneva; among the Grampians you find an entirely different set of ideas from those of Edinburgh: but the same enterprise which makes itself felt in New York and Boston starts up for your astonishment out of all the fastnesses of the Continent. Virgin Nature wooes our civilization to wed her, and no obstacles can conquer the American fascination. In our journey through the wildest parts of this country, we were perpetually finding patent washing-machines among the *chaparral*,—canned fruit in the desert,—Voigtlander's field-glasses on the snow-peak,—lemon-soda in the cañon,—men who were sure a railroad would be run by their cabin within ten years, in every spot where such a surprise was most remarkable.

The portage road is six miles in length, leading nearly all the way close along the edge of the North Bluff, which, owing to a recession of the mountains, seems here only from fifty to eighty feet in height. From the windows of the train we enjoyed an almost uninterrupted view of the rapids, which are only less grand and forceful in their impression than those above Niagara. They are broken up into narrow channels by numerous bold and naked islands of trap. Through these the water roars, boils, and, striking projections, spouts upward in jets whose plumy top blows off in sheets of spray. It is tormented into whirlpools; it is combed into fine threads, and strays whitely over a rugged ledge like old men's hair; it takes all curves of grace and arrow-flights of force; it is water doing all that water can do or be made to do. The painter who spent a year in making studies of it would not throw his time away; when he had finished, he could not misrepresent water under any phases.

At the upper end of the portage road we found another and smaller steamer awaiting us, with equally kind provision for our comfort made by the Company and the captain. In both steamers we were accorded excellent opportunities for drawing and observation, getting seats in the pilot-house.

Above the rapids the river banks were bold and rocky. The stream changed from its recent Niagara green to a brown like that of the Hudson; and under its waters, as we hugged the Oregon side, could be seen a submerged alluvial plateau, studded thick with drowned stumps, here and there lifting their splintered tops above the water, and measuring from the diameter of a sapling to that of a trunk which might once have been one hundred feet high.

Between Fort Vancouver and the cataract the banks of the river seem nearly as wild as on the day they were discovered by the whites. On neither the Oregon nor the Washington side is there any settlement visible,—a small wood-wharf, or the temporary hut of a salmon-fisher, being the only sign of human possession. At the Falls we noticed a single white house standing in a commanding position high up on the wooded ledges of the Oregon shore; and the taste shown in placing and constructing it was worthy of a Hudson River landholder. This is, perhaps, the first attempt at a distinct country residence made in Oregon, and belongs to a Mr. Olmstead, who was one of the earliest settlers and projectors of public improvements in the State. He was actively engaged in the building of the first portage railroad, which ran on the Oregon side. The entire interests of both have, I believe, been concentrated in the newer one; and the Oregon road, after building itself by feats of business energy and ingenuity known only to American pioneer enterprise, has fallen into entire or comparative disuse.

Above the Falls we found as unsettled a river margin as below. Occasionally, some bright spot of color attracted us, relieved against the walls of trap or glacis of evergreen; and this upon nearer approach, or by the glass, was resolved into a group of river Indians,—part with the curiously compressed foreheads of the Flat-head tribe, their serene nakedness draped with blankets of every variety of hue, from fresh flaming red to weather-beaten army blue, and adorned as to their cheeks with smutches of the cinnabar-rouge which from time immemorial has been a prime article of import among the fashionable native circles of the Columbia,—the other part round-headed, and (I have no doubt it appears a perfect *sequitur* to the Flat-head conservatives) therefore slaves. The captive in battle seems more economically treated among these savages than is common anywhere else in the Indian regions we traversed (though I suppose slavery is to some extent universal throughout the tribes),—the captors properly arguing that so long as they can make a man fish and boil pot for them, it is a very foolish waste of material to kill him.

At intervals above the Falls we passed several small islands of special interest as being the cemeteries of river tribes. The principal, called "Mimitus," was sacred as the resting-place of a very noted chief. I have forgotten his name. The deceased is entombed like a person of quality, in a wooden mauso-leum having something the appearance of a log-cabin, upon which pains have been expended, and containing, with the human remains, robes, weapons, baskets, canoes, and all the furniture of Indian *ménage*, to an extent which among the tribes amounts to a fortune. This sepulchral idea is a clear-headed one, and worthy of Eastern adoption. Old ladies with lace and nieces, old gentlemen with cellars and neph-ews, might be certain that the solace which they received in life's decline was purely disinterested, if about middle age they should announce that their Point and their Port were going to Mount Auburn with them.

The river grew narrower, its banks becoming low, per-pendicular walls of basalt, water-worn at the base, squarely cut and castellated at the top, and bare everywhere as any pile of masonry. The hills beyond became naked, or covered only with short grass of the gramma kind and dusty-gray sage brush. Simultaneously they lost some of their previous basaltic characteristics, running into more convex outlines, which receded from the river. We could not fail to recognize the fact that we had crossed one of the great thresholds of the Continent,—were once more east of the Sierra Nevada axis, and in the great central plateau which a few months previous, and several hundred miles farther south, we had crossed amid so many pains and perils by the Desert route to Washoe. From the grizzly mountains before us to the sources of the Snake Fork stretched an almost uninterrupted wilderness of sage. The change in passing to this region from the fertile and timbered tracts of the Cascades and the coast is more abrupt than can be imagined by one familiar with our delicately modulated Eastern scenery. This sharpness of definition seems to characterize the entire border of the plateau. Five hours of travel between Washoe and Sacramento carry one out of the nakedest stone heap into the grandest forest of the Continent.

As we emerged from the confinement of the nearer ranges, Mount Hood, hitherto visible only through occasional rifts, loomed broadly into sight almost from base to peak, covered with a mantle of perennial snow scarcely less complete to our near inspection than it had seemed from our observatory south of Salem. Only here and there toward its lower rim a tatter in it revealed the giant's rugged brown muscle of volcanic rock. The top of the mountain, like that of Shasta, in direct sunlight is an opal. So far above the line of thaw, the snow seems to have accumulated until by its own weight it has condensed into a more compactly crystalline structure than ice itself; and the reflections from it, as I stated of Shasta, seem rather emanations from some interior source of light. The look is distinctly opaline, or, as a poet has called the opal, like "a pearl with a soul in it."

About five o'clock in the afternoon we reached the Oregon town and mining-depot of Dalles City. A glance at any good War Department map of Oregon and Washington Territories will explain the importance of this place, where considerably previous to the foundation of the present large and growing settlement there existed a fort and trading-post of the same name. It stands, as we have said, at the entrance to the great pass by which the Columbia breaks through the mountains to the sea. Just west of it occurs an interruption to the navigation of the river, practically as formidable as the first cataract. This is the upper rapids and "the Dalles" proper,—presently to be described in detail. The position of the town, at one end of a principal portage, and at the easiest door to the Pacific, renders it a natural entrepôt between the latter and the great central plateau of the Continent. This it must have been in any case for fur-traders and emigrants, but its business has been vastly increased by the discovery of that immense mining area distributed along the Snake River and its tributaries as far east as the Rocky Mountains. The John Day, Boisé, and numerous other tracts both in Washington and Idaho Territories draw most of their supplies from this entrepôt, and their gold comes down to it either for direct use in the outfit market, or to be passed down the river to Portland and the San Francisco mint.

I do not lay particular stress upon the mines of Washington and Idaho as sources of profit to the Pacific Railroad. This is for the reason that the Snake River seems the proper outlet to much of the auriferous region, and this route may be susceptible of improvement by an alternation of portages, roads, and water-levels, which for a long time to come will form a means of communication more economical and rapid than a branch to the Pacific Road. The northern mines east of the Rocky range will find themselves occupying somewhat similar relations to the Missouri River, which rises, as one might almost say, out of the same spring as the Snake,—certainly out of the same ridge of the Rocky Mountains.

"The Dalles" is a town of one street, built close along the edge of a bluff of trap thirty or forty feet high, perfectly perpendicular, level on the top as if it had been graded for a city, and with depth of water at its base for the heaviest draught boats on the river. In fact, the whole water-front is a natural quay,—which wants nothing but time to make it alive with steam-elevators, warehouses, and derricks. To Portland and the Columbia it stands much as St. Louis to New Orleans and the Mississippi. There is no reason why it should not some day have a corresponding business, for whose wharfage accommodation it has even greater natural advantages.

Architecturally, the Dalles cannot be said to lean very heavily on the side of beauty. The houses are mostly two-story structures of wood, occupied by all the trades and professions which flock to a new mining entrepôt. Outfit merchants, blacksmiths, printing-office (for there is really a very well-conducted daily at the Dalles), are cheek by jowl with doctors, tailors, and Cheap Johns,—the latter being only less merry and thrifty over their incredible sacrifices in everything, from pins to corduroy, than that predominant class of all, the bar-keepers themselves. The town was in a state of bustle when our steamer touched the wharf; it bustled more and more from there to the Umatilla House, where we stopped; the hotel was one organized bustle in bar and dining room; and bed-time brought no hush. The Dalles, like the Irishman, seemed sitting up all night to be fresh for an early start in the morning.

We found everybody interested in gold. Crowds of listeners, with looks of incredulity or enthusiasm, were gathered around the party in the bar-room which had last come in from the newest of the new mines, and a man who had seen the late Fort Hall discoveries was "treated" to that extent that he might have become intoxicated a dozen times without expense to himself. The charms of the interior were still further suggested by placards posted on every wall, offering rewards for the capture of a person who on the great gold route had lately committed some of the grimmest murders and most talented robberies known in any branch of Newgate enterprise. I had for supper a very good omelet (considering its distance from the culinary centres of the universe), and a Dalles editorial debating the claims of several noted cut-throats to the credit of the operations ascribed to them,—feeling that in the *ensemble* I was enjoying both the exotic and the indigenous luxuries of our virgin soil.

After supper and a stroll I returned to the ladies' parlor of the Umatilla House, rubbed my eyes in vain to dispel the illusion of a piano and a carpet at this jumping-off place of civilization, and sat down at a handsome centre-table to write up my journal. I had reviewed my way from Portland as far as Fort Vancouver, when another illusion happened to me in the shape of a party of gentlemen and ladies, in ball-dresses, dress-coats, white kids, and elaborate hair, who entered the parlor to wait for further accessions from the hotel. They were on their way with a band of music to give some popular citizen a surprise party. The popular citizen never got the fine edge of that surprise. I took it off for him. If it were not too much like a little Cockney on Vancouver's Island who used the phrase on all occasions, from stubbing his toe to the death of a Cabinet Lord, I should say, "I never was more astonished in *me* life!"

None of them had ever seen me before,—and with my books and maps about me, I may have looked like some public, yet mysterious character. I felt a pleasant sensation of having interest taken in me, and, wishing to make an ingenuous return, looked up with a casual smile at one of the party. Again to my surprise, this proved to be a very charming young lady, and I timidly became aware that the others were equally pretty in their several styles. Not knowing what else to do under the circumstances, I smiled again, still more casually. An equal uncertainty as to alternative set the ladies smiling quite across the row, and then, to my relief, the gentlemen joined them, making it pleasant for us all. A moment later we were engaged in general conversation,—starting from the bold hypothesis, thrown out by one of the gentlemen, that perhaps I was going to Boisé, and proceeding, by a process of elimination, to the accurate knowledge of what I was going to do, if it wasn't that. I enjoyed one of the most cheerful bits of social relaxation I had found since crossing the Missouri; and nothing but my duty to my journal prevented me, when my surprise party left, from accompanying them, by invitation, under the brevet title of Professor, to the house of the popular citizen, who, I was assured, would be glad to see me. I certainly should have been glad to see him, if he was anything like those guests of his who had so ingenuously cultivated me in a far land of strangers, where a man might have been glad to form the acquaintance of his mother-in-law. This is not the way people form acquaintances in New York; but if I had wanted that, why not have stayed there? As a cosmopolite, and on general principles of being, I prefer the Dalles way. I have no doubt I should have found in that circle of spontaneous recognitions quite as many people who stood wear and improved on intimacy as were ever vouchsafed to me by social indorsement from somebody else. We are perpetually blaming our heads of Government bureaus for their poor knowledge of character,—their subordinates, we say, are never pegs in the right holes. If we understood our civilized system of introductions, we could not rationally expect anything else. The great mass of polite mankind are trained *not* to know character, but to take somebody else's voucher for it. Their acquaintances, most of their friendships, come to them through a succession of indorsers, none of whom may have known anything of the goodness of the paper. A sensible man, conventionally introduced to his fellow, must always wonder why the latter does not turn him around to look for signatures in chalk down the back of his coat; for he knows that Brown indorsed him over to Jones, and Jones negotiated him with Robinson, through a succession in which perhaps two out of a hundred took pains to know whether he represented metal. You do not find the people of new countries making mistakes in character. Every man is his own guaranty,—and if he has no just cause to suspect himself bogus, there will be true pleasure in a frank opening of himself to the examination and his eyes for the study of others. Not to be accused of intruding radical reform under the guise of belles-lettres, let me say that I have no intention of introducing this innovation at the East.

In the afternoon of the next day we were provided, by the courtesy of the Company, with a special train on the portage railroad connecting Dalles City with a station known as Celilo. This road had but recently come into fall operation, and was now doing an immense freight business between the two river levels separated by the intervening "Dalles." It seemed somewhat longer than the road around the Falls. Its exact length has escaped me, but I think it about eight or nine miles.

With several officers of the road, who vied in giving us opportunities of comfort and information, we set out, about three P. M., from a station on the water-front below the town, whence we trundled through the long main street, and were presently shot forth upon a wilderness of sand. An occasional trap uplift rose on our right, but, as we were on the same bluff level as Dalles City, we met no lofty precipices. We were constantly in view of the river, separated from its Oregon brink at the farthest by about half a mile of the dreariest dunes of shifting sand ever seen by an amateur in deserts. The most arid tracts along the Platte could not rival this. The wind was violent when we left Dalles City, and possessed the novel faculty of blowing simultaneously from all points of the compass. It increased with every mile of advance, both in force and faculty, until at Celilo we found it a hurricane. The gentlemen of the Company who attended us, told us, as seemed very credible, that the highest winds blowing here (compared with which the present might be styled a zephyr) banked the track so completely out of sight with sand that a large force of men had to be steadily employed in shoveling out trains that had been brought to a dead halt, and clearing a way for the slow advance of others.

I observed that the sides of some of the worst sand-cuts had been planked over to prevent their sliding down upon the road. Occasionally, the sand blew in such tempests as to sift through every cranny of the cars, and hide the river glimpses like a momentary fog. But this discomfort was abundantly compensated by the wonderfully interesting scenery on the Columbia side of our train.

The river for the whole distance of the portage is a succession of magnificent rapids, low cataracts, and narrow, sinuous channels,—the last known to the old French traders as "*Dales*" or "Troughs," and to us by the very natural corruption of "Dalles." The alternation between these phases is wonderfully abrupt. At one point, about halfway between Dalles City and Celilo, the entire volume of the Columbia River (and how vast that is may be better understood by following up on the map the river itself and all its tributaries) is crowded over upon the Oregon shore through a passage not more than fifty yards in width, between perfectly naked and perpendicular precipices of basalt. Just beyond this mighty mill-race, where one of the grandest floods of the Continent is sliding in olive-green light and umber shadow, smoothly and resistlessly as time, the river is a mile wide, and plunges over a ragged wall of trap blocks, reaching, as at the lower cataract, from shore to shore. In other neighboring places it attains even a greater width, but up to Celilo is never out of torment from the obstructions of its bed. Not even the rapids of Niagara can vie with these in their impression of power; and only the Columbia itself can describe the lines of grace made by its water, rasped to spray, churned to froth, tired into languid sheets that flow like sliding glass, or shot up in fountains frayed away to rainbows on their edges, as it strikes some basalt hexagon rising in mid-stream. The Dalles and the Upper Cataracts are still another region where the artist might stay for a year's University course in water-painting.

At Celilo we found several steamers, in register resembling our second of the day previous. They measured on the average about three hundred tons. One of them had just got down from Walla Walla, with a large party of miners from gold tracts still further off, taking down five hundred thousand dollars in dust to Portland and San Francisco. We were very anxious to accept the Company's extended invitation, and push our investigations to or even up the Snake River. But the expectation that the San Francisco steamer would reach Portland in a day or two, and that we should immediately return by her to California, turned us most reluctantly down the river, after we had made the fullest notes and sketches attainable. Bad weather on the coast falsified our expectations. For a week we were rain-bound in Portland, unable to leave our hotel for an hour at a time without being drenched by the floods, which just now set in for the winter season, and regretting the lack of that prescience which would have enabled us to accomplish one of the most interesting side-trips in our whole plan of travel. While this pleasure still awaited us, and none in particular of any kind seemed present save the in-door courtesies of our Portland friends, it was still among the memories of a life-time to have seen the Columbia in its Cataracts and its Dalles.

# APPENDIX

## UTAH'S LIFE PRINCIPLE AND DESTINY.

THE great ecclesiastical glory of Mormonism is to be the Temple. This is now in process of erection, but the work is pushed very slowly—probably with a view to the greater soundness of its foundations, as the other reasons common in such cases, lack of money and of labor, can hardly be operative here,—the Church being enormously wealthy, able to control the time of all its disciples, and blessed with a male membership whose large majority is used to physical labor.

The basement of the Temple, as I learned from a Mormon builder, was excavated several years ago, and its foundations partly laid, when Brigham Young discovered in the work something which dissatisfied him, and had it leveled to the ground. The foundations are now well up once more, and the gigantic ashlars are steadily coming in from their quarry in the cañons. The stone used is a handsome compact granite, like the Quincy, but even whiter, and in the more ornamental parts of the superstructure will be associated with marble, and that magnificent crystalline limestone, traversed by veins of pure calc-spar, which, in almost every direction around Salt Lake, is found adjoining the metamorphic strata.

The City is laid out in the shape of an L, whose upright points north and south. "Temple Block" is situated nearly in the inner angle of this L. On the east Brigham Young's, or "the Prophet's" block, adjoins it, with a street intervening. Heber Kimball's stands corner to corner with it, just north of Brigham's. That of George Smith (the original prophet's cousin, and keeper of the sacred archives) is on the west of it. Across the street, on the south of it, is the Council House Block. On the south-east is the block occupied by Mr. Wells, one of the chief apostles, and third of the three presidents, Brigham and Heber[5] being the others; the History Office is also on the same.

The Temple Block is 660 feet square, its lines running due north, south, east, and west, its front being on the east. The front line of the Temple is 78 feet 8 inches from the east line of the block; the length of the building, including towers and pedestal, will be 186½ feet, and its width 118½ feet. I was very much surprised when I learned how comparatively insignificant were the dimensions of a building intended to be the external symbol of God's abode among men, and the architectural glory of a people whose sectarian belief is so closely identified with its national life as the Mormons. The foundation walls, where they reach the surface of the ground, are 16 feet wide. From the surface they slope 3 feet on each side to the height of 7½ feet, having thus on their upper surface a width of 10 feet. On this base begins the true wall, which is 8 feet thick. Measuring from outside to outside of the north and south wall, the width of the body of the building will be but 99 feet—the larger measurement given above including the towers, which stand at each end of the east and west side. Beside these towers at the corners, there are two others, at the centre of the east and west sides respectively. Each of

---

5 Written before Heber's death. With this understanding none of the essential statements are affected.

these towers has pedestals of the same form and proportions as the wall, built of immense rough ashlars laid in lime mortar. Along the north and south sides of the Temple, between the towers, the earth will be sloped into a glacis, or terrace, 6 feet high above the general level of the block; and on its upper surface will begin a promenade with a width varying from 11 to 22 feet, and reaching round the entire building, with stone steps leading up to it from the lower level at convenient intervals along the slope of the glacis. The towers on the four corners start from their footing of 26 feet square, continue to the height of 16½ feet, where they reach the line of the first string-course, and are reduced to 25 feet square. They continue thus 38 feet higher to the second string-course; are then reduced to 23 feet square, and rise another distance of 38 feet to the third string-course. From this course the corner towers become cylindrical, with an interior diameter of 17 feet; those on the east rising to the height of 25, and those on the west to a height of 19 feet, before they reach their own proper string-pieces, or cornices. From these cornices, on all four of them, rise battements 9 feet high. The strings-pieces, save where broken by buttresses, are continuous all round the building, and are massive mouldings from solid blocks of stone. Each of the corner towers has on each of its exposed sides two ornamental windows in their 25 feet square section, two in the section 23 feet square, and one in the highest. The centre towers, on both the east and west ends, start 31 feet square, but are otherwise of the same proportions as the corner towers as high as the third string-piece. From that line the east centre tower rises 40 feet to the top of its battlement, and the west centre tower 34 feet,—each being thus 6 feet higher than its adjoining corner towers.

Each of the centre towers is, furthermore, crowned with a spire; the spire of the east tower rising to the height of 200, and that of the west to 190 feet. All the towers are ornamented at the corners of each story with pinnacled turrets, and each side of the towers is flanked by a pair of buttresses. On the front of each centre tower are two windows, each 80 feet high, set one above the other. It is expected that these will rival the finest abbey and cathedral windows of the Old World. They will be of the handsomest carved stone-work, with stained-glass panes; and there are among the Mormons one or two artists in both these departments, whose talents, judging from small specimens of their work which I saw, are really quite remarkable. It is the intention that all the labor and the art expended on the Temple shall be distinctly indigenous; and the pride which Brigham takes in all home productions tends to the constant development of the very class of abilities needed for this result. The height of the ridge-pole of the Temple will be about 100 feet.

The foundation of the building looks more like that of a fort than of a cathedral. Not only do the massive side walls, 16 feet thick below, 8 feet above, contribute to this impression, but the partitions also, of enormous ashlars, by which the basement is separated into a multitude of rooms. In the centre of the area is the baptismal room, 59 feet long by 35 feet wide, separated from the main north and south walls by four rooms, two on each side, each 19 feet long by 12 wide. On the east and west sides of these rooms are four passages, 12 feet wide; and still further east and west four more rooms, two at each end, 28 by 38½ feet. These rooms are all 16½ feet high, and are to have elegantly ornamented and groined ceilings.

From the basement, by stair-ways in the towers, we ascend to courts 16 feet wide, running from tower to tower, and communicating by doors with all parts of the building. Out of the front or east court, a lofty door-way will enter the principal room of the Temple, 120 feet in length, 80 feet in width, and 38 feet in height to the crown of the ceiling. The ceiling is to be groined; its arches, segments of an ellipse, resting upon columns based on the partition-walls below. These arches will meet in Ogive fashion at the centre, and be as profusely ornamented as possible by saintly artificers. The space outside of the columns supporting the arches, between them and the outer walls, will be divided into sixteen compartments, eight on each side, and 14 feet square, with a passage-way 6 feet wide, running along them the entire length of the building—each of these having in the outer wall (here 6 feet thick) a large elliptical window with the major axis perpendicular.

The next story is to be precisely similar, except that the width of its large room will be one foot wider than that beneath it.

The ornamentation of the building is intended to be symbolical of that employed on the celestial courts above. Its plan is already partially developed to Brigham by revelation through an angel, but will be communicated in all its particulars only as required during the progress of the work. The ungodly understand this arrangement as synonymous among their own uninspired class with waiting to see how things will look; but whatever they may say, I believe that Brother Brigham thinks he receives the plans from an angel. If it be really an angel, we must arrive at the painful conclusion that good taste is not necessarily included in that perfection of human nature which ensues on translation to the celestial state; for such an architectural hotch-potch as that which I have just attempted to describe was certainly never seen on earth, and must render any part of heaven where it existed a very undesirable place of residence to people of cultivation. Among the adornments which are to be executed on the exterior of the barbaric pile are the following, which I quote from the architect's own account of his plan:—

"On the two west corner towers, and on the west end, a few feet below the top of battlements, may be seen, in alto-relievo and bold relief, the Great Dipper, or Ursa Major, with the pointers ranging nearly toward the North Star. (Moral: The lost may find themselves by the priesthood.)

"The pedestals under all the buttresses project at their base 2 feet; above their base, which is 15 inches by 4½ feet wide, on each front is a figure of a globe 3 feet 11 inches across, whose axis corresponds with the axis of the earth.

"Above the promenade, close under the second string-course on each of the buttresses, is the moon represented in its different phases. Close under the third string-course or cornice is the face of the sun. Immediately above is Saturn with his rings.

"The only difference between the tower buttresses and the one just described is, instead of Saturn being on them, we have clouds and rays of light descending.

"All of these symbols are to be chiseled in bass-relief on solid stone. The side walls continue above the string-course or cornice 8½ feet, making the walls 96 feet high and are formed in battlements interspersed with stars.

"The whole house covers an area of 21,850 feet."

While this portentous structure is getting ready to

surprise, if not to scare, the nations, the Mormons residing in the City of Salt Lake worship in cool or cold weather at "The Tabernacle," and in the dog-days at "The Bowery."

The Tabernacle situated on the southwest corner of Temple Block. It is a building of the sun-dried bricks or adobe in such universal use throughout the western half of the Continent,—having its principal entrance in the southern gable, which fronts on the same street as Brigham Young's. Its length is 126 feet, its width 64; and its height disproportionately small as not only to give it a very squat appearance, which its absence of pretension and temporariness of purpose make a matter of no consequence, but to render it almost stifling when the July sun pours down on it,—a matter which, to the 2,200 people whom it can seat at a pinch, is of very great consequence indeed. With the first extremely hot weather, therefore, Sunday religion moves its quarters to "The Bowery," a structure like the booths of the ancient Israelites, or, to descend for illustration into an atmosphere more recent and familiar, like the arbors which used to be in vogue at many of our sea-side watering-places, and are still to be seen fronting some hotels at Long Branch and at Fire Island—a scaffolding of rough tree trunks the diameter of a telegraph pole set firmly in the ground, ten or twenty feet apart, braced together by equally tough string-pieces at the top, and covered with successive layers of boughs green at first, but dried to parchment by the end of August, *felted* into each other, so to speak, until they are quite impervious to the sun. *Rain* in Utah there is but too little need of providing against. The only "fair-weather Christian" must be a cool-weather one. The outer line of posts, in the Bowery, includes a nearly equilateral area of about 14,000 square feet, situated due north of the Tabernacle, and like it, on the Temple Block. I should judge it capable, without difficulty, of accommodating somewhere near 4,000 persons. Its seats are rude pine benches, some with backs, others backless, and provided, by the more luxurious members of the congregation, with hair or cornshuck cushions. On the inner posts hang kerosene lamps for use during the second Sunday service, which is held in the evening through the summer months at least, the afternoon being devoted to Sunday-school. A platform in length and breadth equaling the stage of a good-sized theatre, occupies about half of the northern side (the middle of the stage coinciding with the middle of the side), and affords rather more sumptuous seats than those of the auditorium (cane settees and chairs when I attended service) to a score or more of the principal men of Mormondom. The only approach to a pulpit is a plain drawing-room table, on which lie the Bible, the Book of Mormon, and the Latter-Day Saint's Hymn Book, flanked by a pitcher of water and a tumbler.

On visiting the Bowery at the hour of beginning morning service, about half-past ten, as usual in most of our Eastern churches, I found the seats already well filled, but obtained a good position by the politeness of Brigham's son-in-law, Mr. Clawson. A pleasanter place to attend service in could hardly be imagined. The uninterrupted passage through the leafy covering of a delicious mountain breeze, whose edge, acquired by gliding over the hone of the perpetual snow, had been tempered just to a nicety by the sunshine of a cloudless summer sky, made fans entirely unnecessary; and the liberty of the Gospel was broadly enough construed to admit of several bronzed agricultural saints near me sitting in the spotless freshness of snowy shirt-sleeves. The ladies were generally attired in airy muslin dresses without any over garment, except in a few scattered instances, where a black silk mantilla indicated some member of the Mormon aristocracy; and the children, who were present in large number, were, with striking good taste, dressed comfortably rather than ostentatiously—a course worthy of imitation at the East, and likely, if adopted, to increase greatly the number of youthful Christians who can say without hypocrisy,—

> "I have been there, and still would go:
> 'Tis like a little heaven below."

The stage was occupied by nine or ten dignitaries of the Church, among whom I recognized that stalwart pillar, Brother Heber, Dr. Bernhisel, and a very pleasant-looking man, a bishop, to whom I had been introduced during the week. His name now escapes me, but I shall always recollect his face as expressing more genuine benevolence of nature, sincerity, and good sense than any I saw in Utah, except Brigham's.

The exercises opened with a hymn given out by Dr. Bernhisel, and sung by the whole congregation with abundant fervor, under the leading of a small choir near the stage, accompanied by a melodeon and a violin. The tune was old familiar *Ward*, and in the words of the hymn was nothing which could shock the most fastidiously orthodox of Gentiles.

Some of the hymns in the collection are very curious specimens of sacred and secular rapture commingled, as if the altar fire had been lighted with a coal from the kitchen-range of daily life. One, with which I became acquainted on another occasion, beginning "Upper California—O! that's the land for me!" (written in the early days of the Mormon exodus westward, when California included what is now Nevada, and the Mormons had founded several settlements along the Sierra), was sung to an adaptation of the ancient negro favorite, "O Susannah! don't you cry for me," and contained a vivid description as well as eulogy of the agricultural blessings ensuing to immigrants. It sounded like a melodious prospectus of some new township, with religions and water privileges, the advantage of the Christians and the ten-acre lot treated in the same access of religious spasmody. One jumble particularly entertained me—it went something like this:—

> "Where the blessing of Jehovah is pound out on Jacob's line,
>     And the mountains all are flowing with milk and honey, and
>     saints and wine."

I am not sure that I quote the couplet precisely, except the last line, but that is correct, and the only part of consequence to the fun of the thing.

After the hymn, the bishop of whom I have spoken made an extempore prayer. It was, as I should have expected, a plain, straightforward, honest-hearted appeal to the Divine Being for forgiveness of sins, and thanksgiving for the temporal blessings bestowed on the saintly community. At its conclusion, I was disappointed not to see Brigham rise to address us, but he had come in the week before from making an apostolic tour throughout the southern settlements, where he had averaged one speech a day, sometimes talking in the open air, and had a good excuse for resting his voice to-day. Heber had been out too—accompanying Brother

Brigham through his circuit, and playing Silas to his Paul everywhere. But Heber was a perfect Boanerges, as well as a Silas, and his thunderous utterances no more tired him than the work of keeping the small coal lively tires the leathern lungs which tradition makes it a part of his earlier manhood's career to have operated alternately with the sledge and cold chisel. He needed no rest, and accordingly gave us an address. This time it lacked one of those Heberistic characters which make his sermons as popular among the ungodly as Burton was in his best days—and popular after a fashion even still less congruous with Sunday and sanctities than "*Forty Winks*" or the "*Thousand Milliners.*" It was not indecent. I confess that I felt my curiosity disappointed while my good taste and ethical sense were relieved, for I had braced myself to stand any amount of deviation from the line usually followed by preachers, whether as regards subject selected or treatment employed. In his private conversation, as I had many occasions of noticing, Heber granted himself the largest latitude of reference to matters which are usually tabooed, or, if mentioned of necessity, only behind the screen of friendship's most intimate privacy; and of substituting for the euphuisms and circumlocutions in which such friendship mentions them, the very baldest and boldest literalities of speech. Without resorting to the old-fashioned pedantry of putting such conversation into a Latin note (as if Juvenal and Apuleius had set moderns the example of using their native speech for a cesspool of baleful immoralities that could not flow exposed to common view down the channels of our sunlit Saxon), I cannot report the second President's habitual style of talking. It is sufficient to say that all subjects which, by the common consent of civilized communities in this age, are wholly withdrawn from the currency of talk, were his most favorite and habitual topics of conversation; indeed, I never saw any man who had known him a day without learning his opinions upon some one of these subjects, or hearing him refer to them in the most unvarnished terms and with a peculiar lickerish relish. He is as audacious on the platform as he is in the parlor. I never should have believed possible the reports I have read and heard of his speeches, had they not been authenticated to me by the consenting testimony of numerous most respectable and unbiased men present on the occasions when they were delivered—still more by my own ear-witness of identical language used in private. Heber's favorite audience is one largely consisting of "the beloved sisters," and to this he expatiates by the hour after a fashion which would crimson the cheeks of an assembly of Camilles not utterly lost to the memories of a pure home and childhood. No more overwhelming proof can be offered for Mormonism's degradation of the marriage tie and its extinction of man's chivalric feelings of respect and protection toward woman, than the fact that men of refined, gentlemanly, and scholarly antecedents, like Dr. Bernhisel, for instance, can hear one of their own sex talk in public to their sisters, mothers, daughters, and wives, upon the most private subjects in the most blatant way, and not tear him in pieces where he stands.

On this particular occasion, Heber disappointed the morbid curiosity of such Gentiles as had gone to the Bowery to hear something improper, unless, indeed, their tastes were so simple that disloyalty satisfied them. Heber took no text, but his address was directed at the California regiments under Colonel (now General) Connor, lying camped on the first rise toward the Wahsatch Cañons, about three miles out of the city, and admirably well posted to command it, either as an army of observation, or in a strategic point of view. Heber did not like to have them there; their presence was an insult to the Mormon Government; they were there ostensibly for the purpose of protecting immigration and the mails against the Utes, the rebel split from Washki's Shoshones, the Piutes, the Goshoots, and other hostile Indians of the Range and Desert; but the no less important function they were there to discharge, and the Mormons knew it, was the protection of United States officials, and the preservation of at least a semblance of United States authority, in opposition to the Mormons themselves. From the roof of the Opera House their white line of tents could be seen plainly beyond the rich green foliage that embowered the city, extending like a flock of snowy storks lit in a broad high meadow to rest on their way across the Continent; and in this view were a charmingly picturesque set of objects. But unlike the poetical and migratory birds which they resembled, they were not harmless in their manners nor temporary in their sojourn. They were there to enforce taxes and drafts, if such were resisted; to see that the Territorial Governor received respect, and Gentiles got even-handed justice in lawsuits with saints, through the medium of inviolable United States courts; they were there in fulfillment of Uncle Sam's constitutional pledge to sustain all his nephews in the enjoyment of a republican form of government. Their preparation for the maintenance of all these rights and causes was of the meagrest—a couple of howitzers perhaps, and half a dozen little field-pieces, the heaviest carrying only a twelve-pound ball. But the men behind the guns were the true batteries. Though they might eventually be overwhelmed by numbers,—in fact, *must* be, if smouldering hostility ever broke forth into belligerent flame,—they would burn down the city first, and serve their cannon till the last round was exhausted; then, making their extirpation the costliest job the Mormons ever undertook, die in their first tracks on a mound of their fallen enemies. They were old Californian grizzly hunters, men that had crossed the heaven-piercing barriers, and slid down the soul-dismaying precipices of the Sierra Nevada on snow-shoes; old Indian-fighters, prospecters, forty-niners, and vigilance committee men—men who knew Fear by name, but had never shaken hands with him. Thrice or more had Brother Brigham prayed that these buffeting messengers might depart from him; but Uncle Sam had answered him as a higher power answered the other apostle, thus for, however, omitting to give him grace sufficient to bear them. They wanted to be there, curious to say, as little as Brother Brigham wanted to have them. They had enlisted at the very outbreak of the Rebellion, with the understanding that they were to go east and south to fight the battles of the Union; with most of them, I believe, it was an express stipulation. Judge of their chagrin when they found themselves compelled to settle down in their present life of inglorious ease under the Wahsatch—their only smell of powder coming in skirmishes with Indians; the employment of their seething energies limited to this cat-watching-a-mouse-hole kind of business; the whole gigantic sell resulting from the government's changing its mind as to the economy of giving them transportation to the Potomac, without allowing them to change their minds as to the validity of their enrollment. But though they grumbled (in fact, I don't know but it would be more accurate to say, all the more because they did grumble), they were as stanch and formidable defenders as the Union could have had in Utah.

Heber told his audience that they must cultivate feelings of Christian forgiveness to the blue-coat sojer-men; they were all poor critters that had to do what they were bid, and probably none of them would keer, of their own accord, to be sticking their noses into the business of other people, and be spyin' and smellin' around a community of honest, industrious, respectable people that hadn't never done 'em no harm inowayshapermanner. I don't know that Heber regarded this adverbial phrase as a single word, but he always pronounced it so. Poor critters! he continued,—with a sigh of such peculiar pathos that one felt he would like to eat them to put them out of their misery,—how could *they* know that the time was comin' when they would call on the Wahsatch to cover them, and the devouring flames of the Lord should roast them till the flesh sizzled on their bones, and they should cry out for Death to come; but Death wouldn't have nothin' to do with their lousy carcasses, any more'n you or I, brethren 'n sisters, would touch a lump o' cowyard manure when we'd just washed our hands to go to meetin'. Little good then would their shoddy coats do 'em; the devil, who had a mortgage on them and the contractors that made 'em, wasn't scared at blue jackets and United States buttons. He did sincerely hope to see the day, brethren 'n sisters, when they might all be licked clean up as the small dust of the balance, 'n not one stone left upon another; but till then it was their duty to indulge a sperrit of Christian forgiveness. O yes! them and their wives and their little ones, though they whirled 'em around on their bayonets and stamped the blood of their prophets in the dust, until the terrible day of the Lord should come, and the Saints could sit under their own vine and fig tree with none to molest 'em or make 'em afraid. He was a friend to 'em himself—he was. He didn't want to see 'em ripped open and torn to pieces with just wrath like a gutted catfish. He pitied them, for he thought of the day when the oppressed would hev to rise agin 'em and drive the last footprint of the tyrant from the soil God had given to His people. He pitied the people of the States, all on 'em. They were fightin' their brethren for the sake of the niggers. Talk of niggers! Where were there miserabler niggers than the poor slaves that followed the fanatic Abolitionist leaders at the North? They didn't dare to say their soul was their own; they had to go and fight their brethren and get licked—they always were licked like hell, and he thanked God for it; everybody ought to that went into other people's premises and tried to break up their family arrangements; and slavery was a family arrangement just as much as ours, brethren and sisters. They had to follow their leaders like sheep over a stone wall, and get and get butchered like sheep by the thousands and thousands; but, thank God, the thing was pretty nigh played out, and before long we'd see it. The Union was all gone to hell; there wouldn't be enough left in a few days to bury its carcass decently. There never could be any such thing as a reunion; henceforth and forever the North and South were two separate nations, and the South were much the better fellows of the two. If he had been East at the breaking out of the rebellion,—as the Abolitionists called the Southerners' trying to keep them from stealing their niggers, ravishing their wives, and murdering their old men and babies,—he would have shouldered his musket and marched down to help those brave fellows, the Southerners—you bet! But they didn't need any help; they had no more to do than they could attend to. What was faith? It was knowledge that the Lord God Omnipotent reigneth. It was a belief that things would come to pass. Now, did we, brethren and sisters, believe that things would come to pass? That the proud enemy would be destroyed, yea, smitten, until they that were in the uttermost isles should be proud of his tokens, and Lebanon should not be sufficient for a burnt-offering thereof? Had we that? He hoped we had, though there were some that hung down their feeble knees. This was a great day—there was no doubt but the Lord was moving. He pulled up a new peg and sot down a new peg every day. If we had not faith that brother Brigham, if necessary, could be inspired by the Lord to tumble Ensign Peak into Salt Lake—and we might live to see greater wonders than that, only we hardened our hearts as in the day of provocation—we had no show for heaven at all. It was a grain of mustard-seed, but it filled the whole earth. Wasn't that a miracle? But His arm is not shortened. He was sorry to see that faith was waxing cold. Some of the young sisters needed a sort of stirring up—the brethren too were drowsy—he wasn't talking about the hot weather, though it was so hot he guessed he'd take a drink (took a drink and wiped his mouth on his cuff)—it would be hotter yet, and no drinks neither, if they didn't yearn inwardly and seek the kingdom. Where was he? O yes—stirring up—till they should cry hosannah—with a sharp gad—a ten-foot pole, as he might say of gospel truth and exhortation—until they should repent and do their first works. Why, when they first come out here, weren't there lots of 'em that were glad enough of a peck o' yellow meal to keep themselves, and their wives, and their little ones from starving, and now they were riding around in their spring wagons, and old Buck and Bright that drew the Ark of their Covenant, their family ark, not built out of shittim wood, but ash and hemlock, across from the States—they were changed off for two-forty nags, and everything was to cut a dash; but what they had gained in this respect (here he adopted the famous gesture made by Everett in his "Washington" address, and slapped his breeches pocket till the chink rang), was more'n lost by the fallin' off in sperritooality. But he guessed that what he'd said would bear fruit, and if it didn't he wa'n't to blame—he had done his dooty, and now he guessed he'd wind up. He hadn't made a speech to edification like to brother Brigham's, but he was a horse of another color, and there was plenty in what he'd said, any way, to bring 'em into the kingdom; leastways, if he couldn't carry 'em slap in, up and through, to give 'em a saving hist any how, and might the Lord bless 'em all, forever and ever, amen!

After Brother Heber's sermon was concluded, we had another hymn sung with great earnestness, for it was set to the tune of the "Star Spangled Banner," and there was enough of the American element present to tinge the whole audience with enthusiasm despite the chuckling disloyalty of Heber. It is hard for Uncle Sam's prodigals to forget the old man; Joe Smith does not seem to take his place at all; and all the American Mormons outside the governing class, feel a sneaking thrill for the liberty pole and the spread eagle. One Sunday night a party of Conner's blue-coats got leave to come into service at the Bowery. The Mormon choir happened to select for one of their hymns that evening, this same tune, dear to patriotic hearts, and voices of 2½ octaves compass. The boys who occupied a seat in the back part of the "Meetin'" had listened attentively to all the preceding service—had borne good-humoredly the invariable diatribes against the Government which formed the staple of Mormon sermons; and had conducted themselves with the utmost decency, in accordance with Connor's orders, to avoid all cause of quarrel with the Saints, until the Mormons began to sing the national air. At first they found outlet for their enthusiasm in joining the music, but soon found they did not fadge with the regular attendants on the sanctuary. Not being favorite visitors, they had received from nobody the courtesy of a hymn-book; and not being acquainted with the hymn, they sang Key's original words as they had learned them in camp. Having good out-door voices of their own, valuable rather for strength than skill in *ritenuto* and *piano* passages, they soon smothered the sacred under the profane lyric, and became aware by ominous scowls from the surrounding benches that they were disturbing the worship of the sanctuary. Always desirous to keep the general peace, they forthwith held their own, contenting themselves with such relief to overcharged nervous systems as might be afforded by beating time with their feet and fingers. Just as the choir finished the last verse, their ecstasy becoming incontrollable, burst forth in a volley of applause mingled with hurrahs. This was the feather which produced dorsal fracture in the Mormon camel. "Young men!" said a venerable bishop, sternly, from the rostrum, "you forget that you are in the house of the Lord." "Not a bit of it, ole hoss," one of the boys "spoke right out in meetin'." "What in thunder diye want to sing such all-fired nice tunes for, if you want a feller to sit still and bust himself?"

On the present occasion there were none of the blue-coats present and nobody "bust himself," but after the hymn an elderly gentleman (of sixty, perhaps, or thereabouts) rose and approached the (more or less) sacred desk. He was of good height and had had no quarrel with his cook. His weight might have been two hundred; his general complexion was a cool permanent pink which shaded artistically onto the warmer Magentesque tinge of a large, generously nourished, and globularly terminated nose. His clothes were that gray homespun which told of a Penelope among his wives; and it was right he should have one, for in some respects he was the "πολυμητις Οδυσσευς," the many counseled Ulysses of Mormonism. He was the historian and keeper of the sacred archives, the cousin of the martyr Prophet and Revelator Joseph—George Smith. He wore a pair of silver mounted spectacles; and his hair, which was rapidly turning white, hung in long, flossy strands from about a forehead whose slippery shine and intellectual height and bumpiness reminded me of Patriarch Casby in "Little Dorrit," while it suggested for its refulgence a supernatural explanation. Among prophets and seers we cannot expect to see heads crowned with festal wreaths,—"Caput nitidum *non* licet impedire myrto" (although the nose did look secular and temporal); but this good man's polished poll might perchance be accounted for by the glaze naturally consequent upon the habitual resting on it of saintly halos and tongues of fire.

Mr. Smith spoke very well. I don't know how much inspiration is claimed for the Apostles who speak on Sunday, but if he was not inspired he did not seem to miss it, for much that goes by the name is inferior to his sermon in good sense and interest. He reviewed the Mormon past in a vigorous sketchy way, contrasting it with the present, to show how manifestly the Saints had been the peculiar care of Providence, and how much cause they had for encouragement regarding the future. His references to the early persecution of the sect were remarkably temperate. I was surprised to find in the representative of a family which had suffered more than any other among the Mormons from the rancor of the Gentiles, altogether the calmest spirit manifested by any Saint I heard broach the subject. His mood was humorous and hopeful, and when he concluded his speech his audience were all smiles and cheerfulness. One of the bishops then made a prayer; and after singing another hymn the congregation dispersed.

George Smith's reference to the persecution of the Saints revived in my mind the memory of facts without taking which into account it is impossible to do justice to the Mormon people. We see their polygamy, their disloyalty, their cruelty to immigrants passing through Utah on the way to California, and they become mere devils to us, without one bright spot in the character, one atom of palliation for their spirit and their deeds. They are a people apart from the rest of mankind—not governed by the ordinary laws of human nature—vindictive, treacherous, blood-thirsty, wholly bad. Even among the wildest, most reckless of the neighboring frontiersmen, among persons claiming neither morals nor religion of their own, the Mormons are spoken of as a distinct race of beings, possessing the craftiness of the fox, the ferocity of the bloodhound, the salacity of the baboon, and the absence of all principle which characterizes the brute creation. One of the worst men that I met between the Missouri River and the Pacific spoke to me of them with a shudder, as an area thief would speak of a murderer. People living east of the Wahsatch talked of them with bated breath, if indeed they mentioned them at all—then only after searching scrutiny of me, and glancing in every direction to see if one of their lurking spies might not chance to be within earshot. The Gentile settlers in the mountains seemed to have more fear of them than of the Indians at their worst.

I am inclined to think that this reputation is not so much an annoyance as a satisfaction to the Mormons. It is not the mere result of atrocities which they have committed, though some of these, like the Mountain Meadow massacre, are well calculated to strike terror into every Gentile heart; but part of the Mormon strategic system, invented and carried out in all its manifold complications by that longest-headed of men, Brigham Young. He knows that in some cases not only a good, but a bad name, is better than riches. The current knowledge that a man can snuff a candle with his Derringer, or has repeatedly killed his man on the "field of *honor*," saves him many an insult and many an encounter. Under the protection of a reputation for massacres, Brigham is aware that his people may sheathe the bowie-knife, and attend to the development of their country's more peaceful resources. He chuckles to think how his bugaboo keeps the children out of the sweetmeats'-closet, and his Guy frightens the cows from his corn. Utah needs all the labor she can possibly get in her thirsty fields and her wooded cañons; in her infant shops and manufactories; on her mines of useful and, in some privately known localities, of precious metal; on her road making, her city building, and the foundations of her Temple. Every man spared from defense is gained by industry; and Brigham alone knows how much is saved the Church exchequer in fortresses, military equipments, and militia drills, by the hard earned reputation of his people for ferocity. His capital lies right on the transit line between the two sea-borders of the Continent. Not only peaceful agriculturists but blacklegs and scamps of every kind pass through Salt Lake City, on their way between the Atlantic and Pacific States. All trains camp in or about the city, yet he never needs to reinforce his police; there is never any row or disturbance among them, because an undefinable sense of prompt and certain death hangs over every man who meditates an outrage either against the Mormons or his fellows. The emigrant feels that his steps are dogged by Mormon spies every rod of the way from the Missouri River; that the ranchman on the Plains, anywhere within a thousand miles of Salt Lake, the driver of the stage, the hunter, the guide, even the other emigrant like himself whom he encounters on the way, may be noting all he does and says, to forerun him to the New Jerusalem, and be entered on the Prophet's memorandum-book against his arrival. So his circumspection increases until it amounts to fear, and an absolute awe settles over him as he enters the red defiles of the Wahsatch Cañons.

The abundant portion of the Mormon reputation for ferocity which is true must be read in the light of the past, or injustice will be done a hundred thousand souls who, in spite of their polygamy and disloyalty, are still our fellow-citizens. If the Mormons are vindictive, let us remember what a training they have had. In 1830 the "Church of Jesus Christ of the Latter-Day Saints" was first organized by Joseph Smith, though for ten years previous he had professedly lived in the receipt of communications from angels, Divine inspiration, and all the other signs of Apostleship. Two years after, on the 25th of March, 1832, at Kirtland, Ohio, a mob tarred

and feathered him and his disciple, Sidney Rigdon, for pro-
mulgating their sentiments by word and practice. (This was
long before polygamy had been thought of as a tenet in the
Mormon creed—the Saint's possession of their goods in
common being their most obnoxious principle). The next
year, on the 20th of July, another mob tore down the printing-office of the earliest Mormon newspaper, at Jackson
City, Missouri; tarred, feathered, and whipped the Saints,
and compelled the leaders to leave the town and county;
upon which they returned to Kirtland, there to establish
another paper, and lay the corner-stone of "The Lord's
House." A little more than three months after (October 31
of the same year), ten houses inhabited by converts to the
faith were destroyed by another mob. The persecution continued to rage, with bloody fighting, till the 4th of November,
when all the Saints fled to Clay County, Missouri. In December, the Mormons of Van Buren County, Missouri, were
attacked by their Gentile neighbors. In May, 1836, the Clay
County Mormons were driven out, and went to Carroll,
Daviess, and Caldwell Counties, in the same State—found-
ing in the last of the three a town called "Far West." In
January, 1838, after the failure of their bank, Joseph Smith
and Sidney Rigdon were compelled by a mob to flee for
their lives from Kirtland, abandoning a "House of the Lord"
which had cost the Mormons $40,000. The July following,
about a hundred families, or nearly six hundred people, were
driven out of Kirtland for Mormonism, and fled to Missouri. In August and September, having attempted to elect
members of their sect to county offices in Caldwell and
Daviess Counties, Missouri, they were again mobbed; and
in one instance their winning the election excited the wrath

of the Gentiles to such a degree that the latter turned out from his office by violence the officer elected, and several Mormons, Brigham Young among the number, had to flee for their lives to Quincy, Illinois. On the 1st of October, the Saints were driven out of their homes in Carroll County, after a pitched battle. There was another battle at Crooked River Missouri, on the 25th, in which several Mormons were killed. On the 30th, at Ham's Mills, Missouri, sixteen adults and two boys were slaughtered by a mob, in cold blood, and with no chance or weapons to defend themselves. On the 1st of November, the town of Far West was plundered by a mob, who captured Joseph Smith, his brother Hiram, and forty other Mormons, and after a mock drumhead court-martial sentenced them to be shot; but General Doniphan interposed to prevent the execution of the sentence, and the prisoners were sent to Richmond, Missouri, to be tried. Here the civil authorities released them after a protracted confinement in jail, but they narrowly escaped butchery at the hands of the militia. Many other Mormons in various parts of the State suffered imprisonment about the same time, but were generally released without even the pretense of a trial. In 1839, the sect moved its head-quarters to Commerce, afterward called Nauvoo, in Hancock County, Illinois, where the Saints had rest for a season, and the town increased to a population of 15,000, or considerably over three fourths of the present size of Salt Lake City. In June, 1841, the Missourians attempted to get Joe Smith again into their hands, sending into Illinois a requisition from their Governor. On this requisition he was arrested, but being brought up on a writ of habeas corpus, at Monmouth, Illinois, upon examination he was instantly released. On the

8th of August, 1842, he was arrested on a second requisition, but discharged as before—his arrest being adjudged ground-less. One would have thought this second defeat of his enemies sufficient to discourage them, but it seems not, for a third requisition from the Missouri Governor was sent for him on the 26th of December, in the same year—only to be decided null, as before, on the 5th of the following month, January, 1843. It reads like a joke, but it is the truth that on the 23d of June, Smith was again arrested, to be released on the 2d of July. In 1844 the Mormons made the great mistake of retaliating religious persecution in kind. They had now a home of their own, where their influence was paramount, and might, by circumspect behavior, have established their position beyond the reach of enemies. But as usually and unfortunately happens when ill-luck lets up the persecuted, they used their new-gained power, not to set the ignorant and malignant who had persecuted them a better example of religion and philosophy, but to indemnify themselves for past injuries by inflicting the like on others, as if they had all the while been seeking, not liberty of conscience, but liberty to persecute; as if the salve for their own wounds was to stab some one else; as if an injury were to be remedied, not by trampling it under the feet of the injured, but by passing it on to some one else. The "Excelsior" newspaper having libeled Prophet Smith, was visited by the Mormon marshal and his constables, who smashed its press and burned its types. Messrs. Foster and Law, the proprietors, sued out a warrant against Joe Smith, the marshal, and other Mormons, accessory to the destruction of the property, who resisted the sheriff when he came to serve it, and compelled him to sum-mon the Stale militia to his aid, on the 6th of May, 1844. On the 17th of June, he succeeded in arresting Smith, who, as usual, was released after a few days' imprisonment. Meanwhile the Mormons were ready to defend their Prophet the moment he should give the word. On the 24th of June, the Governor pledged his word and the honor of the State for the personal safety of Joseph and Hiram Smith, and their followers if they would compromise for the sake of soothing the exacerbated people by laying down their arms and going to Carthage to be tried. The Mormons must have been sadly deficient at that time, both in angelic and legal advisers, for a heavenly revelation, or an hour's talk in the back-office of any country lawyer, would have shown them that this pledge in a practical point of view was not worth the breath it was uttered with,—a State, like a private corporation, having no honor, and that of its executive, however valuable in a personal point of view, possessing no official weight whatever. Deserted alike of angels and attorneys, the over-credulous Saints permitted themselves to be disarmed and sent to Carthage, under the escort of a company of militia bitterly opposed to them, and the next day the prisoners were arrested by the authorities of Hancock County, Illinois, on a charge of treason. Two days after, on the afternoon of June 27th, they discovered how little the most sincerely given private pledge could avail for their protection when a mob of Missourians, whose number have been variously stated, but were certainly over a hundred, came to Carthage jail, beat down its iron doors, and butchered both the Smiths, in cold blood, besides inflicting serious injuries upon other of the prisoners. On the 4th of October, Brigham Young succeeded Joe Smith in the first Presidency of the Latter-Day Church, and early in the next year, 1845, "by special revelation,"

decided that the Mormons must leave Nauvoo. This decision was as long-headed as Brigham's usually are, for it
enabled the Saints to say that they had taken the initiative,
and had not been expelled by the action of the State Legislature, repealing the charter of Nauvoo, which took place
nearly ten months after, on September 24th, 1845. Though
they had anticipated this, it was not until it had taken place
that they decided where to go. Immediate settlement of this
question became necessary. Brigham Young and the Pratts—
the latter perhaps the best educated and most scientific men
in the sect, as the former was the man most thoughtful and
capable in an executive point of view—had read with great
interest Captain J. C. Fremont's reports of his Rocky Mountain explorations, which at that time were received by every
investigating mind with the delight of some fascinating
romance, and proposed to the convention appointed to
deliberate upon the future resting-place of their ark, that a
pioneer company should be sent in Fremont's track to prospect for a suitable situation. This counsel prevailed over a
multitude of others, and in 1846, all but a few hundred of
the Saints abandoned Nauvoo for Council Bluffs, Garden
Grove, and Mount Pisgah, in Iowa; one band of 2,000 Mormons crossing the Mississippi on the ice, in the month of
February. In the September following, after a battle of three
days' duration, lasting from the 10th to the 13th, the rear-
guard of the Saints, which had stayed behind to settle up
their affairs, were forcibly driven out of Nauvoo, and now
the entire Mormon body, with the exception of missionaries
and secret agents, whom it has always been the Mormon
policy to keep scattered among the Gentiles, as a sort of
picket-line to watch the movements of the enemy. On the

24th of July, 1847, Brigham Young with his pioneer party of 143 men and 70 wagons entered the Salt Lake Valley, and in obedience to the Lord's revelation, to which I have heretofore referred, delivered to Brigham by an angel, the night previous, on Ensign Peak, selected what was then a wild waste of artemisias and saltworts, tenanted only by sagecocks, badgers, and Goshoot Indians, as the future site of God's kingdom upon earth. The anniversary of this day is the real Mormon independence day, and kept by them with much more éclat than the 4th.

It is not my intention to pursue their history further. I have only endeavored to show that up to the period of their settlement in the land where at present they hold the paramount authority, they had scarcely known rest for the soles of their feet. The question of their theology and their morals does not enter into the consideration. Their tenets were doubtless extremely offensive to their neighbors on this side of the Missouri; they cannot fail to offend the good taste and the religious sense of any people indoctrinated into the principles of Christian civilization. But this does not alter the fact that their perpetual molestation by mob violence during the entire period of their stay in the States, was persecution of the bitterest character. One of the noblest achievements of the very civilization and Christianity which their tenets offend is the doctrine of religious tolerance. The light by whose ray mankind have learned the falsity of those doctrines which constitute the staple of Mormonism, is the very same light by which mankind have discovered the loathsomeness of religious persecution. And whether religious persecution be loathsome or not,—whether or not the Mormons in some cases infringed by the practice of their belief upon the rights of adjoining communities,—they were certainly harassed and injured to a degree which may abundantly explain any bitterness of feeling which they now cherish toward their former neighbors. I have no desire to set myself up either as their advocate or judge; I am only one among the many students of their problem; and it becomes such an one to array all the facts he finds accessible that he may understand every phenomenon of their peculiar existence. Were I one of the early chemists studying the subject of the compound $SO_3$ $HO$, and should find that one of its phenomena was acidity, I certainly should not be thought particularly prejudiced in favor of sulphur because I was stringent in my quantitative analysis of the oxygen and water which are demanded to explain how the sulphur has been changed so as to exhibit an acid reaction. The Mormons, like any other community among mankind, are a compound: many Gentiles who have known them would tell me that I might press the figure still further without breaking its back and call them a sulphurous compound. They are a compound who exhibit in the most decided degree the phenomenon of acidity. If we really care to come at the truth about them, or have any other object than that of gratifying dislike by denunciation, we must consent entirely to dismiss the spirit of the special pleader on either side, and adopting that of the philosopher, to weigh dispassionately all the circumstances through which they have been brought to their present condition of hatred and vindictiveness. This appears to me the only way to study either an individual man or a body of men, and it is in accordance with this way that I have rehearsed the grievances which the Mormons endured in the States,—grievances of such sore and continuous character as might well turn any body of men into Ishmaelites, without regard to the question whether their religion was false or true. When I found a man as dispassionate as George Smith appeared in his recital of the sufferings endured by his sect, and recollected that two of his cousins had been murdered in cold blood by the enemies of whom he spoke; when I recollected how repeatedly Brigham Young had carried his life in his hand, and been driven from home, property, everything a man holds dearest, yet saw that under ordinary circumstances he controlled his temper and seldom spoke revengefully, I could not avoid acknowledging at least in this respect the intellectual greatness of the men, whatever I might think of their views upon theology and religion. If those are false, the triumph of self-control in the men is all the greater, for they achieve it without the help of that great adjuvant to calmness and self-control,—*the being right*. The world's archives furnish their students with many a sad story of people whom the verdict of humanity now calls right using their first hour of freedom to enslave, their first firm foothold to supplant, their first refuge from murder to slay their fellow-men. The gallery of historic paintings in which hang the grandest battle-pieces between Superstition, Tyranny, and Corruption on the one side, Truth, Freedom, and Holiness on the other, contains dark alcoves where the philosopher must turn aside to blush for his race as he sees laid in with a bloody brush pictures of the Protestant just escaped from rack and fagot dragging thither Arian and Skeptic with freshly unfettered hands; and the Puritan importing across the sea the lash and the halter which he had fled from when wielded by Prelacy, to lay them on the backs and tighten them round the necks of Quaker and of Indian. Yet these were good men, and had a strength to rely on, which does not belong to errorists like the Mormons. We cannot wonder at the spirit of the latter when we disapprove it most.

The noble spectacle of a people breaking the yoke of tyranny to make freedom general is preserved for the generations which are to come after. The utmost that history thus far shows us is a people breaking the yoke for their own freedom's sake. Much has been said by popular speakers in praise of the Pilgrim Fathers, as men who crossed a wintry sea and buried themselves in savage forests, to establish the great doctrine of liberty of conscience. Much as those brave men are to be reverenced, such an assertion respecting them seems incorrect. They left their English homes and sought the American wilderness not for liberty of conscience but for liberty of Calvinism. Grant if we will the superiority of their set of doctrines over those of Prelacy; we are still compelled to own that their motive in obtaining freedom was nowise nobler than that of the Laud faction in seeking supremacy. The liberty sought by both High Churchman and Puritan was liberty to worship God as their own consciences dictated— not the liberty of all men to do the same. To acknowledge this is no derogation from the purity of nature, the inflexible uprightness, the truthfulness of soul, which their bitterest enemies equally with their warmest friends must accord to the early settlers of New England. Indeed, it is only doing them justice to define their claims to admiration accurately. We prevent the acknowledgment of their real excellences by taking in their defense an untenable stand on virtues which they had not,—virtues which at that day were possessed by no people on the globe. In the early part of the seventeenth century liberty of conscience as an abstract principle was the

Utopian dream of mild enthusiasts; had it been proposed as a rule of general application of national and ecclesiastical government, it would have been scouted from the benches of Convocation and the seats of General Assembly alike. The furthest attainment that had been made by any people was the discovery that their own beliefs were right, and that no sacrifice of life or property was too great for the sake of securing their unmolested indulgence. This was a great advance from the servility and nonchalance which considered individual opinion a matter of no consequence compared with homogeneous institutions and the smooth working of mankind under one supreme hand and eye, like a vast senseless machine,—a great advance, but it was not liberty of conscience. The age was not ripe for the reception of that doctrine, and to deny its possession even by the brave men from whose veins much of our country's best blood is derived, is merely to confess that they had not reached a pinnacle of intellectual progress which was utterly inaccessible to any people at that day,—a height which we ourselves nearly two hundred and fifty years after them have only just reached, and on which even we stand but totteringly. They are as little to blame for not having attained the doctrine of liberty of conscience as distinct from liberty of their particular conscience, as they are for not making a screw-steamer of their May-Flower, establishing telegraph lines between their Massachusetts settlements, or printing the sermons of Cotton Mather on a ten-cylinder press. There was, therefore, no inconsistency in their persecuting those who differed from them at Plymouth, as they had been persecuted by those who differed from them in London, though they would have been most indefensibly inconsistent had they really set up for defenders of liberty of conscience. Never once did they blame their enemies on the ground of their violating such liberty; their grievance lay simply in the fact that they themselves, possessing the only truth, were oppressed by errorists over whom they should have been supreme; and the moment that they obtained such supremacy, without a thought that they were violating a universal right of mankind, they turned the tables on error and suppressed it with its own weapons.

I do not know where to look for an instance of freedom sought for its own beloved sake—not merely as a personal privilege, but as the franchise of humanity. Even we, the acknowledged color-bearers of liberty—we, the American people, who have fought the fiercest battles of history, borne the bitterest pangs, suffered the hardest deprivations, and won the grandest triumphs, threw off the yoke of England with one hand, while we riveted our own on the neck of Africa with the other. England drove out the Stuarts and subjugated Ireland with fire and sword, under pressure of one and the same popular impulse; Holland was, at the same time, the fruitfulest mother of freemen and the cruelest mistress of slaves; the sound of the lash, and the groans of the tortured bondsman went up to plead with God against her from all her tropical colonies, before the songs of lofty faith, or the cheers of glorious triumph died on the ears of baffled Alva; France rescued herself from the Bourbons and murdered Toussaint L'Ouverture. The philosopher looks in vain through time, and round the world, to find a people dedicated to any liberty except its own; and gives up the hope of beholding such in his day, with a resignation born only of the perception that America, through a succession of fiery furnaces, is surely getting purified to take that place of sub-lime distinction in the eyes of his great grandchildren.

Least of all the persecuted faiths does Mormonism con-template liberty of conscience as a principle of national organization. Nothing but the presence of the United States authority in its symbols of court, camp, and executive, pre-vent Utah from becoming the prey of the most unmingled tyranny which the world ever saw. Even the wisest and most dispassionate of the Mormon leaders look upon popular freedom, both civil and religious, as a very undesirable thing. None of them remember their repeated expulsions from home, the ruin of their fortunes, the murder of their sons, the atrocities of all kinds which they suffered from mobs, as outrageous because they violated a principle, but solely because directed against *them*, the chosen people of God. Had the mob been a Mormon one, its object the propa-gandism instead of the extirpation of Joe Smith's doctrine, and its victims the Gentiles instead of the Saints, its whole moral character in their eyes would have been diametrically different. They put down dissent with the same strong hand which smote them in a country where they held the minor-ity. Nor is this course on their part the result of unreasoning indignation—a mob-method of settling differences like that from which they suffered in Missouri. It is the Mormon the-ory of government—the organic principle of Mormonism.

Herein lies the political crime of the system—here is the ground of inevitable collision between Mormonism and the Government—the ineradicable root of bitterness spring-ing up between the now isolated nationality under Brigham Young and the people of the United States, who surround and have the supremacy over it. Mormonism is a distinct, systematic, dispassionate contradiction of the American idea. Its position is one of avowed and essential hostility to that of the nation. Its leaders find a serious grievance in the delay of Congress to grant Utah the rank and privileges of a State. Here they do not show the practical wisdom and foresight which have characterized their views and decided their action in many other instances. To make Utah a State would be their own inevitable destruction. They desire the State rank as an addition to their own emolument, pride, and power. They would fain possess a State constitution, as the Philistines wanted Samson, for their sport. They would reduce it to the instrument of their pleasure; shearing it of the strength which endangers tyrants; blinding it of the vigilance which protects the people; making it play at their feasts, the guardian of freedom reduced to a minister of their pomp, little dreaming that the blinded giant must surely rise in his wrath, and, bowing on the pillars, bring their Dagon temple to the ground. Woe to Mormonism the day that Utah becomes a State! In the Constitution of our country, in the first clause of the fourth section of Article Fourth it is thus written:—

"*The United States shall guarantee to every State in this Union a republican form of government.*"

These words are the death-warrant of Mormonism. So long as Utah remains a Territory, the way in which its internal affairs are managed, under the shelter of a technicality may be left comparatively undisturbed by Congress, provided only that the national courts are respected, and the national taxes paid. The supreme people of the United States may blink at the fact that its *territorial* citizens are living under the yoke of despotism,—especially while the majority of those citizens accept that yoke,—for the Constitution only pledges its guarantee of a republican form of government to *States*. But once make Utah a State, and the last technical quibble is swept from under the feet of Mormonism. That instant, and it becomes the solemn duty of the nation—a duty which it cannot shirk if it would; a duty whose neglect would violate the organic instrument and principle of its existence; a duty from which it cannot on any plea absolve itself without confessing its imbecility and branding itself with contempt before the world—to extirpate Mormonism as a civil institution from the soil of Deseret forever.

Mormonism is, as I have said, a retrogression toward the ante-Christian ages; a cession of all the ground which has been won from Ignorance and Despotism since the birth of Christ; a surrender of every stronghold and charter of freedom for which patriots and martyrs have shed their blood; a confession that all reform has only been a worse deforming; that progress has been deterioration; that the spread of popular enlightenment has only plunged the world into deeper gloom; that the civil and religious emancipations which have cost humanity during our era tenfold more agony than has been endured, more tears than have been shed, more yearnings and strivings than have been felt for any cause to which its heart can be devoted, are all naught or worse than naught,—as so many steps in a course steadily and continuously wrong since the day that man emerged from the dark portals of Idolatry and Judaism.

On the other hand Republicanism stands forth as the representative and concrete form of human progress. It is the embodied idea of growth; the solid, aggressive assertion of the fact that man has become wiser, better, happier with every step of the Christian era; that the triumph of popular principles is the triumph of God; that the utmost independence of individual thought and action consistent with the enjoyment of equal independence by his neighbor is every man's right, and the most favorable condition for his perfection in goodness; in fine, that the world has bettered and is bettering every year by an equitable distribution of its advantages throughout society, and that man's conscience is inviolable: these are the things which America stands in the lists of nations to affirm; these, if need be, to defend with the right arm of power.

Nothing can bring the Mormon and the national ideas together. There is no more compromise between them than between ice and fire, darkness and light. They are diametrically opposed forces. They are as unmixable as water and oil. Absence of contact between them can alone prevent their collision. Theirs is an irrepressible conflict,—as irrepressible as that between the national idea and slavery,—and this conflict must terminate as that one did, with the triumph of the national idea. The Mormons feel the parallel instinctively and reveal the feeling unconsciously, in asserting, as they often do, and as Brigham Young did to me on the evening of the ball, that the very same spirit which drove them from the East brought on the late war of the rebellion. They realize the fact that "two cannot walk together except they be agreed," and their system is so inherently and utterly obnoxious to that which founds and maintains our free institutions, that agreement is as impossible as it would be between America and an independent state of cannibals, infanticides, or widow-burners, which by some magic had are free to contract fresh alliances. But, supposing that such divorced parties should come into one of the former class of States and select new partners, in this State they would be guilty of bigamy, their former partners not having been separated from them on any ground allowed by the State. Why should not such a case of bigamy be made the subject of Congressional legislation as well as that of Utah? More-over, marriage seems essentially to belong to those matters which are with most propriety settled *in foro conscientiæ*; or, if we regard the importance of that relation in its bearings on the neighbors of the married, as settling to a great extent the happiness and safety of the social system, legislation upon it may most naturally be committed to the community immediately concerned. Those who have favored national legislation against polygamy are in the habit of comparing it with slavery—an institution with which Congress to a cer-tain extent was always obliged to concern itself, and which, finally, it was compelled by ratificatory action, at least, to destroy, in spite of the fact that it was domestic and internal to separate independent States. The analogy, however, is a strained one. In the humanitarian point of view, slavery and polygamy are entirely different. The slave is held compul-sorily; in Utah the wife of the polygamist is not obliged to stay with him a single day after she is dissatisfied. She has merely to go to Brigham Young and inform him that she is unhappy with her husband; upon which, after sufficient investigation to ascertain that her step is deliberate, and not the result of a sudden fit of passion the consequences of which she would repent in her calmer moments, the presi-dent decrees a divorce immediately. Cases have occurred in which a woman entered Brigham's office the wife of one been transplanted from the Marquesas, China, or Hindostan into the place now occupied by Georgia. The safety from disturbance hitherto enjoyed by Mormonism at Salt Lake has been due entirely to its isolation. This cannot continue always. The Pacific Railroad will break it up entirely. When Utah becomes readily accessible, the Gentile element, led by motives of aggrandizement and the sanitary advantages of Utah as a residence, will come pouring in upon the Saints as at Nauvoo. Then the National Government will possess a constituency in the Salt Lake region which will demand its interposition for their defense, and the American and Mormon systems will instantly come together in the shock of a conflict which though much more promptly settled than that from which we have just emerged cannot fail, if the present Mormon leaders are alive, to be as bloody.

I find extreme uncertainty prevailing at the East in regard to the Mormon character and destiny; but on no particular point to a greater degree, than on this—how the collision which I have called inevitable will occur and how it will be settled. Many good and wise men, to whose moral natures polygamy is abhorrent, are still unable to see how it can ever become a valid ground for the interference of the National Government. To such, any governmental disturbance of local customs regarding marriage, looks as tyrannous as dictation concerning statutes of divorce. If Congress is to decide that a man may not marry as often as he pleases, why, they ask, may it not also settle the question as to what constitutes the legal ground of separation? In the majority of the States nothing but infidelity is admitted as such a ground; in a few States the decree of divorce is issued upon the simple proof of marital unhappiness. In the latter States both the divorced parties man and went out of it another's. Nor does polygamy resemble slavery in the expansiveness of its results. The fact that a negro could be made to produce a hundred dollars' worth of cotton on one tenth of the outlay in food and clothes for which a similar amount of labor could be procured from the poorest freeman, tended to depreciate labor throughout the entire country; and when, as often happened, especially among the class of slaves resulting from slavery's favorite practice of "miscegenation," not only brute labor, but a high grade of mechanical ingenuity and artistic skill, could be procured for the still minuter fraction of an equally accomplished white man's wages,—not only muscular strength, but intellectual ability was undersold and degraded through the length and breadth of the land. But the possibility of marrying two wives in Utah affects none of the partners to monogamic marriages in other parts of the country—does not degrade the martial relation, nor alter the sacredness of the tie and the condition of the married woman elsewhere. In fact, the example of a polygamic community operates, by way of warning, to intensify the monogamic spirit of people beyond the boundary of its immediate influence. To say the least, the marriage question is a very delicate and complicated one, and the central power of a Union like our own most hesitate long before it touches the question in any Territory or State.

But there is no need of such an interference. Every end which might be attained by it may be secured without running the risk of establishing a bad precedent—of acting unconstitutionally against the liberty of conscience and popular sovereignty—by a method much simpler, even though less direct, and so far from being open to serious

objections on the ground of our republican principles, certain to be demanded in obedience to those principles, for
the settlement of the Mormon question, at no distant day.
The moment that Mormonism becomes a power dangerous
to the peace and supremacy of the Union, admit Utah into
the sisterhood of States, and fulfill to her people the constitutional guarantee of a republican form of government. For
the attainment of that end, Congress will be compelled to
deprive the Church of all civil authority; and the unhallowed
union of Church and State once terminated, Mormonism
necessarily sinks to the level of any other sect. That sinking
means destruction. Episcopacy and Presbyterianism flourish
still more healthily, as we have seen in this country, when
disentangled from the corrupting embrace of civil power;
no longer state churches, as in England and Scotland, they
become churches of the people, and draw fresh blood from
the great, warm heart of which they were naturally meant
to lie: but Mormonism has no popular basis—it must have
authority, or perish. It is government as much as it is worship—it is a despotism in both; in fine, it is Judaism revived,
or rather, galvanized into a mockery of life, and adapted to
the nineteenth century, in the particulars where it has not
force enough to adapt the nineteenth century to itself.

I have repeatedly asserted that Mormonism is Judaism,
and this seems the best place to examine how far that assertion may be verified. There has always been a Judaizing
tendency at work, with greater or less vigor, in the body of
Christian civilization. It troubled the Apostles, who could
scarcely leave their flocks before Judaistic teachers sprung
up among them, and tried to bring them back under the
former yoke of bondage. It has manifested itself ever since,

in efforts made to substitute cumbrous rituals for the simple worship of a loving nature and righteous living; sacred places like Samaria and Jerusalem, like Rome and the Temple, or the church edifice in general, for the spirit in which God would have men worship Him; special sacred days, fasts, feasts, "new-moons and Sabbaths," for the one unbroken day of a whole devoted life. In the religion of this country the Judaizing tendency has powerfully manifested itself. Noble in its spirit, purposes, and results as Puritanism to a great extent has been, it has greatly favored and fostered this tendency. It has distrusted the mild discipline, the persuasive doctrines of the Christian dispensation, impliedly treating them as too lax for the regulation of human life, and needing to be reinforced by the sterner threats, and more terrible penalties of the Mosaic ages. It has abjured the doctrine of progressive revelation, and confounded the fulfillment of a dispensation intended for the infancy of mankind with insult to that dispensation and its blasphemous degradation from the respect due a revelation of God; forgetting that the Bible itself declares its temporary purpose, calls it at best but a shadow of good things to come, and says that the first generation of our present era should not pass away before every jot and tittle of it was fulfilled. Standing on the untenable ground, that a system which was true for a given time and race, must be true for all times and all races; moreover, influenced by a sombre spirit peculiar to its own moral constitution (without which it would not have fallen into its intellectual mistake), it has favored the introduction among our people of a sort of hybrid religion, which may be called, at the risk of a theological bull, *Old Testament Christianity*. The child brought up under its discipline finds it hard to believe that the Messiah has really come, and cannot see anything but a technical ground of disagreement between Christians and Jews. He hears the Old Testament read at church and in the family quite as often as the New—even oftener than any part but the polemic. He is taught to regard God chiefly as Force; he hears of Him manifesting the passions of humanity, and a very imperfect humanity at that; but is instructed to palliate these manifestations, on the ground that his force is the Supreme Force, his will the Paramount Will. Thus he learns that only in finite matters is "might makes right" an abominable doctrine; that making the terms infinite, the proposition becomes a formula for the expression of the highest holiness of the universe. The Judaistic Christian, as I said of the Mormon,—though in a less degree, because he has not been consistent enough to carry out his views to their ultimate logical conclusions,—has thrown away the results of the last eighteen centuries, and gone back for his spiritual aliment to the crude and half-developed notions of truth and laws of life, which were granted to the imperfect faculties of the ancients, by that Divine Spirit of accommodation which prepares the human race its food in due season—milk for babes, strong meat for men,—and furnishes mankind in any given era only with such pabulum as it can digest. As we said above, the whole error of Puritan theology lies in its obstinate denial of the fact that all Divine dealings with mankind are progressive. It insists on this denial because it fears that a confession of the fact involves the unsettlement of faith—involves an admission that what is true to-day may not be true to-morrow. If it conceded this it must lose its organic existence,—for its axis is not love but belief—not a principle of life, but a set of doctrines. So there is no way of escape for it. It cannot say that God's revelation of himself and of his plan of governing the universe, as given to the Jews, was a very good thing—even the very best thing for the day and the people to whom it was made; that it conveyed the largest amount of truth capable of being comprehended by an infant race, and that to have conveyed more would have really had the effect of conveying less; that just as I say "The sun rises" to a child, whom my utmost effort could not cause to comprehend the phenomena of terrestrial revelation, the Creator may describe Himself and his dealings to a Jew of Joshua's, David's, or Herod's time in a way which was absolutely perfect in its fitness to reveal the greatest amount of truth, and inculcate the highest degree of holiness which the ancient bearer was developed to attain, but which, at the same time, to me with my enlightenment of at least 1870 years plus the ancients', should be no truth at all, and no stimulus in the way of holiness.

Unable to make this acknowledgment without the corollary that revealed doctrine is progressive; unable to grant that corollary without the further conclusion that *life*, not *doctrine*, is the only eternal, unchangeable basis of religion; unable to see that Christ came, not to impart an immutable creed, which in the nature of human intellect is a thing impossible, but to infuse a spirit into the life of mankind, which should keep the soul advancing into grander perceptions of intellectual truth forever, and to implant a deathless germinal principle, whose growth, while it sweetened and purified the moral character, should enable the reason to throw off shard after shard of creed, as it found their capacities successively too narrow to bound and embody the truth which its strengthening vision caught, and its increasing constructive powers formulated,—unable to do thus, Judaistic Christianity is compelled to accept the obsolete *régime* of types and shadows as equally commanding in our present life with the Christian *régime* of perfect day.

It finds the Divine character delineated in the old Hebrew Scriptures by terrible physical symbols, by forcible, but to our present enlightenment, degrading anthropomorphisms. In the Scriptures of the Christian dispensation,—and progressively in the conceptions which have been developed under the influence of its implanted spirit in the general consciousness of our age,—it finds an altogether higher and nobler statement of the relations between mankind and the Divine—of the character of the latter, and the destiny of the former. But pledged by its original mistake it is compelled to carry both ideals, according them equal prominence, granting them equal respect. It therefore sets about finding a compromise. In the effort to make them fit, to reconcile them where they clash, it finds the Judaistic ideals always the most tyrannous, because they are expressed in terms most vehement, and symbols most physically tangible. The result is that Judaism gets a great deal more than its share in the statement, and the hybrid notions resulting from the compromise seem more properly to belong to the Hebrew than the Christian period of the world. The disciple of Judaistic Christianity insists that his rushlight shall not be blown out though the sun stands at high noon, and holds it so close to his eyes that they are too dazzled by its fire and bleared by its smoke to see the sun clearly.

It would startle the old Puritan to charge him with the ancestry of Mormonism—but Mormonism is certainly the outgrowth of those Judaistic ideas which he has insisted on carrying over, past their fulfillment, into the life and thought of the Christian age. Talk with an intelligent Mormon upon the subject of his system, and so long as he does not touch upon polygamy you will be irresistibly reminded in all that he says of many a sermon which you have heard from the representatives of Puritan ideas. He loves as well as Cotton Mather, or his intellectual offspring, to introduce God to you in an atmosphere quaking with Hebrew thunders. He has a perfect arsenal of fiery clouds, and physical hells; he swathes all his metaphors in garments of mysterious horror. He takes the Old Testament, as he takes all the Scriptures, literally, and consistently carries this literal interpretation into his daily life.

Almost without exception, the Mormon leaders passed their childhood under the influence of the sternest Puritan thought. Both Brigham Young and Heber Kimball were brought up in its nurture and admonition. They look back with reverence upon their parents and teachers, as having prepared them for the reception of the full Latter-day glory. I am far from charging upon Puritan theology any intuitional share in the generation of Mormonism; still, any dispassionate man, pledged to no sect, but to the spirit of Christianity in general, cannot fail to perceive that Mormonism is the legitimate outgrowth of its intellectual bias pushed to the extreme. Judaism has been praised, honored, imitated, kept alive in the Christian teaching of the age, until it has at last found disciples to reconstruct it as a living institution.

It is curious to see how the very physical circumstances of Mormonism are a copy of the Jewish. The parallel is not a fanciful or accidental one. The Mormons acknowledge, in some points intend it, themselves. Kirtland and Nauvoo were their settlements in Egypt; Joe Smith was their Moses; and when he died too early for a sight of the promised land, Brigham Young became the Joshua who led them all the way home. They have founded their Jerusalem in a Holy Land wonderfully like the original. Like Gennesaret Lake Utah is a body of fresh water emptying by a river Jordan into a Dead Sea without outlet and intensely saline. The Saints find their Edomites and Philistines in the Indians of the desert, whose good will they can only keep by perpetual tribute under the less humiliating guise of presents (as necessary as the backsheesh you give to a Bedouin, or the ransom you pay to a brigand), and in the Gentile troops of Uncle Sam. The climate is a photographic copy of the Judean; the thirsty fields must be irrigated through long seasons of rainless, cloudless heat, while the ridges of Lebanon, here called the Wahsatch, are covered with snow. The timberless plains, the wooded mountain gorges of Judea are here, and here are the summer-shrunken streams, the dry beds or "wadies," which mark the path of the Syrian traveller. In the City of Salt Lake biblical imagery is perpetually recalled to the mind by the low adobe houses, which resemble the day dwellings of Jewish times, and by the thick refreshing shade of irrigated gardens, where the inmates of the houses rest from the heat of the day, and slake their thirst with the delicious juice of that most oriental among fruits, the melon, which grows as luxuriantly here as in Palestine. I have elsewhere referred to the striking illustration of that passage, "He turneth men's hearts as the rivers of water are turned," when in such a garden I saw the master leading the precious liquid with his foot to the rootlets of some favorite plant by a little extempore channel from the main trenches.

Nature, in Utah, having repeated the physical conditions of Palestine as closely as she ever repeats any of her work, has been assisted to the utmost by the energies of man. Mormonism is intended to be a theocracy like the Jewish. Mormonism *is* a theocracy so far as human agency can make one. The Mormons have shown what can be made of the old Puritan idea carried out consistently to its ultimate conclusions. If the Jewish notions of theology are good for the nineteenth century, they have reasoned, why not the Jewish theory of government? Both being equally of Divine ordinance for the Jews; and one being insisted on as binding upon the conscience of the nineteenth century, why not the other? The Puritans, equally with the Mormons, assented to the conclusiveness of this logic, and attempted to imitate the Jewish theocracy in their government of the early New England communities, quoting the Old Testament to any extent in support of their civil ordinances for the compulsory observance of *Sabbath* (as all Christians with Judaistic tendencies love to call Sunday); their commission of penal authority to the hands of clergymen, deacons, and other ecclesiastical officers; their whole code of religious pains and penalties. But the Puritans broke down in one important particular where the Mormons have triumphantly gone on. They lacked one essential piece of the theocratic machinery— the supernatural. They had no prophets; no miracle-workers; none endowed with the gifts of healing and of tongues. They had a very rampant devil to be sure; and witches innumerable, who in partnership did innumerable grievous deviltries and sore witcheries; but those were all on the debit side of their theocracy—a supernatural which belonged to somebody else, and represented the stock in trade of a hostile

house. Thus they came gradually to find that a Jewish theocracy was not adapted to modern times; that is, their children
so found it—and little by little, the substitution of here a
piece and there a piece of governmental enginery resulted
in quite an enlightened system of Republicanism, such as
prevails in the greater part of New England at this day. If
it were not the sorrowful fact that men's religious ideas are
a matter of much less essential consequence to them than
their ideas of material well-being; and that they will worry
along with a spiritual system that does not fit, a great while
after they would have found intolerable a municipal or a
digestive system, or even a pair of boots of the same character, the inapplicability of the Jewish theocracy to an era
of Christianity and civilization would have been discovered
at the same time with that of the theocracy; and then we
should have had no Mormonism.

The Mormons have been better off than the Puritans.
Through superior gifts of inspiration and faith, or, as skep-
tics prefer to say, of "cheek" and credulity, they have acquired
a supernatural which works as well as any in modern ages.
They have not an empty shrine like the Puritan theocracy;
their divinity has descended to the tripod, and his presence
fills the Temple. They are not compelled to put up with the
meagre make-shift of a few petty selectmen and deacons.
They have wealth of exorcists, and speakers in unknown
tongues: the former being as numerous as the Saints possessed of powerful animal magnetism; the latter, as they are
not compelled to translate, susceptible of indefinite multi-
plication. They have prophets and apostles whose imposition
of hands is infallible; some of them are said by the ungodly
to take away whatever they lay their hands on, be it portable

property or insupportable pains; they have seers who wait on the Lord and are visited by angels; but a rule prevails similar to that posted on the walls of some public institutions, and none of the waiters are permitted to receive anything from visitors, except the head-waiter Brigham. In other words, though the doctrine of open communication between earth and heaven is recognized by the Saints, the only person in the Church who can become the recipient of infallible revelations is the President. With his permission, however, Heber Kimball[6] or General Wells, his colleagues, may act as his proxy.

The supernatural element is used with comparative infrequency. The fact that they possess it is, generally, enough for the Mormons. Now and then, on occasions of great excitement,—like the anti-Gentile assemblies during Johnston's occupation, for instance,—a Saint is suddenly inspired to speak in an unknown tongue. A friend of mine, present at a sort of camp-meeting called together near Nephi in the year 1857, heard one of the saints address the audience to great apparent edification for nearly ten minutes, in language purporting to be that of an ancient Lamanite tribe, called the "Children of Glawdulgrum." My friend took down on the back of an old letter (the only note-book which happened to be convenient) a few snatches from the part which, as he said, interested him as much as any of it. I give one snatch:—

"Kravighi! Karoom! Ro eptepetia hrancobolomei degesh mapsasalbonor. Hokoparŭni Képtepénil senkandra.

6 This assertion was written before Kimball died, but probably holds good for any successor he may have in the co-presidency. It may be as well, to avoid the necessity of any further explanation on the subject, to say here once for all that the entire Appendix supposes Kimball still living, and no substantial misapprehension will occur to any reader keeping this fact in mind.

Moipsópagath genéndlis loludógro tolla? Kedepórkomal
unúnu pegesh sokathdólgoni. Nenopétemi lalaptágro ebo-
dungrŭno. Oheki degesh Wi was! Wi was! Moepne Karoom?
Mopalpártogos lubébe bóttolob lupete bolobilandro?
Manapalbonor Kravighesseros Wi, bagamolu, peneteban-
groni—solugheldepinpin Wi was! Wi was! Hrancobolomei
degesh epsekenkorugu kragashr Molu nongodógragon?
Otse degesh—Wi was! Wi was!"

The therapeutic imposition of hands and the exorcism of
evil spirits are supernatural gifts oftener employed; and their
exercise has been attended with really marvelous results in
well-authenticated cases of nervous and mental disease, such
as chorea, epilepsy, neuralgia, hysteria, periodic mania, and
the like—whose cures, however, the ungodly classify with
the phenomena of animal magnetism acting upon susceptible organizations. Of the more startling class of miracles,
those seeming to contravene some established law of nature
and verifiable by direct experience, the Saints are properly
chary. Brigham Young's splendid executive talents insure
revelation from falling into disrepute, since a project which
he decides to have accomplished, even in circumstances
apparently the most unfavorable to its realization, is either
inherently so feasible or carried through by such tact and
force of will, that his followers have no difficulty in believing
that he acts under Divine guidance.

Possessing the supernatural as the credential and prop of
its authority, the Mormon theocracy wields more unlimited
power than any despotism on the globe. Here again it is a copy
of the Jewish. As the High-priest, after consulting the Urim
and Thummim, was infallible, and to be disobeyed only on
pain of death or being cut off from one's people, so is Brigham

in any case, for he carries his Urim and Thummim in his own breast—a judgment perpetually flooded with divine light, and always accessible. He is therefore the concentrated will, on all subjects which he chooses to assume the right of deciding, of more than one hundred thousand people.

He nominally occupies no despotic place. Many a Mormon will indignantly deny that his power is any more absolute than that of the President of the United States. The external shows of Republicanism are so far preserved that the unthinking part of the population really imagine themselves under a free government. Their head is a president, not an emperor; but Louis Napoleon might be glad if his supremacy over the French were a fraction of that wielded by Brigham Young over the Mormons. His acts are called neither ukases, nor pronunciamentos, nor decrees; but no Asiatic tyrant ever issued such irresistible expressions of his will as does Brigham in publishing the orders of the Church. He, ostensibly, is nothing but the Church's mouth-piece; yet as the Church has no other mouth-piece, and the Church is absolute, Brigham Young is the most indisputable tyrant on earth. In Japan—hitherto supposed the ideal representative of a pure despotism—the supreme power is weakened by division; the spiritual and the temporal rulers may fall out and the people get their own; but Brigham Young, under the skillfully painted disguise of "the Church," is Tycoon and Mikado in one; he holds in his hand the gathered heart-strings and purse-strings of the whole nation,—the wires which control and more the mechanism of their entire interests for time and for eternity.

A page of illustration is worth a chapter of mere statement. Let me suppose my reader a subject of the Mormon government, and take him through the career which every such an one is liable to run; showing him the nature of the theocracy by the manner in which it may legitimately act upon the individual. I will expose him to no exceptional hardships. I will make him the victim of no peculiar oppressions, such as result in every nation—even in our own sometimes, as we must blushingly acknowledge—to the subordinate who incurs the dislike of the powers that be. He shall suffer only from the natural workings of the Mormon system—in most respects as all Mormons suffer daily—in all respects as some one of them suffers every month or every year. I shall exaggerate nothing; suppose nothing to have happened which has not happened in every essential point repeatedly, and been known to happen by the great body of the Mormons themselves.

Mr. Polypeith (my reader can well excuse my hiding him under a Greek name when I have already gone so far as to take the liberty of Mormonizing him) determines that he will leave his pleasant home in the Eastern States, and cast in his lot with the Saints of the Salt Lake basin. He learns at the New York Agency, by one of whose officers he was converted, that a train of the brethren is expected to leave Atchison or Omaha early during the next month. He converts all his property into cash, save a couple of thousands which he spends in getting his own and his family's outfit. This consists of a large Plains' wagon with a canvas tilt, a load of furniture and provisions, a few cattle, and four mules whose value will be about doubled when they reach Salt Lake, or more than doubled if after they have drawn his wagon there he sends them on to California. The Polypeith family penetrate the Wahsatch by Emigration Cañon, and proceed to the public square, situated at the centre of the city. Here the Church, in the person of one of the presidents, or an elder appointed by Brigham,—perhaps, as happens on some occasions, though more rarely than in the early days of emigration, in the person of Brigham himself—meets Mr. Polypeith, makes him an address, and gives him the right hand of fellowship. He is then appointed quarters until he can look about him and prepare for his family permanent accommodations consistent with their circumstances, and the will of the Church. His wagon is unpacked, his goods are stored, and if it be warm weather, his cattle may be delivered to the charge of the Church herder, who makes a note of their marks and that afternoon takes them down to Church Island. After he has the dust washed out of his pores and the bruises of his jolting ride across the mountains hare turned a healthy color, he receives a billet from the Church (Brigham), commanding him to report himself at the office in Prophet's Block at 11 o'clock A. M. on the following Tuesday. Obeying the mandate, he finds himself at the appointed time in a small plain room, like that appropriated by the recorder of deeds in a rural eastern county, where he is confronted with the Church in the shape of a peculiar but pleasant-looking man in pepper-and-salt clothes, who asks him a variety of questions, and with a younger man who puts down his answers in a sort of ledger, belonging, when at rest, on a shelf flanked by tin boxes. His name, age, and place of nativity are carefully noted; likewise those of his family, and their total number. Then the Church (still Brigham) desires to know the avocation he has pursued before leaving the States. He replies that he has of late kept a grocery, but was formerly a cabinet maker by trade—he thought of going on with the grocery business here. Where did he prefer to settle; in Salt Lake City or in one of the outer settlements—Nephi, Ogden, or Rush Valley, for instance? He had meant to settle in Salt Lake City—the chances for his kind of business would probably be better there; besides, there were greater advantages there of society and for the education of his children. The Church in pepper-and-salt takes an attitude of deep thought—hm—hm—will Mr. Clerk reach down from the shelf among the deed-boxes Book B? The Church whispers—there is more thought. Mr. Polypeith waits in silent veneration until the Prophet speaks again.

"Brother Polypeith—The Church, being as nearly as possible dependent on its own internal resources, is obliged to distribute them with discretion so as to use every brother to the very best advantage. The Church has no room for any more grocers in Zion itself. That branch of industry is abundantly stocked at present. Without prejudice to the right of changing his avocation at some future time, if he is still so drawn, and the Lord opens the way to another grocery, Brother Polypeith may be of use to the Church in his former profession. Zion needs another cabinet maker. Or (Book B is consulted again). Brother Polypeith may find occupation, if he have agricultural leanings, in the development of the indigo of Zion. Or, there is a grist-mill sorely needed at Tuilla. But really the best opening seems to be that of the furniture."

The result is that before he has at all worn off the novelty of his position—standing a full-grown American citizen of means and family, to receive absolute dictation upon the method he shall adopt to employ those means and support that family—Brother Polypeith has changed, or gets changed for him, the channel of his entire energies and his future destiny in the community where he must live. He entered the Church office a grocer, to go out of it a cabinet maker. But the questions are not done; before he goes he must answer further.

How much property does he bring to Utah? The entire savings of a small tradesman's hard life, he answers—and these amount to the sum of twenty thousand dollars. Is Brother Polypeith ready to make oath to that effect? He is and does so. Brother Polypeith is then informed that the Saints, from Brother Brigham himself down to the humblest cattle-boy, own nothing—that the Church owns all, and has a right to do what it will with its own. Furthermore, that twenty thousand dollars is a larger sum than the Church can availably embark in the cabinet maker's trade just now; part of the sum can be employed for the interests of the Church better elsewhere. The Church will accordingly receive from Brother Polypeith, to be employed in advancing the spread of the kingdom, the sum of five or ten thousand dollars, as the case may be. There is no invariable rule for the sum taken; it depends on the needs of the Church, or the wealth of the individual, and on the amount which, considering the interests of the Church, can be beneficially employed in the owner's especial branch of business. The opinion of the chief party in interest (as we should call him according to our unenlightened Republican and common law ideas) is of no weight whatever in contributing to the conclusion. It often amounts to a quarter, sometimes to a half of the entire property brought into Utah. It is now too late to back out (I am supposing the Polypeiths already baptized), and very likely there is no desire to back out;

the Polypeiths have perhaps known long ago the Mormon tenets in regard to the residence in the Church of all titles to individual property, or if they have not, their conversion was too thorough to be shaken by the discovery; at any rate, here they are, in the Mormon power, of their own free will Mormons themselves; they have taken the irrevocable step—and Mr. Polypeith has no alternative. So he forks over—we will say ten thousand dollars. That sum forthwith goes into the coffers of the Church (to wit, Brigham's Herring safe), and neither Mr. Polypeith, his heirs, nor his assigns, ever hear from it in the shape of principal or interest thereafter.

He receives the ten thousand which the Church graciously accords him from his own former possessions, and sets up the furniture business. During the first week or two of his life in Salt Lake City nothing occurs to make him sensible of the difference between the Mormon *régime* and that under which he lived in the States. Yet none the less is he becoming enmeshed in the secret toils of a system as unlike the free, open-air spirited government of our noble republic as the Council of Three, Jesuitry, or the Vehm-Gericht. Each of the twenty wards into which the city of Salt Lake is divided has a ruler of its own, who takes charge both of its temporalities and spiritualities with the title of bishop. He exercises supervision over the tithes due from citizens under him to the Church treasury; has general charge of the Church's financial interests in the ward, and registers marriages, deaths, and births. But surpassing importance all his other functions is that of secret investigator. He stands responsible to the Prophet President for the private lives— the most intimate circumstances and doings of his people. It is a principle of Mormonism that the President must be omniscient. The inmost secrets of every household must be revealed to him; he must know what is whispered in the bride-chamber, the nursery, in the consultations of the lawyer and the doctor, in the lover's courtship, and on the dying bed. Fouché never knew as much as he must know, nor does the Superior of the Jesuit College. Fouché bothered his head with religious secrets, the Superior concerns his with political ones, only as subsidiary to other ends. Brigham Young must know all secrets; and to attain this end indefinitely multiplies himself through bishops and their subordinates. The bishop is supposed to visit the members of the Church in his ward in the New England pastoral sense; but his visits are sometimes of a much more formidable character than those mild interviews for prayer and religious conversation which the Eastern clergyman indulges in with his flock at periodic intervals. The bishop's crosier abroad has a hooked and a sharp end, each with its several office,—"*Curva trahit mites—pungit acuta rebelles.*" The Mormon bishop has no crosier, but he can prick as well as pull, and some of his visits are judicial though others be pastoral. He has proxies or deputies whose sole business it is to furnish him with that stream of knowledge of which he is the President's channel: plausible informers who enter families as guests, or watch them through windows and key-holes, like burglars making their preparation for a "crack"; spies who climb trees and grape trellises to eavesdrop, or lie all night on ladders at second story shutters; who accept confidences to betray them, and employ all the black arts of the detective policeman to possess themselves of the very most trifling particular which may sometime be needed as a clew to the sinner against ecclesiastical authority. From this espionage even the most innocent life is no freer than that of the once detected der-elict. The Mormon, like the Jew, has to learn that the God of a theocracy is a jealous God.

In the States Mr. Polypeith's family has always been such a blameless one that the suspicion of suspicion never crosses their minds. They live with the same guileless free-dom that has characterized their behavior everywhere. They little know that not in Milan before the Austrians were expelled, not in Havana at the present day—that nowhere among hunted Carbonari, Mazzinists, Fenians, Huguenots, Lollards, or proscribed French Loyalists, ever existed any people so closely watched in the house and by the way-side; so minutely known in all their goings out and comings in; so tracked and noted and booked down to the smallest par-ticular of their conduct at bed and board; subject to such scrutiny of the hands they clasp, the lips they kiss, the eyes they smile into, and the infinitesimal shades of expression which they unconsciously throw into clasp, kiss, and smile, as they themselves—this self-same blameless Polypeith family. So the first fortnight goes on in making acquaintances at home, stocking and working the shop on Main Street. Mrs. Polypeith, who still remains without a colleague, gets along pretty well at Mormon house-keeping by the aid of her two daughters, after discharging her "help" because she became too impudent to put up with, as frequently happens with her class at Salt Lake, owing to the fact that promotions out of it to a wifely rank in the household are sufficiently common to destroy any vestige of distinction between mistress and servant, which among the more unsophisticated may have survived the transit of the Plains and Rocky Mountains. It is not to be supposed that a buxom Mormoness will take much pains in doing up another woman's cap when she is occupied in setting her own for that woman's husband. Mrs. Polypeith has, however, given some quiet little teas in spite of her domestic trials, and Mr. Polypeith has celebrated his birthday by a modest dinner.

Early in the week following the dinner he receives an invitation to call on the bishop. He cheerfully accepts it—perhaps flatters himself on the courtesy with which he is treated by so high a functionary thus early in his saintship. He is ushered into a private room, where he finds himself confronted with the bishop and two or three elders beside. To his astonishment the object of the interview is not hospitality but judgment. He has been accused by somebody (and this is the nearest approach to definiteness with which he ever knows his accuser; it may have been the "help" who was dismissed by Mrs. P., after having failed to win Mr. P's affections, and thus seeks to avenge the "spretæ injurium formæ"; it may have been a guest at the dinner party, who was at the same time an agent of the Mormon Vehm-Gericht) of having taken, on the festal occasion last alluded to, a drop of his own liquor more than was good for him. Does he deny the charge? Does he ask to be set face to face with the informers? Mormonism never "goes back" on its spies. The name of the accuser is of no consequence. Besides, he is brought up not for trial, but for sentence. The bishop takes care of all his flock without any assistance from themselves. The trial has been conducted with as much regard to his interests as if he were present, and the brother, more especially as he is a new-comer and this his first offense, will be dealt with in a spirit of the utmost leniency consistent with the salvation of his own immortal soul and the welfare of the Church—that absolute theocratic proprietor, which owns him "neck, crop, and gizzard," from the tips of his boots to the forelock he has pomatumed for his visit to the bishop. Or, does he make a plea, as the old common law hath it, "in confession and avoidance," acknowledging that on the occasion referred to he may have crooked his elbow once too often, but then the superfluous draught was on his own birthday, in his own house, and from his own bottle? Ruled out! The Church knows no festivals, no privacy, no proprietorship but its own. As in "Le Diable Boiteux," so in the romance of Mormon Life; as there with Asmodeus, so here with the Devil (or Angel, according as you be Saint or Gentile) of the Latter-Day Church, all the roofs of the houses come off like the cover from a soup-tureen; he catches the cover by the knob of the chimney or the cupola, and looks down on the family simmering in its wickedness, or refreshes his nostrils with its odorous steam of sanctity, and not an ingredient in the pottage escapes his omniscience. No man's house is his castle in a theocracy. Thus was it with the Jewish; thus with the Puritan; and it is thus with the Mormon. Acknowledge that God can have deputies who rule in his name, and they must be gifted with the prerogatives of God. He does not leave the citizen at his door-sill—neither can they. No Mr. Polypeith! You have left behind you the pestilent atheism of Republican government; you are enjoying the blessings of that system which so many good men at the East have tried in vain to bring back; you are forced to be religious whether you will or no. This is no community where a man with impunity can go home and get drunk in the bosom of his family. So Mr. Polypeith leaves the bishop's with a face longer by an inch; a mind wiser by a revelation; a pocket lighter

by ten dollars—exactly the sum which he often used to read
of in the police reports column of his morning paper as paid
promptly, "after which the magistrate advised the offender
to take better care of himself in future, and he left the court-
room in company with his friends"; or, in default of which,
"the prisoner was sent up for ten days." He used to read such
accounts with a shudder, did Mr. Polypeith; or, perhaps he
thanked God, like the Pharisee, that he was not like other
men—at least, not like this victim of the Publican, enjoying
his visit at the generous city's island country-seat. Now he,
the self-same Eusebius Polypeith, stands mulcted in the self-
same sum—a degraded man—mulcted for drunkenness!
He groans from the bottom of his being—goes home—and
does not tell Mrs. Polypeith. Where does that fine go? To
the Church: namely, to the Herring safe in Brigham's office.

A year has elapsed since he came through Emigration
Cañon. He has been tolerably successful in business. One
morning he receives another missive; the bishop wants a
statement of his profits, concealing, abating nothing, under
the penalty of Ananias and Sapphira—a statement verified
by his oath. There is something in the preparation of such a
statement that makes any man brought up with Republican
notions wince and feel humiliated,—even when he is doing
it as a war necessity for the sake of supporting a National
Government in whose stability he has coequal interest with
every neighbor of his. I do not believe that the most patriotic man in the United States ever receives the assessor's
peremptory order to return his income without an instinctive feeling that he is suffering a sort of grand national
indignity—as if the collective sovereign people had given
him a collective sovereign tweak o' the nose; or searched

his pockets like a collective sovereign constable, or looked over his shoulder while he was balancing his ledger with a collective sovereign impudence which it requires all his philosophy and patriotism to excuse, and of which he says to himself, as he sits down to obey the assessor, "I *do* hope that Congress will before long invent some less obnoxious way of collecting the national revenue!" But in making our returns to the United States assessor most of us have the relief of considering that we voted to support the best government the sun ever shone on; that we are in reality only collecting the tax from ourselves; that, furthermore, we, through the representatives our ballots sent to Washington, shall have our say as to the manner in which the money shall be spent. Mr. Polypeith has no such relief. He is the subject of a theocracy. In 1884, long before he had heard of Mormonism, Joseph Smith the Prophet, and Oliver Cowdery (one of the three witnesses to whom the Angel of the Lord showed the plates of the Book of Mormon), met in Clay County, Missouri, and made a covenant with God that they would henceforth pay into his treasury, for the advancement of the heavenly kingdom upon earth, tithings of all that they possessed—imitating the Jewish theocracy in this respect as closely as all the others. Thenceforth all the Saints were expected to contribute likewise, and the custom which binds Mr. Polypeith has no other foundation than this thirty-two years' prescription. Nor has he any voice, directly, or by vote, in the disposal of his property after it goes into the Church coffers, to wit, Brigham's safe. The Church uses its money—i. e., Brigham spends it—without taking counsel of the taxed, but by Divine command, and that command is revealed to Brigham alone, while only the Divine Revelator has the right of looking over his accounts. There is, therefore, not one alleviating circumstance in the necessity under which Mr. Polypeith sits down to make out his exhibit of income for the bishop. Nevertheless, he winces his way through the task, and sends back the following:—

"Salt lake city, *July 24th*, 1866 }  Being the 37th year of the Church
of Jesus Christ of Later-Day Saints.

Eusebius Polypeith: Income return for Year ending at Date.
  Resulting from Cabinet Ware business                    $1,520.00
  Dividends on Stock held in Railroad Companies              125.00
  Dividends on Stock held in Insurance Companies             245.00
Money paid Wife by executors of her Mother's estate in Mass   300.00
Total                                                      $2,190.00
*Attestatur,* E. Polypeith."

A few days after this return has been handed to the Bishop, Mr. Polypeith gets his order to repair to the Tithing Office and pay into the Church treasury (the Henning safe again) the sum of two hundred and nineteen dollars. Or, it is possible that he may receive instead one of those pleasant episcopal invitations with which he became acquainted earlier in the year, and on repairing with a heavy heart to his pastor's house find out that the terrible charge of making a false return has been lodged against him. He feels as guiltless of the wrong as a child a month old. He may discover that, in the opinion of the authorities, he has overvalued the original cost to himself of some of the articles on which he has estimated his profits. In this case he will, perhaps, be startled to have copies of his wholesale dealers' charges and vouchers presented to him. Or, he may have omitted in making his return to include the advance which he has received during the year on the original price of a pair of draught horses left behind at the East to be sold, whose proceeds were forwarded to him. The transaction has totally escaped his mind—not so the Church's! There, in black and white, he reads all its particulars—more precisely drawn out, it may be, than he could have done them by referring to his own private papers. A sickening sensation comes over Mr. Polypeith's soul as he realizes the omniscience and ubiquity of that power into whose grasp he has voluntarily resigned himself irretrievably—forever! If he is really innocent of all intent to cheat, Brigham reads character too skillfully not to know it; and, instead of the fearful doom which awaits such as are foolhardy or green enough to attempt defrauding the great Fraud of the Universe,—the outlawry, the delivery to the buffets of Satan, the vague, unnamable terrors, the lurking death,—he gets off with a solemn warning and a mulct which may amount to the duplication of his tithes.

Suppose that, instead of having succeeded in his annual business by the time the next tithing day comes round, he has in reality sold nothing, but has accumulated either by manufacture or importation five hundred Boston rockers. He has no money to give the Church; but the Church takes toll out of every grist, and all is grist that comes to its mill. The Church is not fastidious; it will take fifty of his five hundred rockers, and call it square. What can it do with them, d'you ask? A Church founded upon a rock, one might think, can have no call for rockers, but it has. Mr. Polypeith is instructed to deliver them in the great Tithing Store-house, right under the personal eye of the Church, *scil.* Brigham. Then, if he has never had occasion to call there before, he sees a sight which surprises him. There are carts and rude Utah-made ranch-wagons standing at the gate to unload tithes of every description of product created by human industry. The shelves and the deep ware-rooms of the all-devouring theocracy groan and bulge with everything which it is conceivable that mankind should sell and buy on this side of the Rocky Mountains. Here are piles of rawhide, both cow and mustang, or even pig-skin; bins of shelled corn, and cribs foil of corn in the ear; wheat and rye, oats and barley; casks of salt provisions; wool, homespun yarn, and home-woven cloth in hanks and bales; indigo; cocoons and raw silk; butter, cheese, and all manner of farm produce; even the most destructible of vegetable growths,— not only potatoes, turnips, and other root crops, but green pease and beans, fruit, and young cabbages; hay, carpenters' work, boys' caps, slop-shop overalls, hemp-rope, preserves, tinware, stogies, confectionery, adobe bricks and tiles, moss and gramma mattresses; buckskin leggings, gloves, moccasins, hunting-shirts, and complete suits, the manufacture of which the Mormon women make a specialty, arriving at a degree of excellence in their preparation, and beauty in their adornment, surpassed nowhere in the world,—not even among the Snake Indians. These are but a minute fraction of the contents of the Church Tithing Stores. I have seen day laborers who were too poor to pay their tithes in any lumped form at the end of the year, bringing them in at sundown in the shape of a tenth of the poor, flabby-meated gudgeons which they had caught in their day's fishing along the Jordan. The Church, under the wonderful management of Brigham, somehow or other succeeds in disposing of all that it receives in this way to the best advantage, and is not only a self-supporting, but a money-making concern of the most brilliant character. By consenting to receive the tithes

THE HEART OF THE CONTINENT

in form, wherever the Mormon finds it easier to bring the literal tenth of his possessions instead of their money value, it effects three most desirable ends. It secures the certain payment of its tithes, since the products of a man's industry are tangible, accessible, unconcealable, and therefore within its grasp as no notes or specie can be; it acts as a perpetual stimulus to Mormon industry by affording one certain outlet to every man's products,—a market through which he can dispose of at least a part of such products, however loth private dealers may be to run the risk of buying them; and it adds another resemblance to the old Jewish theocracy, which tithed the property of the people in kind, to the multitude of similarities on which it bases its claim to the successorship of Israel as the repository of the Urim and Thummim, the possessor of the Original Priesthood and the Eternal Truth, and the sole Architect of God's temple and kingdom upon earth. At the same time, Brigham's talents as a Rothschild being none less than as a Moses and a Richelieu, the Church loses nothing pecuniarily by taking Brother Clod's cabbages, and Brother Polypeith's chairs.

Mr. Polypeith's diary for the next few years contains nothing more startling than the marriage of his two daughters to a well-to-do elder of the Church, possessing, besides five hundred head of cattle and a nice ranch in the region of Parley's Park, a trifle of two previous wives, who live harmoniously, not being able to quarrel, as one of them understands nothing but Norwegian, and the other possesses no lingual accomplishments beyond her original Shoshonee. To Mr. Polypeith it seems a little odd at first to have a man paying attention to both his daughters at once; early associations are difficult to conquer, and an only partially regenerate right leg of his twitches uneasily at the memory how it would have kicked such a suitor down-stairs at the East; but grace triumphs when he reflects that after all the elder does not mean any such thing as trifling with young affections of the girls, since he proposed to Hannah Rebecca on Thursday, and to Lucetta Plumins on the Sunday following; moreover, it is a great deal less wearing and expensive to order a wedding for two and get one's family nicely provided for in a single evening, than to string the paternal anxiety along, States-fashion, through two separate courtships, and disburse for two entirely distinct sets of presents and wedding-cake. So he says, "Bless you, my children—bless you!" and, to use the choice patriarchal vernacular, the elder "gits" with the lot.

If polygamy at any time, during the progress of these occurrences, seem to Mr. Polypeith any harder of deglutition because the two wives of saintly son-in-law stand to each other in the sisterly relation, he may lubricate the morsel by that sage consideration which has doubtless been suggested to every dissatisfied person since the foundation of the world, "How much worse it might have been." He may have made the acquaintance of a family such as I myself became aware of while in the Mormon Zion. Passing with a very zealous believer through one of the streets in that city, I had my attention called by my companion to a comfortable residence, belonging, apparently, to some person of more than average condition in the community. "There!" said the gentleman emphatically,—"there lives one of the very best men we've got in Salt Lake City." "How so?" I asked him. "The most noble-hearted, whole-souled, liberal fellow I ever knew. Doesn't stand at anything when he can do a generous action. Here's an instance. Two years ago his partner in business died insolvent, leaving two widows and three daughters without a leg to stand on. He was very well off himself and a bachelor. So what does he do but go right over to his partner's house, see the two widows and three daughters—make it all right—and marry the whole of 'em. That's what I call a right down liberal action!" I have seen it indignantly denied by Mormon defenders, that marriages of this sort are permitted in Utah; but such a denial on their behalf would be scornfully repudiated by the Mormons themselves, who rather favor such marriages than otherwise, on the same ground that benevolent and sage old slave-holders, in the halcyon days of the Eastern and Southern Patriarchal Institution, used to buy whole families, to wit, that they live much more contentedly together than when they are separated. A mother and a daughter who are wives of the same man, or two sisters similarly situated, are more apt to be patient with each other and freer from jealousy than strangers.

I must now give a page Mr. Polypeith's diary, which is so painful that he himself would gladly have blotted it out with his heart's blood—which I, indeed, would gladly suppress, were it not that I am writing the truth and have not the romancer's privilege of yielding to sentimental motives. Mr. Polypeith's family, after the daughters were married, consisted of himself, his wife, and one son nineteen years old—a fine, handsome, frank-natured young fellow who for some time had been a valuable assistant to his father in business, and whom he was rearing to take his place when age should release him from the harness of active life.

Among the neighboring families was one of an elder, whom the Church, shortly after Hiram Polypeith's nineteenth birthday, had appointed to go forth upon a foreign mission—a tour for the collection of converts in Sweden, Denmark, and Norway, which would keep him abroad for two years—indeed, until he could bring a ship-load of fresh Saints from the Baltic to New York, and thence across the Mississippi, and the Mountains to Salt Lake. The elder was a well-to-do man of fifty; and it might have seemed just as advantageous to the interests of Zion to send a younger brother, with youthful energy, the "roving drop in his veins," the love of adventure, and the desire of making his way in the world, to sustain him through the labors of a mission, and less extensive family ties to bind him at home; for besides being a little past middle age, he possessed a large property, five wives, and a score of children. Among all his wives, as frequently happens, he doted most on the last and youngest one, to whom he had been married only about six months when the order came for his departure. The mandate grieved him sore, but theocracies know no sentiment save that of obedience to revelation, and though he would gladly have paid the expenses of a proxy and stayed at home with his little Zilpha and the others, he was compelled to bid them all adieu and fare forth one morning by the overland stage.

The elder's family and that of Brother Polypeith had been intimate from the first year of the latter's settlement in Zion. They frequently met each other in the exchange of hospitalities. Mrs. Polypeith was weekly invited to tea at the Salmudys', and the Salmudys, on the principle of its being inconvenient to move large masses, were reinvited in squads at a rate which went through them all in about one lunar period. When the elder came to go away, Mrs. Polypeith mingled her tears as she had her tea with the Mistresses Salmudy; and Mr. Polypeith, grasping Elder Salmudy's hand with emotion, told him that during his absence he would endeavor to be such a friend to his family, as he would ask Elder Salmudy to be to his in case their positions were changed.

There was one member of the Polypeith family who did not partake to the full extent in the general affliction felt at Elder Salmudy's departure. This was Hiram Polypeith—the handsome, spirited lad with the curly hair, red cheeks, and bright boyish eyes—who had his reasons. As the Salmudys lived next door to the Polypeiths on the right side, so did the Crandalls live next door on the left side. From the day that Mr. Polypeith took his house, his garden and the Crandalls' had opened into one another by a little wicket in the partition fence, and the relation of the two families had been as intimate as that of the former with the Salmudys'. The wicket almost always hung ajar, and the children of both households had held the inclosures in common playing tag together, around the gravel walks, dressing dolls and making-believe tea-fight under extempore houses rigged up beneath the cool shadows of acacias, quaking asps, cottonwoods, end rock-maples transplanted from the cañons. The youngest child of the Crandalls was a pretty golden-haired girl, with laughing blue eyes and merry temperament—the pet of everybody, and a gleam of sunshine wherever she went. She was the little sweetheart of Hiram Polypeith from the time they first played together; she was enough unlike him in every respect, except the fact of beauty and mutual attraction, to bring out the strongest positive characteristics of the boy, and awaken an intense feeling of chivalry in him, which manifested itself in every way—from fighting her battles with ruder and stronger children to carrying her tiny dinner when he went to school, and being her invariable guard of honor at all picnics to Black Rock or the Lake in the Mountains. She returned his feeling with one of absolute confidence and admiration—was never so happy as when she nestled against his side, and, whenever her light heart thought of the future at all, never imagined a place in it whose centre was not her boy-gallant. One of their most frequent plays (as I suppose is the case with all children of every place and age) was "getting married'; and the romantic tenderness of Hiram's love for little Zilpha Crandall was shown by the fact that while the other little male-Saints had polygamic plays, he never added to his list of wives, but incurred the temporary suspicion or even infantile religious persecution of his mates as a bad Mormon, by remaining sternly monogamic and marrying Zilpha over and over and over again.

But they could not always remain children and play under the acacias. Zilpha, being just Hiram's age, as was woman's right, blossomed first, and became a demure, marriageable little Mormoness in long dresses (or, as a perverse Gentile friend used to call Mormon little girls, a "*Mormoniculess*," Mormon little boys being similarly, "*Mormonicles*)," while Hiram was blushing at the shortness of a roundabout, which he felt still more ashamed to exchange for that uneasily self-conscious garment, a coat with tails. Before either of them knew it, the golden-haired beauty had attracted the attention of that multuxoriverous mammal, Elder Salmudy,—a splay-footed quadrigenarian, with beetle brows, a raucous voice, which one would have as soon thought of as a frog's for the vehicle of love-making, and vast expansiveness below the epigastrium without adequate diameter

THE HEART OF THE CONTINENT

of legs to sustain such a superstructure. Already, too, as the Gypsy Queen denominated Rector Racktithe, married the third time, he was "*a mighty waster o' women*," having four Mistresses Salmudy to watch for his martial footfall at the close of the laborious day. To adapt *Louis* in "Richelieu," "Fine proxy for a gay young cavalier!" But why linger over the hagglings of the marriage market? Salt Lake is no better than New York or London, though it does pretend to be, and Mormon parents sell their daughters for a "bon parti" just as ours do,—though not as universally as was the case in the much desiderated Hebrew theocracy. The Crandalls were poor—Elder Salmudy was rich—Hiram Polypeith was only a boy—Zilpha was an obedient daughter. She cried bitterly—vowed she would always love Hiram—and married the multuxoriverous monster. As for Hiram—he gnashed his teeth in secret—that most helpless, uncommiserated, most laughed at of all human beings—a boy indulging a hopeless passion. What could he have expected? He would not be ready to marry for years—Zilpha was a grown-up woman—did he suppose she was to be bound by the plays of a baby-house? Pshaw! So he crawled into the straw of his father's barn and wept out his heart-break, not even pitied by the hen whom his grief had driven off her nest on the beam, and who scolded at him with the crossest of cackles.

Time will insist on healing such wounds for us though we swear he shall not, and despise ourselves as brutes for finally yielding to him. What was at first the bitterest ingredient in the boy's cup—the fact that his little Zilpha lived next door to him in his successful rival's house—became a sort of sad delight—gradually a delight with only a faint *soupçon* of sadness, for he saw a great deal of her without the elder, and cherished in his heart that fearful torpedo, liable to explode at any moment, the old love for her without the old right. Just as he was beginning to go about his work with some sort of equanimity, and to answer the criterion which old country women suppose infallible for the question whether a hopeless passion exists or not, by "taking his three meals reg'lar," Salmudy received the mandate to depart. Hiram could have gone to Brigham Young and hugged him round the knees! It almost seemed as if the President had known his heart and intended to do him a personal favor. He did not dare to accompany his father to the stage office, lest instinct should be too strong for conventionalism, and the real sunshine of his heart at Elder Salmudy's parting break through the hypocritical clouds upon his face. So he stayed at home, hiding in the barn, and through a knot-hole saw with a quickened pulse of delight little Zilpha feeding her chickens from the back porch—heard her singing blithely while she scattered the crumbs—as light-hearted as if it were indifferent to her whether her six-months' lord went to Copenhagen or Jericho, and it would be quite the same to her if he never came back from either. Already he began to calculate the chances against the elder's return: his years were against him; the journey was full of exposures; there were several sea-voyages to make; the ocean baffled, there were still the Sioux, the Arrapahoes, and the Snakes on the way across Plain and Mountain—he blushed, catching himself suddenly, just about to enter a chamber of thought which was the vestibule of murder.

Papa Polypeith's promise to keep a fatherly eye on the bereaved Salmudys gave Hiram constant occasion to run in next door. He went to see if his mother could help them; if there was butter wanted; if the flour was getting low; if the cattle were getting on nicely; if his father could transact any business for them; if they wouldn't like to read the last New York papers; if the flower-beds needed weeding; if *he* could do anything; if anything was wanted—yes! something was wanted—wanted all the time, by one of that household. And O! perilous gift!—he brought it—brought all the strong, passionate, flaming love which he fancied he had raked out and buried under—the love which by God's law was his right and hers to whom he gave it, though man had set on it his black seal of execration.

Neither knew when it came. The curves of danger are so gradual—its inclines so smooth. The two thought they were reviving innocent childhood's playtime. They sat under the acacia as of old; they talked of the houses he made for her to live in, and laughed at their baby-housekeeping. Did she remember when he stood in the cedar clump to be married to her with a big doll for a bridesmaid? did *he* remember what he did as soon as the ceremony was over? She blushed as she recalled it and dropped her moist eyes; he folded her to his heart and did it again. But they did not feel as they had in childhood—their lips parted slower—his arm was harder to unclasp.

Day after day of delicious dreamy peril went on, in house and garden—part of it right before the eyes of the parental Polypeith; but they, remembering what attached playmates the children had been, and like all parents so slow to realize the fact that *their* child could grow up, saw the two walking and talking together, saw them inseparable in their stud-ies, their amusements, even their work, so far as they could help each other, and never warned them of a danger that they themselves did not suspect. Other eyes, however, were not so fondly blind. The other four wives of the elder had never been one with that excellent man in his admiration for Zilpha. One of them, moreover, was the spiritual wife of the bishop of that ward, and on more than one occasion had shown her devotion to the Church and to the man who should be her husband in the celestial mansions, by acting as eyes for him and the Vehm-Gericht. She was bound by the holiest of ties, therefore, to let no iniquity pass her scrutiny without revealing it directly to the bishop. Within the first month after her earthly husband's departure she had repaired to the house of her spiritual one, and told him that she saw mischief hatching. His only reply was, "*Watch.*" So she did watch. As for the other three, their feeling toward the pretty little Zilpha was of a less tragic and religious nature; they hated her and waited to catch her tripping because they were unpleasantly homely; had long and slabby or stocky and dumpy figures; were without grace or womanly development in either spirit or physique; were bald, sallow, wrinkled, uneducated, uncouth, while in every particular she had the impudence to be exactly the reverse; because no handsome young man came to console them for the absence of Brother Salmudy, therefore they hated her with that poisonous petty hate which nothing can create in a woman but the degradation to which she has always been subject in a theocracy. Thus both the Church and Personal Jealousy—Artificial Evil and Native Evil—were arrayed against the two young lovers, and searched out their most secret communings, their most intricate paths, with fiery eyes that never drooped in weariness or were damped by pity. Yet the lovers, wrapped in the isolation of that heavenly dream which made them the two only human beings in the universe, toyed on like mating wrens, just over the fanged jaws of the black-snake.

As innocent of evil intent as Francesca da Rimini and her lover, the two thought of nothing but the fact that they loved. They knew that they were each other's—they had no room, no politic coolness for the thought how to get it acknowledged that they were. They talked as if life were to be all an endless now; as if Time were put to sleep for them, Age forbidden to approach them, the world banished from them, the elder never coming back from Copenhagen. What they would do when he did come back, was a thought which seemed so far away, that to have roused them to it from their trance of love would have seemed an impertinence of the same kind as waking a man from the middle of his night's sleep to decide the choice of a name or a profession for his great-great-great grandson. They did not even reflect that Brigham was noted for his urbanity and kindness to unequally yoked wives, and that Zilpha's unhappy lot might be changed in an hour by going to his office with her story as soon as the elder returned and had a chance to be notified of her wish for the separation, so that he should not feel as if a trap had been sprung on him. Marriage they did not think of, for in the childhood with which their present lotus-eating life was continuous, had they not been married dozens of times? How many times we toll lovers to be prudent—prudent even if only for the sake of their love! But who obeys—who *can* obey that mandate? There is something in love itself which takes policy out of the most politic head—and floods the veins with childlike heedlessness. Love is so necessary to the lover's existence—so vital an air to him, that it seems as if all around him must be loving too, and if so, that they can have no time and as little heart, to meddle with his happiness.

One night, Zilpha stole out by the kitchen and the back porch, from the glum society of her four elder "sisters." Two of them were busily engaged in rocking separate cradles, each containing a young Salmudy of nearly the same age; another was knitting stockings for her part of the family feet; and another was reading the "Deseret News" report of Brother Brigham's last sermon, which a face-ache had kept her from hearing with her fleshly ears. Such of the children as were not married and permanently out of the house, or in the cradles biting the gum ring of infancy, were either in bed up-stairs in a sort of phalansterian nursery, or out in town somewhere at social or religious meetings, or engaged in the favorite rural occupation of New England male-evenings, which has survived the transit of Rocky Mountains, seated around a stove with their feet on the fender ring, squirting tobacco juice between the legs, or joining with idiomatic old men in muzzy fur caps, talking politics and relating reminiscences. The women folks and the one inadequate astral lamp on the centre-table seemed one and all to need fresh filling if they were ever to be expected to shed light on anything, and diffused about them such an atmosphere of dejection that one would think they might have sufficiently well understood why a bright little girl like Zilpha could not stand it any longer in the room with them. Evidently, however, the tallest and stiffest sister could not accept these facts as sufficient to account for Zilpha's retreat, since she folded up her "Deseret News" with spinster-like precision, and followed the junior wife out like a chaperone. She was too late to find her in the kitchen or on the porch.

The moon was at its second quarter and shed the peculiar, uncertain lunar twilight characteristic of that phase; melting into each other the lines which at the planet's full come out silver-edged and distinct as strands of filagree; the very light for lover's meetings, since it does not betray them to their enemies like the broader radiance, but tinges their faces to each other with a sweet enamoring mystery, and reveal them with a tender half-disclosure which leaves room for the imagination, always delisting in the adornment of the beloved with its own ideals, to make every feature and expression thrice beautiful, thus giving a new meaning to the poet's words,—

> "As darkness shows us worlds of light
> We never saw by day."

After the elder girt his loins and fared on his mission, Hiram had constructed a little wicket in the fence between the Salmudys' and his father's garden like that which existed on the side toward the Crandalls. Toward this, through the half-moonlight, Zilpha made her way. Hiram stood ready to open it for her. He led her in, latched it after her, put his arm around her waist, and led her down the gravel walk to the shade of the acacias. For an hour they sat murmuring into each other's ears the sweetest words that are ever spoken on earth; they forgot time, space, earth, all but the heaven of an immeasurable love that even on the outer sill of its vestibule had no place for an elder of fifty with four other wives. Before the last good-night embrace, a pair of those red, vengeful eyes, by aid of which the Church is omniscient, turned away from the sight of the young lovers' rapture, which for the last half-hour they had been burning through the shrubbery to mark and chronicle. They turned away, and a pair of stealthy, cat-like feet with them, just in time; for, stricken with sudden consciousness, and thinking that they heard a noise near the house, the two arose from beneath the shadow of the acacia, and hastened to the wicket. Just in time, for as they reacted it, a gaunt dark figure unseen by them, got safely within the screening darkness of the elder's back porch. After breakfast the next morning, the lady who was reading the "Deseret News" on the night before, called upon the bishop of the ward, who complaisantly granted her an hour's private interview. All such readers as are too sensitive or squeamish to bear the whole truth regarding Mormonism, whatever depths of moral ugliness it may disclose, will please dismount from my narrative at this stopping place; and, while I pursue the main road, cross the stile, and make a short cut by turning over a leaf, to meet me and get aboard again a few paragraphs on.

Neither Zilpha nor Hiram know that their secret has been discovered. The former goes on with his business, the latter performs her share in the household duties of the absent elder's *ménage*—they both meet and part as blithely as ever. To be sure, the young girl sees sour looks following her everywhere from those whom it is a Mormon "triumph of grace" to call "*sisters*"; but then she always received those, and having at the commencement made up her mind to pay no attention to them, is not now troubled by the question of more or less. As for Hiram, neither in human face, nor word, nor deed— neither in his own thought, nor in outside warning—is there anything to tell him that the Philistines are upon him.

Now it is the full of the moon—a fortnight after that sweet secret meeting under the acacias—and he has a long walk to take for the assistance of his father's business. Old Brother Polypeith has to pay a note to-morrow, and Hiram must go on a collecting tour to the outskirts of Salt Lake City on the Camp Floyd Road. He promises the old couple that he will be back by eleven o'clock at the furthest. They need not sit up for him after that. If he comes back later, he will stop at a friend's of his who lives on the southern suburb.

He carries nothing with him but his locust-switch,—a mere sapling, not for use, but for ornament; his revolvers are left behind, hanging at the head of his bedstead—why should he take any weapon? He has no personal enemies, and it is the Mormon's boast that Salt Lake City is safer after dark than any town of its size east of the Rocky Mountains. Moreover, the full moon makes it as light as day, and if, in all the Mormon Zion, there could be such a *lusus naturæ* as a robber or an assassin, he certainly would not select this time of the month to ply his nefarious trade. If he whistles as he walks, therefore, it is because he remembers a favorite tune which Zilpha used to sing under the acacia when the "Mormonicles" and "Mormoniculesses" were married in play:—

> "Thus the farmer sows his seeds;
>   He stands erect end takes his ease,—
>   Stamps his foot end claps his hands,
>   Turns around, and thus he stands!"

The air is full of blithe influences. He walks as if by will, without muscle, singing and whistling by turns—full of a pleasant peace, and always thinking of Zilpha. He bows now and then to an acquaintance—once or twice speaks to an intimate one. Everybody likes him—everybody seems kind to him. When was there a boy not yet twenty years old, who had made so many friends and no enemies? What a pleasant moonlight this is! There are no clouds over it here, in the summer sky, as there are at the East. He looks up at it and walks unconsciously—his feet on the earth—his heart in the heavens. What if Elder Salmudy should never come home? The sea is dangerous. But then, even if he does come home, the same power which sent him on a mission can take away from his horrible old bear-paws the one ewe-lamb that has been his—Hiram's very own from the beginning. That is one blessing! Brigham is good about divorces. What a sweet little home they can have by and by!

> "Waiting for a partner!
> Waiting for a partner!
> Open the ring and let her in,
> And kiss her when you've got her in!"

He stops whistling again to twine the Wistaria and Madeira vine, the wild honey-suckle and the passion-flower about the porch of that sweet little home they shall have—when—when—and then, thinking *when*, he goes off into a reverie too sweetly transcendental to put into words.

The town's thickest streets are reached; he observes for the first time how lonely it can be,—how dark and hidden in a secluded suburb, even under the full moon. Two furlongs off he can see the house where he must present his largest bill; its candles sending out through the panes two red streaks to struggle with the great silver flood, and finally get lost, utterly beaten out in the ocean dropping down from on high. Long shadows of barns, black as midnight for all the moon,—nay, by reason of the moon, whose contrast they are, lie across the road; and the sand-heaps along the fences, but half-lighted through the picket-slits and rail-gaps, are checkered with oblongs of swarthy penumbra. Though the moon is so bright above, she leaves spots below in which it is dark enough for murder to be done. There is an eddy of blackness behind that corner ranch, long ago deserted in the troublous "Johnston times," where a corpse might drift ashore out of the silver stream that washed the road-way, and though a procession passed all night long, not be seen till morning.

"Now you are married, you must obey."—

Scarce has he again begun to whistle the old memories back from under the acacia, when—"Phiu-u! phiu-u-u!—phiew!" there comes a triple whistle from another mouth, and of a sharper shrillness. Another, like it, answers it from out that black hollow, where all midnight and blackness seem hiding from the moon; than the lad hears a rush of feet, then a sack is thrown over his head, his mouth is stuffed with a wad of rags, and with pinioned arms he is dragged he knows not whither, as in a nightmare.

Brother and Sister Polypeith sit cosily chatting on their door-step until after the appointed hour. It is past eleven; neighbors have come in and joined them—gone, home, and been succeeded by others who in their turn went home. The good old couple finally resolve to shut up the house. They are prepared for the alternative of Hiram's failure to return. He has probably, say they, spent the night at Brother Labys, with Joe. So they enter the homestead and bar the door; sure that their boy will find it no hardship in such a summer night as this, to nestle down in the hay, if he does come back after all. For a little while, tender-hearted Ma Polypeith lies awake to hear her boy slam the gate; but that sound failing her, and her conscience troubling her naught, she presently gives over watching and sleeps the sleep of the just.

The next morning they take their lonely breakfast with regret; but certainly without alarm at Hiram's absence. There is no doubt about Papa Polypeith's debtors, and if Hiram *has* stayed to breakfast with the Labys, he will go right round to the shop with the checks in time for his father to meet the notes. So saying, Pa Polypeith lights his after-breakfast pipe and by the side of Ma Polypeith strolls down the front gravel-walk to the gate, intending to saunter leisurely down to his Main street place of business.

His hand is on the latch-rod, when an old and coarse-looking ranch wagon stops in front of his house. A Mormon ranchman, who sits on a board in front, reins in his mules with one hand, and silently beckons with the other. Hay, wood, vegetables, an order for cabinet ware; these are the ideas that flash through Pa Polypeith's mind in an instant. But no! The contents of the wagon are too meagre for produce, and the ranchman does not look like a saint well-to-do enough to want fresh furniture for his house. The wagon-load is only about six feet by two and a half, and it is covered with an old quilt. Pa Polypeith advances. "Well?" says he to the ranchman. That person simply points with the unoccupied hand over his shoulder. Then Pa Polypeith steps up on a spoke and turns down the quilt. The next moment he falls from the spoke and grasps the side-board with both hands. "What is it?" cries Ma Polypeith, curiously. She only sees his back; and the white horror, that makes his face suddenly unmeaning, has spread into his very heart and throat, making him so bloodless that he cannot answer. She sees that something strange is under the quilt. She runs out and lifts it for herself. She gives a bitter cry that might tear the heart of a hyena—a devil—anything but a theocracy; and climbing into the cart, with a man's strength takes up to her breast her only boy.

*Dead!* is he?

No! O God, no! *Worse!* For as the strength which was not quite bled out of him while he lay in that eddy out of the moonlight just enables him to say, he has suffered the most fiendish wrong which Hell can invent—the wrong after which the leaving of life itself is a demoniac refinement of wickedness. The theocracy has inflicted on him that vengeance which was inflicted on Abelard by the uncles of Eloise—has robbed him of manhood's self because he loved his rightful wife, even in the clutches of a wretch who had four wives already!

Hiram lived—most horrible part of the story—he *lived!* Two months pass by but he did not leave the house. Others who had suffered from the theocracy like him, went crawling like lepers along the shady side of the Salt Lake streets, ashamed to meet their kind. But he would never know the scorn of men. The shook which his mind had suffered had made him a confirmed idiot. The horrible truth was slow in coming to the ears of the only woman he had ever loved in his life. But it did come, and the next morning she was found quite beyond the reach of the sour-faced "sister" who had done her duty to the Church, beyond Elder Salmudy, beyond the bishop, beyond the theocracy itself with an empty laudanum bottle by her side, and her soul under trees more unfading than the acacias; all of which was delicately referred to in a paragraph in the "Deseret News," headed "Terrible affliction of an absent missionary,—Brother Salmudy."

Mr. Polypeith was by no means a young man when he came to Utah, and this crowning trouble of his life aged him to such a degree that the most intimate of his Eastern friends would not have known him: (Here the reader, who from motives of delicacy has objected to knowing the worst of Mormonism, may remount the car of my narrative.) The country which he had fondly hoped to make his Paradise, had become his Inferno. He could not endure the sight of a face that he had known in Utah. The people he met on the street seemed to stare at him sidelong, with cold curiosity, or humbling pity. He had no heart for his work—he missed the deft hand, the cheery whistle, the sunny face that used to be beside him. He should never, never, never have any child to succeed him in his business now. Everything he now did, was only for two broken old people, who would soon be in their graves. Why should he work to keep up a business which could be left to no one? Neither he nor Mother Polypeith had any interest in themselves. All that they wanted was the chance to scrape together enough of their property to leave a comfortable trust fund for the support of their poor wrecked boy when they should be gone; and to get into some quiet place where none of them should be known; where, without notice, they might nurse and tend him while they lived, and, seeing him provided for, lay their tired bones in the earth.

So Mr. Polypeith sold his warehouse, stock, good-will, tools and all, and began making ready to go to California. There he might purchase some quiet little ranch, along the upper waters of the Merced or the Sacramento, and lead the secluded life of a vaquero. He knew nothing of agriculture,—he was too old to learn; but comparatively little training was necessary for the pastoral life, and the three of them could live on the proceeds of the yearly cattle sales, which was all that he now aimed at or cared for.

Of course he could not make this resolution known. He distrusted his very daughters. They had become so identified in all their interests with the theocracy, and that vast power so entirely swallowed up all private relations, obliterated all personal and family ties, that he was not sure, poor old man, that even these children of his own loins—these sisters of a worse than murdered brother—would be faithful to his secret. They might not be able to, even if they would; their husband was high in the Church; one of those whose duty it is to know everything, and he probably possessed means of marital pressure which could extort the truth from the two girls, like a Spanish torture-boot or thumbscrew. So it would be not only wiser for the three who were going, but more merciful to those left behind, if he kept the fact of his intended flight a profound secret even from them; so they might honestly say they had no knowledge of it, and be spared a great deal of trouble.

Nothing of his property now remained unconverted into the portable shape, except the house he lived in. After much casting about for a way to turn this into money without exposing himself to the suspicion of meditating an exodus (and he needed every cent he could raise for the accomplishment of his purposes), he finally hit upon a way by which, as he congratulated himself, he could secure the double end of saving all he owned, and, at the same time, lull any suspicions which might have been aroused in the omniscient mind of the theocracy, by the somewhat hasty and unexpected sale of his business. A rich neighbor, Elder Steatite, had repeatedly solicited him to sell his house, and still retained his fancy for it, keeping open the original very liberal offer he had made for it; and signifying his readiness to close on cash terms whenever Mr. Polypeith should change his mind. To Brother Steatite, Brother Polypeith now repaired, and told him that as he had sold out his business, finding it too much care for his growing years, he wanted to purchase a ranch, already stocked, in the Tuilla Valley, where he might settle down comfortably as an agriculturist for the remainder of his life. For this, he needed money, and if Brother Steatite would lend him something less than the sum he had offered to buy the house outright, he would give him a mortgage on the latter property to be exchanged for a deed in case he found anything in Tuilla to suit him. Brother Steatite was pleased with this opportunity of getting at least a contingent hold on the property, and loaned him what was a pretty fair price for it.

It was agreed in the secret consultations of the sorrowful old couple, that they should move such portions of their household goods as they found desirable to take with them, by slow degrees, to a "cache," or hidden place of deposit, among the sage brush and rocks, few rods off the emigrant road that led by the way of Black Rock; and whenever a trusty teamster could be found in the trains that weekly, in some seasons almost daily, camped outside the city, he should be let into the secret of the cache, and hired to stop and take up the articles hidden there; and then carry them on with him, and leave them in store at one of the Humboldt settlements, to be called for by the Polypeiths as they went through. Accordingly, one by one they moved the few things which they could, without attracting attention to their absence, Mr. Polypeith depositing one lot in the cache each time that he went on his pretended prospecting tour to Tuilla. Finally, having removed all they dared, they made ready to go themselves. They had, fortunately, bought a team of mules and a large wagon for lumbering purposes, two years before, when an unusual run of good luck had given them the means and awakened in them the ambition to extend their business,— so the purchase of that essential requisite was not now to add another to the chances of having their flight suspected.

They stocked their wagon with provisions for two months; taking the most condensed form of everything which they could get: such as canned meats, fruit and vegetables, prepared milk and coffee, Shaker apple sauce, hard-tack, and soup-biscuit. Though the expense of their outfit was considerably greater than if they had taken the ordinary salt pork and beef, they were able thus to provide for a much longer journey; and insured themselves against the disaster of running short on the terrible tract which they must cross between Salt Lake and the fertile country about Lassen's.

They came to their last Sunday in Salt Lake. At first, it seemed as if they could not bring themselves to go to the Tabernacle, for they should see the girls there; and how could they look in those faces which had nestled against her bosom, and his bearded cheek, in the perfect trust of babyhood—how could they clasp those hands which had tenderly stroked their hair; and hear the voices which had cooed up at them out of the cradle—knowing that it was for the last time, yet not disclosing it to them, in cries of heart-rending agony? But they must do it, somehow. The care of poor Hiram had kept them at home a good deal on recent Sundays; and the theocracy of Mormonism, like that of the Jews and the old Puritans, lays a severe penalty on absentees from service. Mr. Polypeith had once before, when his wife and children were ill for six weeks with typhoid fever, been put on the list of suspects, and possibly disloyal persons, who were to be dragooned with the sharp end of the Episcopal crook into worshipping God, and to be roundly fined for their past delinquencies. They could ill afford now to incur suspicion or expense; so Mrs. Polypeith went to have her heart lacerated in the morning, and Mr. Polypeith in the evening.

The principal morning sermon was delivered by the Prophet himself, and had for its subject, the Church's absolute proprietorship in all that its members have or are. Brigham took as his test, "Ye are bought with a price"; and his aim was to make his flock feel grateful that the Church was graciously pleased to accept tithes of what they possessed, instead of stripping them naked, as it had an undoubted Divine right to do, skinning them afterwards to tan their hides. After sermon, the prophet told his flock further, that it had been revealed to him from on high that he must raise a militia regiment of able-bodied saints for the protection of the Territory against invasion from those children of hell, the Gentile soldiery; and that the necessity of equipping them, and purchasing the most reliable kind of shooting-irons for their use, would compel him to levy on them an extra assessment beside the tithes already paid this year—it would probably amount to one fifth the amount usually collected in tithing. Whatever it was, he knew his people would hearken to the voice of the Lord; and he wished that they might be prepared. Nobody grumbled or pulled a wry countenance. These extra assessments to cover suddenly arising needs of the Church were of too frequent occurrence to be regarded as any particular annoyance. The people's chronic religious complaint in Utah, is hemorrhage of the portmonnaie.

After elaborating this theme a little further, Brigham suddenly changed his voice to a sterner tone, and a look of grim solemnity settled in his face, which would not have done discredit to Balfour of Burley.

"Brother Spotsby,"—said he, addressing the bishop in whose ward the Polypeiths lived,—"I have something to say to you which makes me very sorry. In your flock there is a goat who must be separated from the sheep; in your garden there is a root of bitterness which must be plucked up, lest many thereby become defiled; in your division of the body of professors of religion, is one who must be delivered over to the buffetings of Satan. I can stand an open enemy! I can endure even one of those sneaking Gentiles in Kossuth hat, roundabout with braided sleeves, skim-milk blue pants, and brass soldier buttons,—those wolves who have entered the fold of the faithful, down to Camp Floyd,—I can bear anybody that hates the Lord's truth right straight out, fair and square; but I cannot away with an apostate! Brother Spotsby, there is a man in your ward who must be dealt with without budging! He seeks to defraud the inheritance of the Lord; he must meet the fate of Ananias and Sapphira! Before we meet again in this place, he must be sent to hell 'cross lots! Brother Spotsby, after meeting you may come round to my office, and I will further impart to you the revelation in this matter."

Though this speech moved the assembly somewhat more than it had been moved by the news of an extra assessment, their emotion was but a trifling and transient ripple compared with that thundering and rocking breaker of feeling, like the bore of some East Indian river, which would have swept over the same body of men and women at the East who should hear such words and understand their full purport. There were some there, and among these was Mrs. Polypeith—some women, children, and new-comers into the blessedness of the Saint's Rest, to whom the speech was figurative; to whom it wholly and simply portended excommunication, with its attendant isolation from sympathy, its outlawry, and all the evils which may easily be imagined as attendant upon it in a new and sparsely settled country, where men are so mutually dependent for the safety and happiness of every hour. But many—most, indeed, of those who heard the prophet's address to the bishop—knew that it meant the slaughter of one of their fellow-men; the cool premeditated, pitiless killing of a human being (he might be a stranger to some of them, but was also doubtless the intimate friend of some), for the crime, not of taking another's life into his private hands, not even of sinning against his neighbor's rights of property; for nothing that violated natural justice or social order, but for changing his mind!—for coming to the conclusion after a long experience, it might be, of such doubts, perplexities, and trials as had agitated many a breast in that multitude, that Mormonism was not God's truth, but the Devil's lie! And now, when the tearless, merciless, unreasoning, irresponsible Sanhedrim of his rulers was to prove he was right in this conclusion by slaying him, there was not a man in all that theocracy-ridden assembly stirred enough to rise and protest against the crime of his brother's blood! They were all old to such impressions; they had heard and known such things until every man's heart was calloused; though once the wave of passionate indignation which swept them, listening to a speech like the prophet's, in its surging rebound, must have swept the whole fabric and personality of Mormonism into the night and darkness from which they came at first. Thus did the old Jews sit and see Achan murdered with all his innocent family; thus did the young man Saul stand by and witness the stoning of Stephen, holding the assassins' clothes and consenting to the martyr's death; thus did the old Puritan behold the tender flesh of women seethe and crackle in the fires of the stake,— uttering no cry of horror, feeling no tear wet his stony cheeks; and thus do men lose the humanity and the divinity of their natures under a theocracy everywhere.

Mrs. Polypeith, as I have said, never dreamed of the meaning which really lay in the prophet's speech. Possibly she thought that the proposed excommunicate might be her husband—but he had already resolved to excommunicate himself; and before the sentence could be promulgated, he and she with their poor boy, would be where such a sentence was mere empty wind. So, in her tenderness for a heart already too heavily weighted, she carried home no account of Brigham's speech. Besides, she knew as well as anybody can know, in a country where one hardly dare trust his own sister for fear she may be a spy, that there were several malcontents in the ward beside her husband; some of them comparatively reckless and much more prominent: the person referred to might be one of these.

The partings were over; the old couple had not betrayed themselves to their daughters. Sunday, Monday, Tuesday had gone, and in the darkness of Wednesday morning, about one o'clock, the three Polypeiths left their Mormon home forever. They drove slowly through the town, so as to attract no straggler who might be awake at that hour; and were soon on the desolate plain beyond the fens of the Jordan. Here they dared to go more rapidly, and before dawn broke, had reached the shore of the Lake and passed the point of the Oquirrh. Still they did not tarry. They might have aroused some one as they passed Black Rock Ranch, and they felt like guilty people fleeing from a murder; they trembled at every sound of the lake plashing along its stony beach, and the stunted cedars took the shape of crouching men. To think that these were American citizens, in United States territory, who had violated no natural right, no law of their country, and yet they were obliged to move thus! Let us not look abroad for the missionary objects of Republicanism. Austria, a more terrible Austria than that which crushed Venice, is nourished at our own breast.

The Polypeiths had seen an emigrant train bound for Oregon pass through the city about noon of the day before. They were in hopes of reaching it some distance this side of the Tuilla settlements; of merging themselves in it, and so travelling on unnoticed by any of the Mormon ranchmen, who, seeing them alone, might possibly identify them as belonging to Salt Lake, until they had got safely across the boundaries of Utah. A little before sunrise, the mules began to lag; and poor Hiram awakened from the vacant melancholy which now habitually shrouded him, to moan for food like a child. So, driving a few hundred yards off the track, Father Polypeith picketed his mules to a pair of stout sage stalks, to let them browse for a couple of hours, and building a fire of the scrubby sage brush and greasewood he had collected with his hatchet, assisted his wife to prepare breakfast. While they were eating this meal, the two congratulated each other on the thought that before noon, they would in all probability come up with the train and be comparatively out of danger. Their old hearts glowed with a momentary warmth; they pictured to themselves the quiet nook which they might reach in California, and though it was only a place to die in, still they had suffered such entire loss of all which brightened life, that this prospect was a kind of substitute for happiness. The sun was two hours high, when they again put the mules in the wagon and resumed their journey.

They had travelled but a couple of miles further, when they came upon fresh tracks; and presently they saw the still smoking ash-heap which indicated a recent camping-place. Here the train had probably made its night-halt, and from the looks of the fire and the hoof-marks, it could not be very long since it started out again. They took fresh courage, chirruped to their mules, and went on as briskly as the sandy road and their heavy wagon would permit. Rising a little hillock, they had their eyes rejoiced, by seeing through the clear, dry air, which on these plains, everywhere out of the immediate neighborhood of the Lake, has a sort of telescopic property, a long white serpent whose joints were wagons, tapering from the nearer rear to the far-off van, slowly winding under a thin tawny cloud of dust, and through the gray sage about two miles before them, toward the Tuilla Valley. Their hearts leapt into their throats with the joyful thought of such close safety; they laughed like children; even poor Hiram seemed to understand them, and snapped his fingers over his shoulder, as if defying the Saints and the whole theocracy they had left snoring behind them in Salt Lake City.

Descending the opposite slope of the hillock they lost sight of the train, but knowing that every step brought them nearer it, considering the leisurely way in which emigrants travel, it kept its place as a stimulant in their fancy's eye, and they cheerfully pushed their mules through the sand, sure of overtaking their escort before it reached Tuilla. Their way now led through a narrow pass, with a low rocky ledge projecting from the bench-land on either side of them, shaggy with sage, and broken into fantastic crags and notches. Mr. Polypeith sat alone on a cushioned board across the front of the wagon; his wife and son were comfortably lodged upon bags and mattresses under the tilt, with a pile of boxed household wares for the back to their seat. Just as they turned the corner of the pass and were again emerging upon the open sage plain, a sharp crack, and "ping!" broke the golden morning stillness; the old man's hands went up and the reins fell from them; then, without a word, he fell backward into the wagon, while a red rivulet tripled over his temple and dropped from his gray hairs into the lap of his wife. With a shriek that might have pierced a fiend's heart, she caught him to her breast and dragged him back upen the mattress,—sprung to the board and caught the reins; but before she could lash the team into a gallop two bull-necked wretches with painted faces had seized them close by the bits, and drawing each his revolver, fiercely ordered her to dismount. But strength failed her. Her brain reeled; and only less dead than her husband, she fell upon his stiffening body, clasping Hiram her arms. The assassins drew the mules to the side of the road, secured them, and entered the wagon. They lifted the dead man and threw him out into the brush as if he had been the carcass of a beast. Then they tore the boy from his mother's unconscious grasp, and sneering at his blank face of mindless terror, tumbled him to the ground

THE HEART OF THE CONTINENT

after his father. Not even age and the helplessness of woman found mercy from them. The mother was dragged from the wagon after the son, and pitched in a limp, unresisting heap upon the corpse. Hiram, ignorant of all that was doing, first stood and looked curiously on his prostrate parents, then obeying the instinct of mere animal fear, turned to flee into the sage. One of the assassins deliberately raised his pistol, and as he was running, shot him through the back. As he lay weltering in blood and struggling in his death-agony, his moans pierced through his mother's unconsciousness and reached her heart. She began to show signs of returning from her swoon.

"Look out, Bill!" spoke one of the Danites hurriedly; "the old woman's a-comin' to. Why not make a job of it?—*she's* no use! What'll we do with her, anyhow?"

"That's so!" replied the other. "We can't take her back; there's nowhere for her to go to, and she'll raise worse hell with the Gentiles than any o' the tribe, you bet. I believe it's only doin' the Church justice, and her a mercy, to send *her* to Californy too, alonger the rest 'o 'em. Here goes, anyhow"—

She had opened her eyes and raised herself on one palm; in this position, looking out of glassy, unmeaning, bedazed eyes, like one waking from a nightmare. The last speaker coolly put his revolver to her ear, pulled the trigger, and the last of the Polypeiths had forever escaped from the theocracy. The Danites dragged the three bodies out a hundred rods into the brush, made a great heap of sage and grease-wood, laid their victims on it, and setting the whole on fire, calmly sat near and smoked their pipes, making blasphemous jokes the while, till every earthly trace of their crime was consumed. This final act of the horrible tragedy over, they turned the heads of the mules and drove them back toward Salt Lake, arriving there the next day. The wagon and its contents went into the Church store-house, to be sold; while the entire sum of money resulting from the conversion of the Polypeiths' property, found in a belt around the old man's body, was passed directly into the iron safe in the Prophet's office. The married daughters only knew that their parents and their brother had fled from Utah;—whither they went, how far they had gone, and what had become of them, they never learned, for the Church not only allows its members to have no secrets from itself, but keeps all its own as inscrutably as the Sphinx. Thus ends the story of the Polypeiths. And the promise which I made when I began it, I can now assert that I have kept. I have made not one single statement which is either false or exaggerated; have supposed nothing to happen whose parallel has not repeatedly happened in Utah.

If the wholesale assassination of the Polypeiths stagger the belief of any calm Republican Christian, dwelling at the East without the pale of theocracy, what will he think of the massacre, universally known in Utah, of a whole wagon-train—emigrants on their way to California? I have before referred to this bloody affair, and will now briefly fulfill my promise to give its details.

In May, 1857, Parley Pratt, one of the family whose name figures so conspicuously in the Mormon annals,—a man of superior education and marked ability, who has contributed many hymns besides numerous other productions to the literature of the Latter-Day Church,—was slain in Van Buren County, Arkansas, by a citizen of that State named Hector McLean, for having proselyted McLean's wife and

taken her to himself, during his apostleship in the Chero-
kee Nation Country.

This act and the fact that McLean was largely aided in the
pursuit and capture of his insulter by residents of that part of
Arkansas, greatly incensed the Mormons against the people
of that State, and determined them upon taking speedy vengeance for the killing of Pratt, who was very popular in Utah.

Their opportunity did not arrive until the next autumn.
On the 4th of September a train of 150 Arkansas emigrants,
comprising many entire families on their way to California, with about sixty wagons, a large herd of horses, mules,
and beef-cattle, and the entire stock of household goods,
provisions, and merchandise for barter, usually carried by
such trains, amounting in value, as was estimated, to nearly
$200,000, reached a spring and camping-ground at the
west end of the Mountain Meadow Valley. Here they were
surprised and attacked, while corraling their stock inside a
circle of wagons, as is customary when on the halt, by an
overwhelming force of men in the garb and paint of Indians.
Here I must digress a little for explanation.

In every Mormon settlement the traveler finds a number of men with long black hair, dark skins, and black eyes,
whose slouching gait, sidelong, restless look, and entire style
of make-up so suggest the native savage that he might easily
mistake them for half-breeds tamed to the life of a white
community. They are in really pure-blooded white men,
belonging to the Mormons, and selected on account of their
strong natural resemblance to Indians, as well as their love of
adventure and skill in adapting themselves to savage modes
of living, as go-betweens, to conduct the intercourse of the
Mormons with the tribes, whom they pretend to regard as

former true believers, and call by the pretentious title of their Lamanite brethren. These men usually know several of the Indian languages, are enured to fatigue, fine fighters and hunters, cunning in every branch of forest-craft, acquainted with the mountain trails as thoroughly as the Indians themselves, and devote themselves especially to keeping up friendly relations with the savages; part of the time living in their dens with them, making them presents contributed by the Church, conciliating them in every way, and in many instances acquiring unbounded influence over them. Whenever the Mormons want a cat's-paw for purposes so nefarious that their own appearance on the stage of accomplishment would make them obnoxious to the whole world; when they want an exploring party cut off, a mail rifled, a Gentile settlement raided on, or wholesale assassination and plunder committed, these men have only need to stain their faces, strip themselves to skin hunting-shirt, or breech-clout and moccasins, and drumming up a sufficient party of the savages they have brought under their control, to lead them out to loot and massacre. I believe that in the earlier part of this work I have referred to atrocious expeditions of this kind in which (as in the Sweet-water raids, for example) a large number of the seeming Indians, undistinguishable from true savages in any other respect, were detected to be Mormons, from their using German, Irish, and other white brogues in conversing with each other during the onslaught. Such, at least in large part, were the Indians who attacked the emigrants at Mountain Meadow.

For about a day the brave Arkansians kept off their murderers by lying behind their embanked bales and boxes, with their wagons corraled in a circle around them, their women and children inside of this rude extempore fortification; and using their rifles vigorously all the time. Their enemies however had much the best of them, for they could lie almost entirely out of sight in the brush, and were besides between the emigrants and water, so that the latter and their families suffered severely from thirst. Still, though vastly their superiors in number, the savages did not gain an inch. They would probably have been obliged to retire disheartened without accomplishing their object, had not some of the Mormons thought of a stratagem by which they succeeded as they never could have done by force.

Just at this juncture, the beleaguered Arkansians had their eyes gladdened by the sight of an approaching body of white men, who had not before appeared on the scene, and seemed to be strangers crossing the mountains and wholly unconnected with the attacking party. After a parley with the Indians, the latter ceased firing long enough to let them go into the emigrant camp and have an interview. They told the Arkansians that they were settlers in the neighborhood who had always conciliated and been friends with the Indians, and that they possessed so much influence with them that they had persuaded them to cease hostilities and let the emigrants proceed under their (the whites') escort, if they would only at a concession to the exasperated feelings of the savages permit that escort to take possession of their arms and ammunition. The Indians, they said, had recently lost some of their most valuable men by the hand of whites, who murdered them in cold blood and out of sheer wantonness, so that it was now with the greatest difficulty they could be persuaded not to attack every white man they met.

The reasoning and propositions of their new-found friends appeared so plausible, and their disposition so friendly, that after consultation, the Arkansians concluded to accept their advice, and deposited with them all the arms and ammunition belonging to the entire train. Scarcely had they stripped themselves of their means of protection, when at a prearranged signal, all the savages rushed in, and joined by the white men,—among whom the well-known Mormon Elder Haight seems to have been the most prominent,—began butchering the helpless men, women, and children;—nor did they stop pursuing them for several miles, and keeping up a running fire all the way, until they had killed 120 or more of the train. The last of the unfortunate men managed to get to Muddy Creek, forty or fifty miles away, but was tracked by the insatiate devils and shot down. Some of the deeds of the white savages rivaled anything in the annals of Indian cruelty; such, for instance, as the ease of one young girl, who was caught by the hair of her head while running, and at she knelt crying for mercy to her Mormon captor, had his bowie-knife drawn across her throat from ear to ear. The smallest children, boys and girls, from earliest infancy to ten years of age, were spared by the assassins and dispersed among the settlements to be taken into various Mormon families and brought up in the Mormon faith. Seventeen of these were afterward found by Mr. Forney, whom the government empowered to investigate the matter, and returned to their parents' friends in Arkansas. The wagons, cattle, and goods were parted among the Mormon actors in the massacre, and no successful effort at searching out any portion of this property had been made when I left Salt Lake. One wagon which had belonged to the train was then in the barn

THE HEART OF THE CONTINENT

of a well-known Mormon citizen, and another well-to-do, much esteemed Saint, who had participated in the massacre and had taken one of the children to bring up, I met in the streets of Salt Lake repeatedly. He looked as jolly as you please, as if neither conscience nor digestion troubled him.

The position which the United States government holds in Utah may be inferred from the fact that although the prominent participators in this, one of the blackest outrages of modern times, are perfectly well known in Utah, they go about among their fellow-men to this day with unblushing and fearless impunity. The Hon. Mr. Cradlebaugh, former delegate from Nevada, laid the case before Congress in a speech eloquent with terrible fact, and a United States Court (held I believe at Camp Floyd, under the protection of Johnston's guns) was convened to try the offenders, but as a matter of course they all slipped through. The cases had to go before a jury, and the panel had to be drawn from among the Mormons themselves. If there happened to be one Gentile juror drawn, it was only at the risk of his life that he could vote guilty; and if he did, his comrades would be certain to disagree with him. It is evident that until martial-law is proclaimed, no Mormon can ever be punished in Utah for a crime against a Gentile,—Gentiles having no rights there which a Mormon is bound to respect. I am not advocating the declaration of martial-law in the Territory; of the necessity which justifies such an extreme measure I do not pretend to be a judge; but I am sure that unless the United States intends to give over the entire Territory to the possession of a single sect, and virtually forbid all citizens who do not belong to that sect from settling in the Territory; if it ever intends that its citizens shall be equally protected everywhere within its boundaries, their form of religious belief notwithstanding; if it does not intend to cede to the settlers of every new territory as part of their local franchise, analogous with state rights, the power to establish despotism more cruel than any in Asia or in Europe, and compel all new-comers to choose between bowing their necks to the yoke, being assassinated, or abandoning their claims in the territory: then the United States Government will be compelled to take the opposite horn of the dilemma and open courts-martial in Utah for the trial of all such desperadoes as now threaten Gentile life in Utah with the certainty of acquittal by a jury of their peers.

Doubtless, trial by jury is a palladium of liberty; but in preserving the palladium let us be sure that we are not holding it as a screen for murder to stab behind; let us take care lest we leave no liberty for the palladium to shield.

If we can sufficiently purge ourselves of indignation and other personal passions to look at Mormonism with the calm intellectual eyes of the philosopher, it will present to us the most curious object of study which the world at present affords. Its life is an hourly anomaly. The fact that the system continues to exist, is as strange a one as it would be if the Falls of Niagara should begin pouring up instead of tumbling down. As we have sought to show, it is a violation of all moral and intellectual laws of gravitation. It is a perpetual defiance to the progress of the age. We are irresistibly driven to the questions, What upholds it? What has carried it through trials well-nigh as fiery as any which ever assaulted the Christian Church, and placed it in a position of such prosperity that it is capable of setting at naught successfully the will of the Government, the spirit of American Republicanism and the strongest people upon earth?

Its element of cohesion is not to be found where superficial students usually look for it,—in the fact that its system provides full swing for the baser passions of mankind in the institution of polygamy. One of the strongest of the Mormon leaders, Colonel Kinney, is not a polygamist at all, and the institution itself, so far from being an original element in the system, is but a recent importation into it Besides, the Mormons are by no means a grossly sensual people; quite as far from that, everybody who has lived among them will bear them witness, as the old Puritans or Covenanters. Their polygamy, of course, offers opportunity for the gratification of sensual men without the stigma which in civilized and Christian countries attaches to sexual inconstancy; but it is a stem religious institution, not a voluptuary one. The grace and poetry of Athens, the sensuous languor of oriental lands, are entirely absent from it. The Mormon is a polygamist not for indulgence, but from conviction. He hedges around his many marriages with a sterner legislation than that with which we protect our one. He marries repeatedly, because every time he is adding to his importance, elevating his position in the hierarchy of heaven; because every father has in the kingdom of God a principality proportionate to his number of children. There cannot be imagined any country less favorable for the residence of a voluptuary than Utah. There is no such thing possible as promiscuous passion in Salt Lake City. Not only are the statutes severer against such practices, but the feeling of the people is more opposed to them than in any place on the globe. The man who wishes many objects of his attachment, must marry them all, and burden himself with a responsibility at each successive marriage for which even the most frantic sensualist could find no compensation. Moreover, a great mistake is frequently made at the East in supposing that the "spiritual marriages" so often heard of in connection with the Mormons, correspond to those promiscuous and illicit relations gilded by Free Love with that once sacred name, and are merely an extension of the sensual area of the persona contracting them, without the necessity of his assuming any of the burdens of the husband. How impossible it is that this should be, may be perceived by putting together the facts that on the one hand all such relations outside the marriage tie are severely punished; and when the transgressor not only violates social order in general, but trespasses on the close of some other man, that punishment takes the horrible form which (some of) my readers have read in the history of the Polypeiths; and that on the other, a great many women in Utah are the physical and temporal wives of one man, the spiritual and eternal wives of another. The spiritual marriage is a ceremony of great intended solemnity, purporting to seal a woman to be the wife of a man after this life,—a contract and covenant ratified by the Church, and capable of being solemnized by Brigham Young alone,—that she shall form part of his celestial household and live with him in heaven forever. This involves no union of any kind on earth after the marriage ceremony is over.

Nor is the element of strength in Mormonism any liberty of any kind, granted to the people of Utah, but not granted to other people elsewhere. The very reverse is true. The power resides in the hands of an exceeding few—really, and finally, I ought to say, in but one hand. The *people,* elsewhere in this country the sovereign people, are here the veriest creatures of despotism. They are no more a power than were the

Venetians under Francis Joseph; but they are ready to die in defense of the chain that binds them.

The strength of Mormonism is this,—Mormonism is a one-man power. Mormonism is Brigham Young. The people are generally collected from the lowest, the most credulous, the unthinking stratum of Europe. And Brigham Young is one of the most remarkable men of any age, of any country. Next to Louis Napoleon he possesses the vastest executive ability, the highest talent for government, which this century has seen; and when I consider the disadvantages under which he has labored, his lack of a great name, like the elder Bonaparte's, behind him to give his very mistakes prestige; his deficiency in education beyond the meagre help which he might receive from a common school in the early settlement of Western New York; his being obliged to associate all his life with the gross, the ignorant, and the superstitious,—I do not know why I should make a reservation, when I speak of him superlatively, in the French Emperor's favor. Perhaps the best expression for the difference between the two would be to say, that he is Louis Napoleon plus a heart and intense moral convictions. There are some circumstances under which the addition must be a despotic ruler's weakness; but then again there are other cases—and in Utah, among that wild, fiercely mobile nation of fanatics, these are not few—where it is a positive advantage.

Brigham Young's power with the Mormons is a cause of inexpressive astonishment to every thinking mind which visits Utah. They do not seem to know it; he works their hundred and twenty thousand wires (for that is probably not far from the right number of his subjects), sitting at his table in his plain little office, as a telegraph operator works a single line with a single key. He has acquired absolute ascendency over them. His power is the most despotic known to mankind. The Mormons would think of disputing a law of nature as soon as his will; and that, probably because he works like nature, without any apparent selfishness, without anger, but inevitably, and with an almost invariable result of success and general beneficence. The people amuse themselves with the fiction that they, like us Gentiles at the East, have a voice in things; that their votes elect their officers; that they are a representative government. But Brigham always knows who is going to Congress. I asked him if Dr. Bernhisel would be likely to get into Congress again. "No," he replied with perfect certainty, "we shall send Colonel Hooper as our delegate." When the time came Brigham would send in his name to the "Deseret News," whose office, like everything else valuable and powerful, is in his inclosure. It would be printed, of course,—a counter-nomination is a thing unheard of among the Mormons, and the Gentile residents have not the slightest show for a candidate of their own,—and on election day, the man Brigham named would be delegate as sure as the sun rose. Here is the crack in which the lever must be inserted when Mormonism rushes to its suicide by challenging collision with the United States authority. Here may it be pried off its base, for no administration can be caitiff enough to hold that a congress-man or delegate elected in this fashion belongs to that Republican form of government which the Constitution guarantees to all the States.

All Mormondom is Brigham's. As the irresponsible trustee and treasurer of the Church, its first officer in all things, secular and religious, he possesses absolute control of all the property of the Church,—and we have seen how vast that property is,—including the tithe of every man's private property, as a matter of course, and regular; the right at will to sequestrate any further proportion of such property for Church purposes; the gigantic Building Fund, for a temple and any other edifices he may choose to erect, of whose plan, specifications, and disbursements he is sole arbiter; the Emigration Fund, still vaster, from which are made the advances necessary to bring poor proselytes from all the regions of Europe visited by Mormon missionaries, and into which those proselytes after their settlement in Utah are compelled to pay back that advance, by installments, to the uttermost farthing of principal and interest, in addition to their tithes. One's mind becomes staggered at the immensity of the financial interests which this single man wields unquestioned. His supreme relation to both the secular and religious governments of Mormonism and the *unreporting* character of such a relation, makes it impossible for any outsider to draw the line between his private possessions and those of the Church; but he is for all practical purposes the owner of all the Church has. I heard many estimates of the amount of his personal fortune among those (which to be sure is not saying a great deal) who had as good opportunities as anybody else, and all of them made him by far the wealthiest man in America; one, indeed, of the wealthiest men in the world. Since he has been in Utah, a single New York house is stated upon competent authority to have invested sixty millions of dollars for him in foreign securities.[7] The Gentiles regard this as an evidence of his

---

7  His British possessions alone make him to-day (1870) the third largest
   depositor in the Bank of England.

sagacious anticipation that the whole Mormon fabric, so far as America is concerned, is destined to tumble in his time; and that his practice of the principle "L'église c'est moi" is not meant to extend to identification with his sect's downfall. But among all the eyes watching him, none have ever accused him of peculation or dishonesty of any kind in his office, if we disregard, as we ought, the mere baseless and proofless innuendoes of his avowed personal enemies.

The mountain-stream that irrigates the city, flowing to all its fields and gardens, through open ditches on each side of the highway, passes through Brigham's inclosure; if the Saints needed drought to humble them, he could back the waters to their source. The road to the only cañon where firewood is easily attainable, runs through the same close, and is barred by a gate of which he has the sole key. A family-man wishing to cut fuel, must ask his leave, which is generally granted on condition that every third or fourth load be deposited in the inclosure for Church purposes. Thus everything vital, save the air he breathes, reaches the Mormon only through Brigham's sieve. What more absolute despotism is conceivable? Here, again, is the *pou-sto* for Government interference. The mere fact of such power resting in one man's irresponsible hands, is a crime against the Constitution. At the same time, wonderful as it may seem, this power is controlled for the common good. His life is all one great theoretical mistake, yet he makes fewer practical mistakes than any other man, so situated, whom the world ever saw. Those he does make are not on the side of self. He merges his whole personality in the Church with a self-abnegation which would establish in business a whole century of martyrs having a better cause.

The people believe in him because he believes in himself. He can slay them when they apostatize: they only quote Joshua and Achan, Moses and Korah, or some other bloody theocratic analogue. He may be privy to the Mountain Meadow affair: Samuel hewed Agag in pieces. He has in his Lion and Bee houses, in the Prophet's inclosure (called after the sculptured symbols which they bear on their central pediments), and in other dwellings, over seventy wives after the flesh; while it is so much the fashion to marry him spiritually, that he himself has no idea of the number of those who will share his *ménage* in heaven,—many married on earth to other husbands having gone away from his office just after the ceremony, never to speak to him again until the resurrection. It is amusing to think how perpetually the usher at the door of his celestial saloon will be occupied for the first few years succeeding the Prophet's translation to bliss in the announcement of fresh "Mrs. Brighams." The last time anybody took the trouble to count the register, the number of these spiritual wives of his had run up to something like 5,000. But with all these, and more especially the 70-75 earthly ones, no one thinks of calling him a sensualist. He believes in himself and his doctrine, so the people believe in both. He is the best and most enlightened helper of all his people's industries; he knows so well the worth of labor to the dignifying of the man, that a few years ago, when many of the poor people after a bad season came to him almost starving, to ask the help of the Church funds, he set them building a clay wall around the city to keep out hypothetical Indians, that they might feel they *earned* the aid afforded, and not learn to eat the bread of idleness. What I have before stated of his ingenuity in extemporizing a homemade

gilt chandelier for his opera-house, is true in every department of business. He has made himself familiar with all the
resources of Utah, and studies night and day to make them
avail to the utmost. He has established in the more southern
part of Utah the cane, cotton, and indigo culture; and I had
the pleasure of seeing a beautiful silk scarf, which would not
have done discredit to the Chinese looms, sent him as the
first fruits of that valuable branch of industry which he had
established near Nephi; distributing the cocoons and trea-
tises on rearing the worms, together with plans for wheels
and looms, among the people in the neighborhood when
he went there on a preaching tour. But all these excellences
of executive ability, this boundless versatility and activity of
mind, do not produce one tithe the confidence in him which
is awakened by the universal belief in his sincerity of nature.
He believes so strongly in Mormonism and *Brigham Young*,
that he is the magnet by which Joe Smith has suspended six-
score thousand souls.

Perhaps the Mormon question will ultimately settle itself
without a collision between Utah and the Government. If
Brigham Young dies, it will be settled speedily. He is the
key-stone of the arch of Mormon society. While he remains,
these increasing thousands of the most heterogeneous souls
that could be swept together from the by-ways of Christendom will continue to be builded up into a coherent
nationality. The instant he crumbles, Mormondom and Mormonism will fall to pieces at once, irreparably. His individual
magnetism, his executive tact, his native benevolence, are all
immense; but these advantages would avail him little with
the dead-in-earnest fanatics who rule Utah under him, and
the entirely persuaded fanatics whom they rule, were not his

qualities all coördinated in this one *absolute sincerity of belief and motive.* Brigham Young is the farthest remove on earth from a hypocrite; he is that grand, yet awful sight in human nature,—a man who had brought the loftiest Christian self-devotion to the altar of the Devil, who is ready to suffer crucifixion for Barabbas, supposing him Christ. Be sure that were he a hypocrite, the Union would have nothing to fear from Utah. When he dies, at least four hostile factions, which now find their only common ground in deification of his person, will snatch his mantle at opposite corners. Then will come such a rending as the world has not seen since the Macedonian generals fought over the coffin of Alexander; and then Mormonism will go out of geography into the history of popular delusions. There is not a single chief, apostle, bishop, or elder, except Brigham, who possesses any catholicity of influence. I found this tacitly acknowledged in every quarter. The more enlightened, fore-looking of the people seem like citizens of a beleaguered town, who know they have but a definite amount of bread, yet have made up their minds to act while it lasts, as if there were no such thing as starvation. The greatest comfort you can afford a Mormon is to tell him how young Brigham looks; for the quick unconscious sequence is, "Then Brigham may last out my time,—*après moi le déluge!*" Those who think at all deeply, have no conjecture of any Mormon future beyond him, and I know that many Mormons (Heber Kimball included) would gladly die to-day rather than survive him, and encounter that judgment-day and final perdition of their faith which moat dawn on his new-made grave.

# ACKNOWLEDGEMENTS

The editors benefited from the attention and kindnesses of Fitz Hugh Ludlow's alma mater, Union College. Thanks to Jill Murphy, Assistant Professor of English & American Literature, for her arrangement of our lecture on campus, a classroom workshop, and general encouragement for the project. Thanks also to Ethan Pearce, K.A. in C.C., for his introduction to Professor Murphy.

Thanks India Spartz, Head of Special Collections & Archives, for approving access to the collections and even babysitting one of our transcription assistants. Thanks Annette LeClair, Director of Collection and Technical Services, who gave us the key introduction to the HathiTrust project.

The HathiTrust Digital Library is a national treasure. This project would have taken five years without it. Thanks also to the University of Michigan, our partner institution for access.

While not used directly on this project for digital versions, the Atlantic Monthly and Harper's magazines are to be commended for having so much of their historically important archives available in digital forms; these archives were very helpful in research and organization for this project. The New York Public Library was also important for similar reasons. We also thank the University of Virginia's Albert and Shirley Small Special Collections Library for permission to print an image from Ludlow's letter to Edward Stansbury.

Despite the advances of digital archiving, there were still hundreds of pages of documents that had to be manually transcribed, despite occasionally poor source copies. Thanks to Teddy Dulchinos for the excellent job on the *Masks and Music* broadsheets, to David Olio for the work on the Helen Ludlow manuscript book of poems, and Krystina Crimi and Diana Fowler for their intrepid work on the sadly deteriorated *Due South* diaries.

As every editor knows, a good proofreader is worth his or her weight in bitcoin, and while digital scanning introduces peculiar typos of its own, our readers also had to contend with Ludlow's idiosyncratic and often archaic spelling and punctuation; exotic place names that had not yet achieved a consensus spelling; and his Twain-esque attempts to depict various American dialects and immigrant accents. The latter engendered several nightmares in which single quotation marks loomed menacingly. Thanks to our proofreaders Mindi Meltz, Becky Shipkosky and Krystina Crimi.

And special thanks to Jack Emery Taylor for the beautiful cover art and Susan Yost for her skillful and gorgeous layout, cover design and illustration work.

Rather than update all of Ludlow's spellings into contemporary American English, our method was to keep the older spellings as much as possible to keep the 'flavor' of his writing, and only change place names that were not clear, and update alternate spellings that 'look' like typos, to keep the reader's distractions to a minimum. Obviously in a project of this scope there will be cracks, but the editors can only hope that that will be how the light gets in.

# ABOUT THE EDITORS

DONALD P. DULCHINOS is the author of *Pioneer of Inner Space: The Life of Fitz Hugh Ludlow*, *Forbidden Sacraments: The Survival of Shamanism in Western Civilization* and *Neurosphere: The Convergence of Evolution, Group Mind, and the Internet*. He has found time between these projects for a career in the information and telecommunications technology industry.

STEPHEN CRIMI is the author of *Katabatic Wind: Good Craic Fueled by Fumes from the Abyss*; the editor of two collections of talks by biodynamic pioneer Alan Chadwick, *Performance in the Garden*, and *Reverence, Obedience and the Invisible in the Garden*; and the publisher of Logosophia Books. He lives with his wife Krys in Asheville NC, where he continues to mid-wife literature amidst the splendor of her gardens.

Dulchinos and Crimi graduated three years apart from Union College in Schenectady, NY, where they followed Fitz Hugh Ludlow as members of the Kappa Alpha Literary Society, and walked the same campus where Ludlow had his visions more than a century earlier.

*Designer's Note on Font Selection*

THIS SERIES OF COLLECTED WORKS by Fitz Hugh Ludlow is set
in Adobe Caslon Pro to capture the spirit of Ludlow's era.

The Caslon font was originally cut by William Caslon (1692-1766)
circa 1722 in London, and was used prolifically throughout the
American colonies and England in eighteenth century printing.
Early versions of the American Conſtitution and Declaration
of Independence were set in Caslon, and it was a favorite of
Benjamin Franklin who applied it in his own print shops.

Of the many modern variants, the Adobe version, created by
American designer Carol Twombly from 1990-1992, is one of
the few that remain trueſt to the original design.

Caslon is considered an English Baroque typeface, apparent in
its elegant swashes and ligatures. Robert Bringhurſt in his book
*Elements of Typographic Style* describes it as "rich with aɛtivity and
takes delight in the reſtless and dramatic play of contradiɛtory
forms."

An intereſting characteriſtic of the original cut is that it did not
contain a bold ſtyle. Inſtead, a larger size, italic, small or large
cap was used for emphasis.

CPSIA information can be obtained
at www.ICGtesting.com
Printed in the USA
BVOW08*0742250118

505360BV00001B/5/P